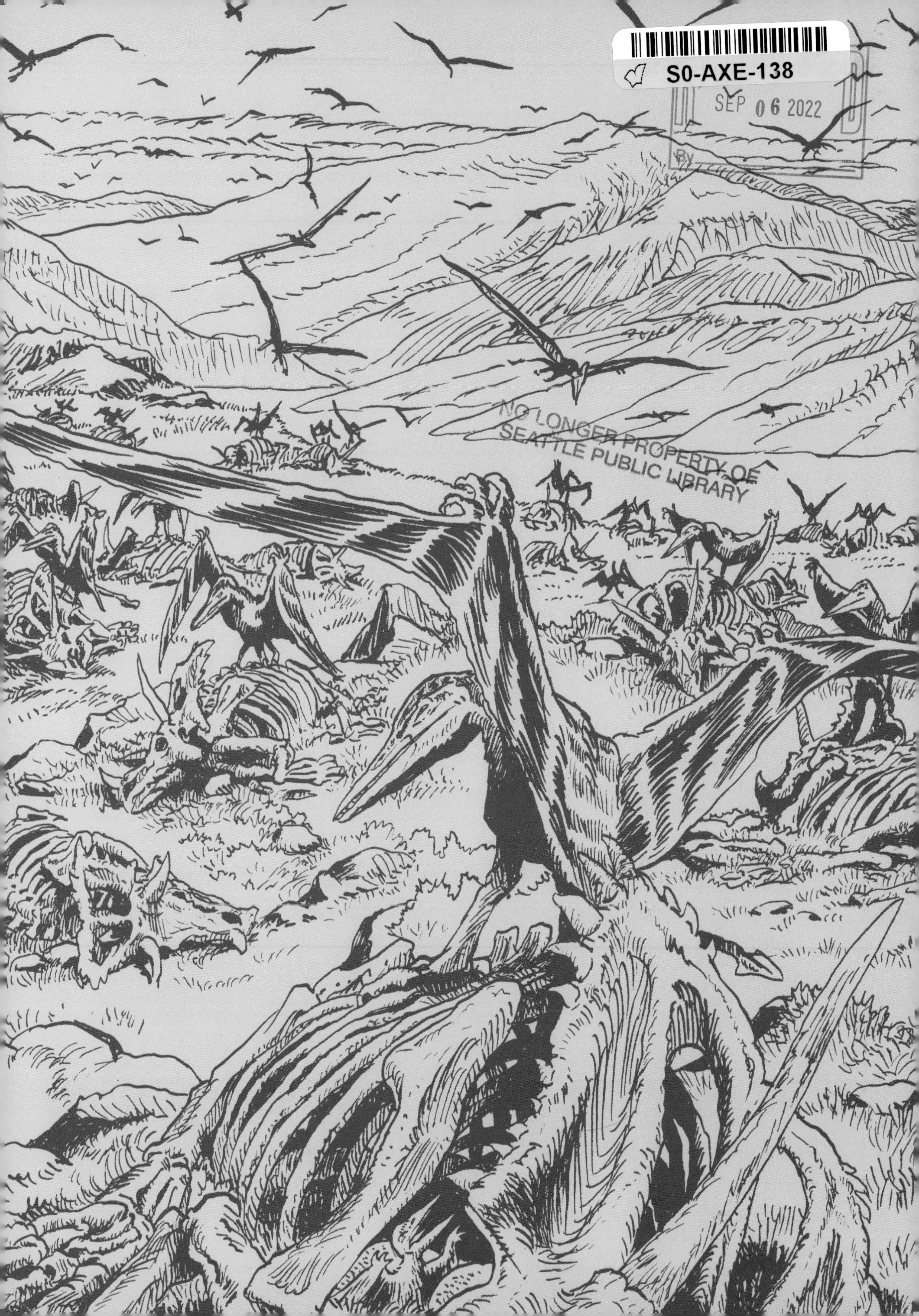

NEGALYOD

THE GOD NETWORK

TITAN COMICS   STATIX PRESS

TITAN COMICS

GROUP EDITOR
JAKE DEVINE

DESIGNER
DAN BURA

EDITORIAL ASSISTANT
CALUM COLLINS

PRODUCTION MANAGER
JACKIE FLOOK

PRODUCTION CONTROLLERS
CATERINA FALQUI &
KELLY FENLON

ART DIRECTOR
OZ BROWNE

SALES & CIRCULATION MANAGER
STEVE TOTHILL

PUBLICIST
PHOEBE TRILLO

DIGITAL & MARKETING MANAGER
JO TEATHER

ACQUISITIONS EDITOR
DUNCAN BAIZLEY

PUBLISHING DIRECTOR
RICKY CLAYDON

PUBLISHING DIRECTOR
JOHN DZIEWIATKOWSKI

OPERATIONS DIRECTOR
LEIGH BAULCH

EXECUTIVE DIRECTOR
VIVIAN CHEUNG

PUBLISHER
NICK LANDAU

NEGALYOD: THE GOD NETWORK

ISBN 9781787734708

Originally published in French as:
Negalyod by Vincent Perriot © Casterman 2018

Published by Titan Comics, a division of Titan Publishing Group, Ltd. Titan Comics is a registered trademark of Titan Publishing Group Ltd. 144 Southwark Street, London SE1 0UP.

A CIP catalogue record for this title is available from the British library.

10 9 8 7 6 5 4 3 2 1

First published June 2022
Printed in China

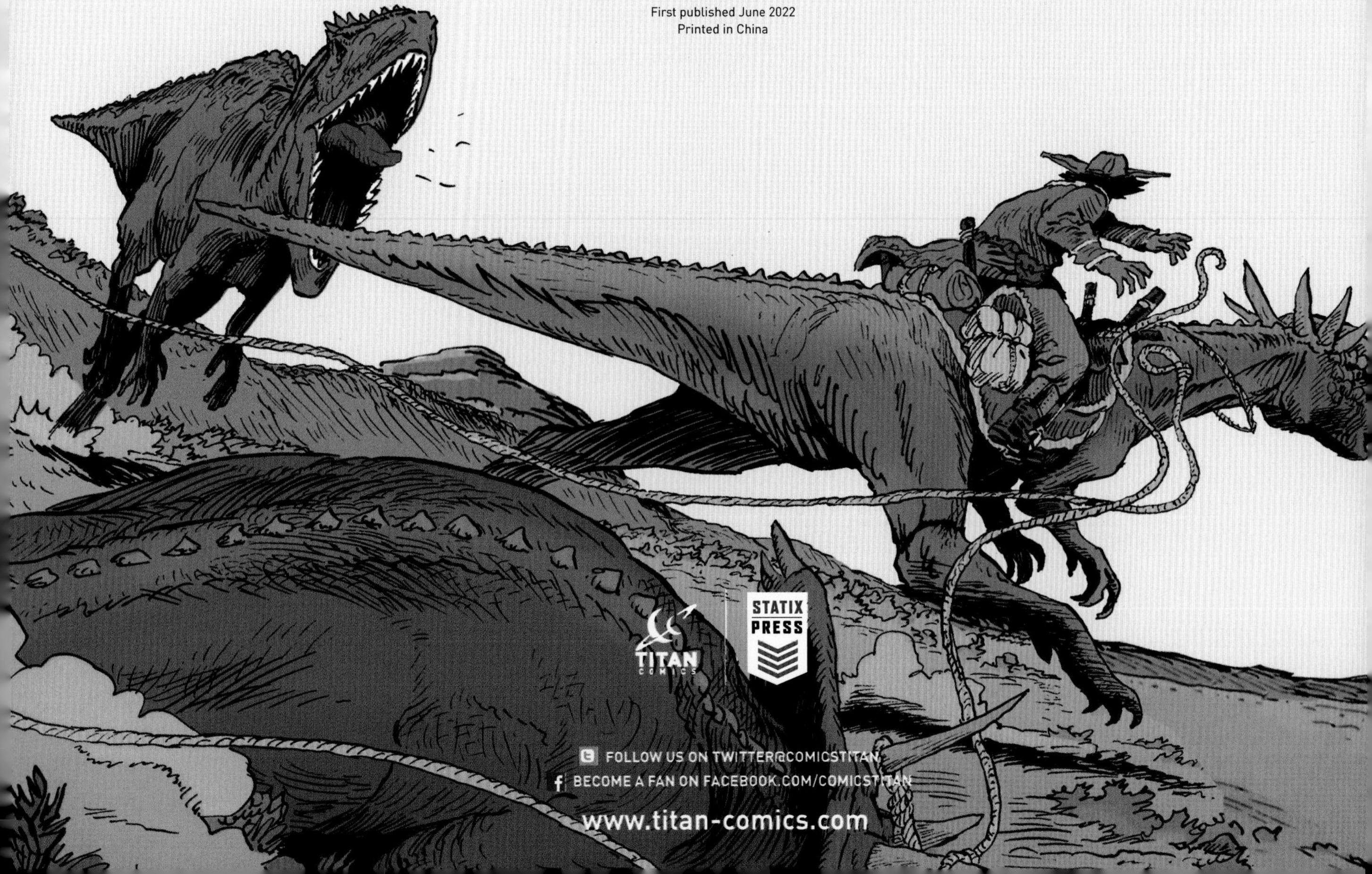

STATIX PRESS

Titan Comics

FOLLOW US ON TWITTER @COMICSTITAN
BECOME A FAN ON FACEBOOK.COM/COMICSTITAN

www.titan-comics.com

— NEGALYOD —
THE GOD NETWORK

WRITER & ARTIST
VINCENT PERRIOT

COLORS
FLORENCE BRETON

TRANSLATOR
MONTANA KANE

LETTERS
LAUREN BOWES

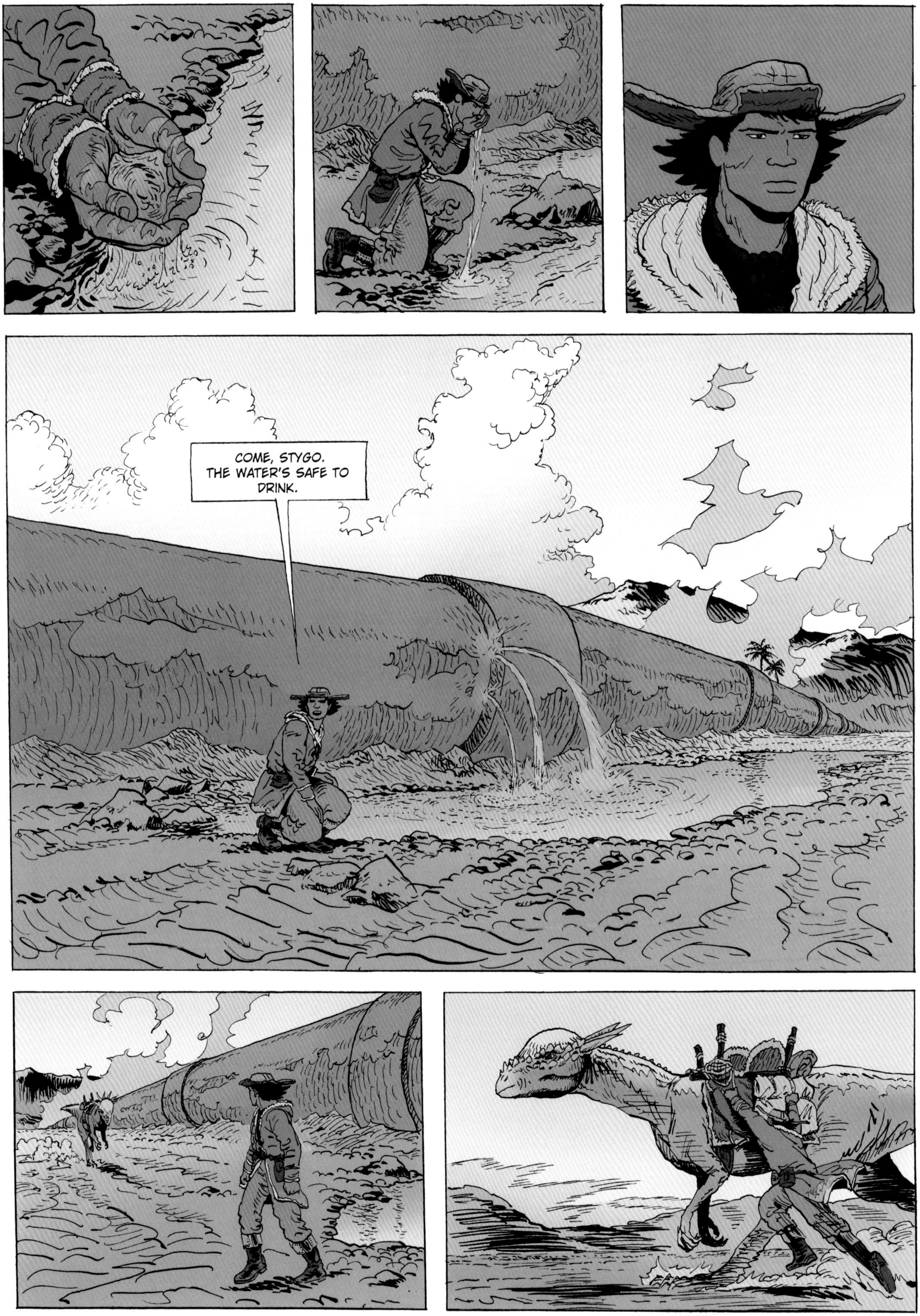
COME, STYGO.
THE WATER'S SAFE TO
DRINK.

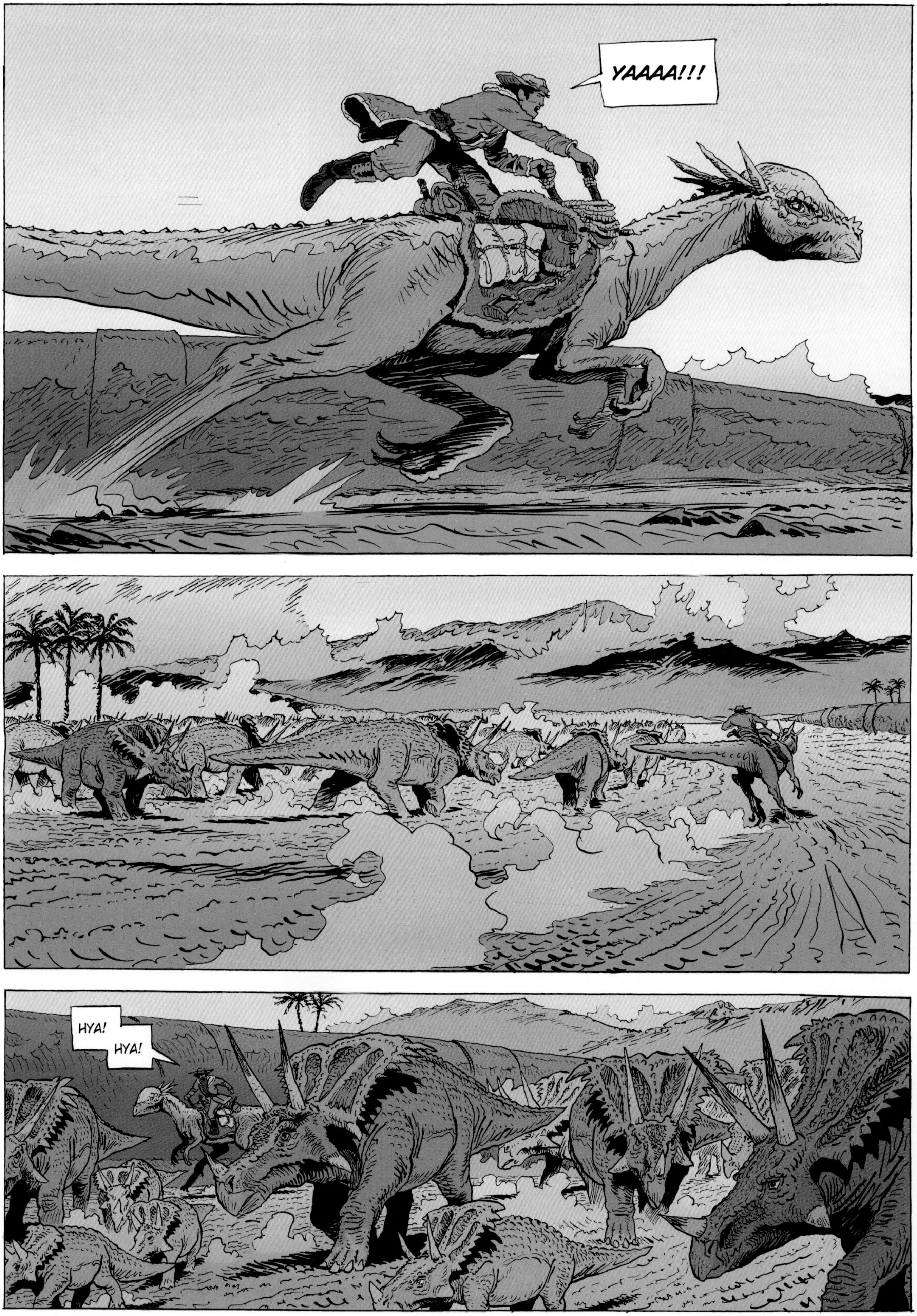
YAAAA!!!
HYA!
HYA!

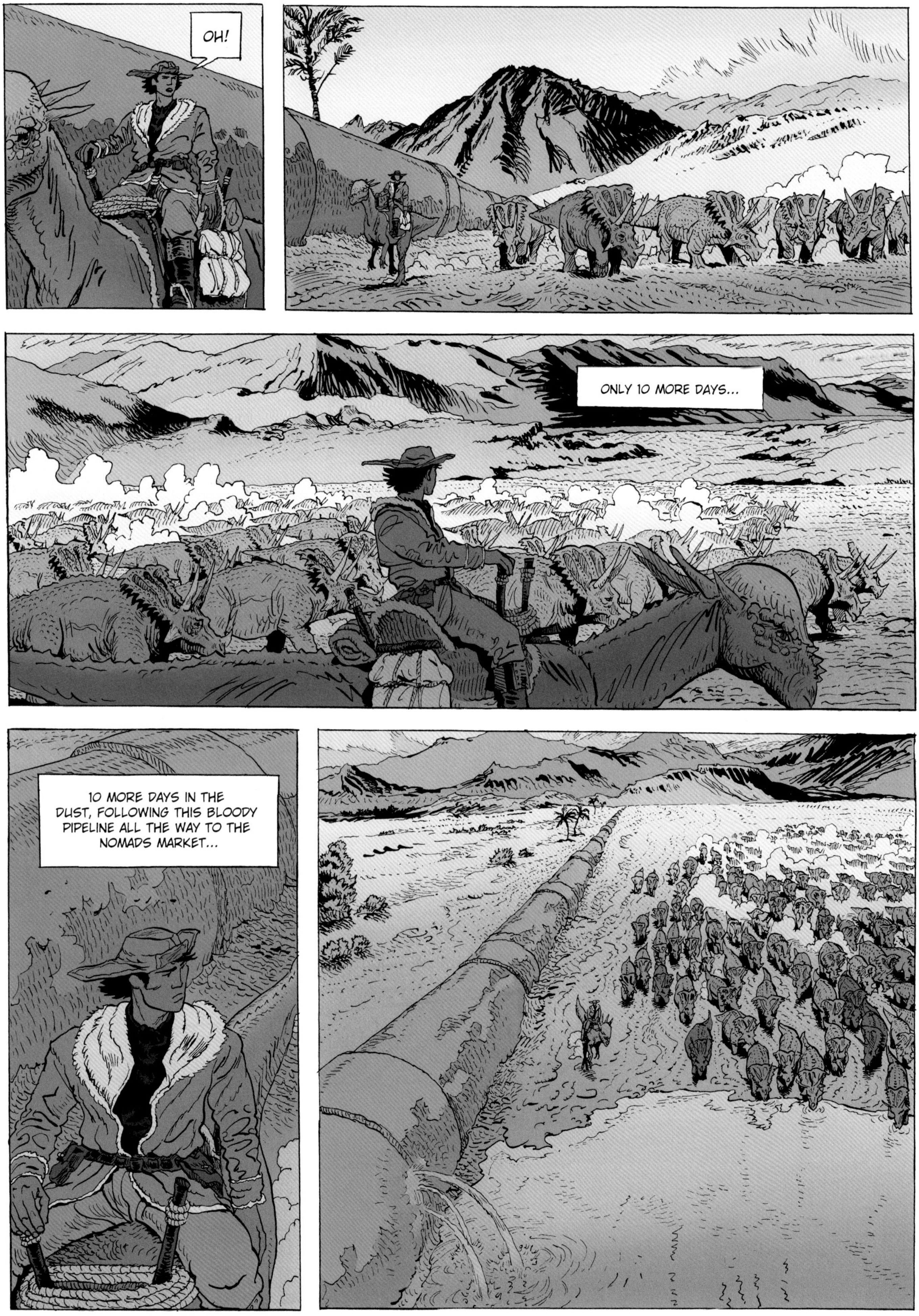
OH!
ONLY 10 MORE DAYS...
10 MORE DAYS IN THE DUST, FOLLOWING THIS BLOODY PIPELINE ALL THE WAY TO THE NOMADS MARKET...

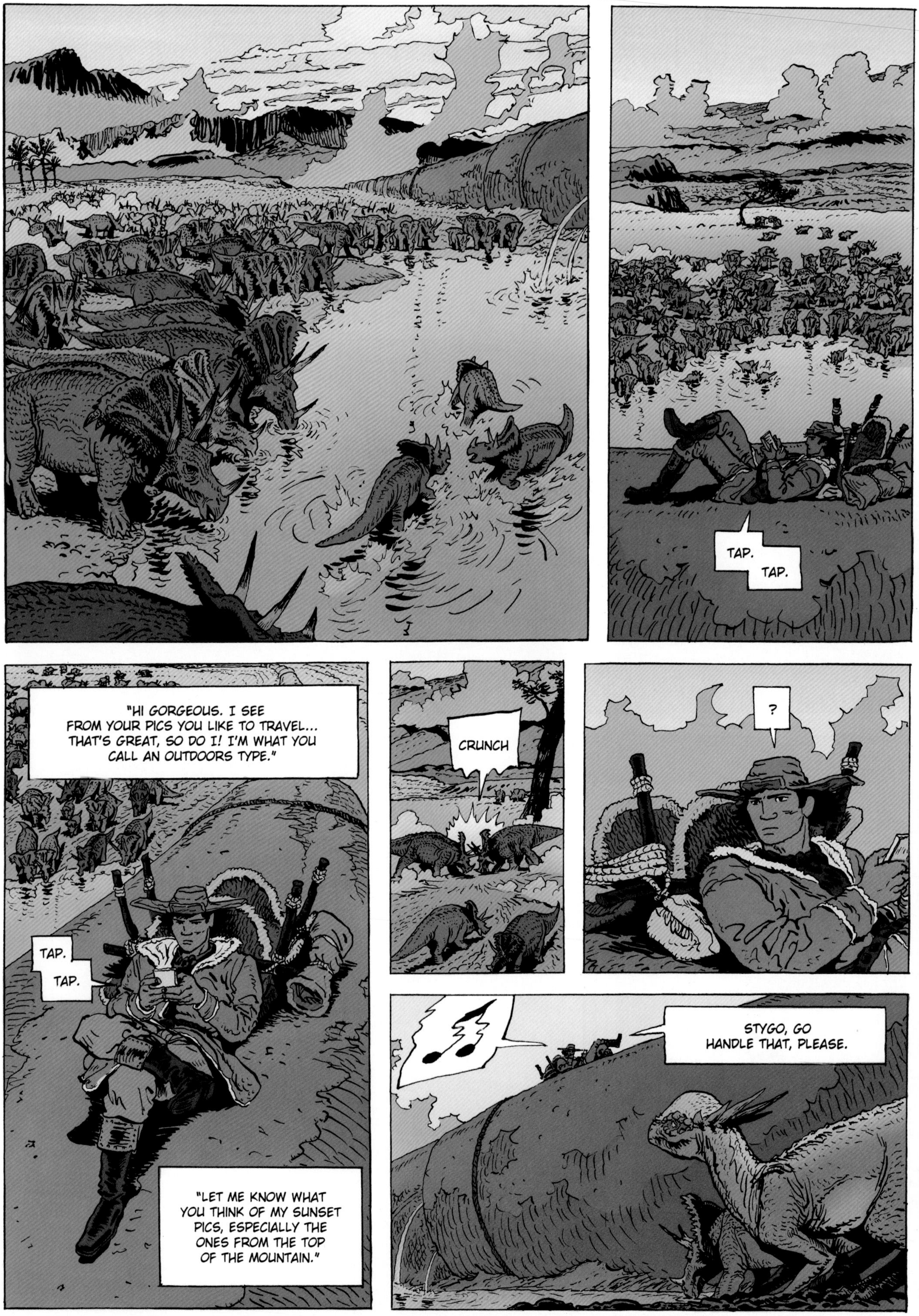
TAP.
TAP.
"HI GORGEOUS. I SEE FROM YOUR PICS YOU LIKE TO TRAVEL... THAT'S GREAT, SO DO I! I'M WHAT YOU CALL AN OUTDOORS TYPE."
TAP.
TAP.
"LET ME KNOW WHAT YOU THINK OF MY SUNSET PICS, ESPECIALLY THE ONES FROM THE TOP OF THE MOUNTAIN."
CRUNCH
?
STYGO, GO HANDLE THAT, PLEASE.

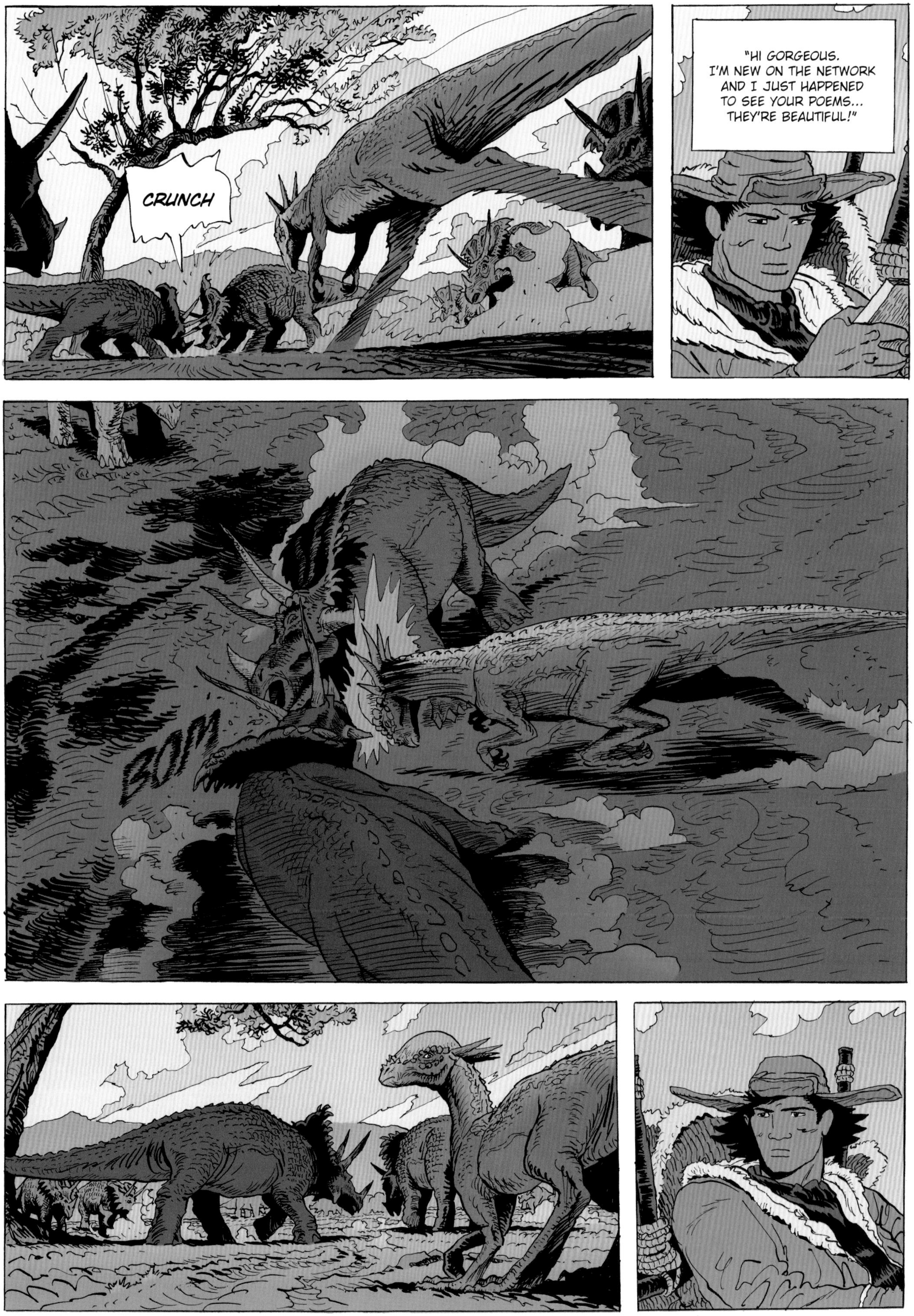
CRUNCH
"HI GORGEOUS. I'M NEW ON THE NETWORK AND I JUST HAPPENED TO SEE YOUR POEMS... THEY'RE BEAUTIFUL!"
BOM

FORGET IT. JUST LET THEM FIGHT, IF THAT'S WHAT THEY WANT.

THANKS, STYGO. I DON'T KNOW WHAT I'D DO WITHOUT YOU. I SOMETIMES WONDER WHAT THE HELL I'M DOING OUT HERE IN THE MIDDLE OF NOWHERE.

THE CHASMOSAURUSES ARE FREE, BUT THEY CHOSE ME TO GUIDE THEM...

THEIR SURVIVAL IS AT STAKE IN THIS ENDLESS DESERT...

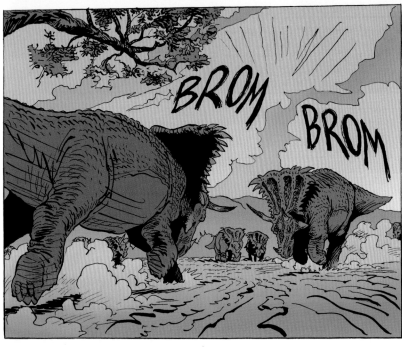

BROM

BROM

CRUNCH

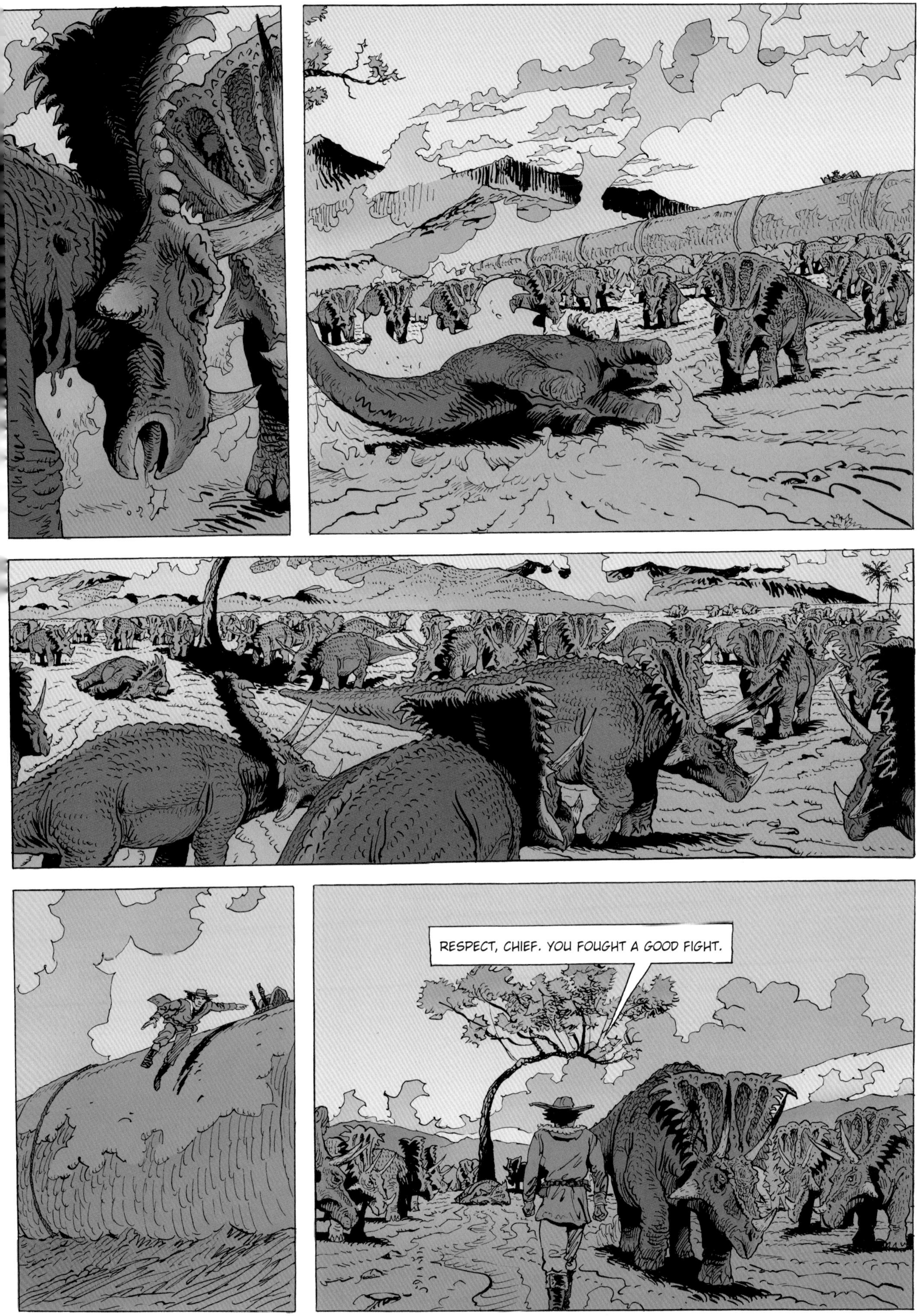
RESPECT, CHIEF. YOU FOUGHT A GOOD FIGHT.

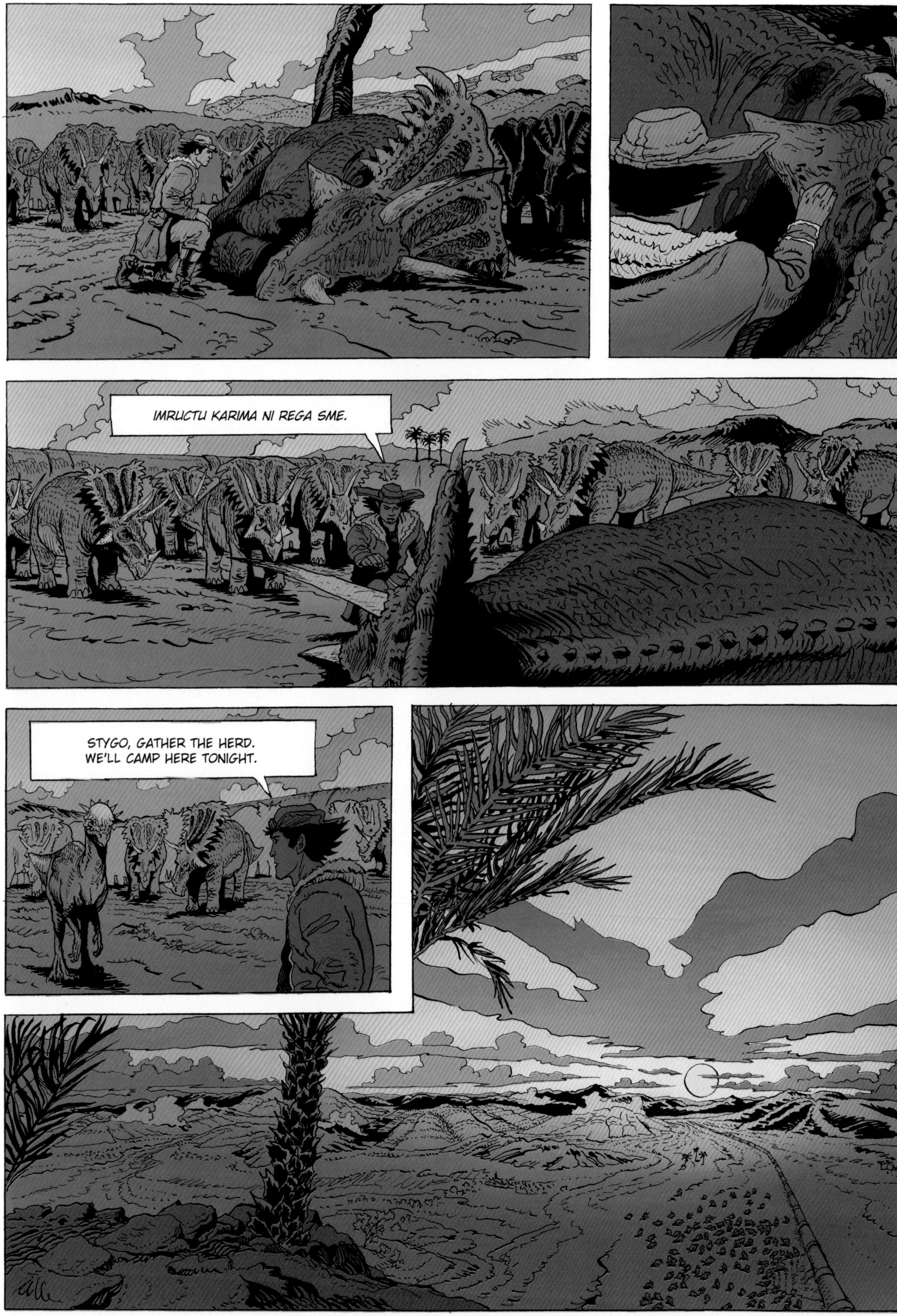
IMRUCTU KARIMA NI REGA SME.
STYGO, GATHER THE HERD. WE'LL CAMP HERE TONIGHT.

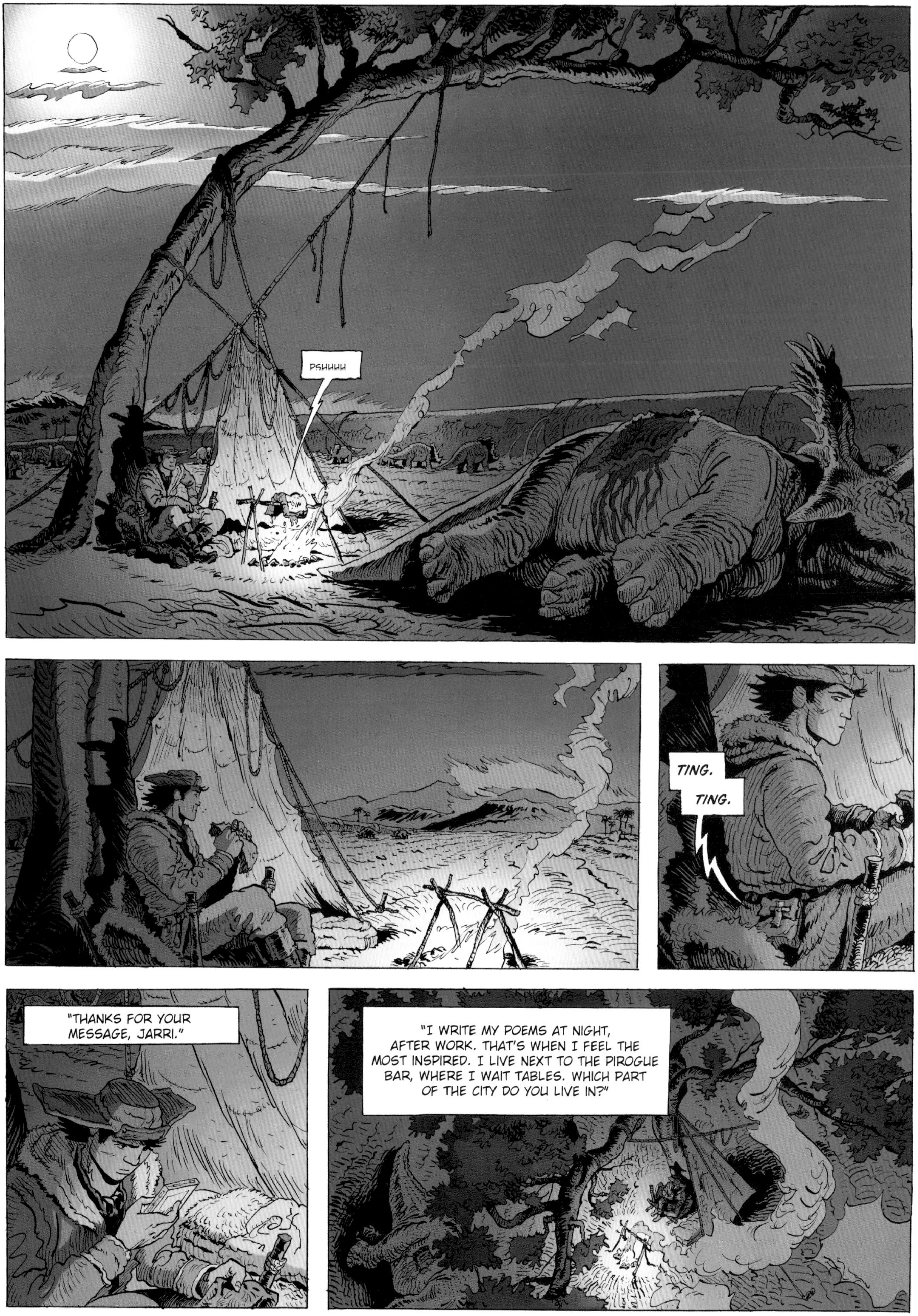
PSHHHH
TING.
TING.
"THANKS FOR YOUR MESSAGE, JARRI."
"I WRITE MY POEMS AT NIGHT, AFTER WORK. THAT'S WHEN I FEEL THE MOST INSPIRED. I LIVE NEXT TO THE PIROGUE BAR, WHERE I WAIT TABLES. WHICH PART OF THE CITY DO YOU LIVE IN?"

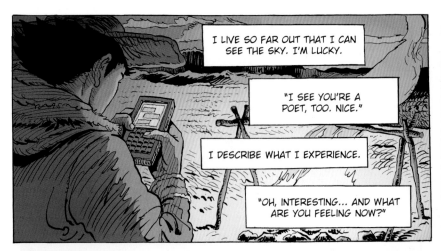

I LIVE SO FAR OUT THAT I CAN SEE THE SKY. I'M LUCKY.

"I SEE YOU'RE A POET, TOO. NICE."

I DESCRIBE WHAT I EXPERIENCE.

"OH, INTERESTING... AND WHAT ARE YOU FEELING NOW?"

THE DUST BILLOWS UP TOWARDS THE SLEEPING STARS, THE SUN CRIES OUT, I COME TO YOU...

MY LOVE...

SIGH WHY ISN'T SHE ANSWERING?

SCHTAK!

SCHTAK!

SCHTAK!

SCHTK

SCHTK

SCHTK

I SHOULD HAVE LIED, AND AT LEAST SCORED A FEW PICS. SO MUCH FOR BEING A POET.

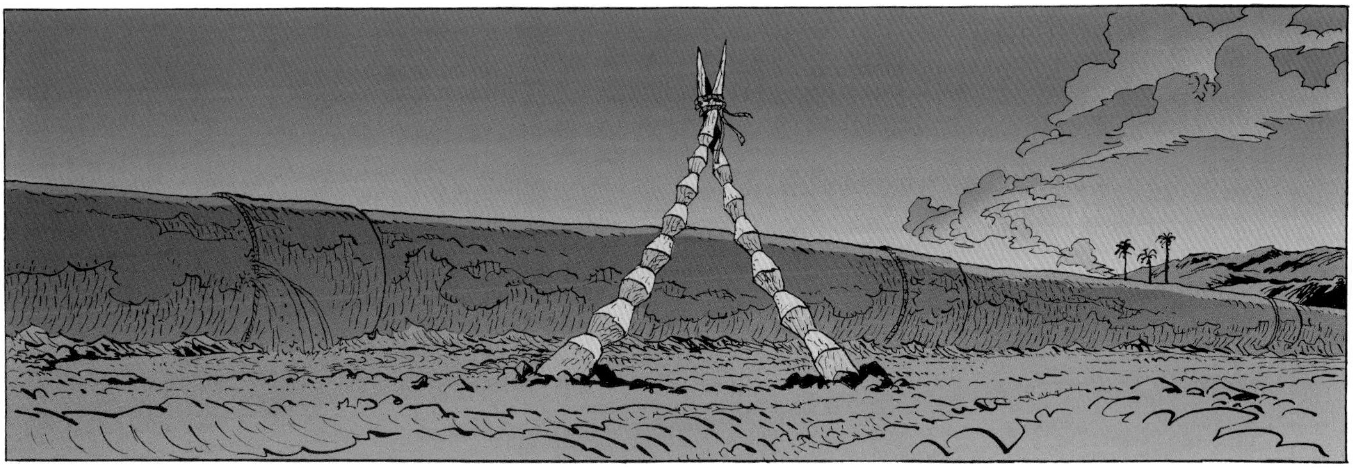

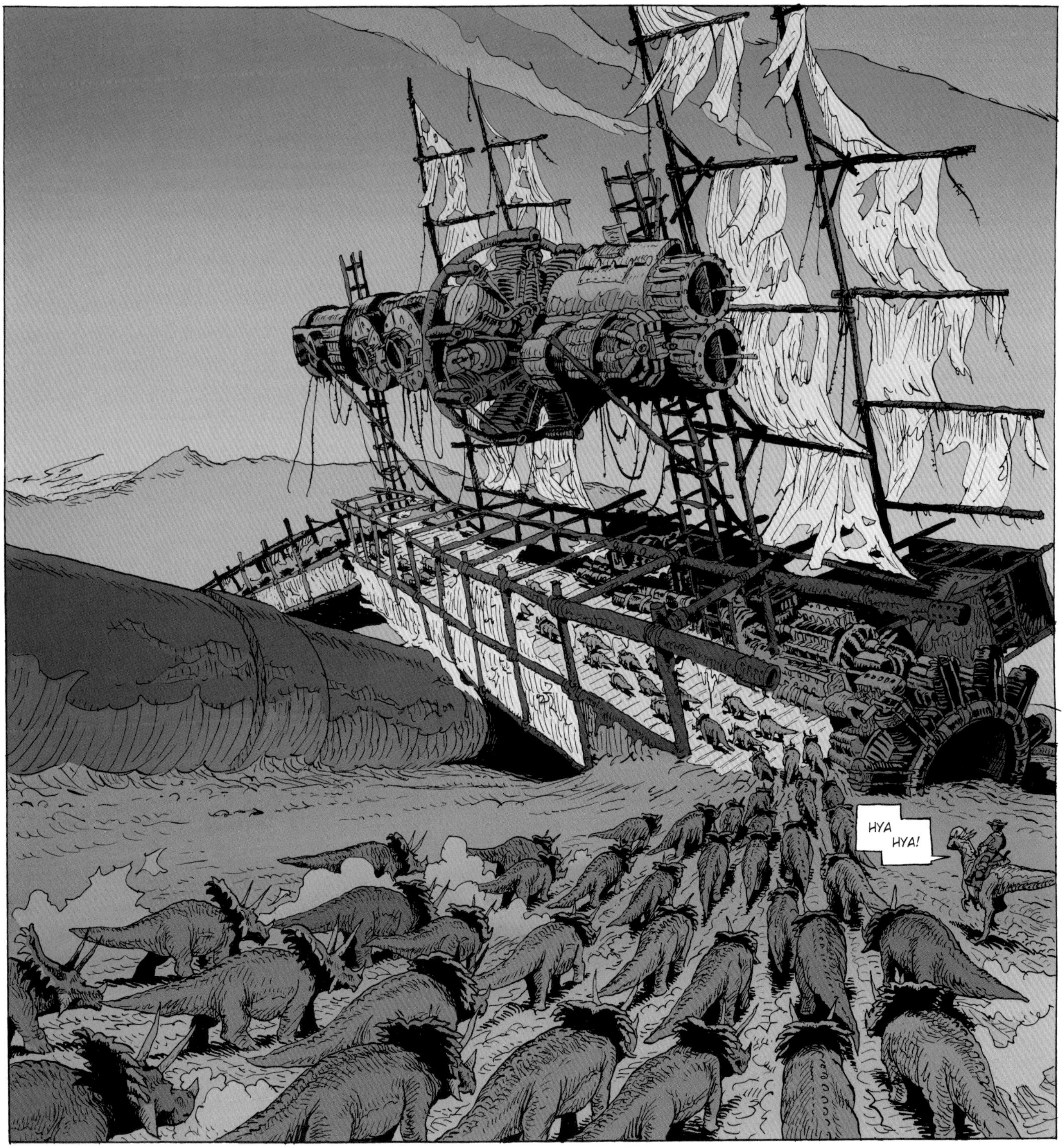
HYA
HYA!

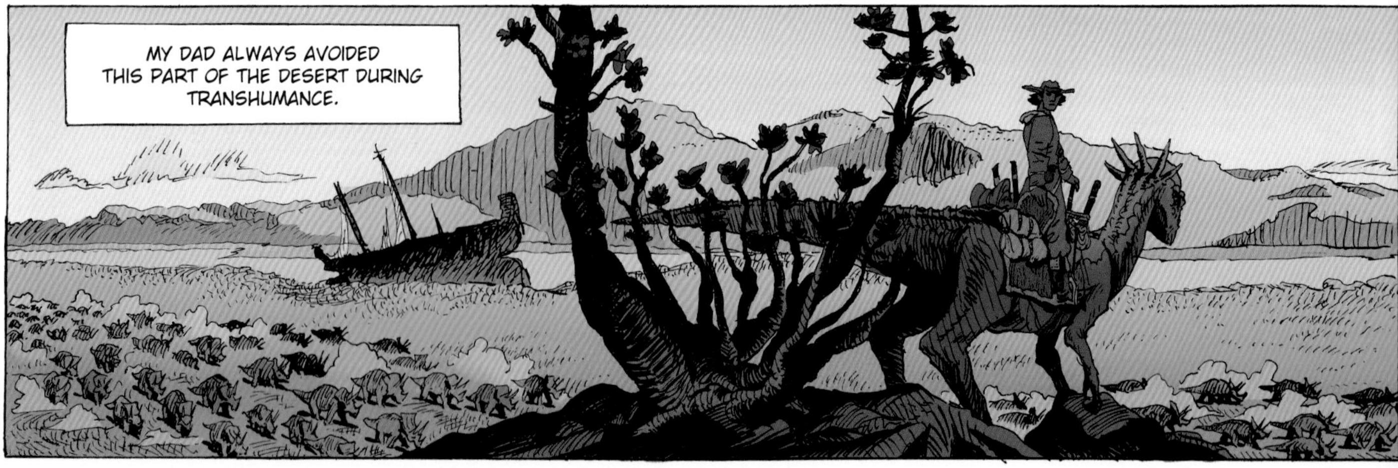
MY DAD ALWAYS AVOIDED THIS PART OF THE DESERT DURING TRANSHUMANCE.

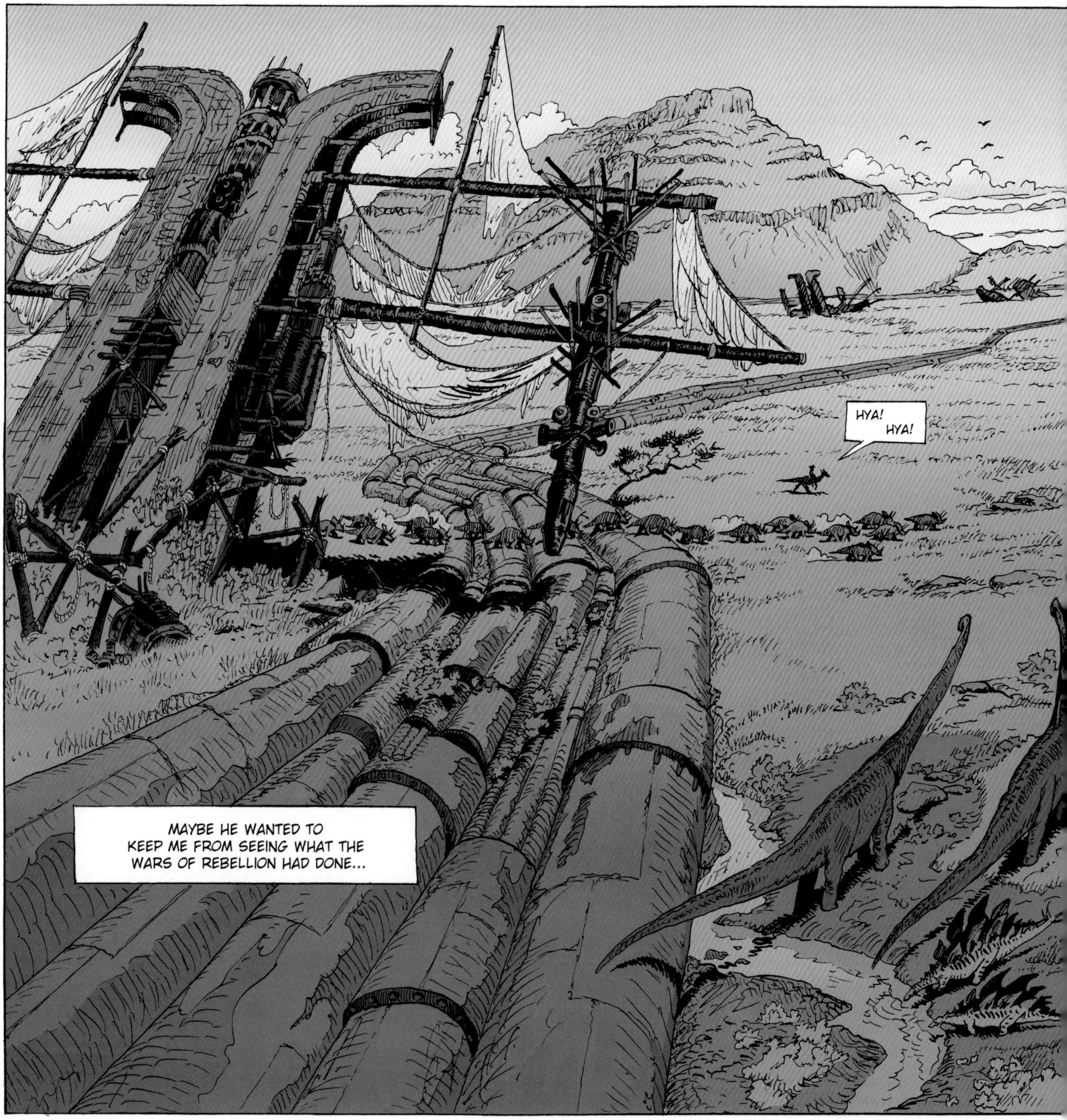
HYA! HYA!
MAYBE HE WANTED TO KEEP ME FROM SEEING WHAT THE WARS OF REBELLION HAD DONE...

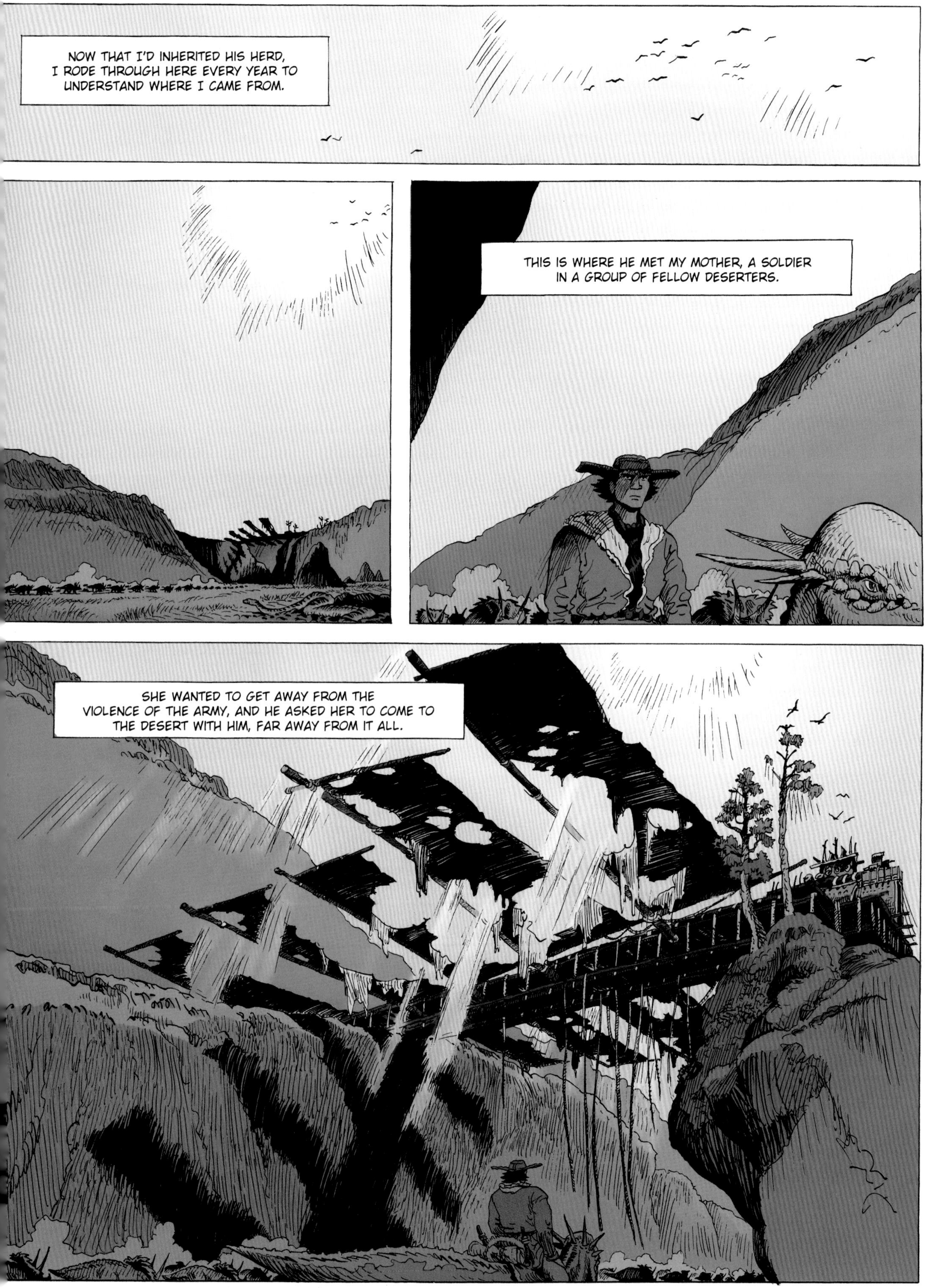
NOW THAT I'D INHERITED HIS HERD, I RODE THROUGH HERE EVERY YEAR TO UNDERSTAND WHERE I CAME FROM.
THIS IS WHERE HE MET MY MOTHER, A SOLDIER IN A GROUP OF FELLOW DESERTERS.
SHE WANTED TO GET AWAY FROM THE VIOLENCE OF THE ARMY, AND HE ASKED HER TO COME TO THE DESERT WITH HIM, FAR AWAY FROM IT ALL.

ONE DAY, WHEN I WAS
JUST A TEEN, THE ARMY FOUND MY
MOTHER AND TOOK HER. THAT'S THE
LAST TIME I EVER SAW HER.

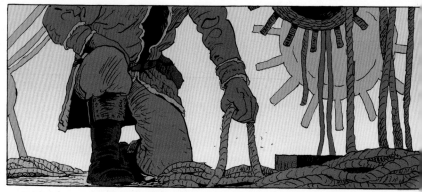

FRRRT!

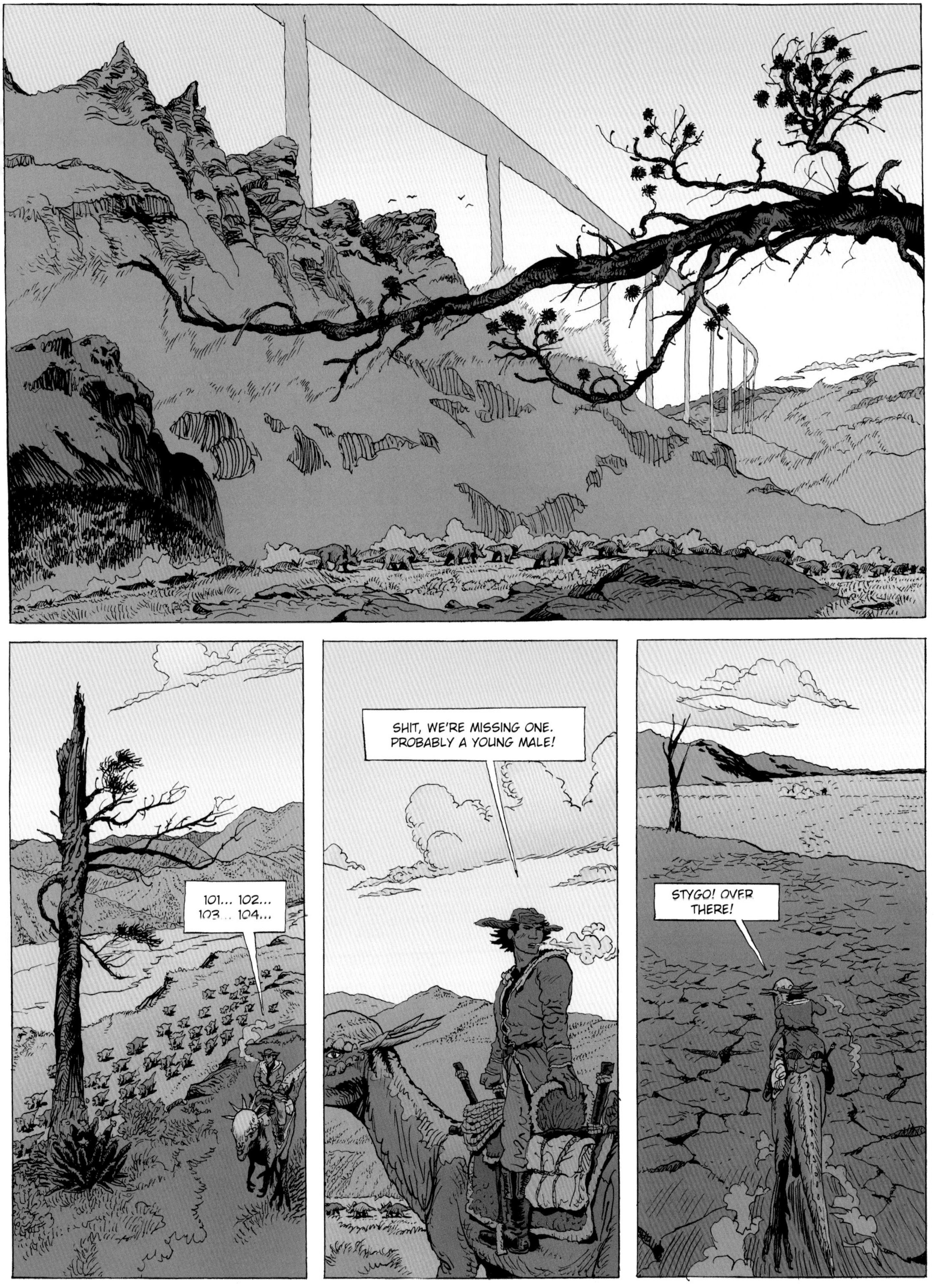
101... 102... 103... 104...
SHIT, WE'RE MISSING ONE. PROBABLY A YOUNG MALE!
STYGO! OVER THERE!

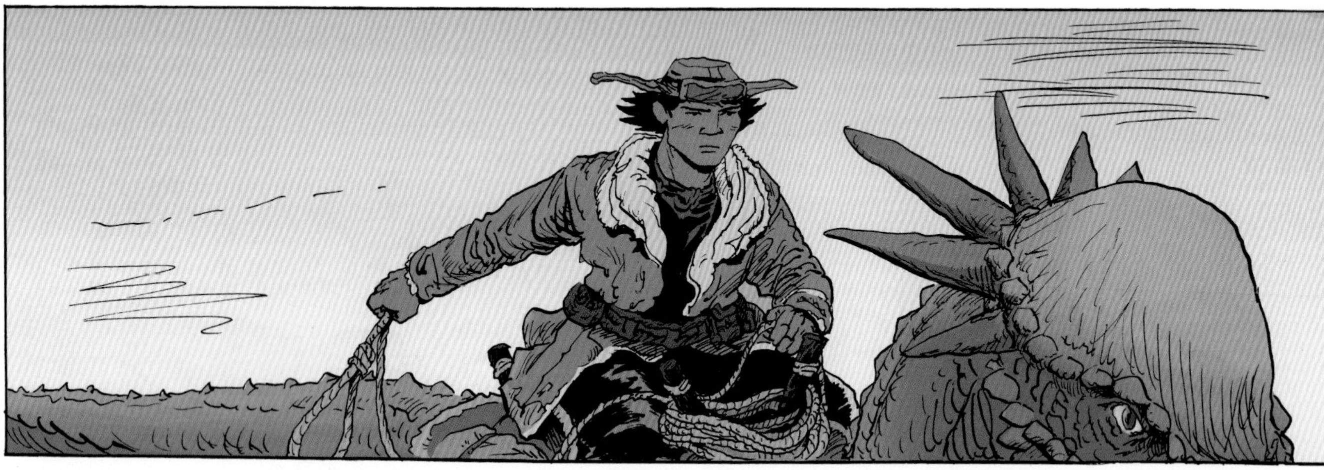

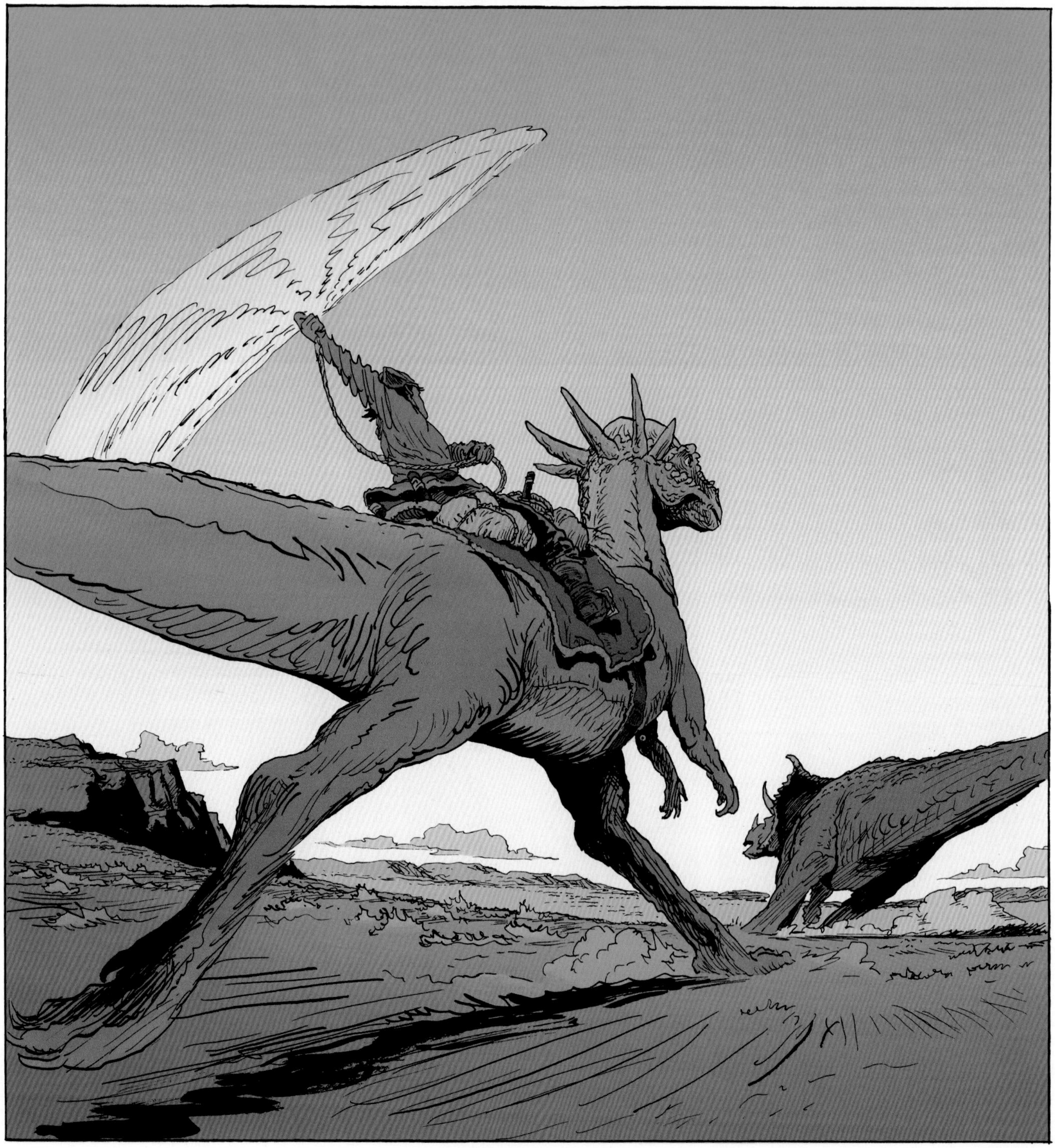

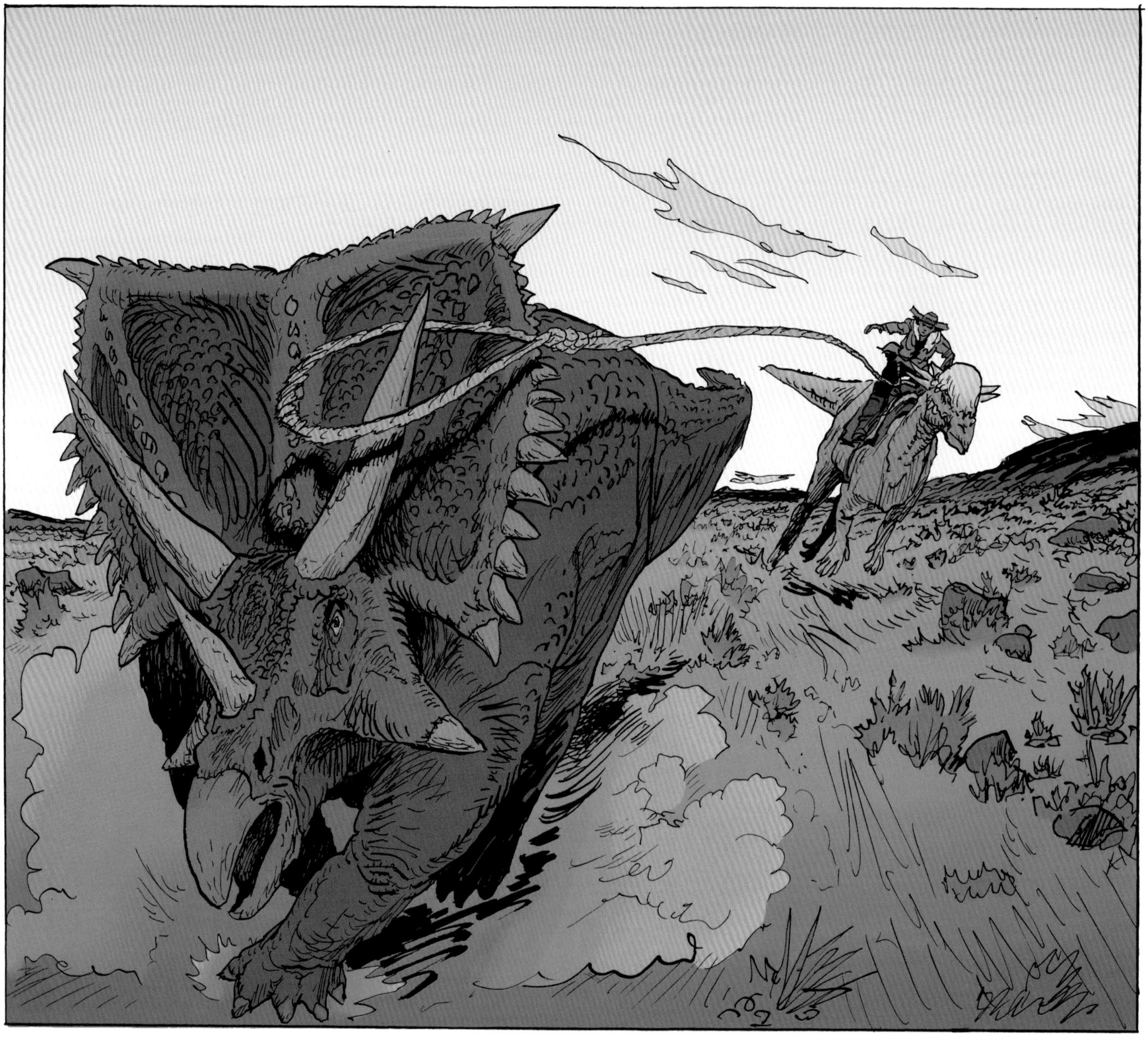

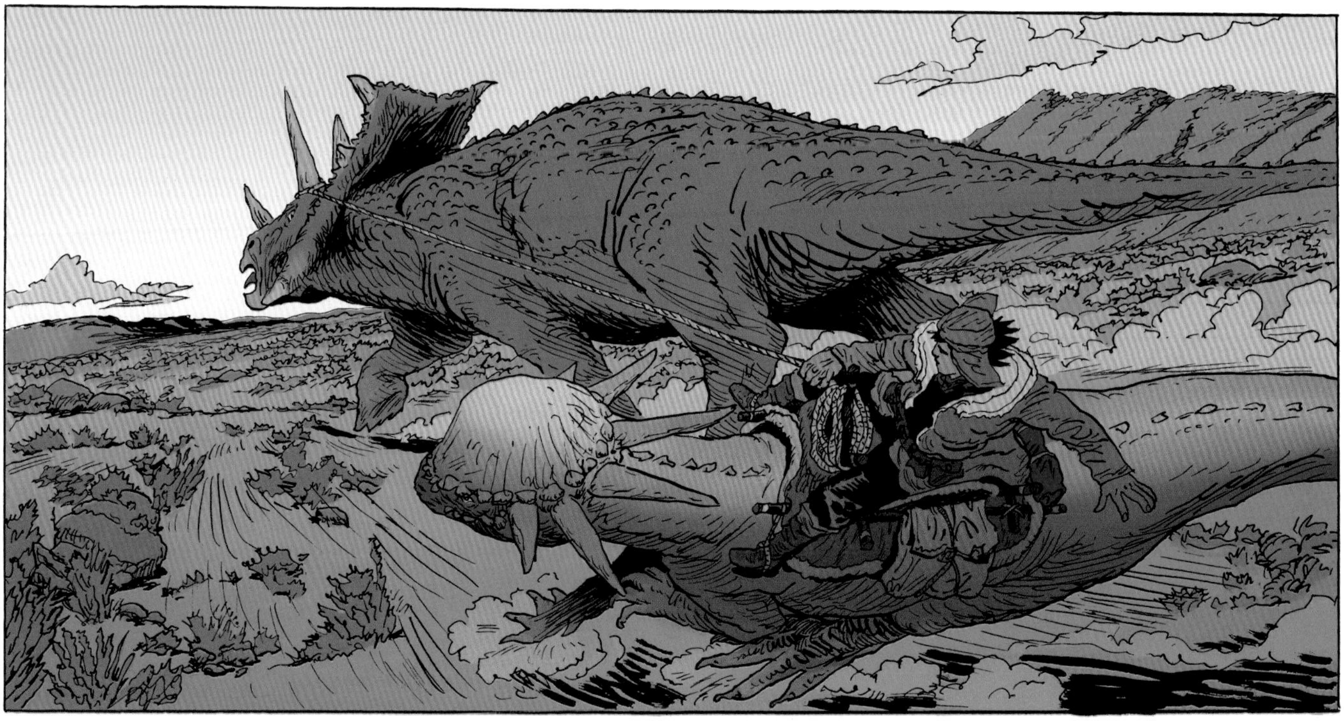

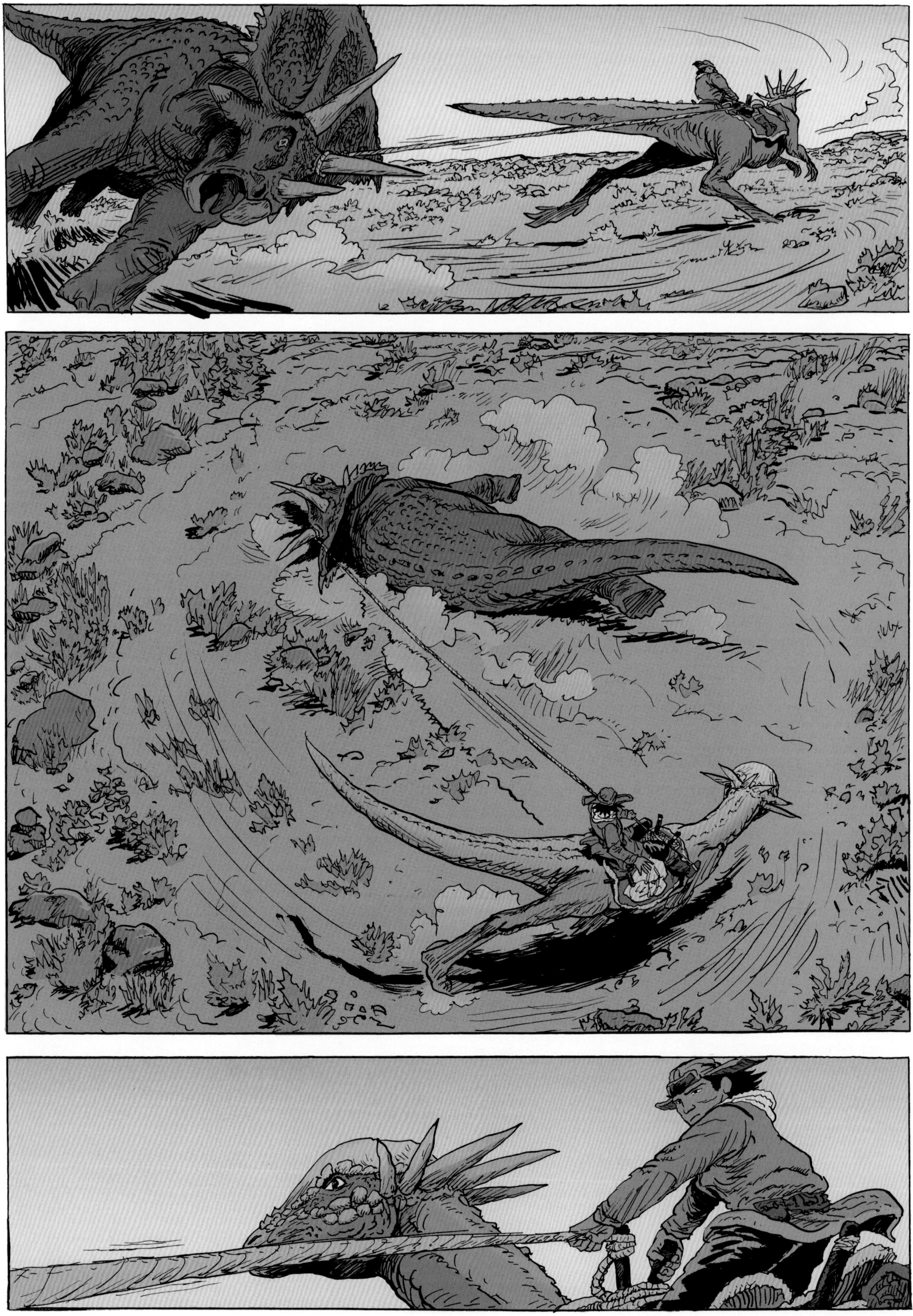

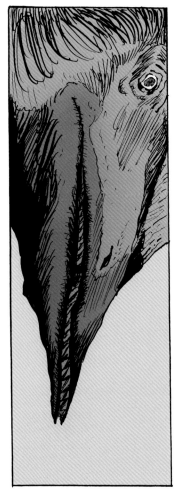

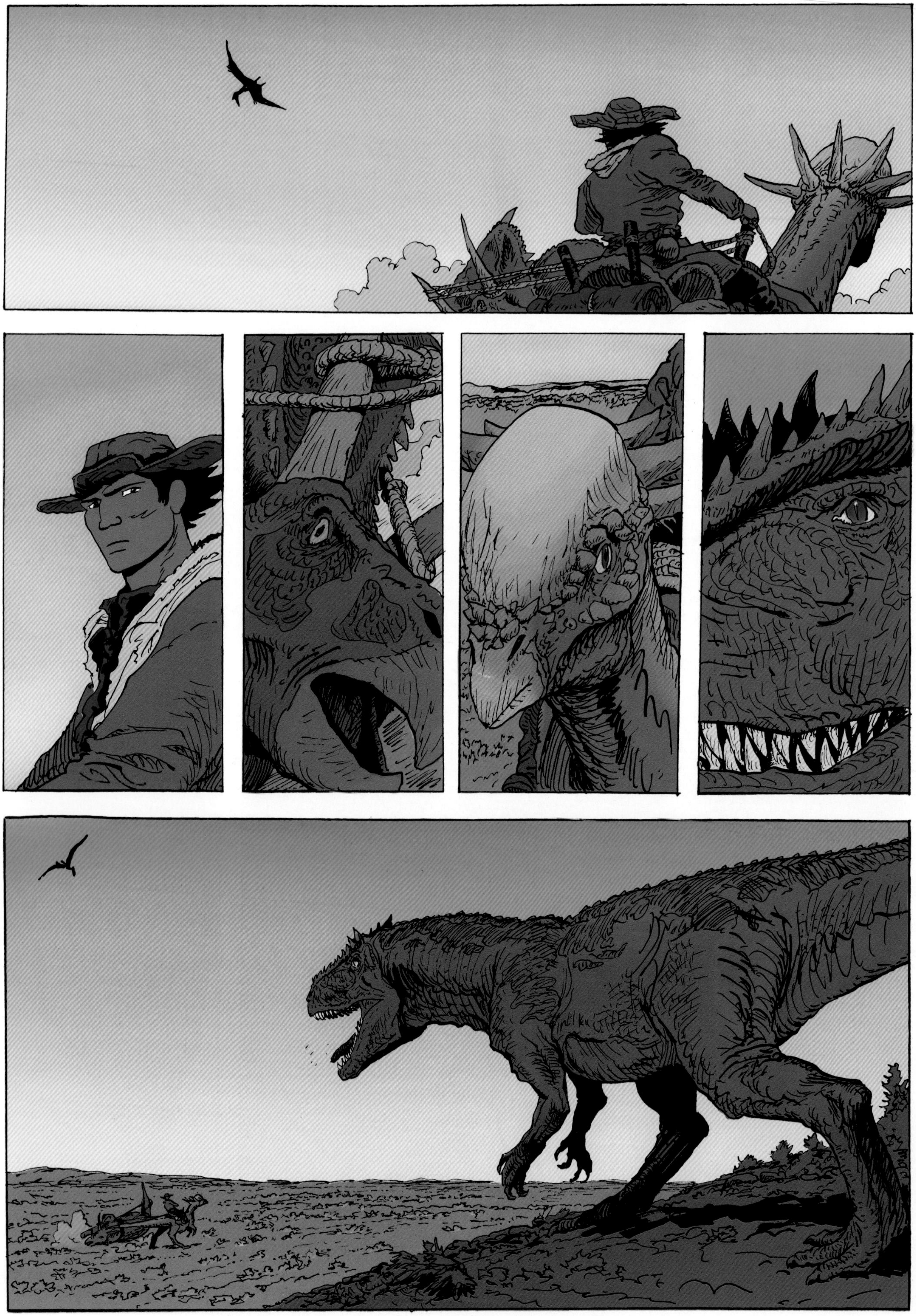

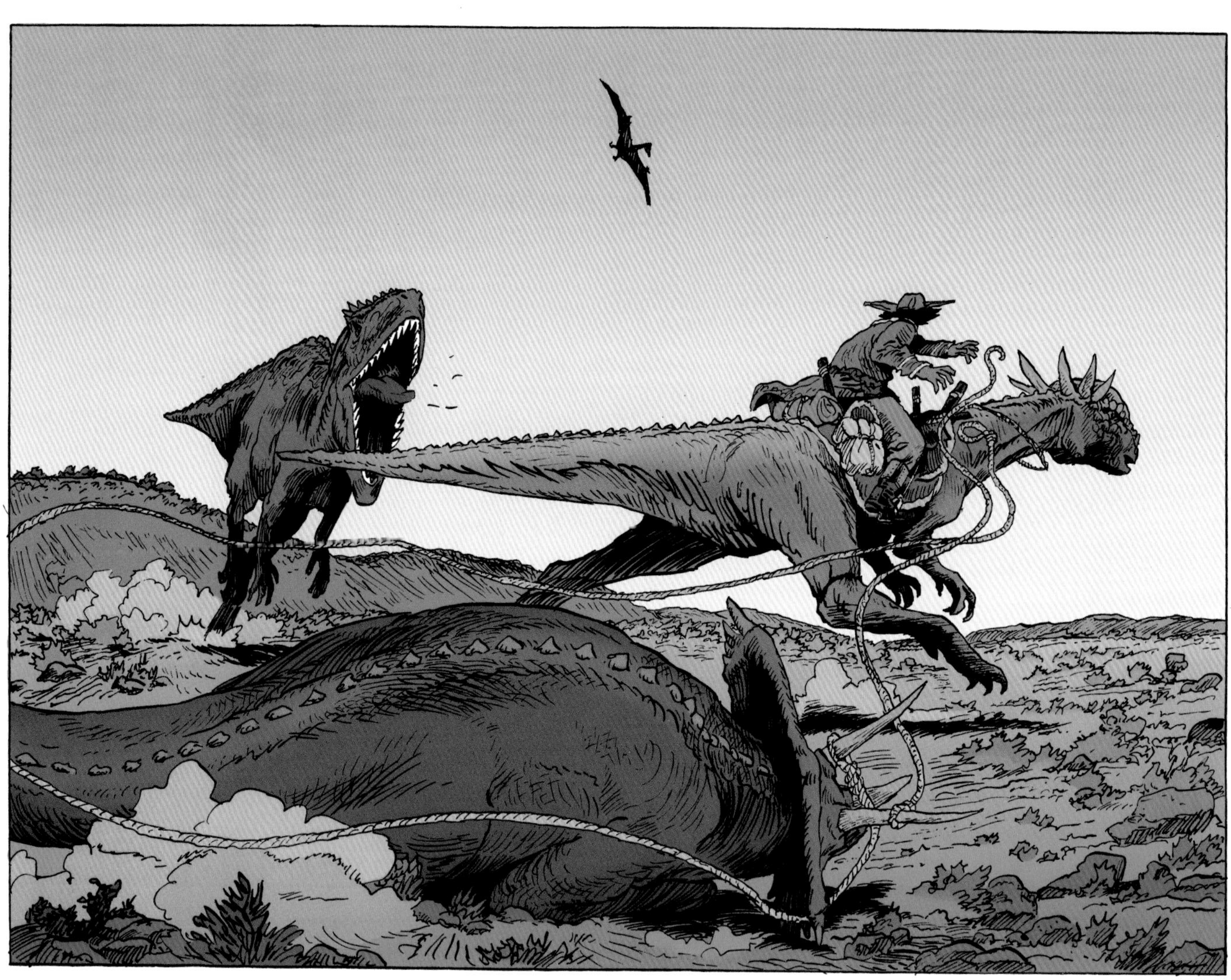

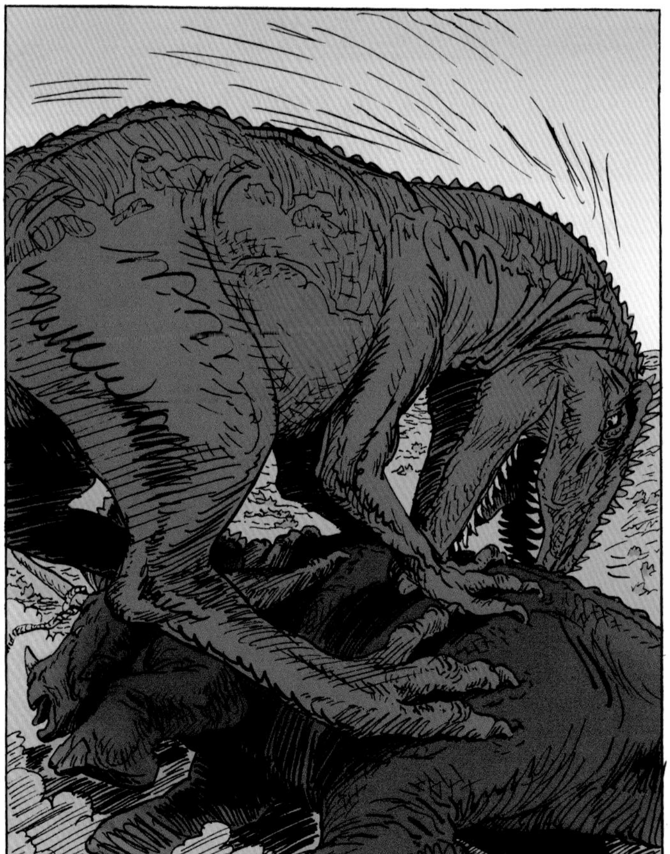

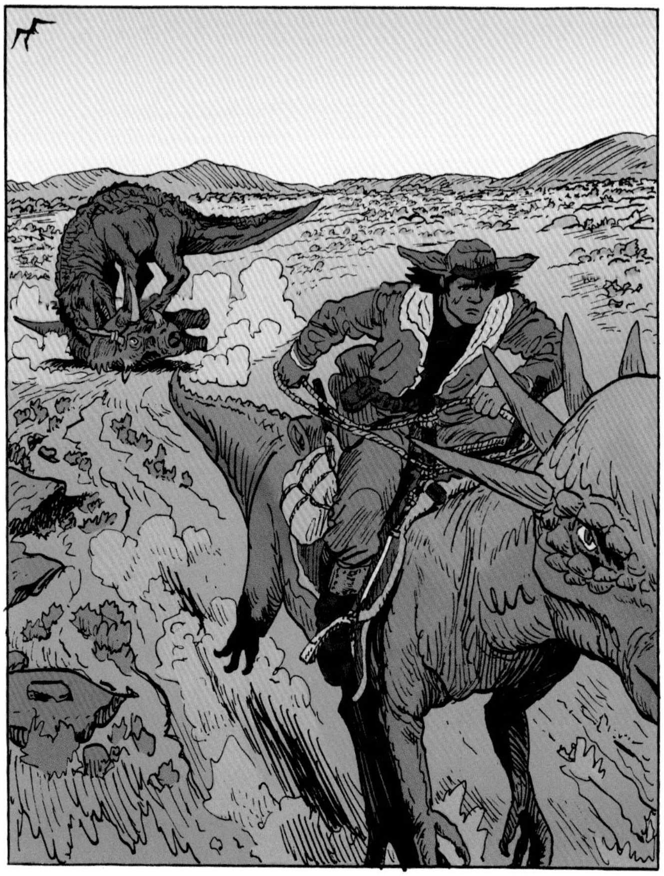

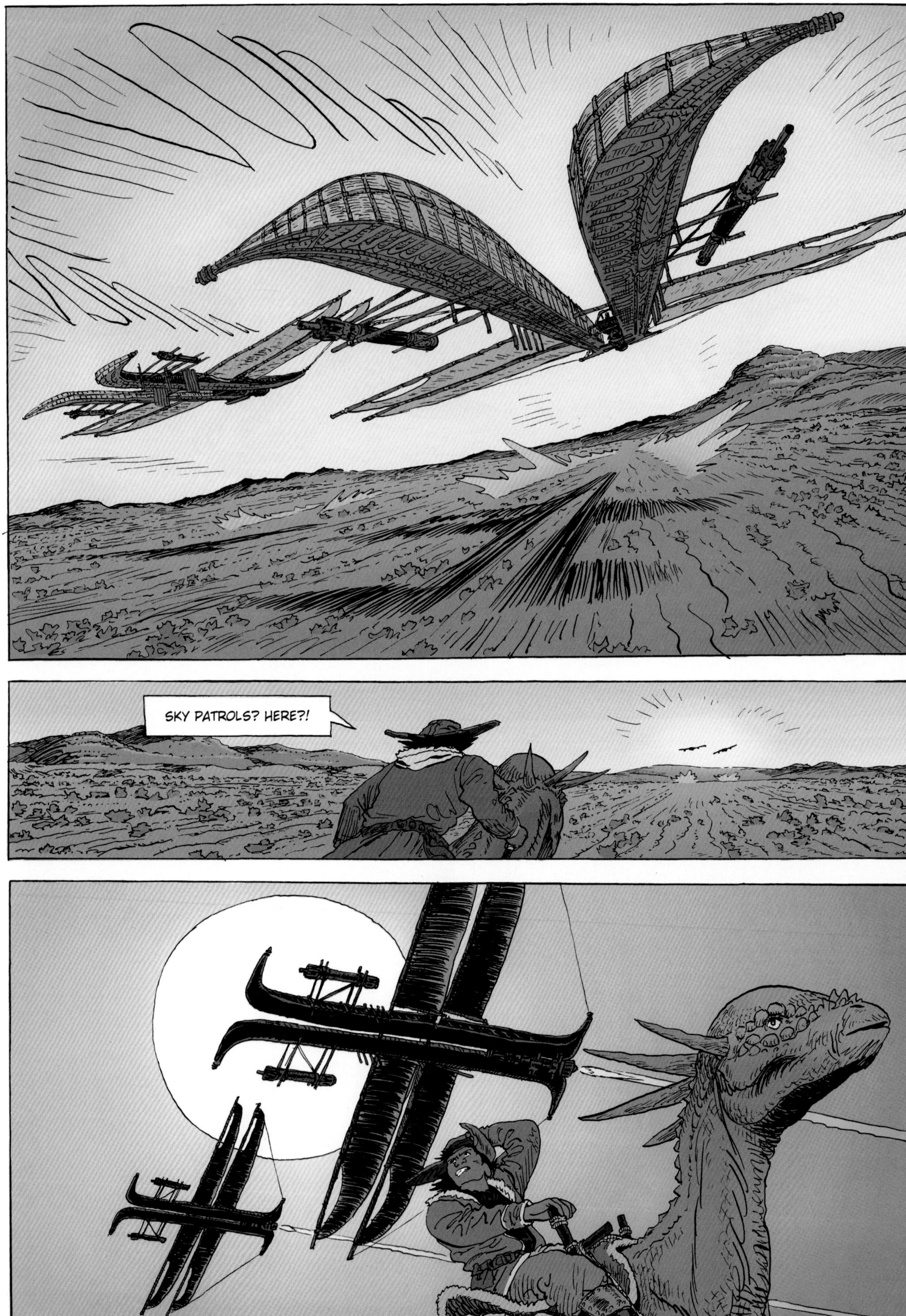
SKY PATROLS? HERE?!

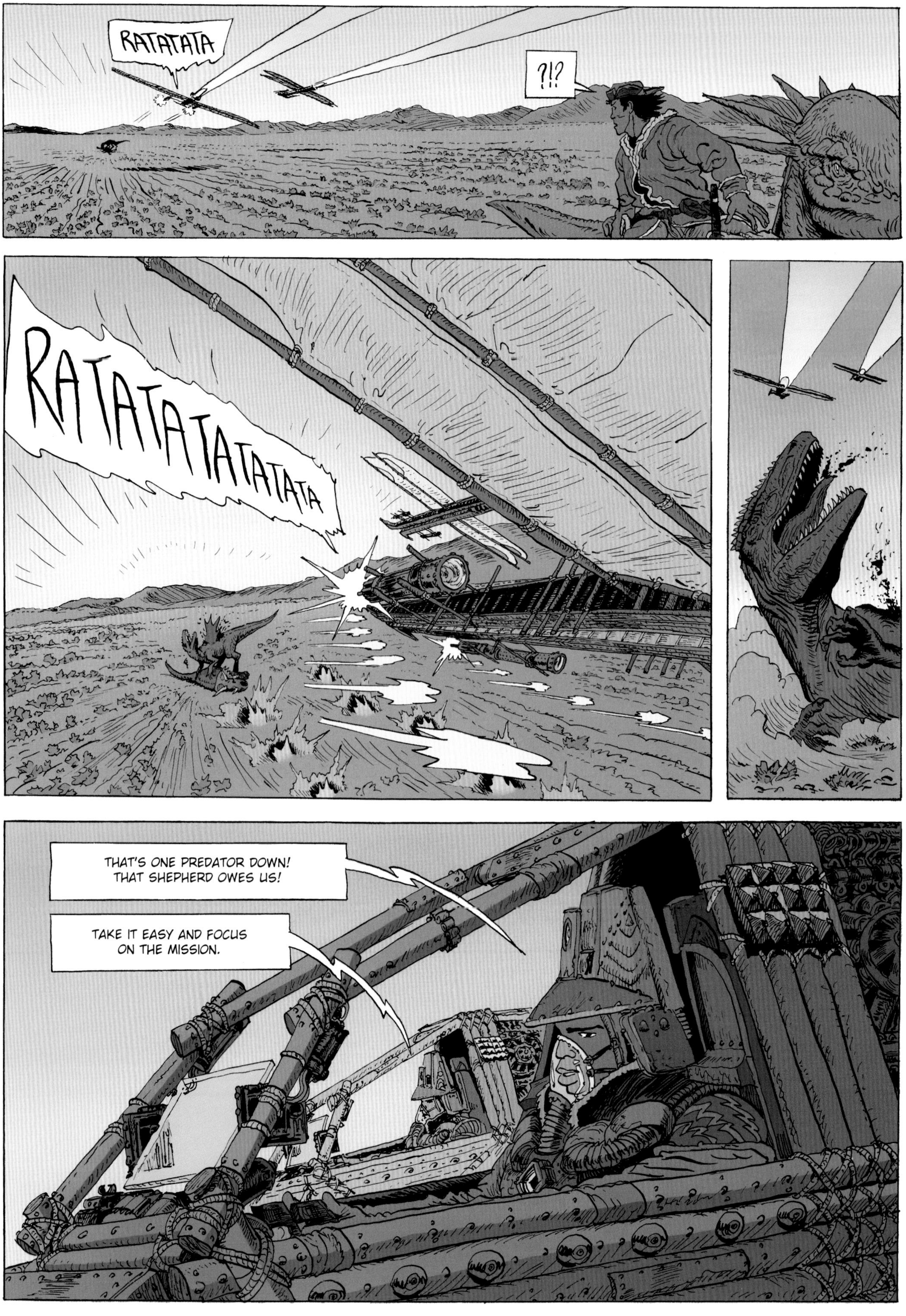
RATATATA
?!?
RATATATATATATATA
THAT'S ONE PREDATOR DOWN!
THAT SHEPHERD OWES US!
TAKE IT EASY AND FOCUS
ON THE MISSION.

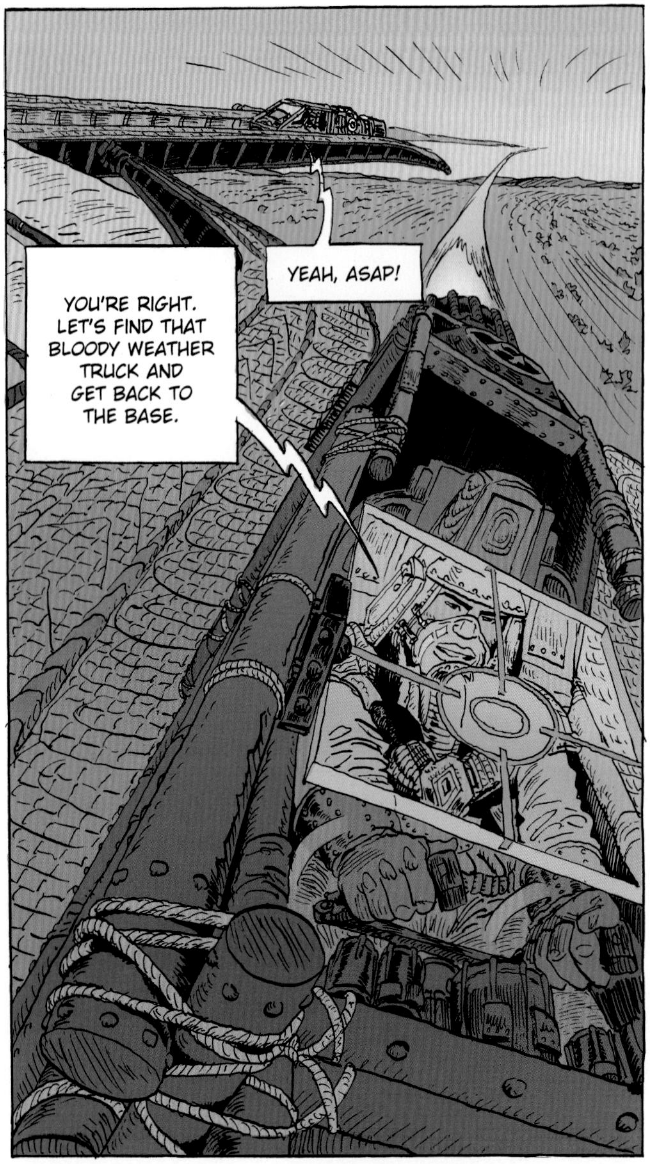
YOU'RE RIGHT. LET'S FIND THAT BLOODY WEATHER TRUCK AND GET BACK TO THE BASE.
YEAH, ASAP!

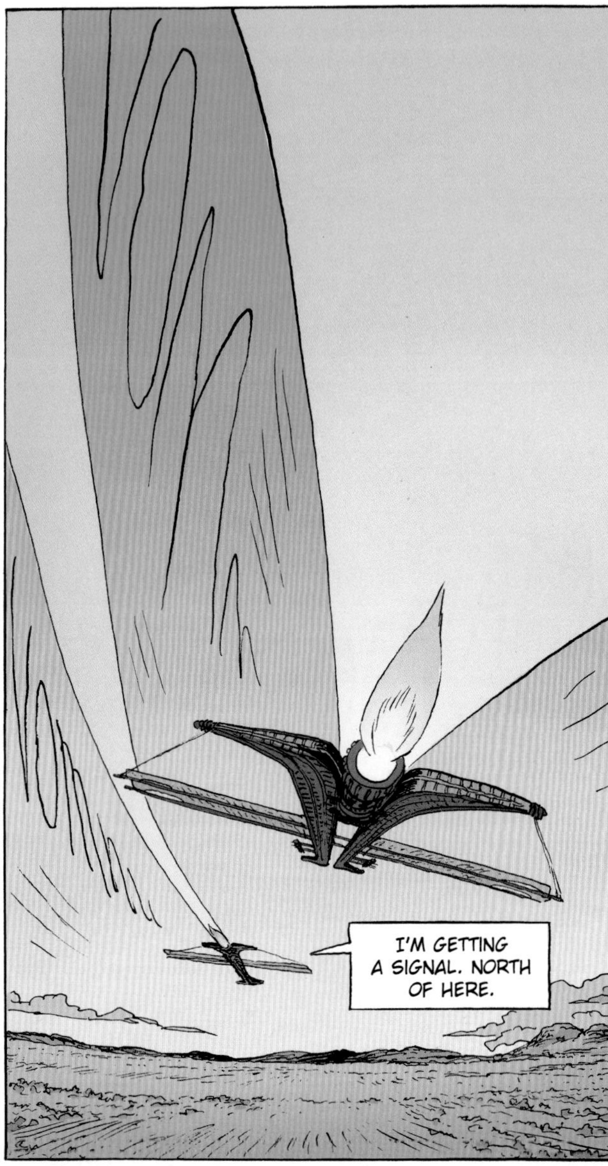
I'M GETTING A SIGNAL. NORTH OF HERE.

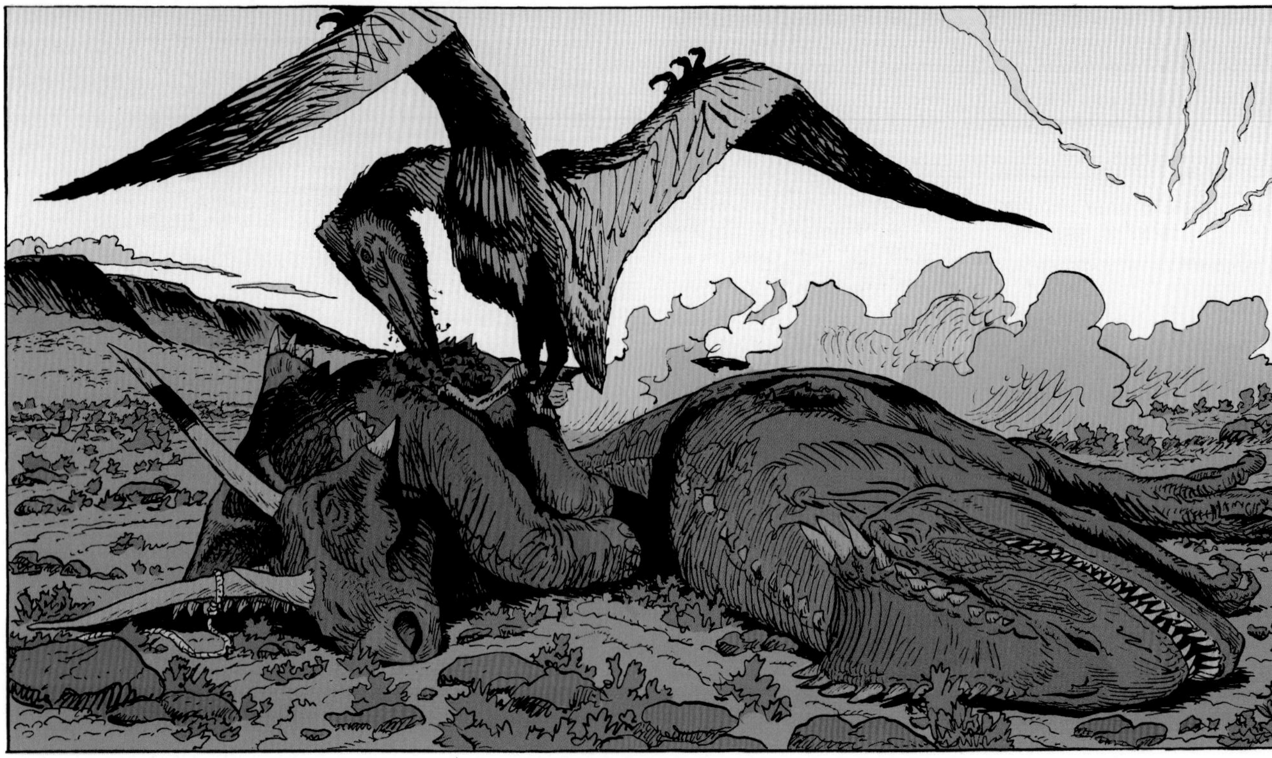

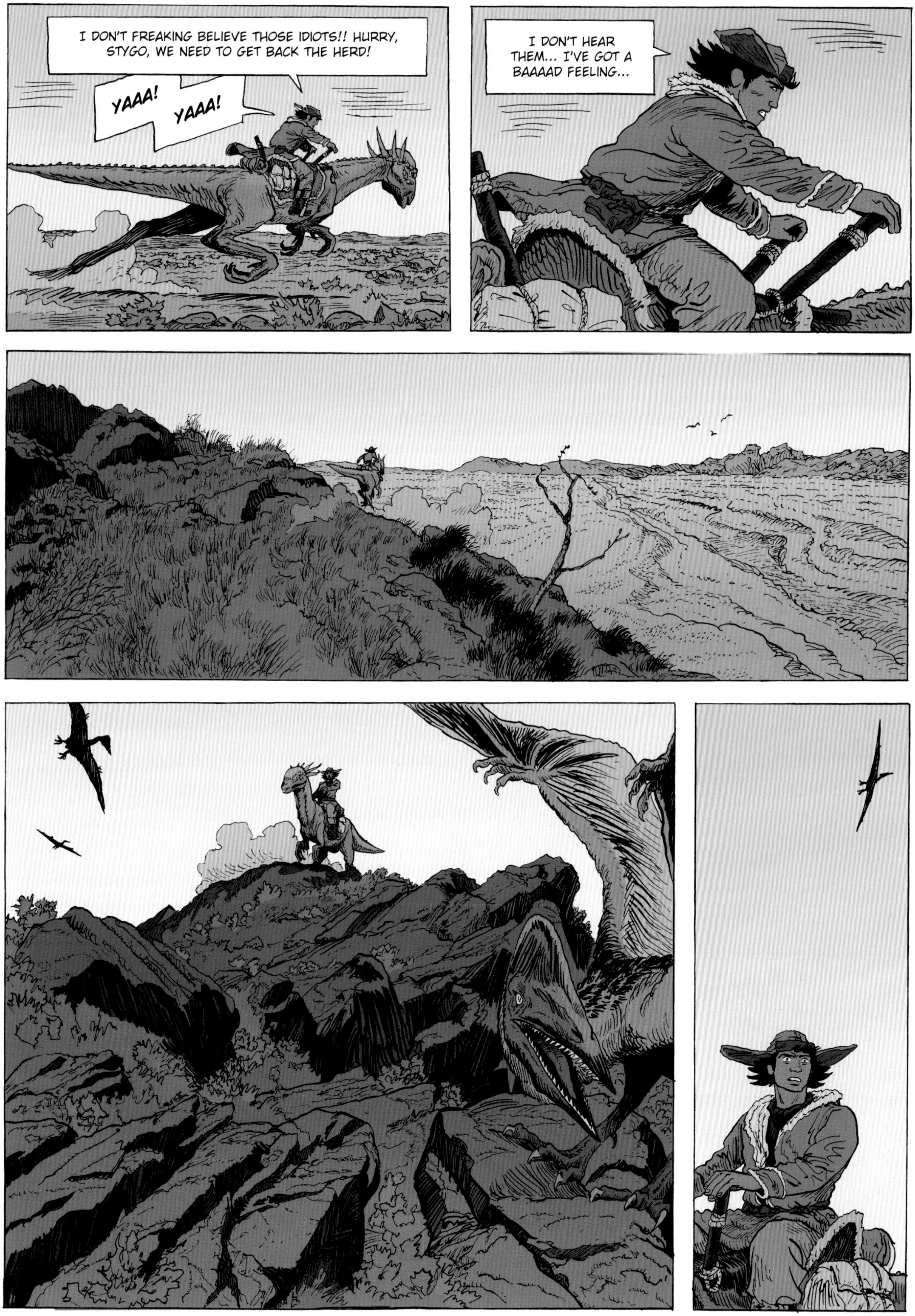
I DON'T FREAKING BELIEVE THOSE IDIOTS!! HURRY, STYGO, WE NEED TO GET BACK THE HERD!
YAAA!
YAAA!
I DON'T HEAR THEM... I'VE GOT A BAAAAD FEELING...

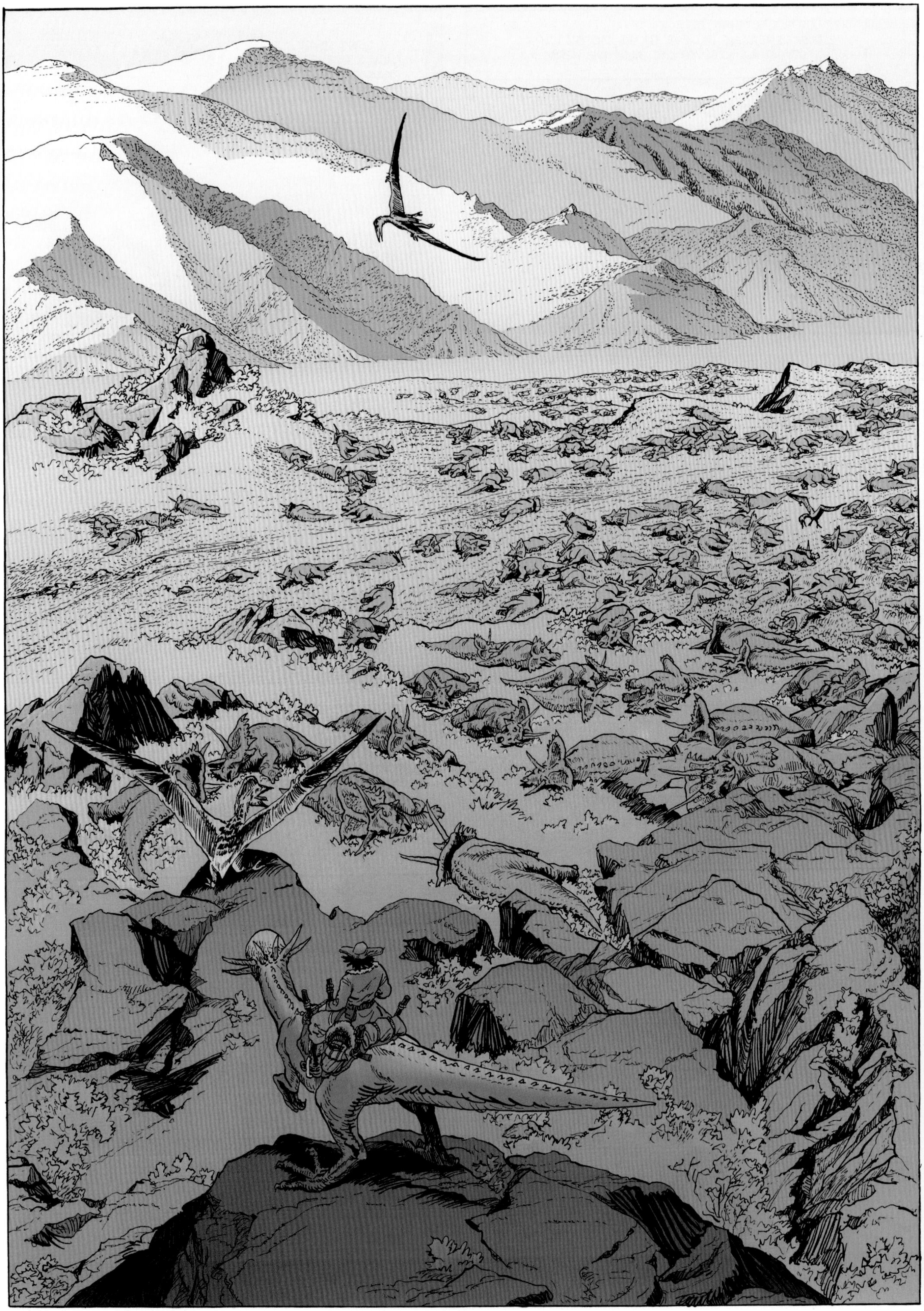

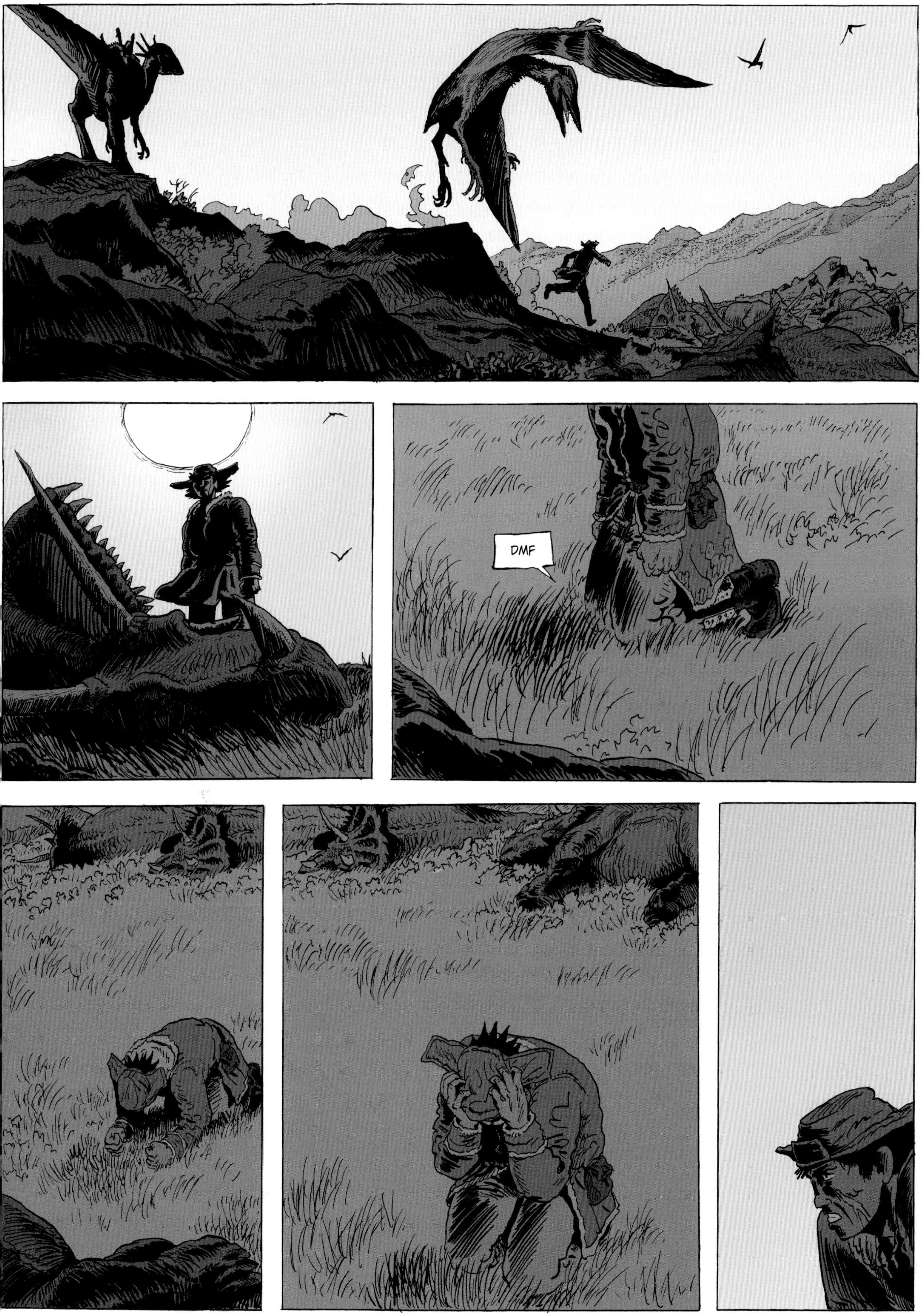
DMF

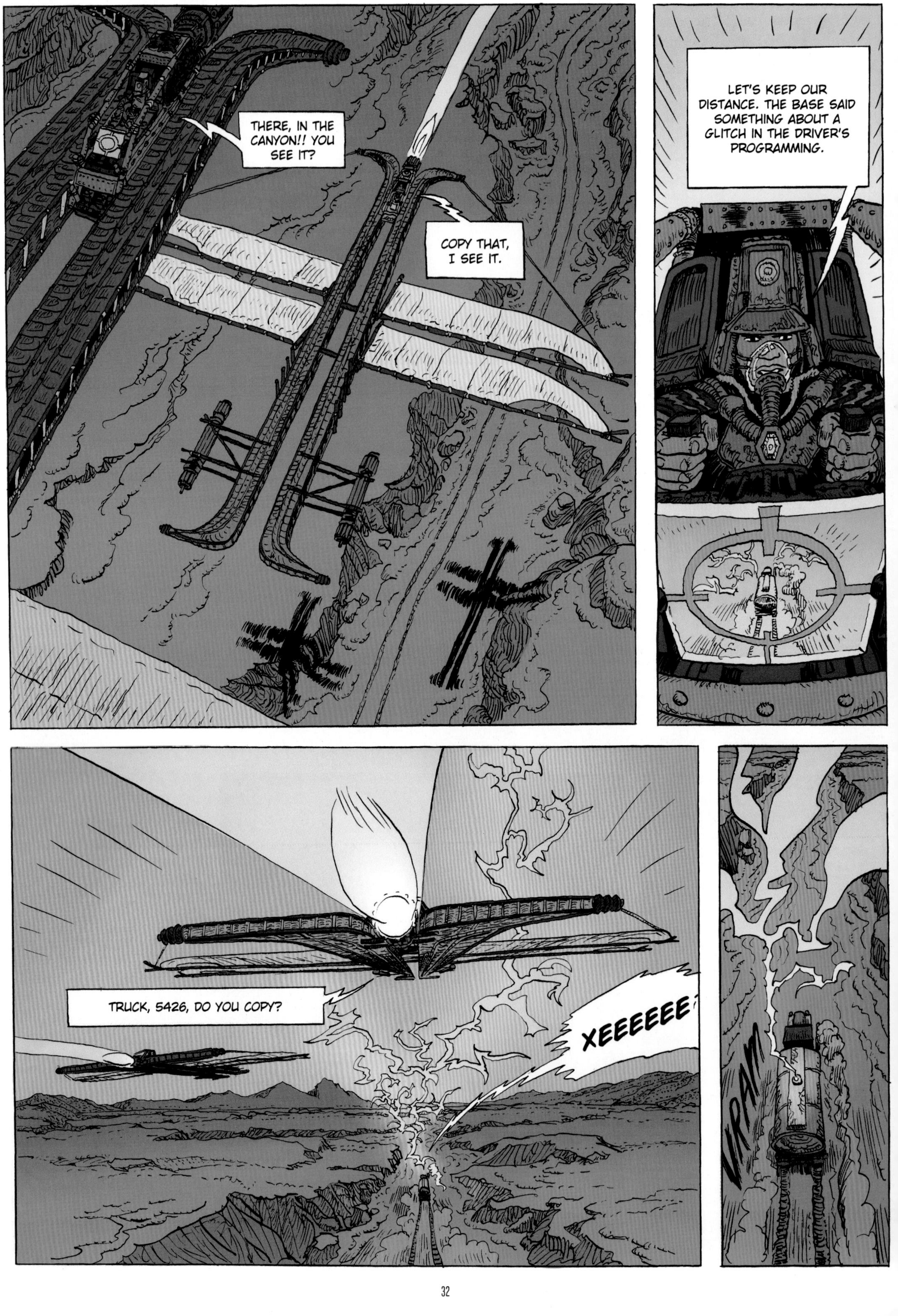
THERE, IN THE CANYON!! YOU SEE IT?
COPY THAT, I SEE IT.
LET'S KEEP OUR DISTANCE. THE BASE SAID SOMETHING ABOUT A GLITCH IN THE DRIVER'S PROGRAMMING.
TRUCK, 5426, DO YOU COPY?
XEEEEEE
VRAM

REPEAT -- TRUCK 5426. DO YOU COPY?
IT'S USELESS. LOOKS LIKE HE'S LOST CONTROL!
CAREFUL! THE POWER'S CRANKING UP!!
WE'RE GONNA LOSE HIM!!
SSKRI

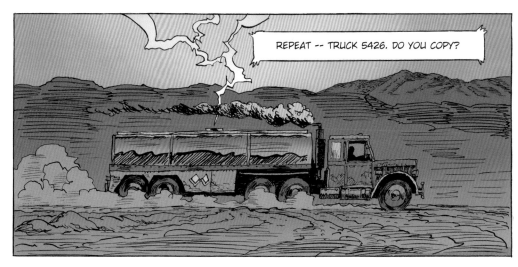

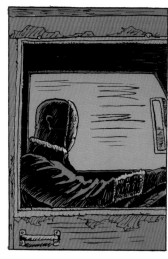

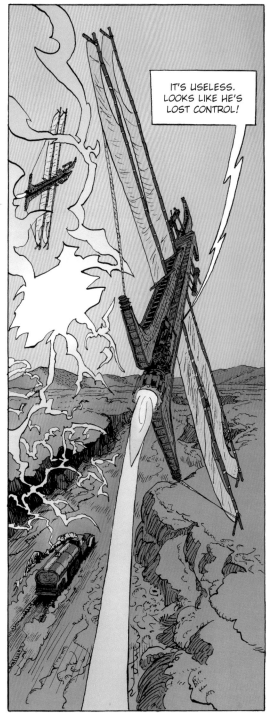

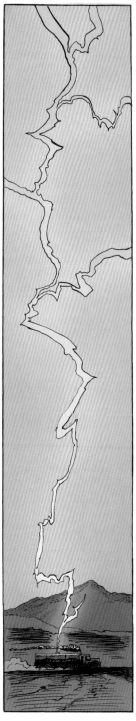

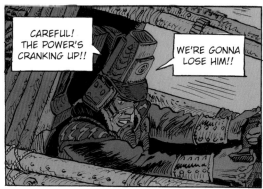

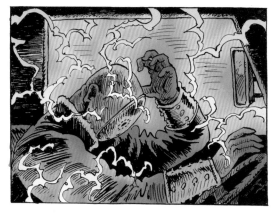

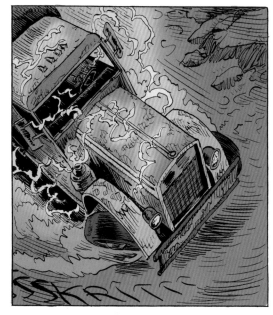

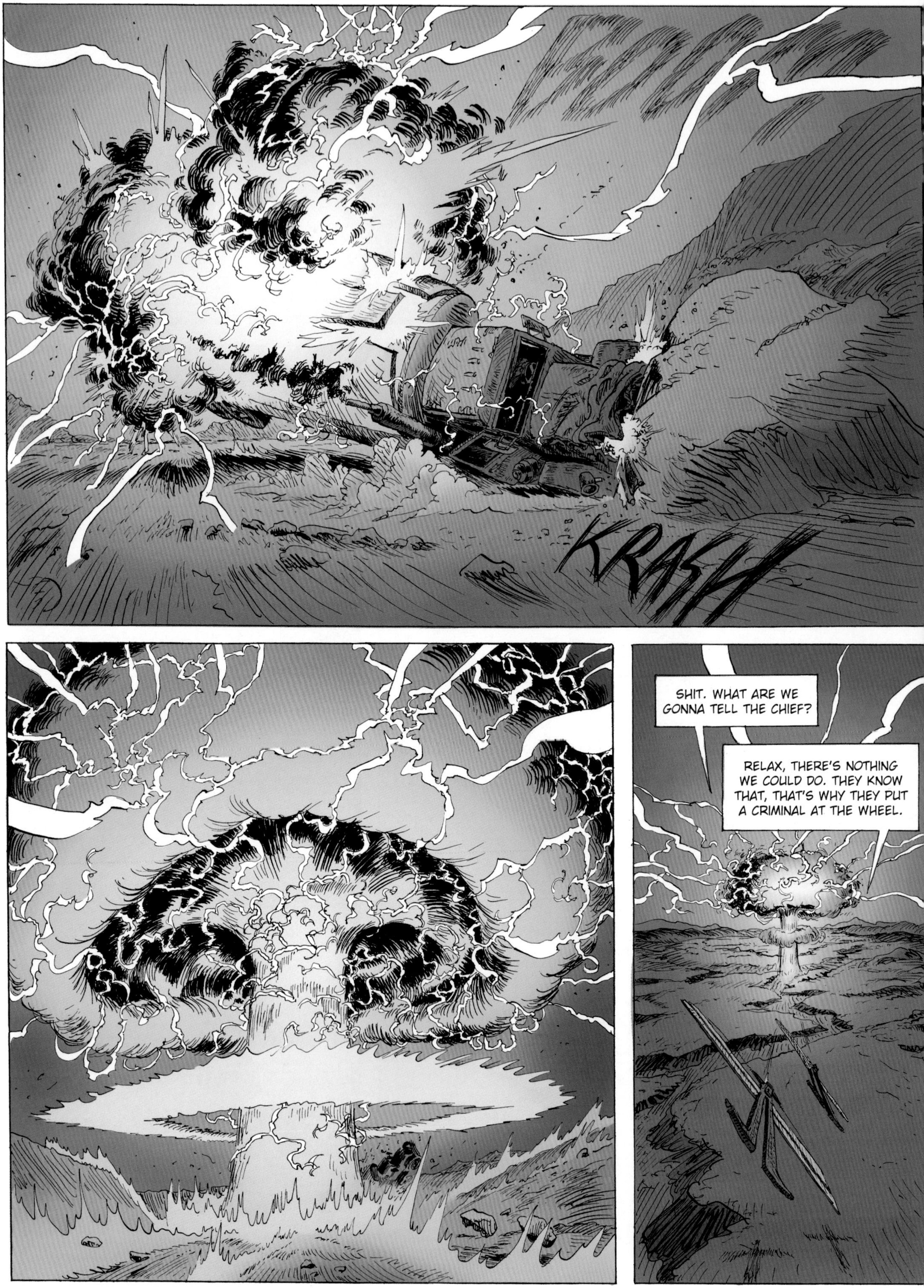
KRASH
SHIT. WHAT ARE WE GONNA TELL THE CHIEF?
RELAX, THERE'S NOTHING WE COULD DO. THEY KNOW THAT, THAT'S WHY THEY PUT A CRIMINAL AT THE WHEEL.

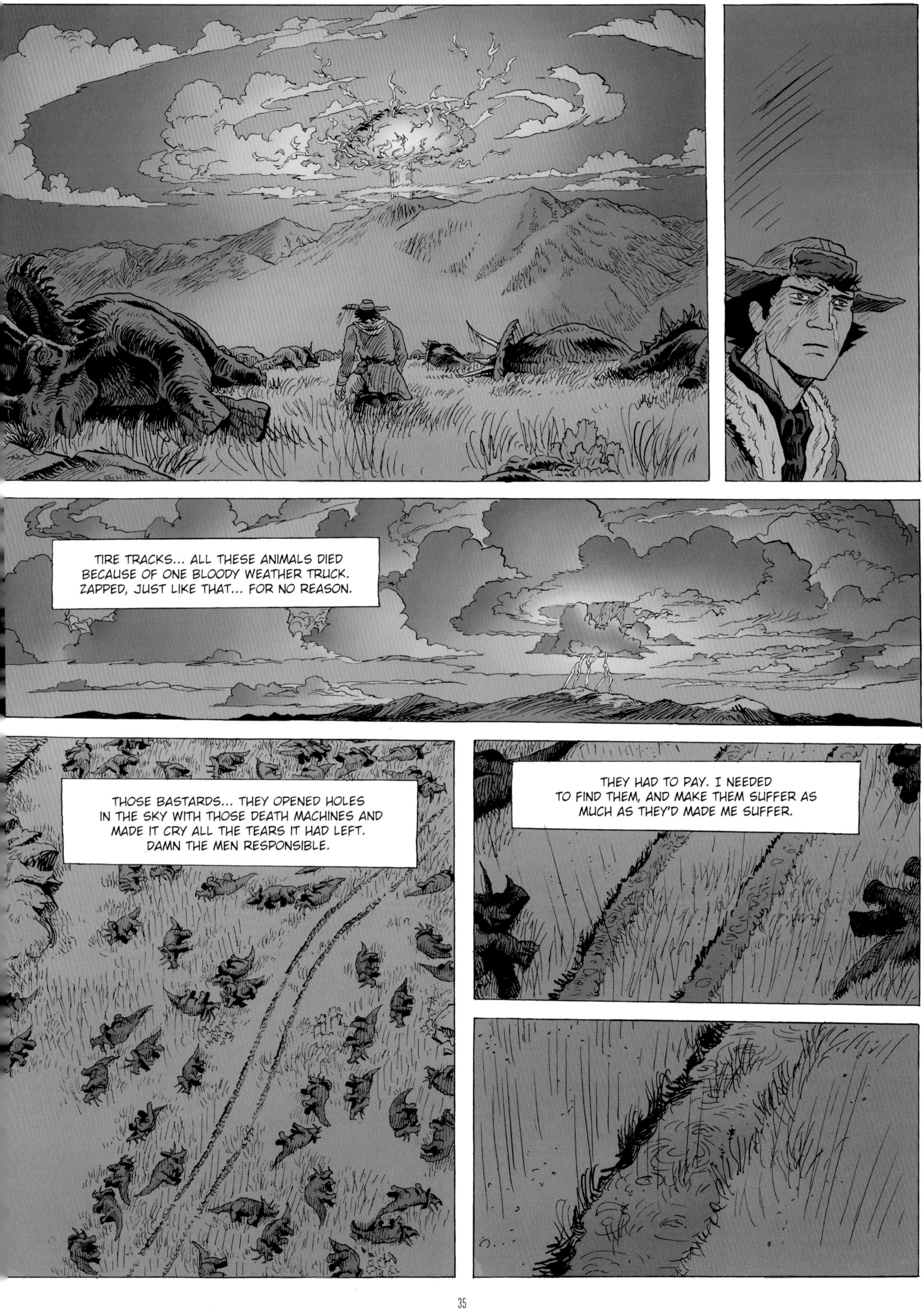
TIRE TRACKS... ALL THESE ANIMALS DIED BECAUSE OF ONE BLOODY WEATHER TRUCK. ZAPPED, JUST LIKE THAT... FOR NO REASON.
THOSE BASTARDS... THEY OPENED HOLES IN THE SKY WITH THOSE DEATH MACHINES AND MADE IT CRY ALL THE TEARS IT HAD LEFT. DAMN THE MEN RESPONSIBLE.
THEY HAD TO PAY. I NEEDED TO FIND THEM, AND MAKE THEM SUFFER AS MUCH AS THEY'D MADE ME SUFFER.

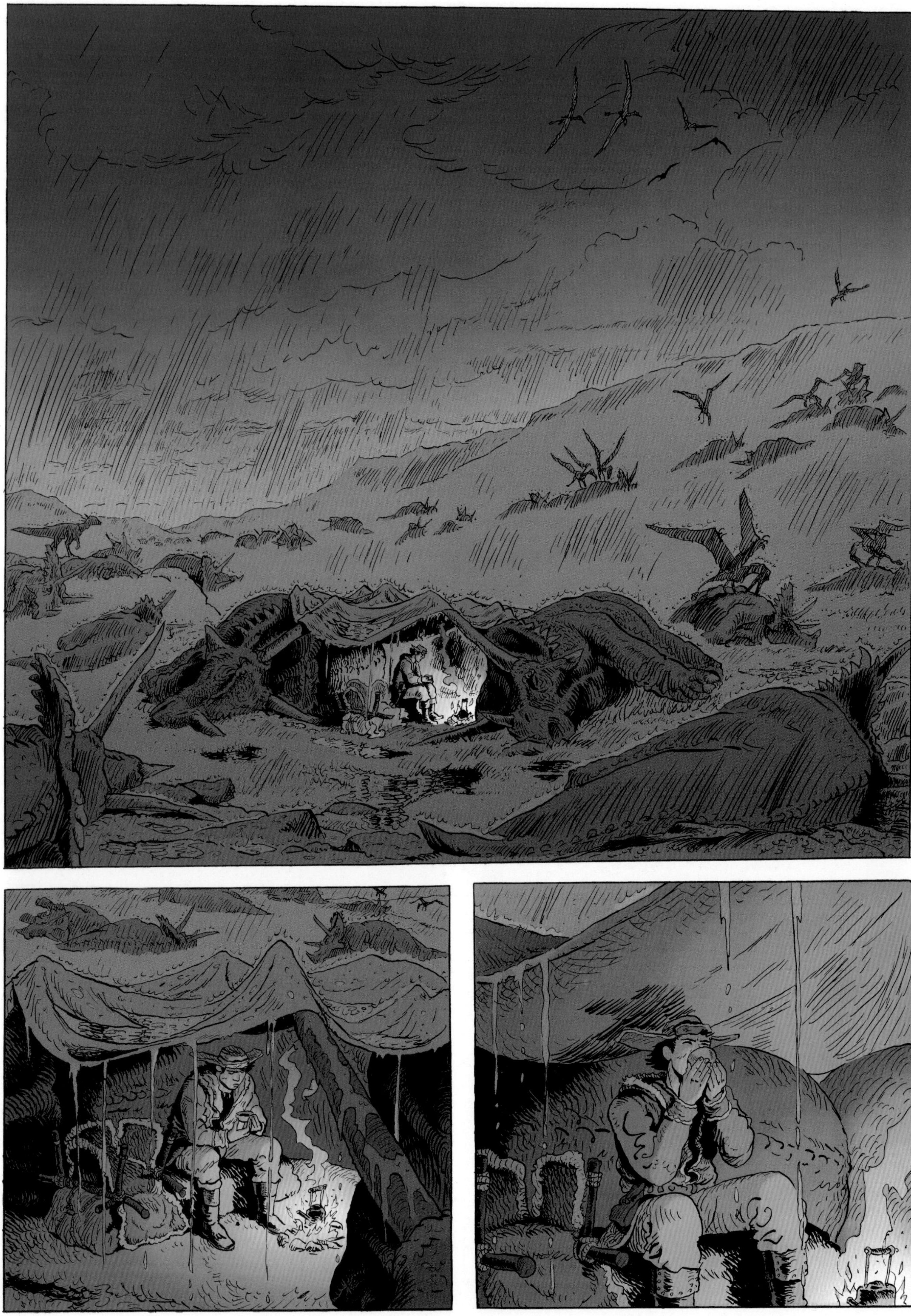

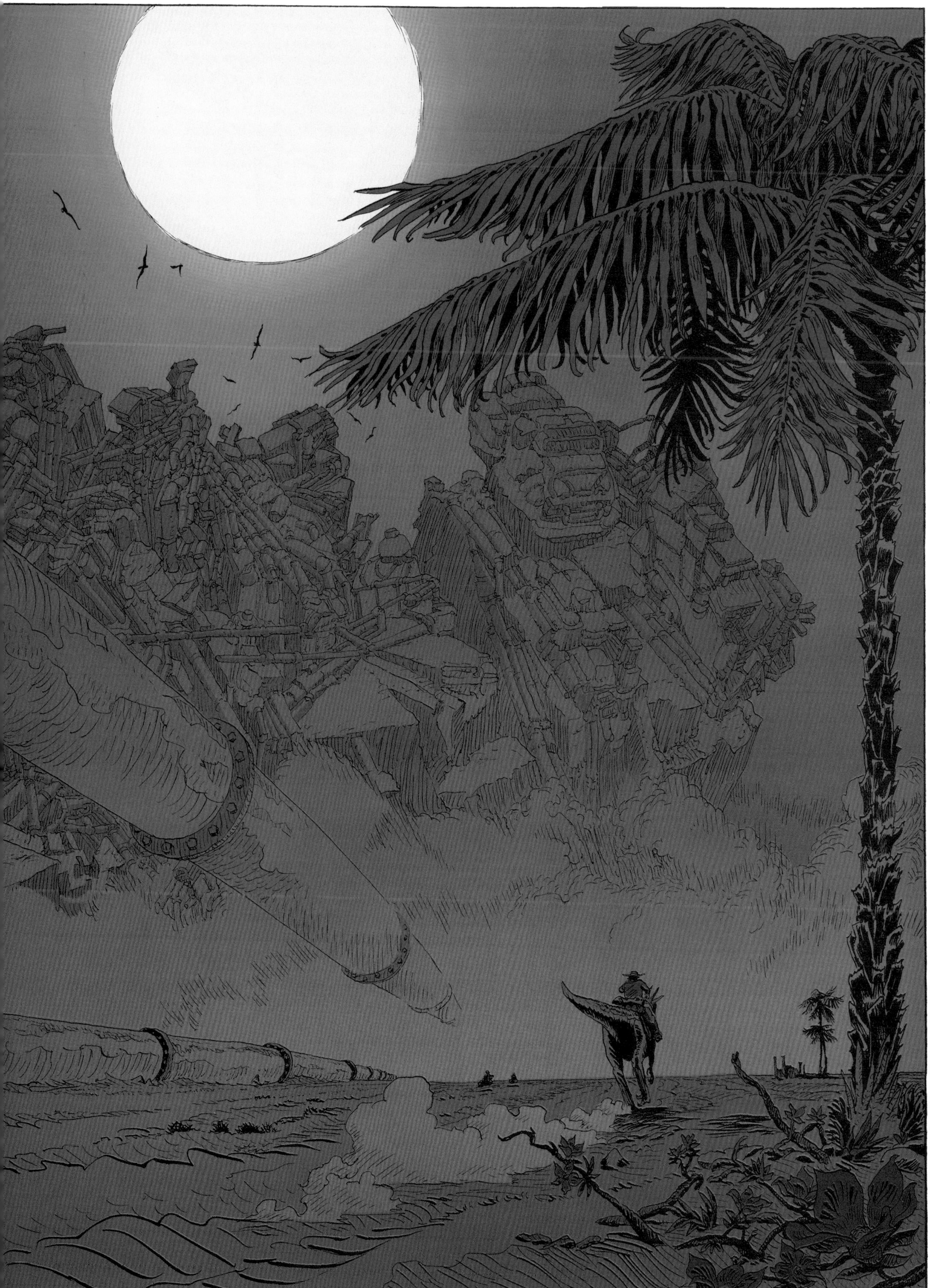

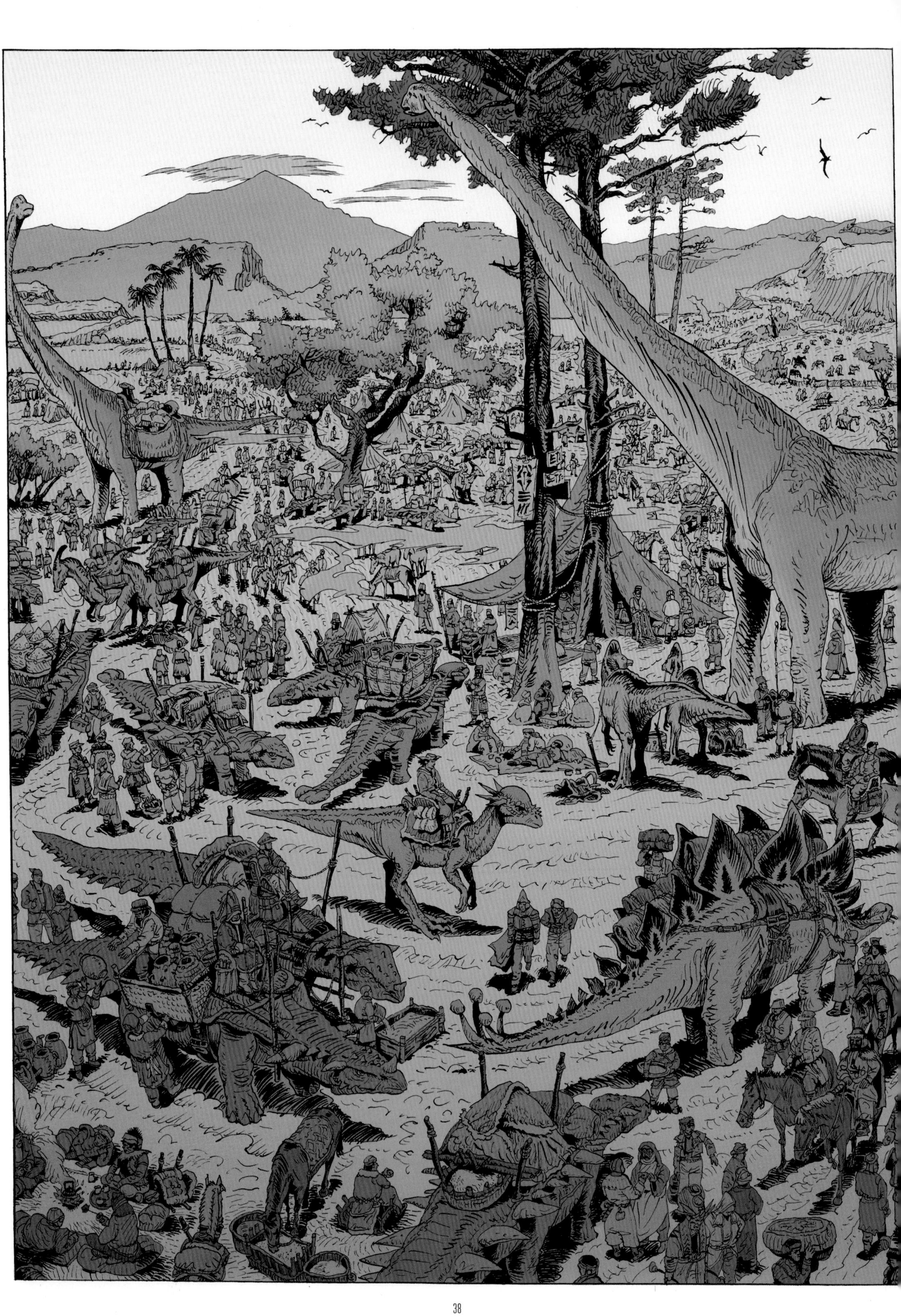

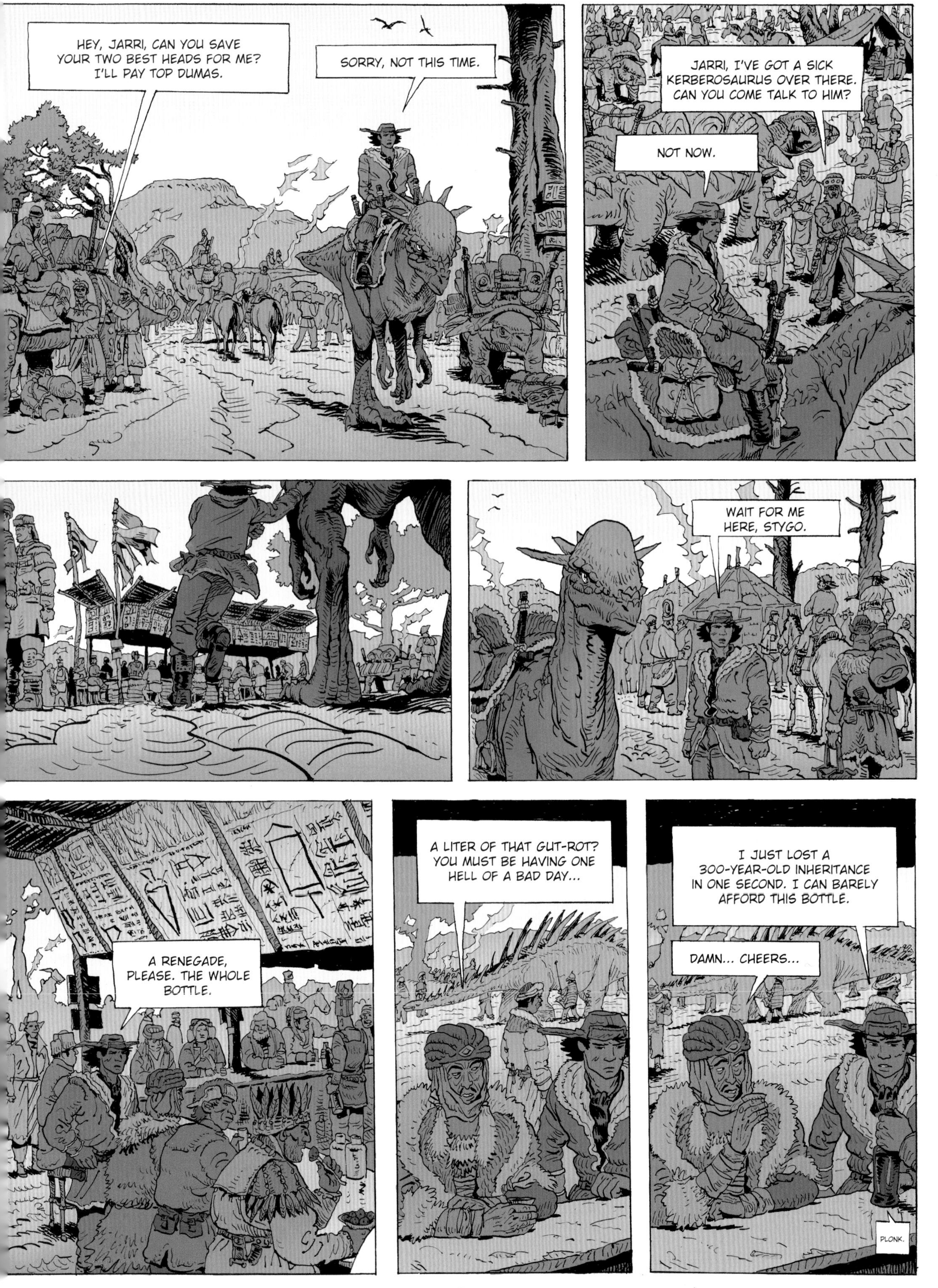
HEY, JARRI, CAN YOU SAVE YOUR TWO BEST HEADS FOR ME? I'LL PAY TOP DUMAS.
SORRY, NOT THIS TIME.
JARRI, I'VE GOT A SICK KERBEROSAURUS OVER THERE. CAN YOU COME TALK TO HIM?
NOT NOW.
WAIT FOR ME HERE, STYGO.
A RENEGADE, PLEASE. THE WHOLE BOTTLE.
A LITER OF THAT GUT-ROT? YOU MUST BE HAVING ONE HELL OF A BAD DAY...
I JUST LOST A 300-YEAR-OLD INHERITANCE IN ONE SECOND. I CAN BARELY AFFORD THIS BOTTLE.
DAMN... CHEERS...
PLONK.

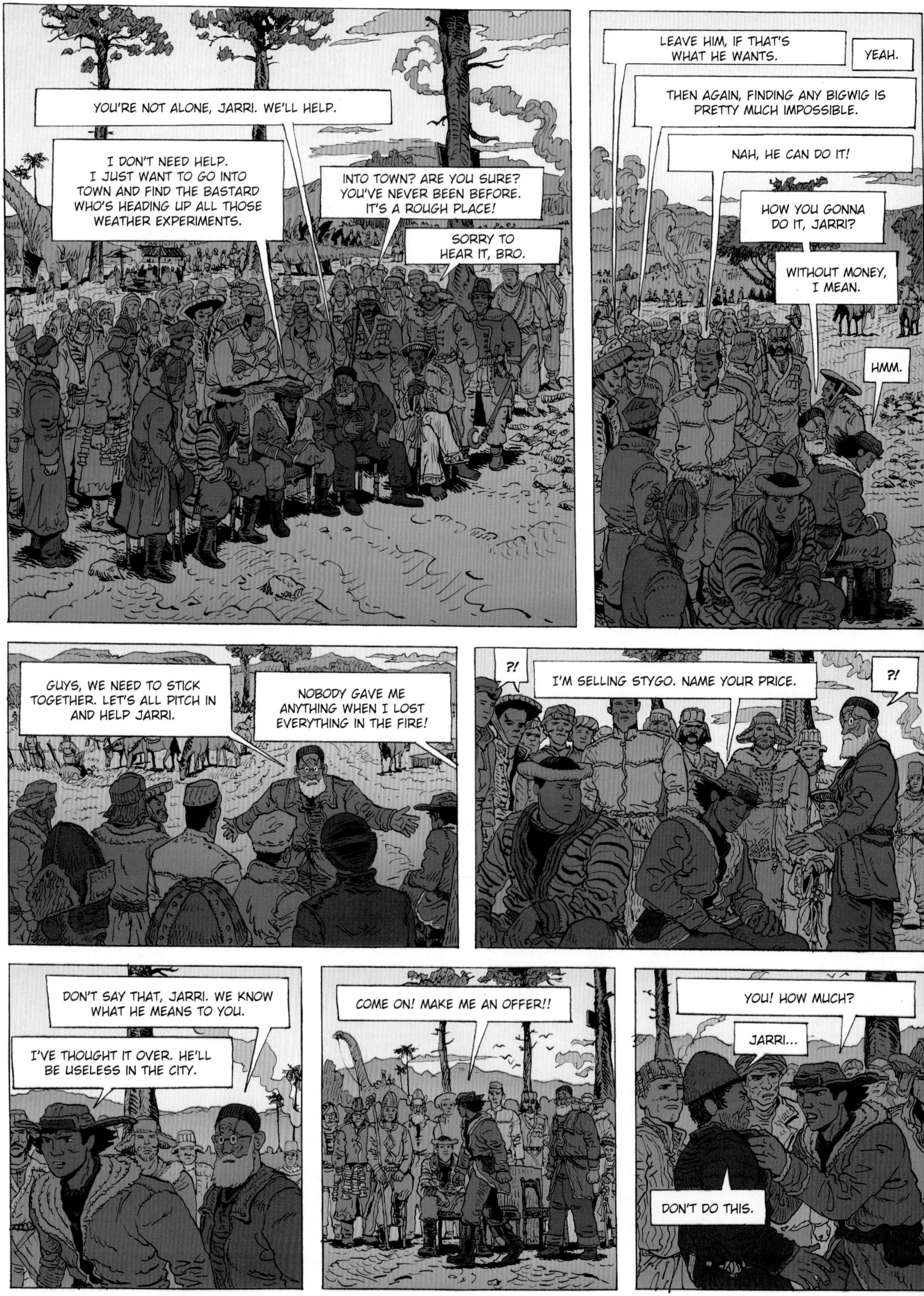
YOU'RE NOT ALONE, JARRI. WE'LL HELP.
I DON'T NEED HELP. I JUST WANT TO GO INTO TOWN AND FIND THE BASTARD WHO'S HEADING UP ALL THOSE WEATHER EXPERIMENTS.
INTO TOWN? ARE YOU SURE? YOU'VE NEVER BEEN BEFORE. IT'S A ROUGH PLACE!
SORRY TO HEAR IT, BRO.
LEAVE HIM, IF THAT'S WHAT HE WANTS.
YEAH.
THEN AGAIN, FINDING ANY BIGWIG IS PRETTY MUCH IMPOSSIBLE.
NAH, HE CAN DO IT!
HOW YOU GONNA DO IT, JARRI?
WITHOUT MONEY, I MEAN.
HMM.
GUYS, WE NEED TO STICK TOGETHER. LET'S ALL PITCH IN AND HELP JARRI.
NOBODY GAVE ME ANYTHING WHEN I LOST EVERYTHING IN THE FIRE!
?!
I'M SELLING STYGO. NAME YOUR PRICE.
?!
DON'T SAY THAT, JARRI. WE KNOW WHAT HE MEANS TO YOU.
I'VE THOUGHT IT OVER. HE'LL BE USELESS IN THE CITY.
COME ON! MAKE ME AN OFFER!!
YOU! HOW MUCH?
JARRI...
DON'T DO THIS.

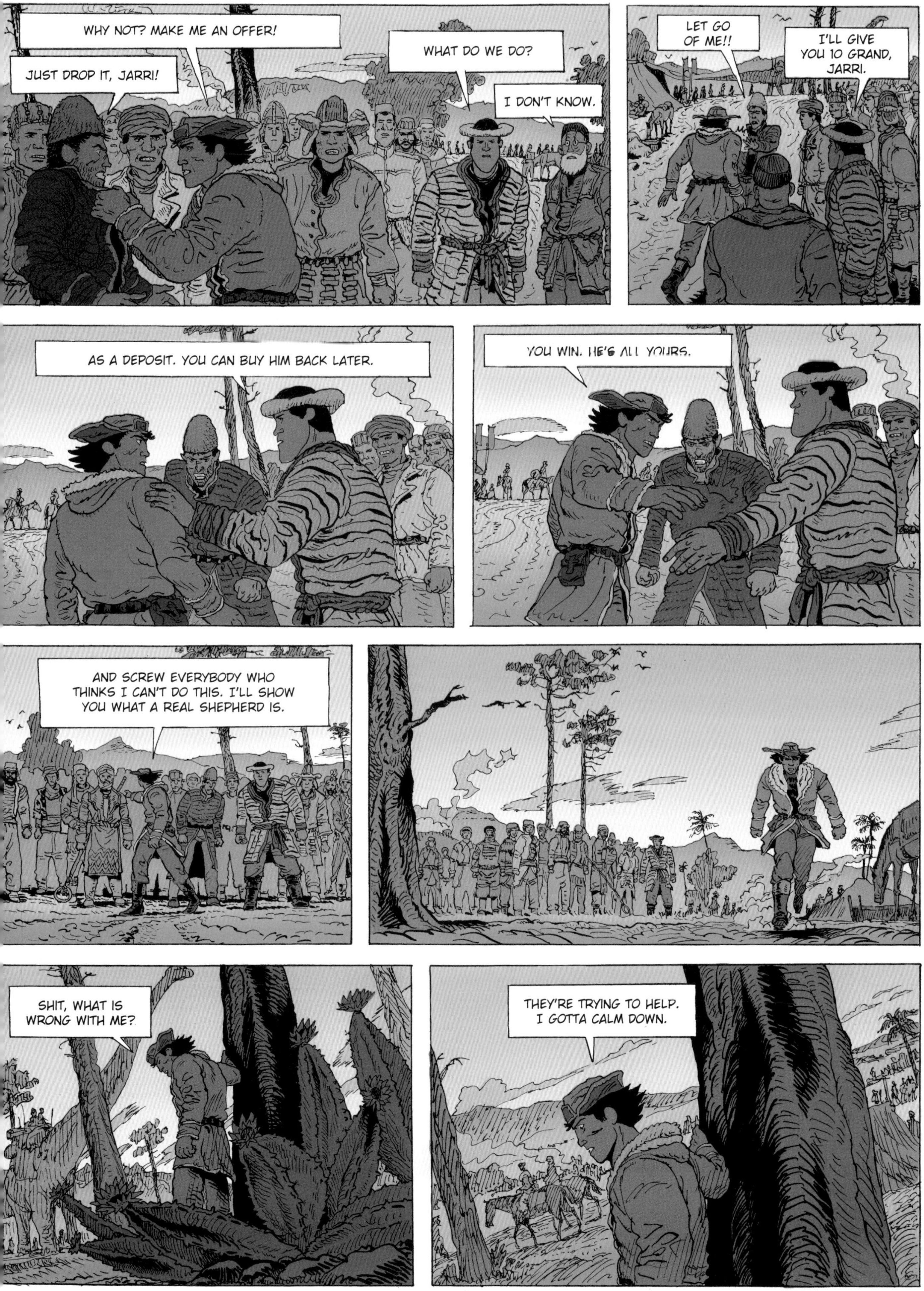
WHY NOT? MAKE ME AN OFFER!
JUST DROP IT, JARRI!
WHAT DO WE DO?
I DON'T KNOW.
LET GO OF ME!!
I'LL GIVE YOU 10 GRAND, JARRI.
AS A DEPOSIT. YOU CAN BUY HIM BACK LATER.
YOU WIN. HE'S ALL YOURS.
AND SCREW EVERYBODY WHO THINKS I CAN'T DO THIS. I'LL SHOW YOU WHAT A REAL SHEPHERD IS.
SHIT, WHAT IS WRONG WITH ME?
THEY'RE TRYING TO HELP. I GOTTA CALM DOWN.

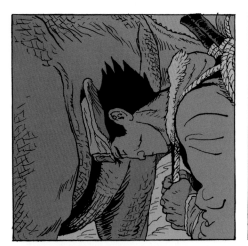

I'M SORRY, STYGO.

I'LL COME BACK, I PROMISE.

HE'S IN GOOD HANDS, DON'T WORRY. JUST WATCH OUT FOR ALL THE HUSTLERS THERE. THEY DON'T ALL HAVE OUR VALUES.

AND TAKE NORTH CANAL 381 TO STATION 3703. YOU AVOID THE ROADBLOCKS THAT WAY.

GOOD LUCK, JARRI!

YEAH, RIGHT.

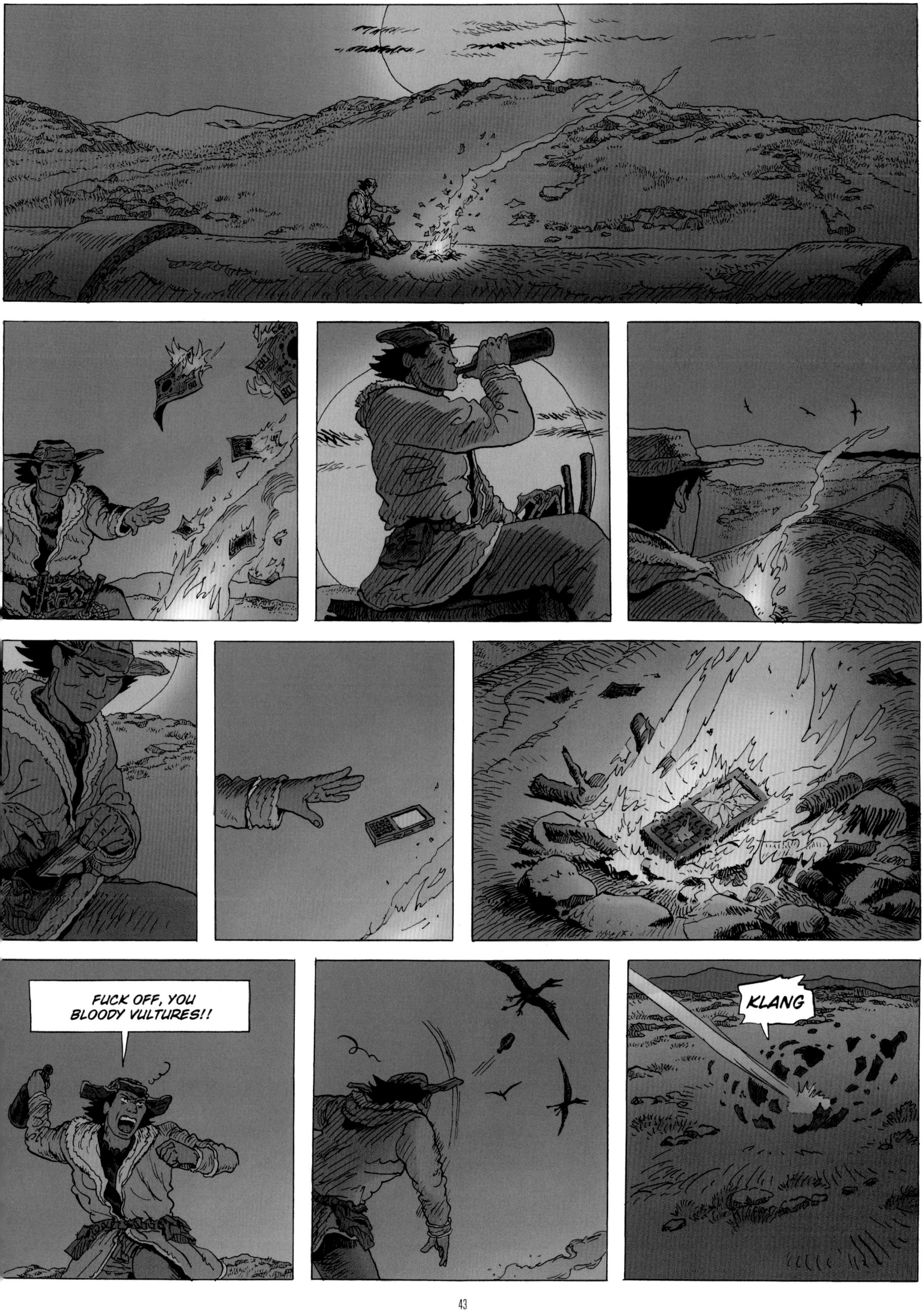
FUCK OFF, YOU BLOODY VULTURES!!
KLANG

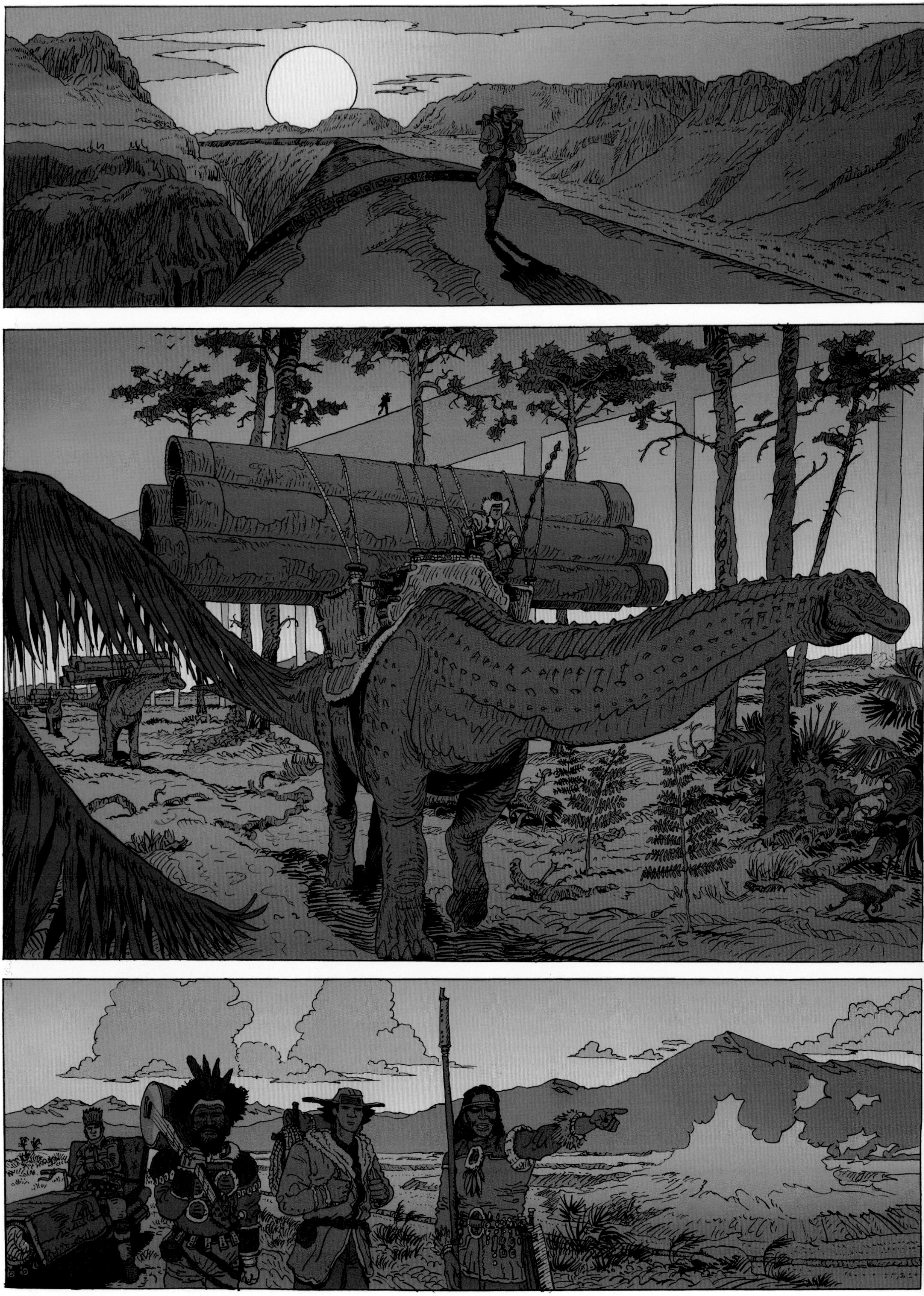

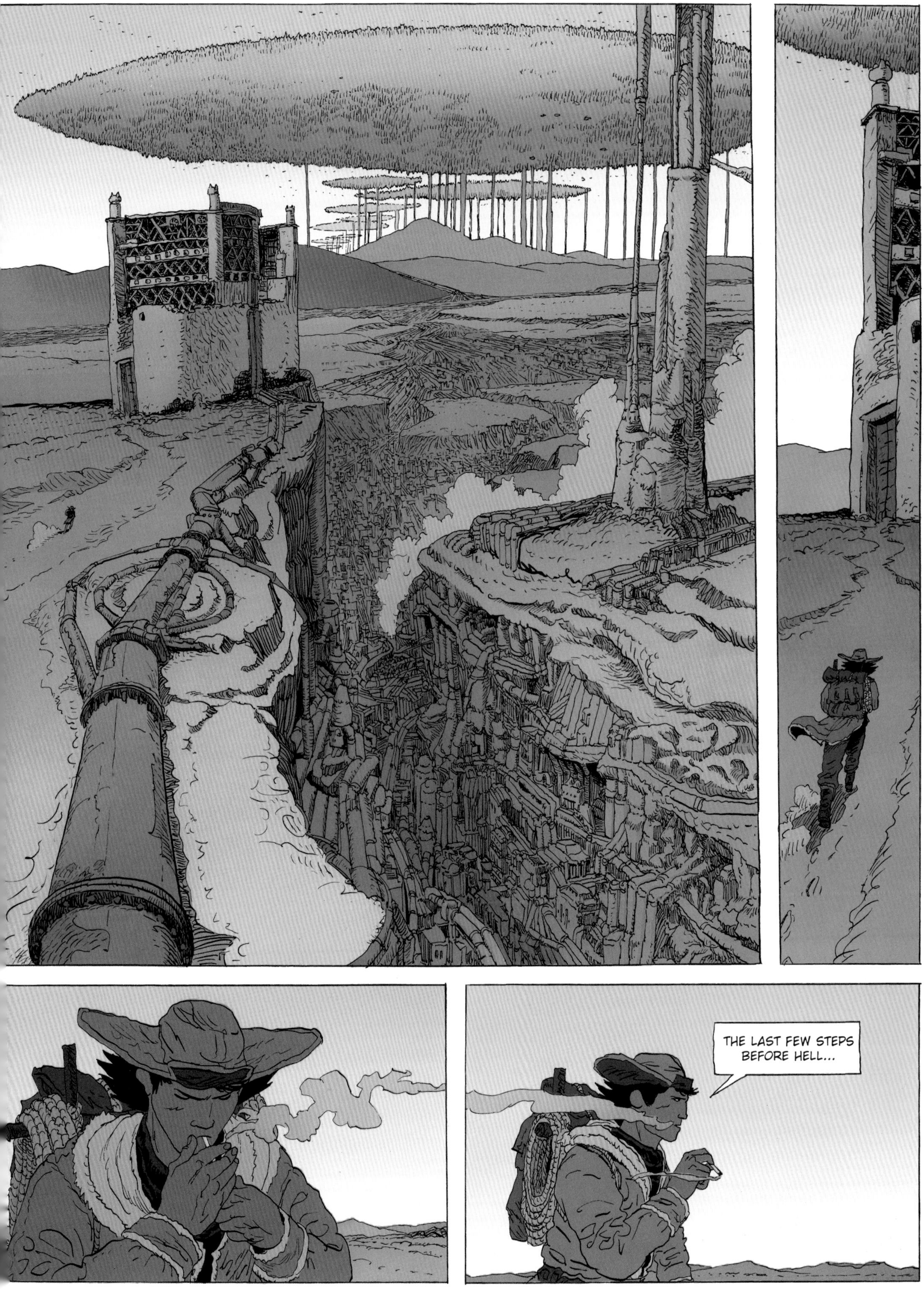
THE LAST FEW STEPS
BEFORE HELL...

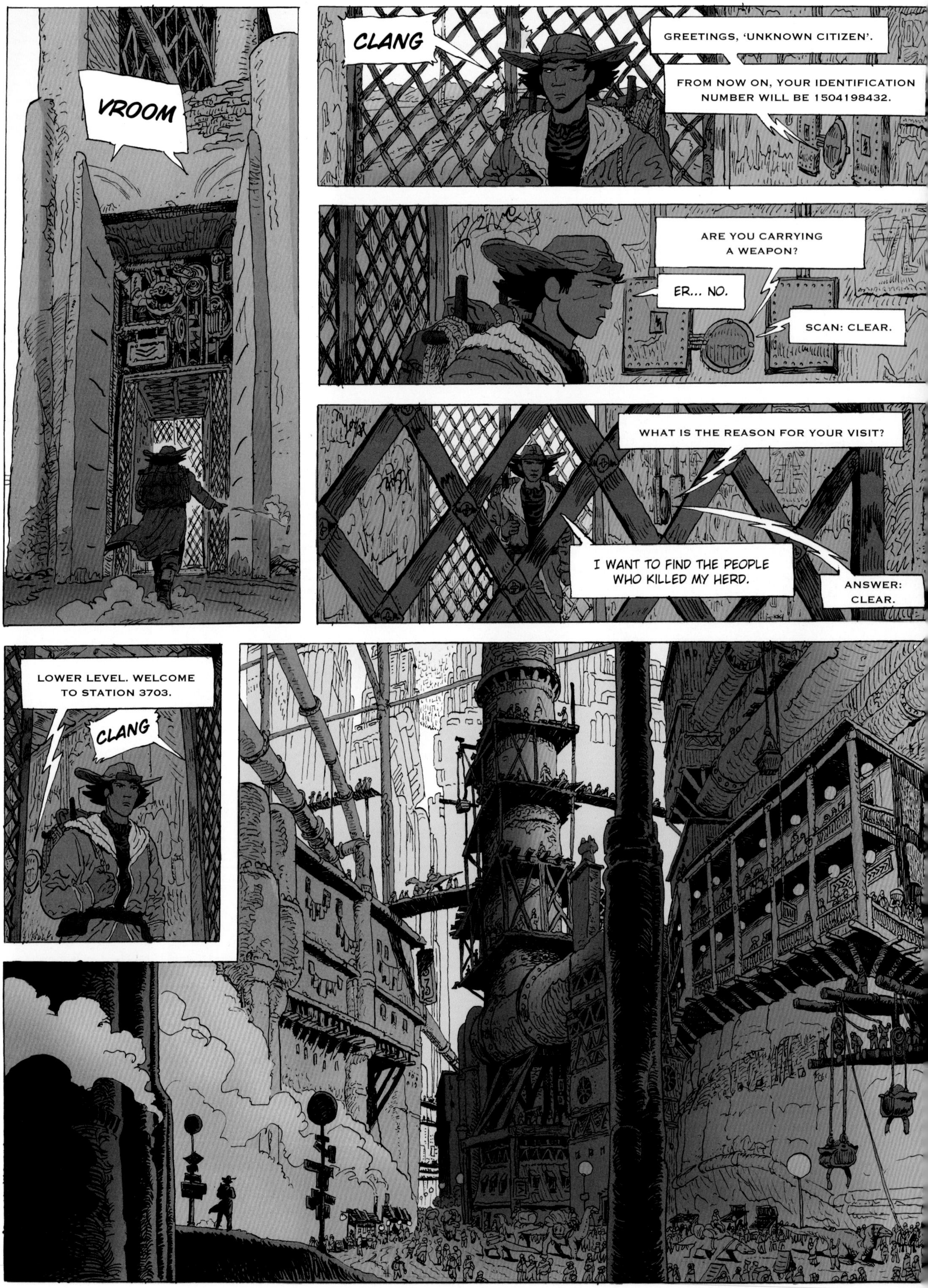
VROOM
CLANG
GREETINGS, 'UNKNOWN CITIZEN'.
FROM NOW ON, YOUR IDENTIFICATION NUMBER WILL BE 1504198432.
ARE YOU CARRYING A WEAPON?
ER... NO.
SCAN: CLEAR.
WHAT IS THE REASON FOR YOUR VISIT?
I WANT TO FIND THE PEOPLE WHO KILLED MY HERD.
ANSWER: CLEAR.
LOWER LEVEL. WELCOME TO STATION 3703.
CLANG

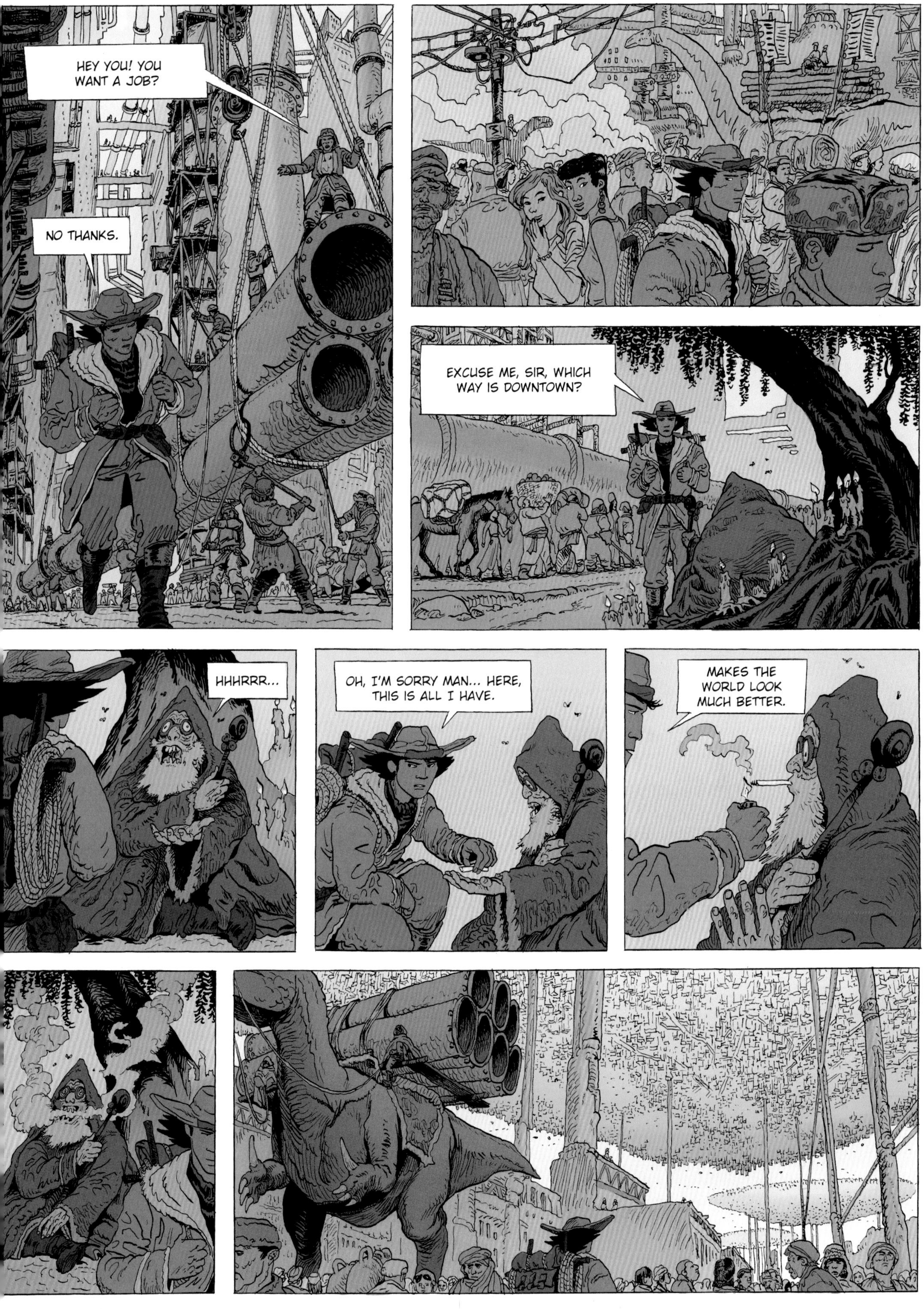
HEY YOU! YOU WANT A JOB?
NO THANKS.
EXCUSE ME, SIR, WHICH WAY IS DOWNTOWN?
HHHRRR...
OH, I'M SORRY MAN... HERE, THIS IS ALL I HAVE.
MAKES THE WORLD LOOK MUCH BETTER.

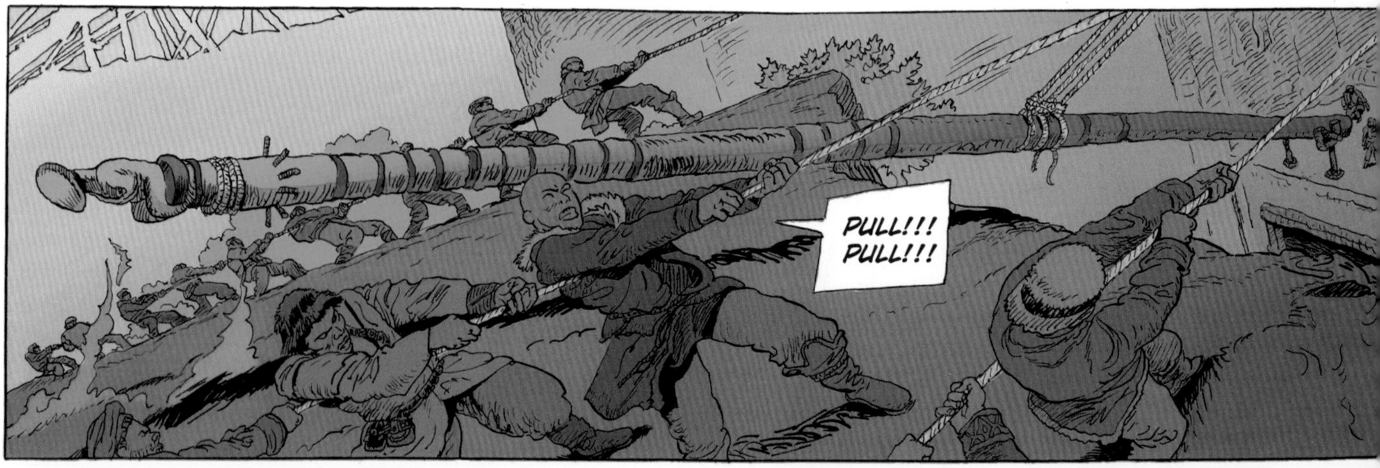
PULL!!!
PULL!!!

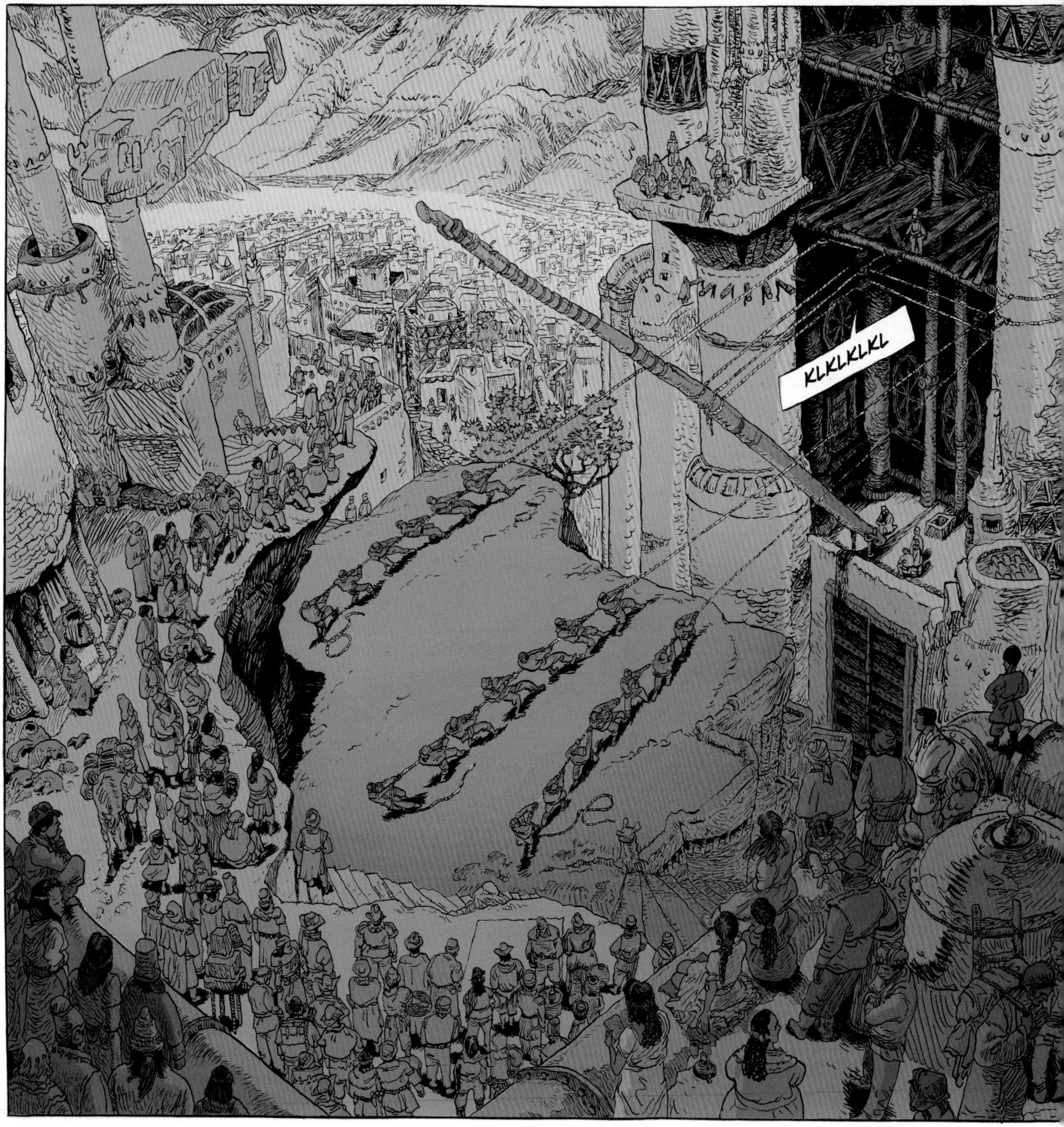
KLKLKLKL

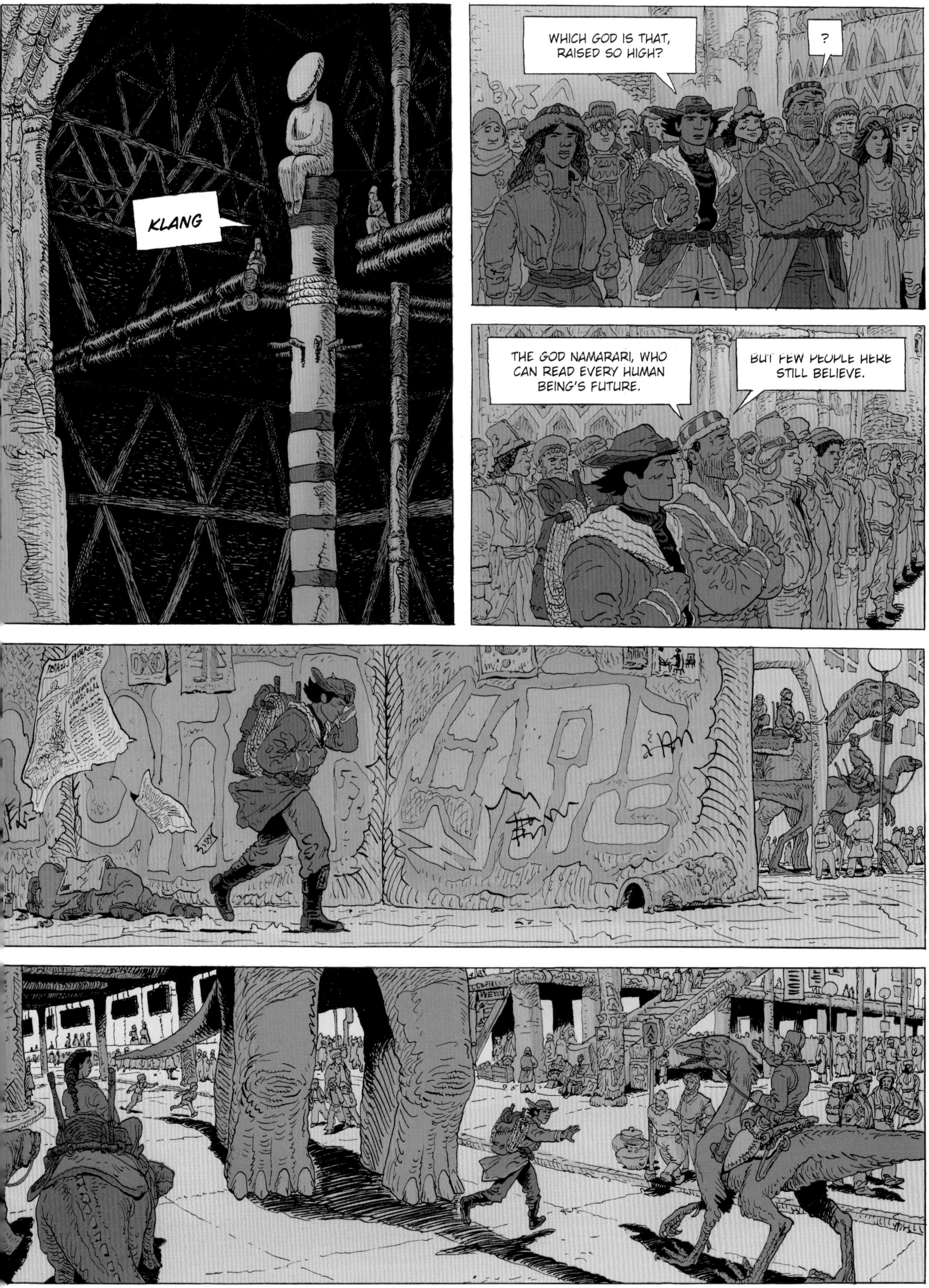
KLANG
WHICH GOD IS THAT, RAISED SO HIGH?
?
THE GOD NAMARARI, WHO CAN READ EVERY HUMAN BEING'S FUTURE.
BUT FEW PEOPLE HERE STILL BELIEVE.

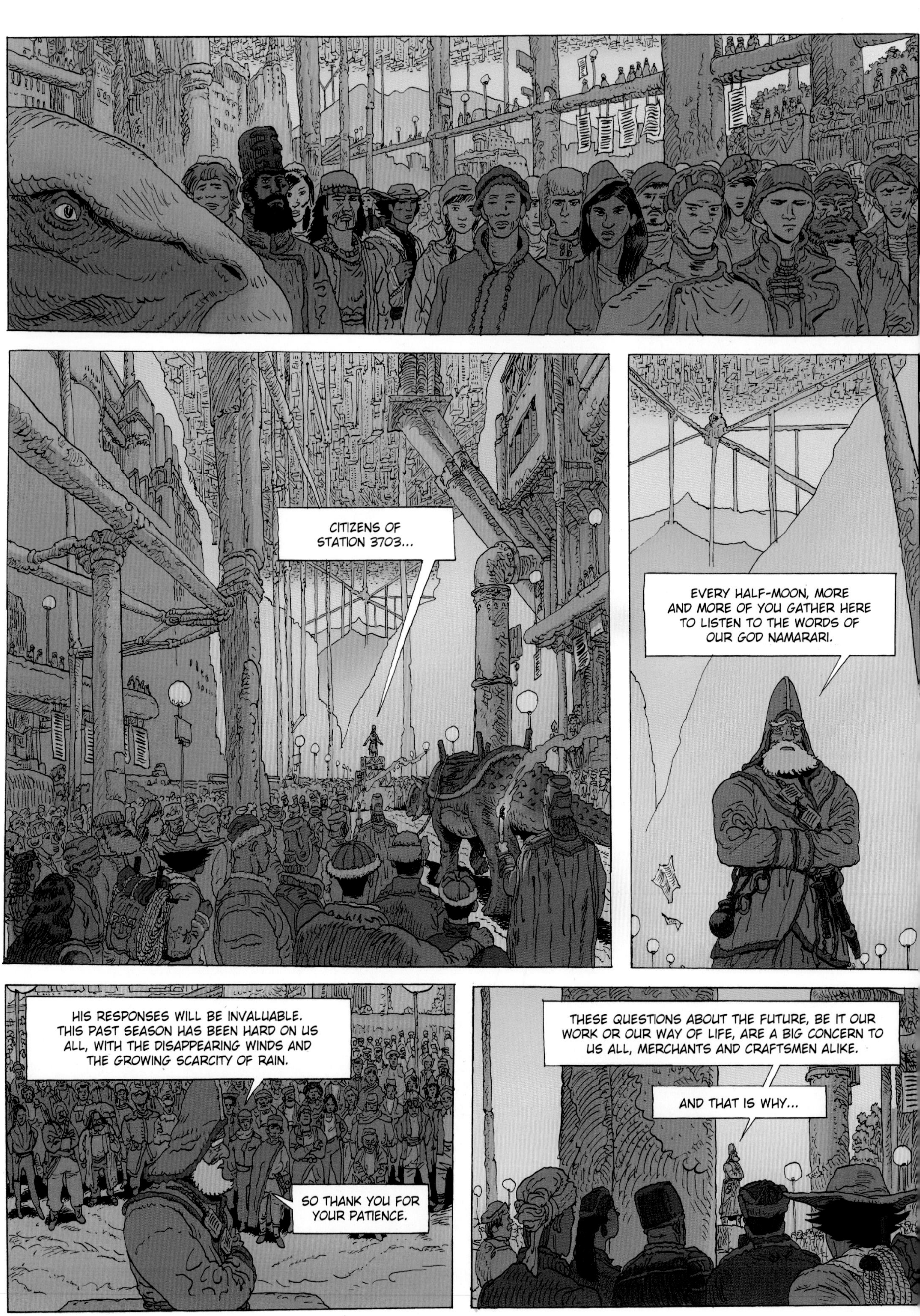
CITIZENS OF STATION 3703...
EVERY HALF-MOON, MORE AND MORE OF YOU GATHER HERE TO LISTEN TO THE WORDS OF OUR GOD NAMARARI.
HIS RESPONSES WILL BE INVALUABLE. THIS PAST SEASON HAS BEEN HARD ON US ALL, WITH THE DISAPPEARING WINDS AND THE GROWING SCARCITY OF RAIN.
SO THANK YOU FOR YOUR PATIENCE.
THESE QUESTIONS ABOUT THE FUTURE, BE IT OUR WORK OR OUR WAY OF LIFE, ARE A BIG CONCERN TO US ALL, MERCHANTS AND CRAFTSMEN ALIKE.
AND THAT IS WHY...

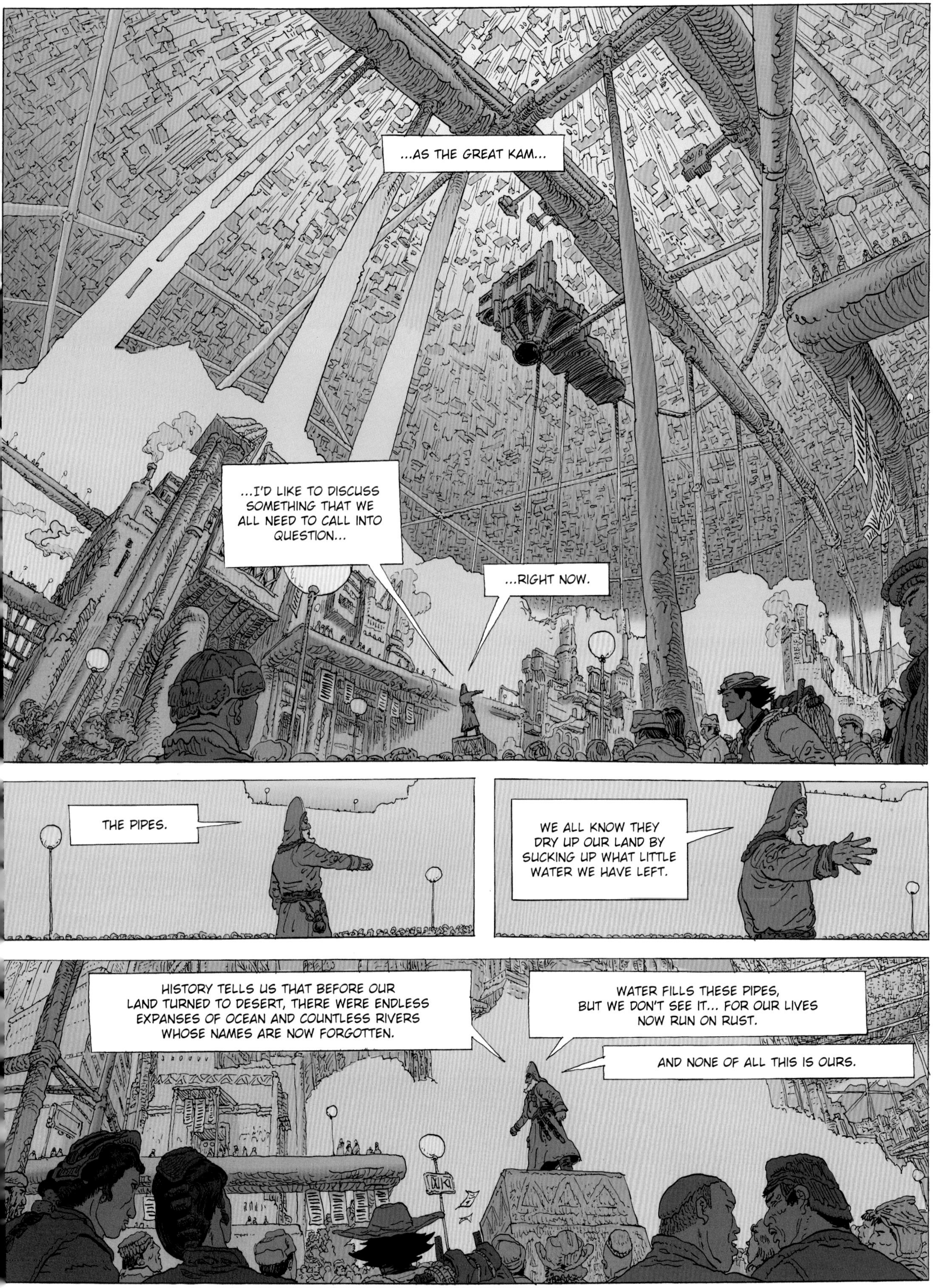
...AS THE GREAT KAM...
...I'D LIKE TO DISCUSS SOMETHING THAT WE ALL NEED TO CALL INTO QUESTION...
...RIGHT NOW.
THE PIPES.
WE ALL KNOW THEY DRY UP OUR LAND BY SUCKING UP WHAT LITTLE WATER WE HAVE LEFT.
HISTORY TELLS US THAT BEFORE OUR LAND TURNED TO DESERT, THERE WERE ENDLESS EXPANSES OF OCEAN AND COUNTLESS RIVERS WHOSE NAMES ARE NOW FORGOTTEN.
WATER FILLS THESE PIPES, BUT WE DON'T SEE IT... FOR OUR LIVES NOW RUN ON RUST.
AND NONE OF ALL THIS IS OURS.

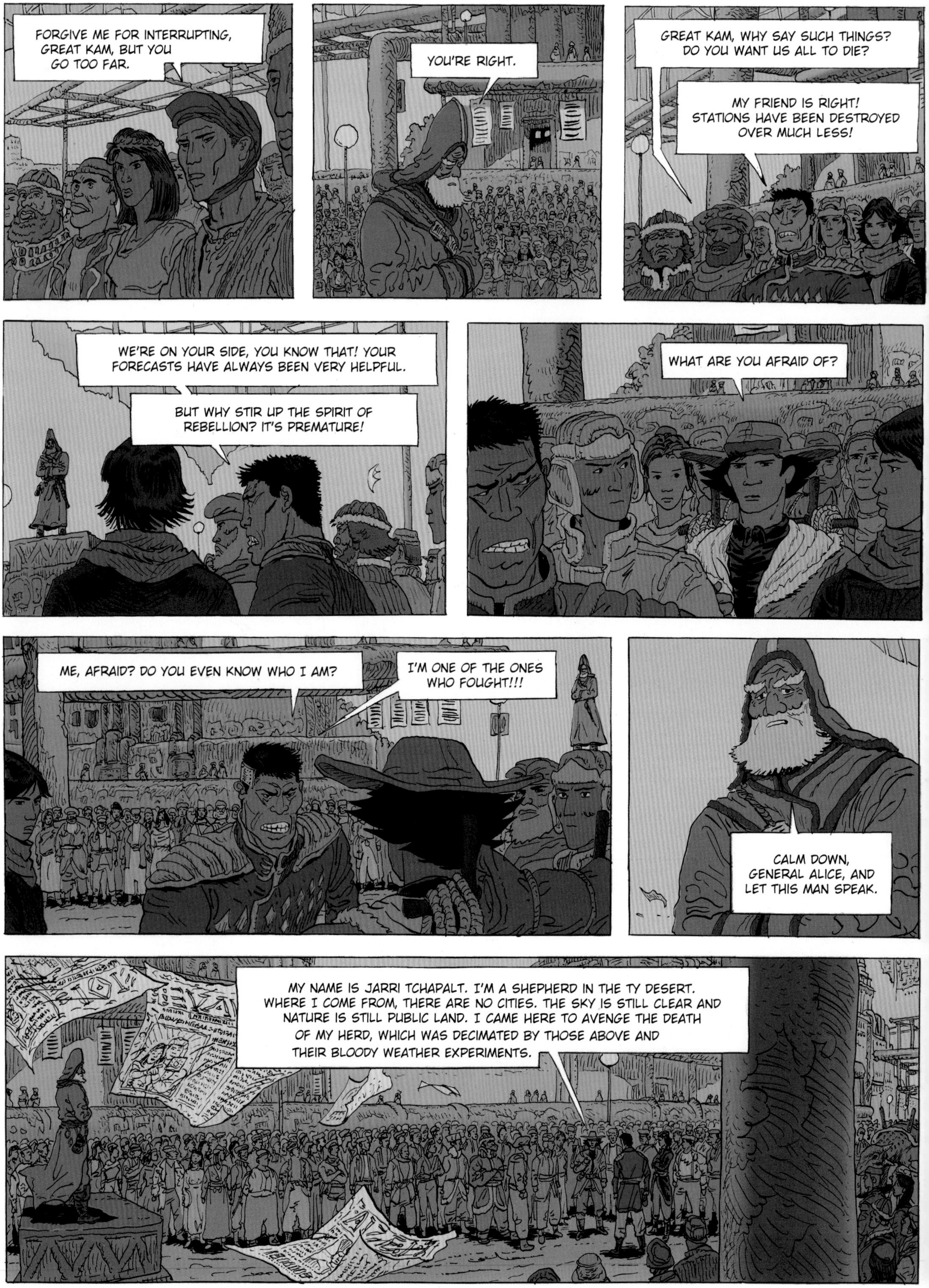
FORGIVE ME FOR INTERRUPTING, GREAT KAM, BUT YOU GO TOO FAR.
YOU'RE RIGHT.
GREAT KAM, WHY SAY SUCH THINGS? DO YOU WANT US ALL TO DIE?
MY FRIEND IS RIGHT! STATIONS HAVE BEEN DESTROYED OVER MUCH LESS!
WE'RE ON YOUR SIDE, YOU KNOW THAT! YOUR FORECASTS HAVE ALWAYS BEEN VERY HELPFUL.
BUT WHY STIR UP THE SPIRIT OF REBELLION? IT'S PREMATURE!
WHAT ARE YOU AFRAID OF?
ME, AFRAID? DO YOU EVEN KNOW WHO I AM?
I'M ONE OF THE ONES WHO FOUGHT!!!
CALM DOWN, GENERAL ALICE, AND LET THIS MAN SPEAK.
MY NAME IS JARRI TCHAPALT. I'M A SHEPHERD IN THE TY DESERT. WHERE I COME FROM, THERE ARE NO CITIES. THE SKY IS STILL CLEAR AND NATURE IS STILL PUBLIC LAND. I CAME HERE TO AVENGE THE DEATH OF MY HERD, WHICH WAS DECIMATED BY THOSE ABOVE AND THEIR BLOODY WEATHER EXPERIMENTS.

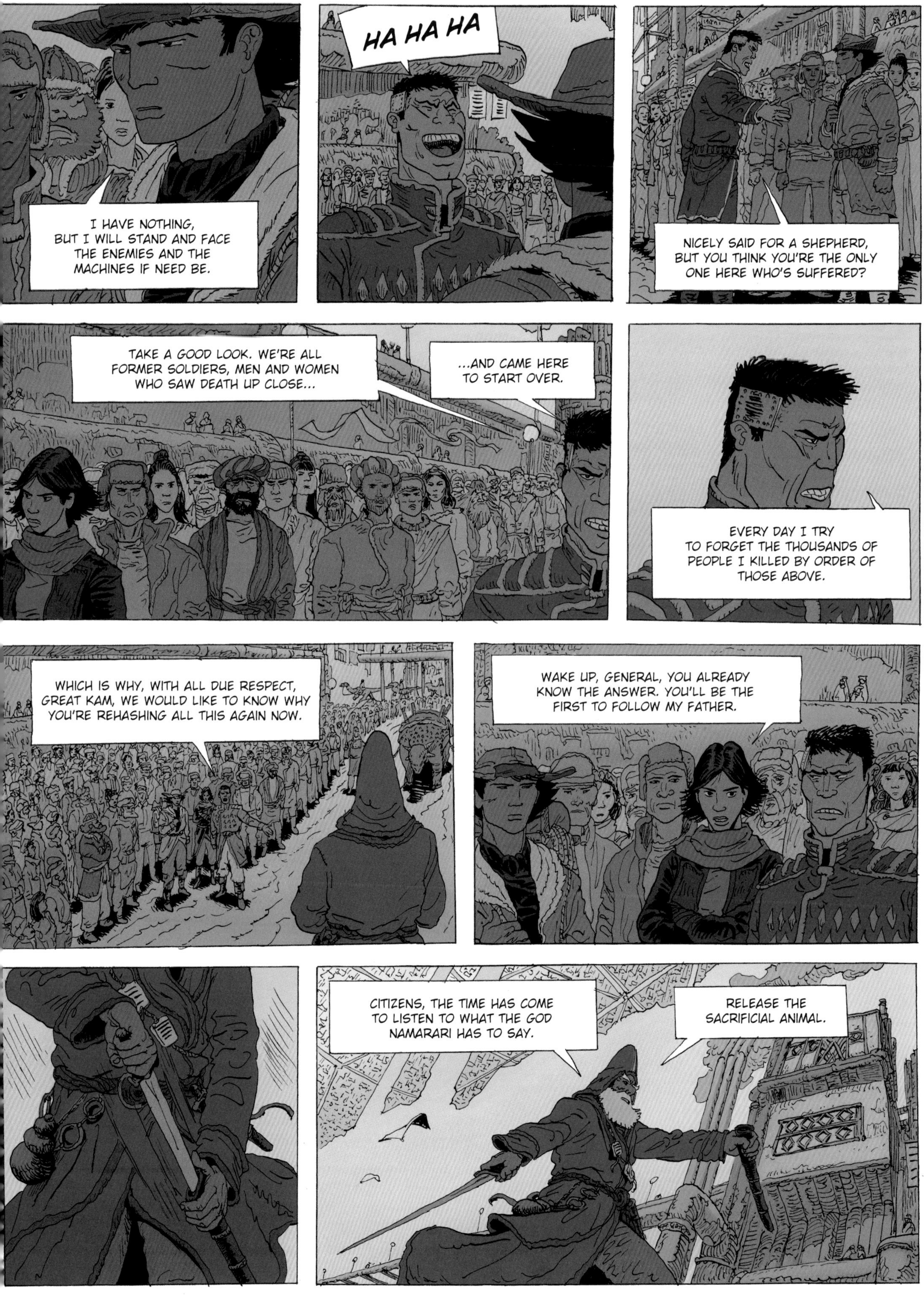
I HAVE NOTHING, BUT I WILL STAND AND FACE THE ENEMIES AND THE MACHINES IF NEED BE.
HA HA HA
NICELY SAID FOR A SHEPHERD, BUT YOU THINK YOU'RE THE ONLY ONE HERE WHO'S SUFFERED?
TAKE A GOOD LOOK. WE'RE ALL FORMER SOLDIERS, MEN AND WOMEN WHO SAW DEATH UP CLOSE...
...AND CAME HERE TO START OVER.
EVERY DAY I TRY TO FORGET THE THOUSANDS OF PEOPLE I KILLED BY ORDER OF THOSE ABOVE.
WHICH IS WHY, WITH ALL DUE RESPECT, GREAT KAM, WE WOULD LIKE TO KNOW WHY YOU'RE REHASHING ALL THIS AGAIN NOW.
WAKE UP, GENERAL, YOU ALREADY KNOW THE ANSWER. YOU'LL BE THE FIRST TO FOLLOW MY FATHER.
CITIZENS, THE TIME HAS COME TO LISTEN TO WHAT THE GOD NAMARARI HAS TO SAY.
RELEASE THE SACRIFICIAL ANIMAL.

COME CLOSER, NAMARARI...

THE PEOPLE ASK TO HEAR YOUR WORDS ON THE FUTURE OF STATION 3703!

WILL THEY FREE THEMSELVES OF THE CONTROL OF THOSE ABOVE ONE DAY?

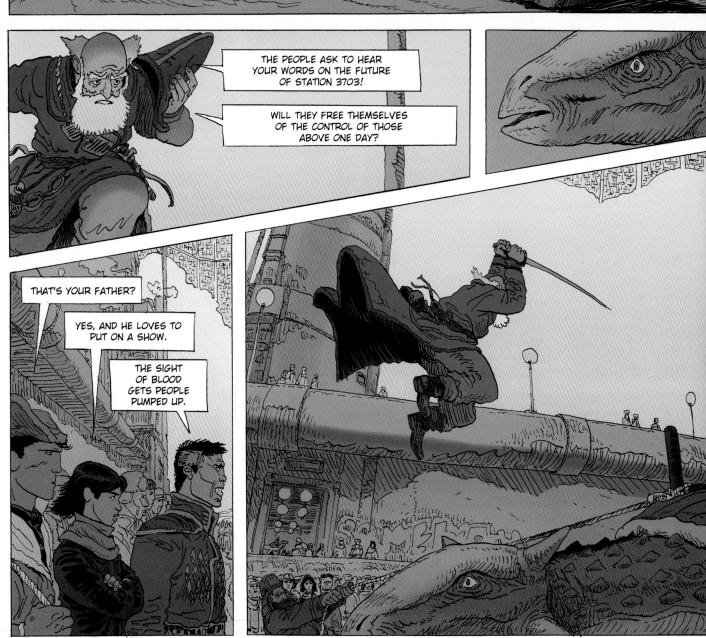

THAT'S YOUR FATHER?

YES, AND HE LOVES TO PUT ON A SHOW.

THE SIGHT OF BLOOD GETS PEOPLE PUMPED UP.

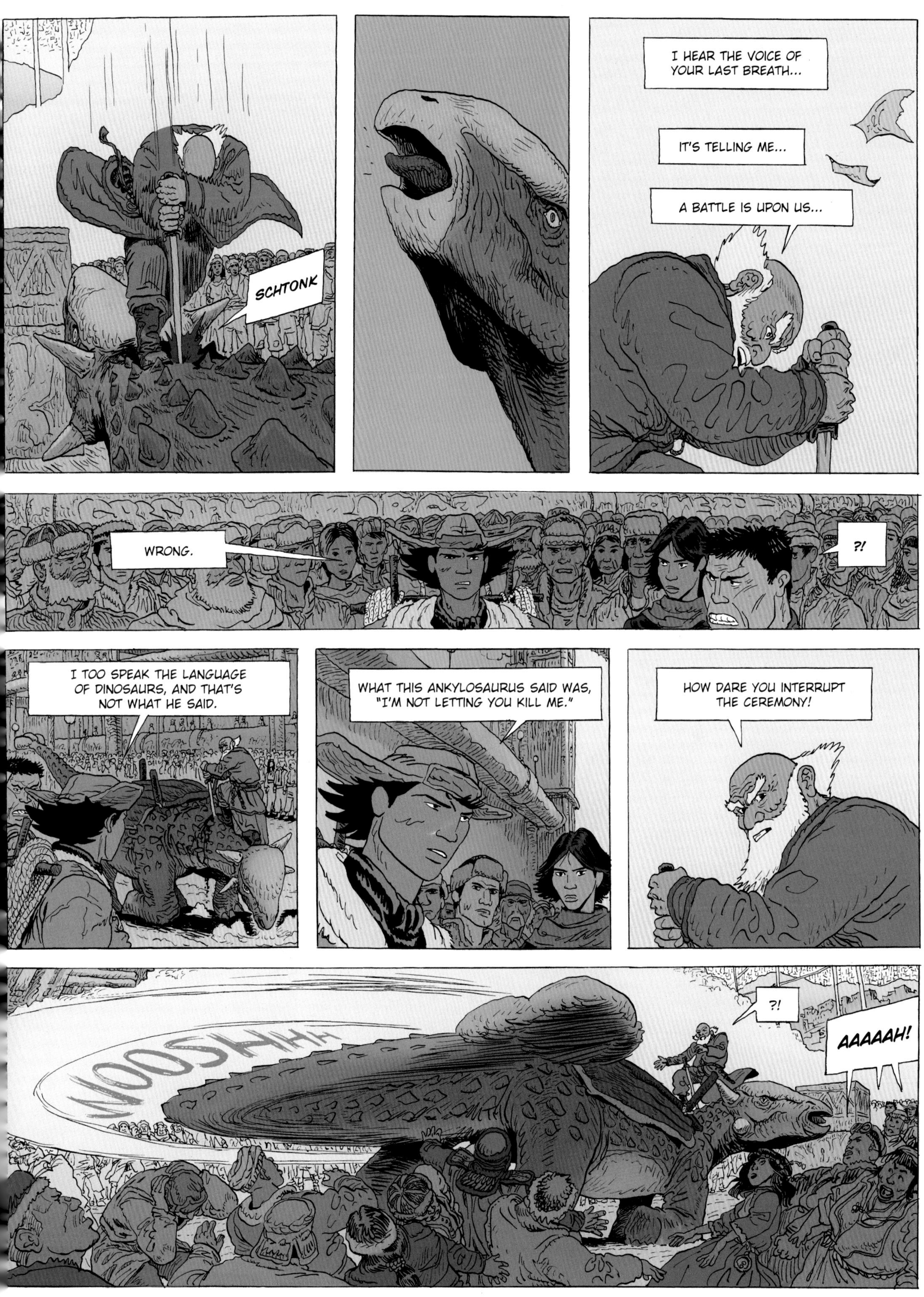
SCHTONK
I HEAR THE VOICE OF YOUR LAST BREATH...
IT'S TELLING ME...
A BATTLE IS UPON US...
WRONG.
?!
I TOO SPEAK THE LANGUAGE OF DINOSAURS, AND THAT'S NOT WHAT HE SAID.
WHAT THIS ANKYLOSAURUS SAID WAS, "I'M NOT LETTING YOU KILL ME."
HOW DARE YOU INTERRUPT THE CEREMONY!
WOOSHHH
?!
AAAAAH!

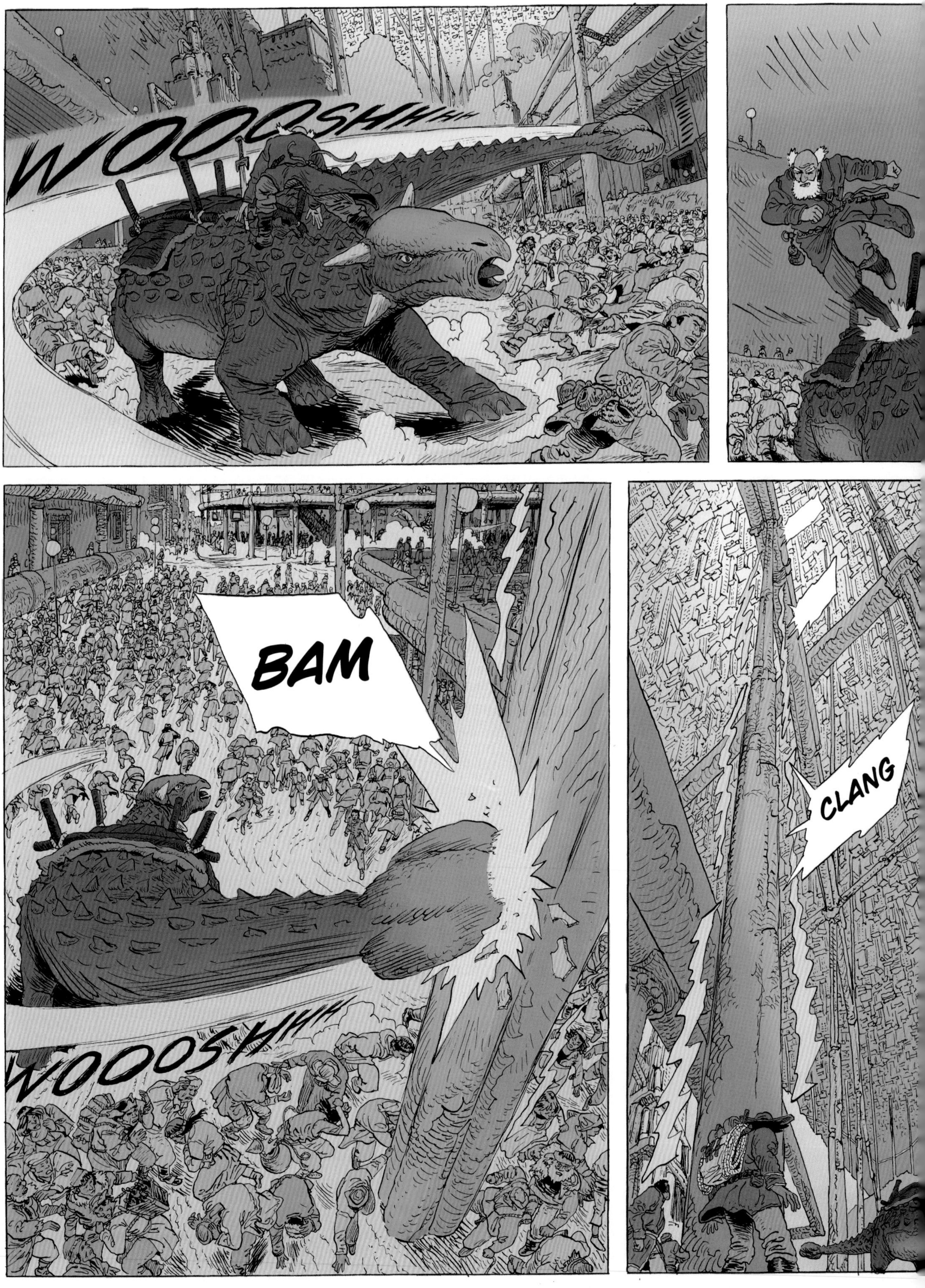
WOOOSHHHH
BAM
CLANG
WOOOSHHHH

THE SPIRIT OF THE GOD NAMARARI IS ANGRY! KILL THAT BEAST SO HE CAN BE RELEASED!!

STAND ASIDE, GENERAL.

SCHWWWW

SCHWWWW

BAM

SFFFFF

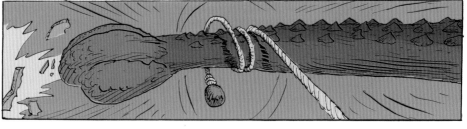

57

SWISH

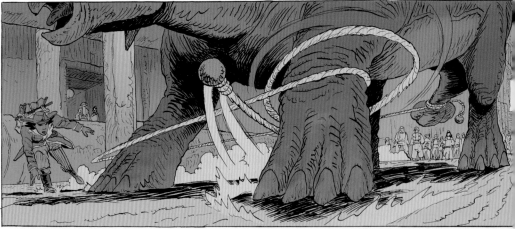

WHO TAUGHT YOU THE ART OF THE ROPES?

IT'S NOT WHAT YOU THINK.

CHIEF, LOOK!

LET'S CLEAR OUT! NOW!!

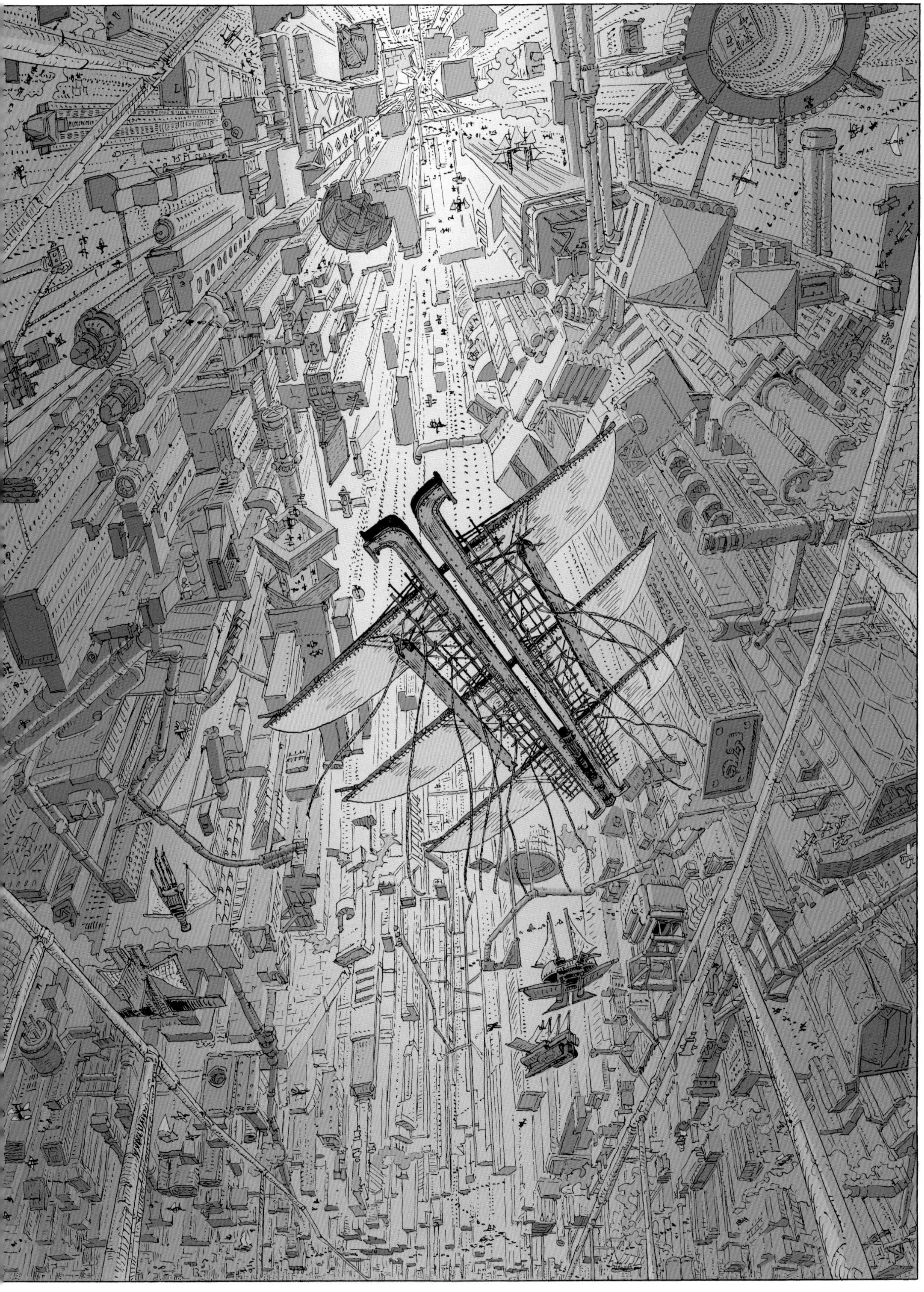

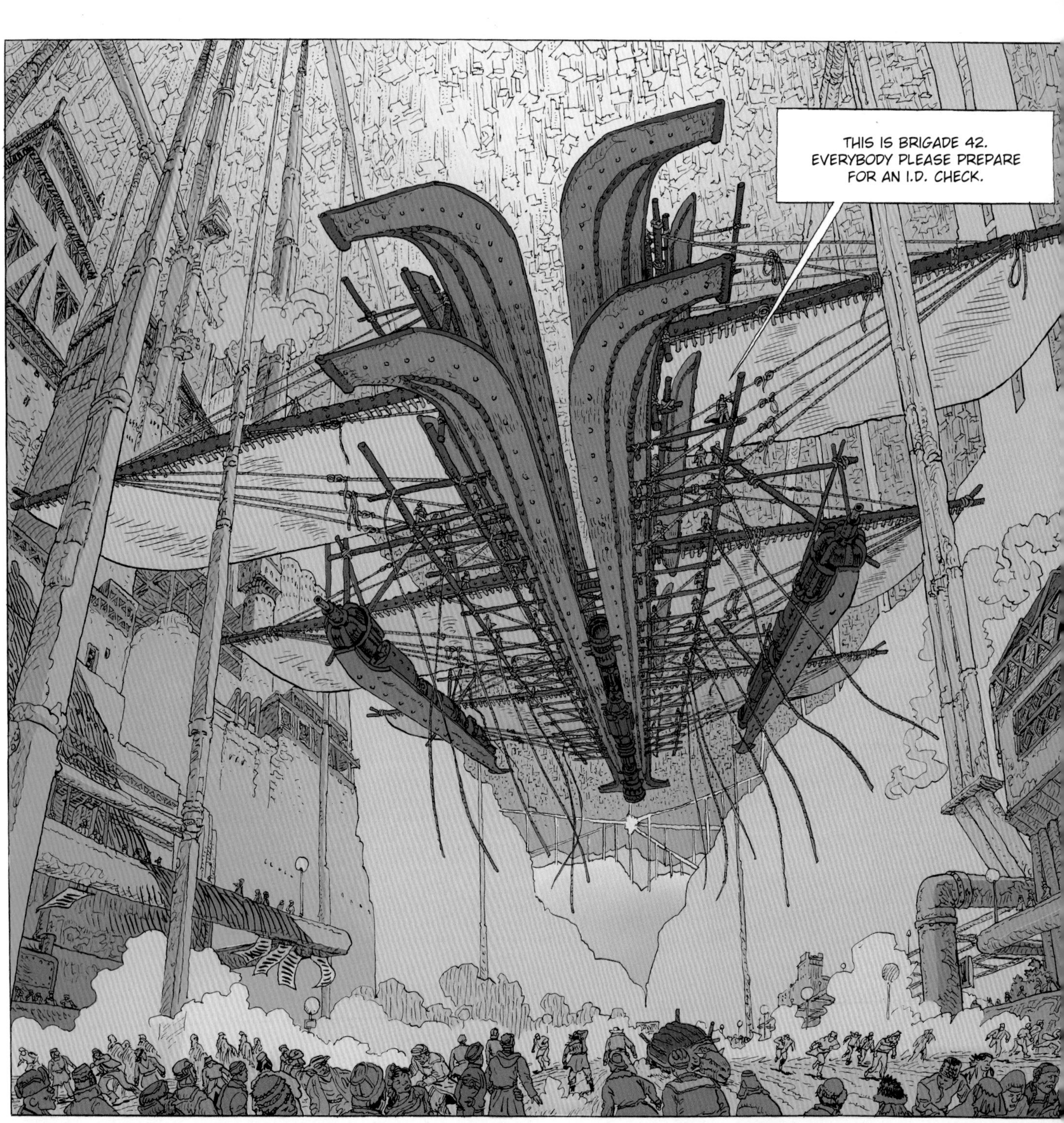
THIS IS BRIGADE 42.
EVERYBODY PLEASE PREPARE
FOR AN I.D. CHECK.

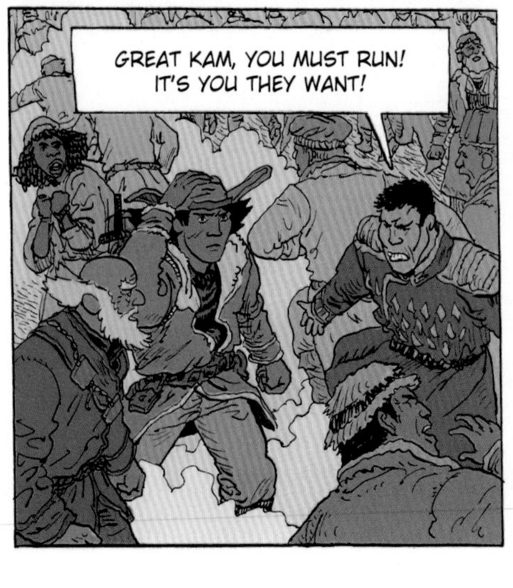
GREAT KAM, YOU MUST RUN!
IT'S YOU THEY WANT!

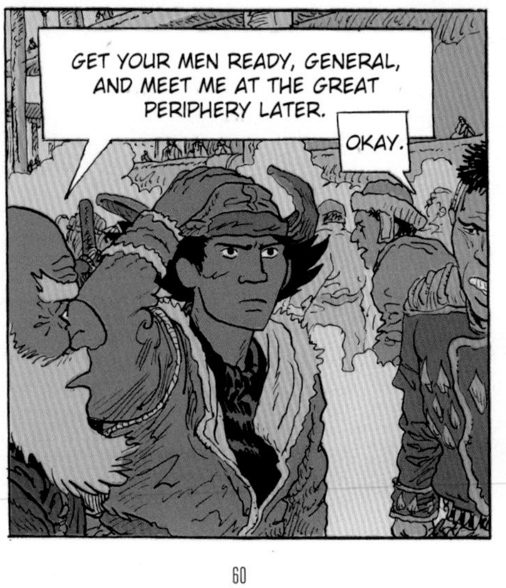
GET YOUR MEN READY, GENERAL,
AND MEET ME AT THE GREAT
PERIPHERY LATER.
OKAY.

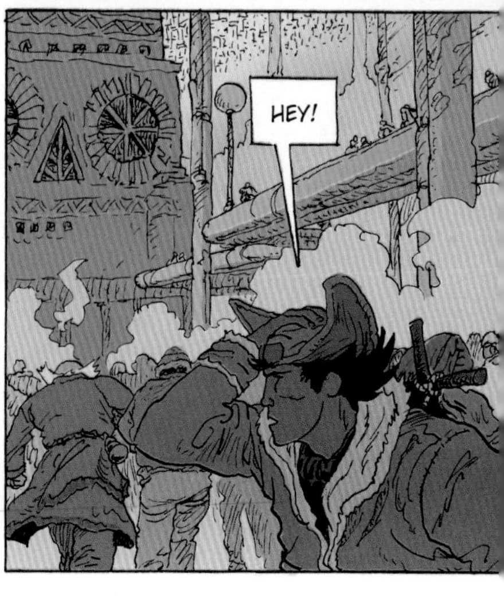
HEY!

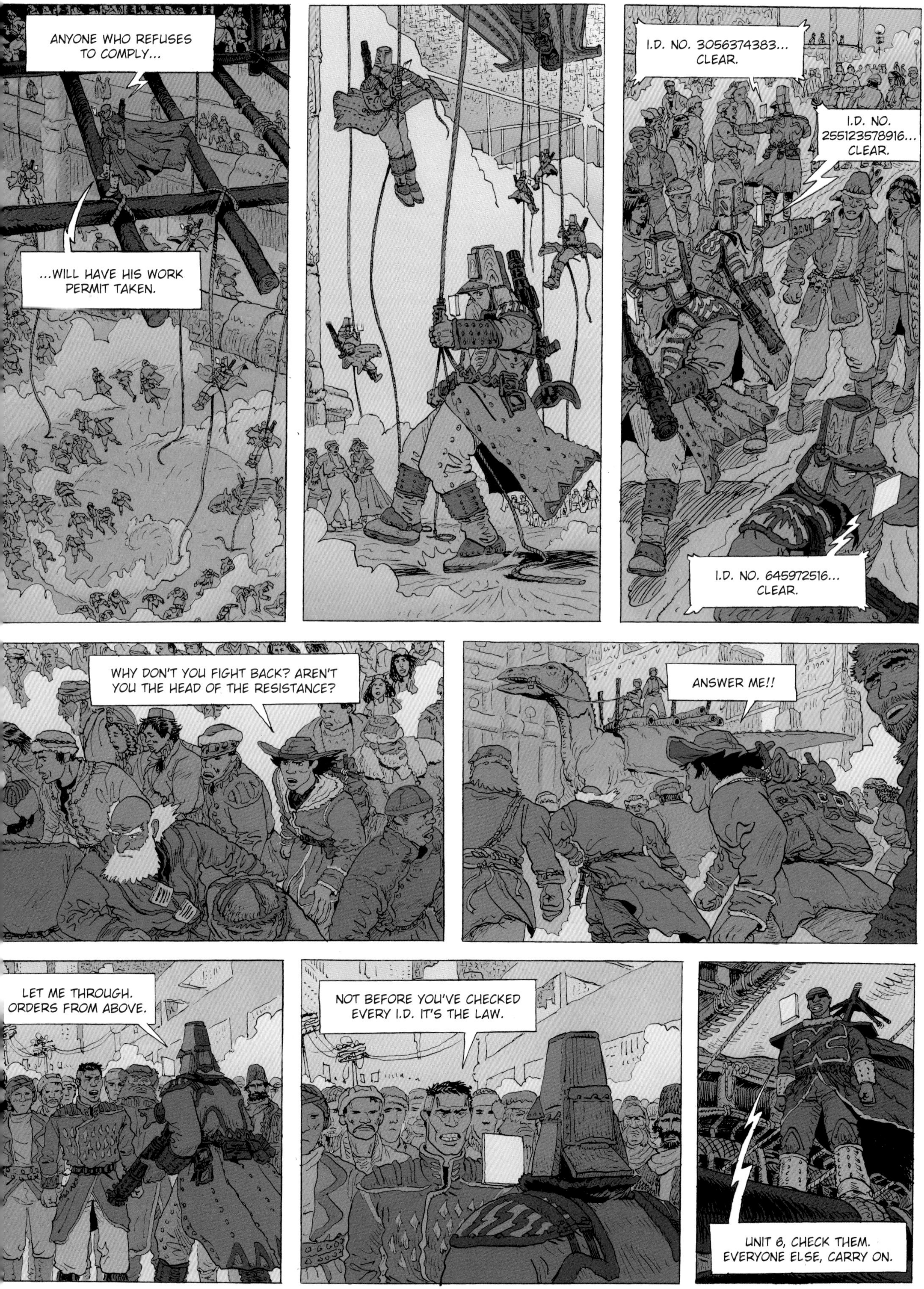

ANYONE WHO REFUSES TO COMPLY...
...WILL HAVE HIS WORK PERMIT TAKEN.
I.D. NO. 3056374383... CLEAR.
I.D. NO. 255123578916... CLEAR.
I.D. NO. 645972516... CLEAR.
WHY DON'T YOU FIGHT BACK? AREN'T YOU THE HEAD OF THE RESISTANCE?
ANSWER ME!!
LET ME THROUGH. ORDERS FROM ABOVE.
NOT BEFORE YOU'VE CHECKED EVERY I.D. IT'S THE LAW.
UNIT 6, CHECK THEM. EVERYONE ELSE, CARRY ON.

WAIT!!!

STEP ASIDE!

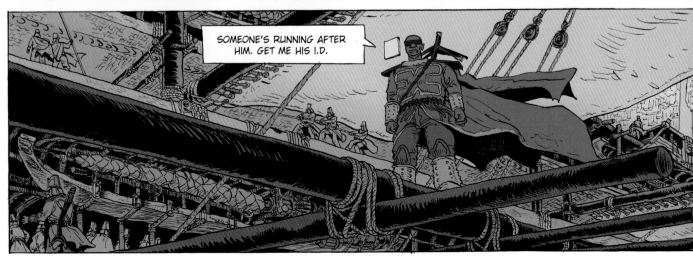

SOMEONE'S RUNNING AFTER HIM. GET ME HIS I.D.

62

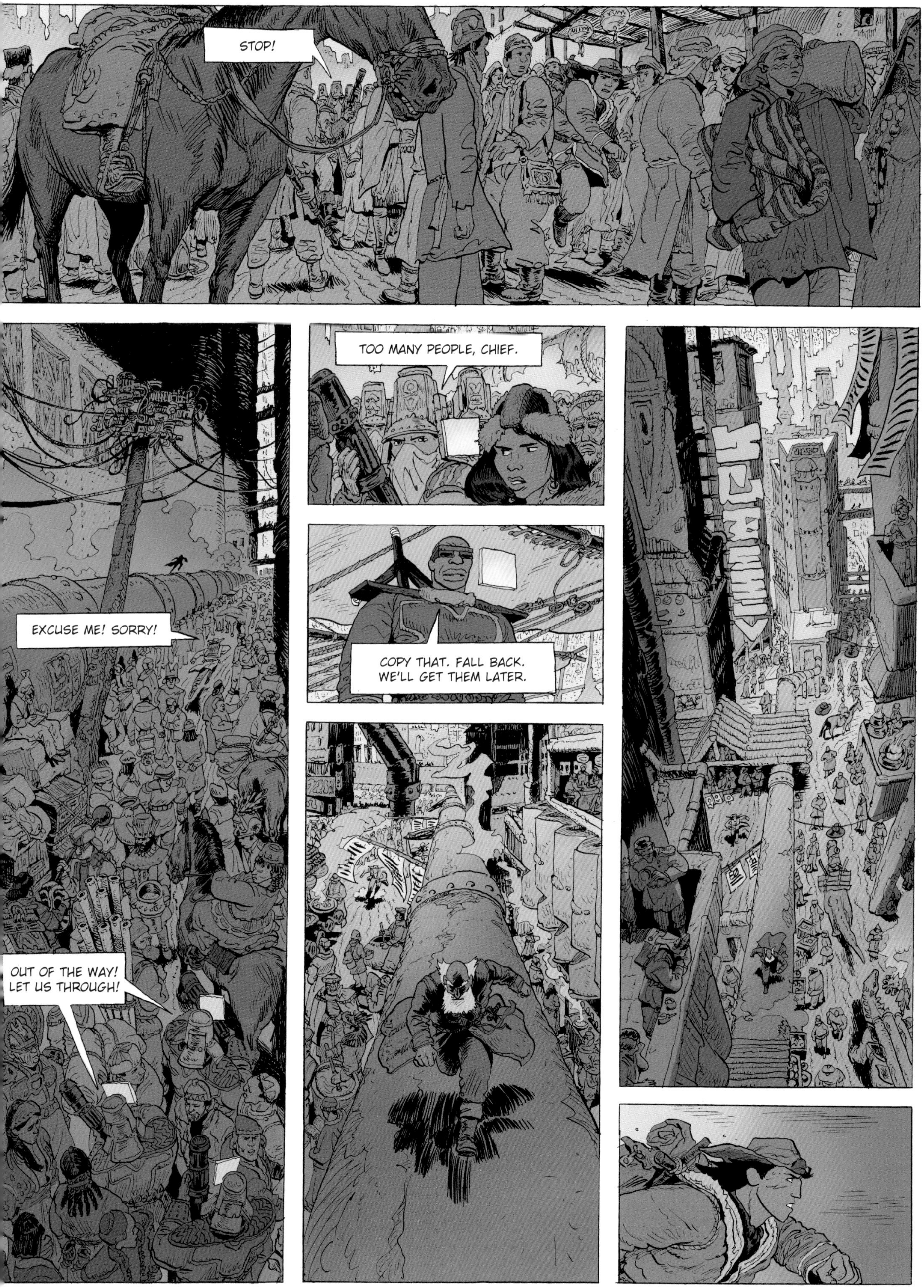
STOP!
EXCUSE ME! SORRY!
OUT OF THE WAY! LET US THROUGH!
TOO MANY PEOPLE, CHIEF.
COPY THAT. FALL BACK. WE'LL GET THEM LATER.

SORRY! JUST PASSING THROUGH!

?!

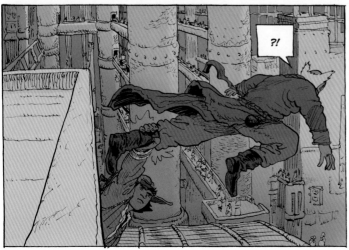

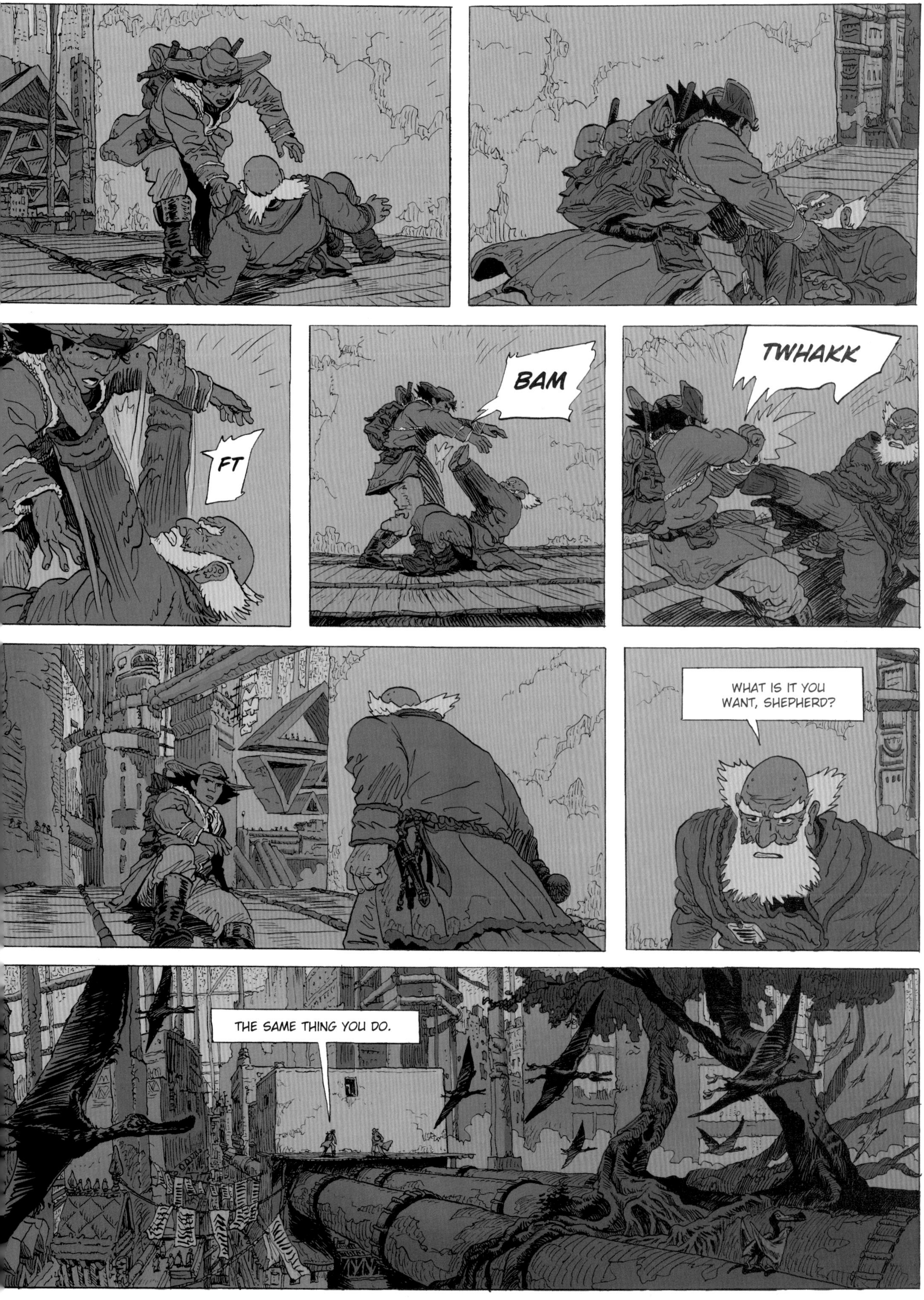
FT
BAM
TWHAKK
WHAT IS IT YOU WANT, SHEPHERD?
THE SAME THING YOU DO.

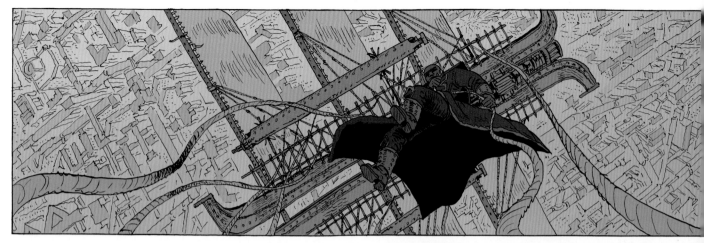

WE MEET AGAIN, GENERAL ALICE.

GETTING CHUMMY WITH THE RESISTANCE, I SEE?

TO THINK YOU WERE ONCE SO PROMISING.

WHAT ARE YOU DOING HERE, GENERAL YURLUNG, ASIDE FROM GETTING YOUR BOOTS DIRTY ON SOLID GROUND?

YOU KNOW THE RULES. IT TAKES VERY LITTLE FOR THE NETWORK TO REACT AGAINST THOSE WHO MAKE THE WRONG CHOICE.

SOME CHOICE!!

THE STATION'S NEVER BEEN UNDER SO MUCH SURVEILLANCE!!

DON'T YOU THINK IT'S HARD ENOUGH FOR US AS IT IS?!

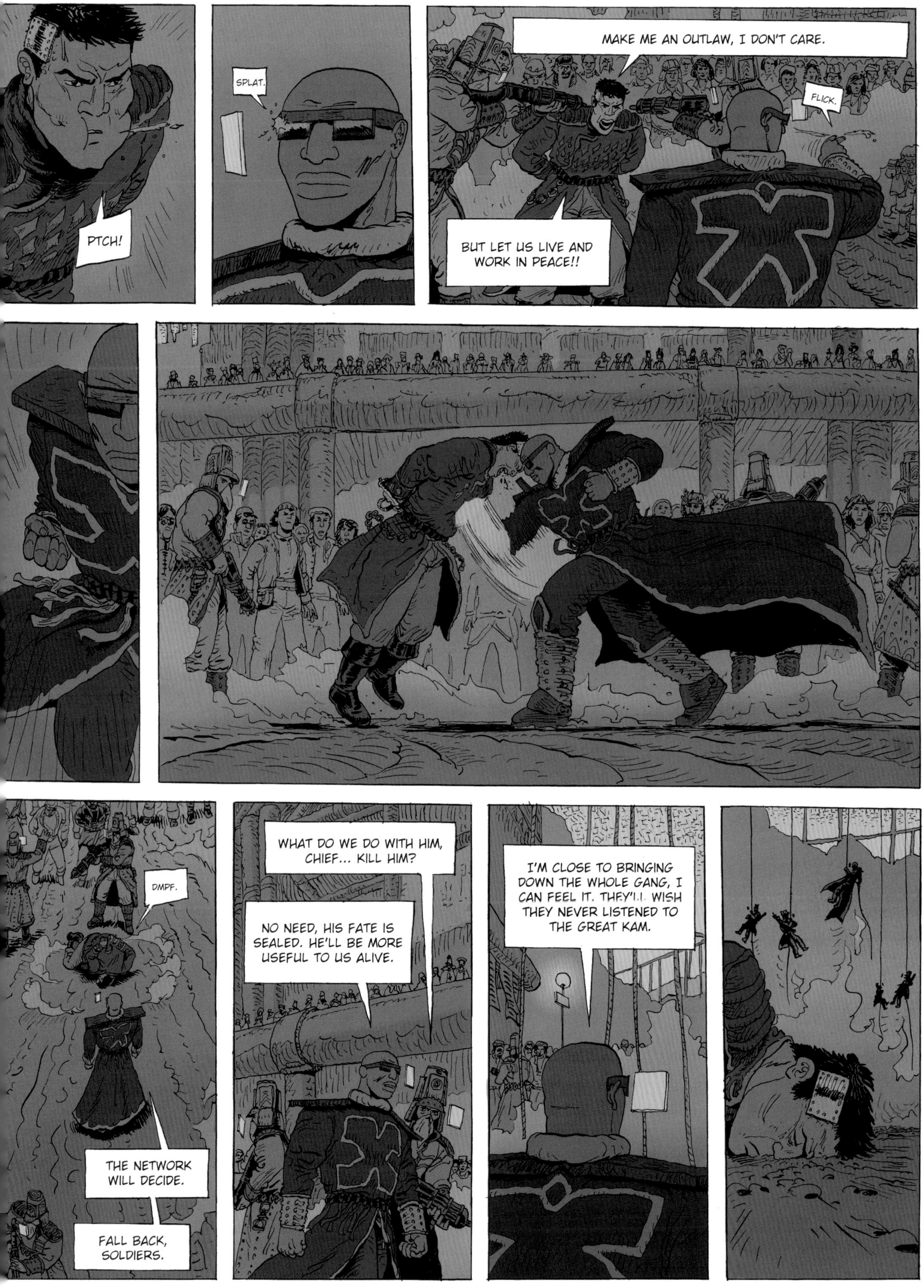
PTCH!
SPLAT.
MAKE ME AN OUTLAW, I DON'T CARE.
FLICK.
BUT LET US LIVE AND WORK IN PEACE!!
DMPF.
THE NETWORK WILL DECIDE.
FALL BACK, SOLDIERS.
WHAT DO WE DO WITH HIM, CHIEF... KILL HIM?
NO NEED, HIS FATE IS SEALED. HE'LL BE MORE USEFUL TO US ALIVE.
I'M CLOSE TO BRINGING DOWN THE WHOLE GANG, I CAN FEEL IT. THEY'LL WISH THEY NEVER LISTENED TO THE GREAT KAM.

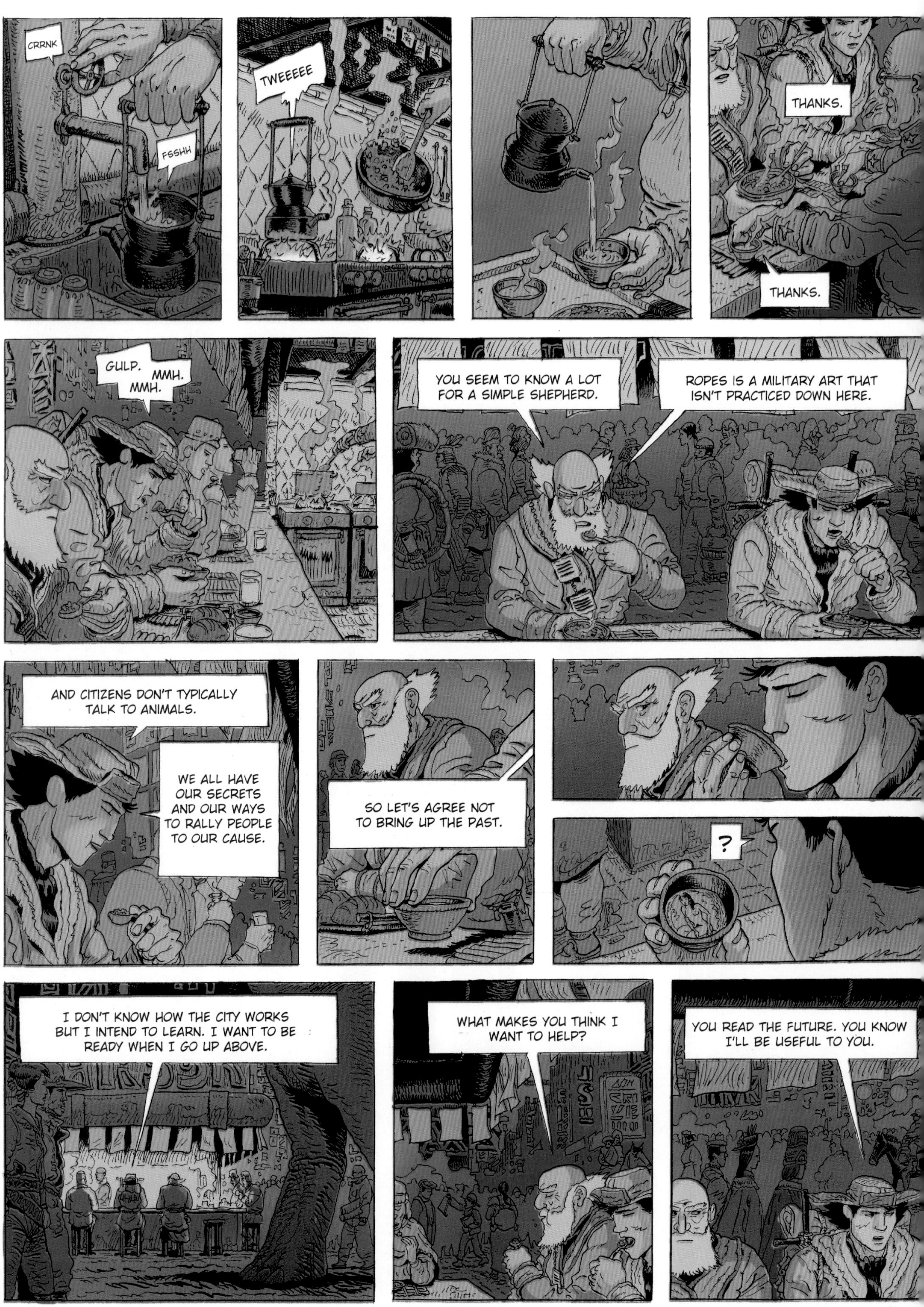
CRRNK
FSSHH
TWEEEEE
THANKS.
THANKS.
GULP.
MMH. MMH.
YOU SEEM TO KNOW A LOT FOR A SIMPLE SHEPHERD.
ROPES IS A MILITARY ART THAT ISN'T PRACTICED DOWN HERE.
AND CITIZENS DON'T TYPICALLY TALK TO ANIMALS.
WE ALL HAVE OUR SECRETS AND OUR WAYS TO RALLY PEOPLE TO OUR CAUSE.
SO LET'S AGREE NOT TO BRING UP THE PAST.
?
I DON'T KNOW HOW THE CITY WORKS BUT I INTEND TO LEARN. I WANT TO BE READY WHEN I GO UP ABOVE.
WHAT MAKES YOU THINK I WANT TO HELP?
YOU READ THE FUTURE. YOU KNOW I'LL BE USEFUL TO YOU.

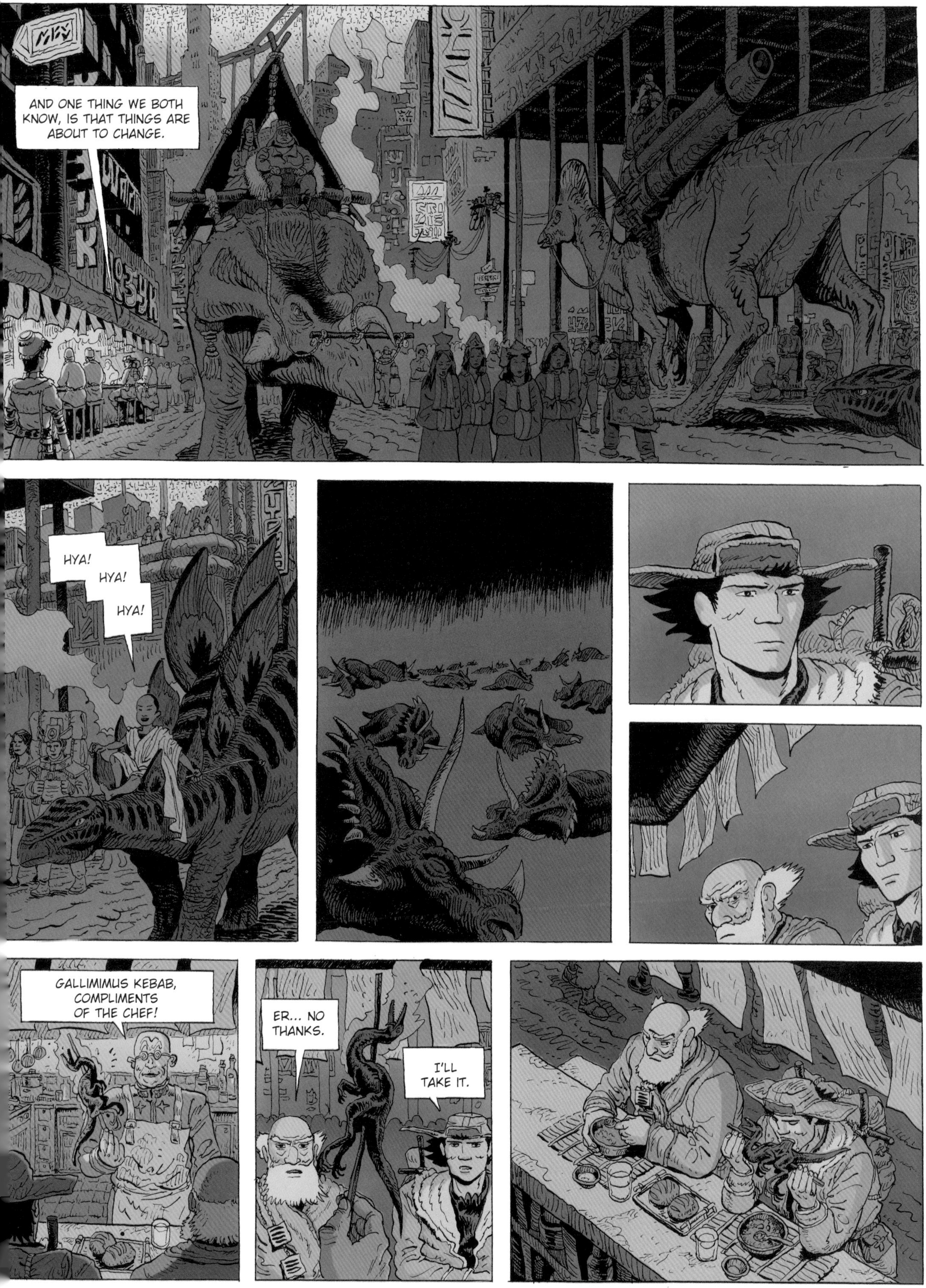
AND ONE THING WE BOTH KNOW, IS THAT THINGS ARE ABOUT TO CHANGE.
HYA!
HYA!
HYA!
GALLIMIMUS KEBAB, COMPLIMENTS OF THE CHEF!
ER... NO THANKS.
I'LL TAKE IT.

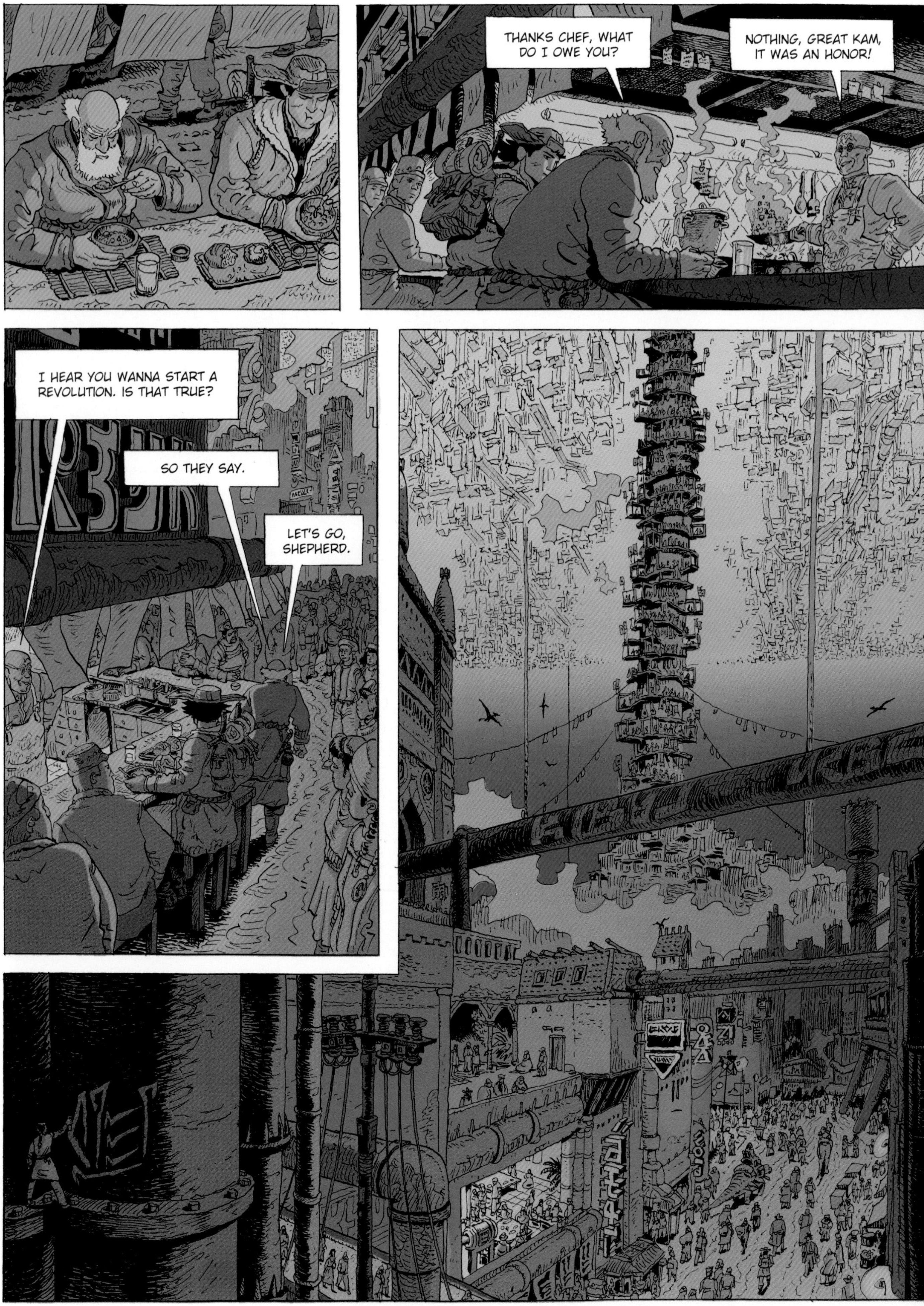
THANKS CHEF, WHAT DO I OWE YOU?
NOTHING, GREAT KAM, IT WAS AN HONOR!
I HEAR YOU WANNA START A REVOLUTION. IS THAT TRUE?
SO THEY SAY.
LET'S GO, SHEPHERD.

I.D. NO. 0741278540I... CLEAR. YOU CAN GO THROUGH.

I.D. NO. 852I43I67355... CLEAR. YOU CAN GO THROUGH.

DON'T HOLD UP THE LINE.

EASY FOR YOU TO SAY, WE'VE BEEN WAITING 20 HOURS!

KEEP IT MOVING!

MOM, I'M HUNGRY.

I KNOW, SWEETIE. HERE, HAVE SOME FRUIT.

STOP PUSHING!

WRITE DOWN YOUR NUMBER UNTIL WE CAN REVIEW YOUR CASE.

IS THAT REALLY THE ONLY WAY UP THERE?

NO, YOU CAN ALSO FLY UP, BUT THE NETWORK MONITORS ALL THE SHIPS. THEY'VE GOT EYES EVERYWHERE.

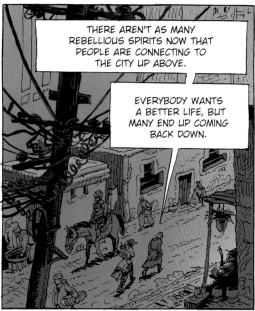

THERE AREN'T AS MANY REBELLIOUS SPIRITS NOW THAT PEOPLE ARE CONNECTING TO THE CITY UP ABOVE.

EVERYBODY WANTS A BETTER LIFE, BUT MANY END UP COMING BACK DOWN.

HOW MUCH FOR A GOURDE OF WATER, MA'AM?

TWO DUMAS, GREAT KAM.

I'LL TAKE TWO.

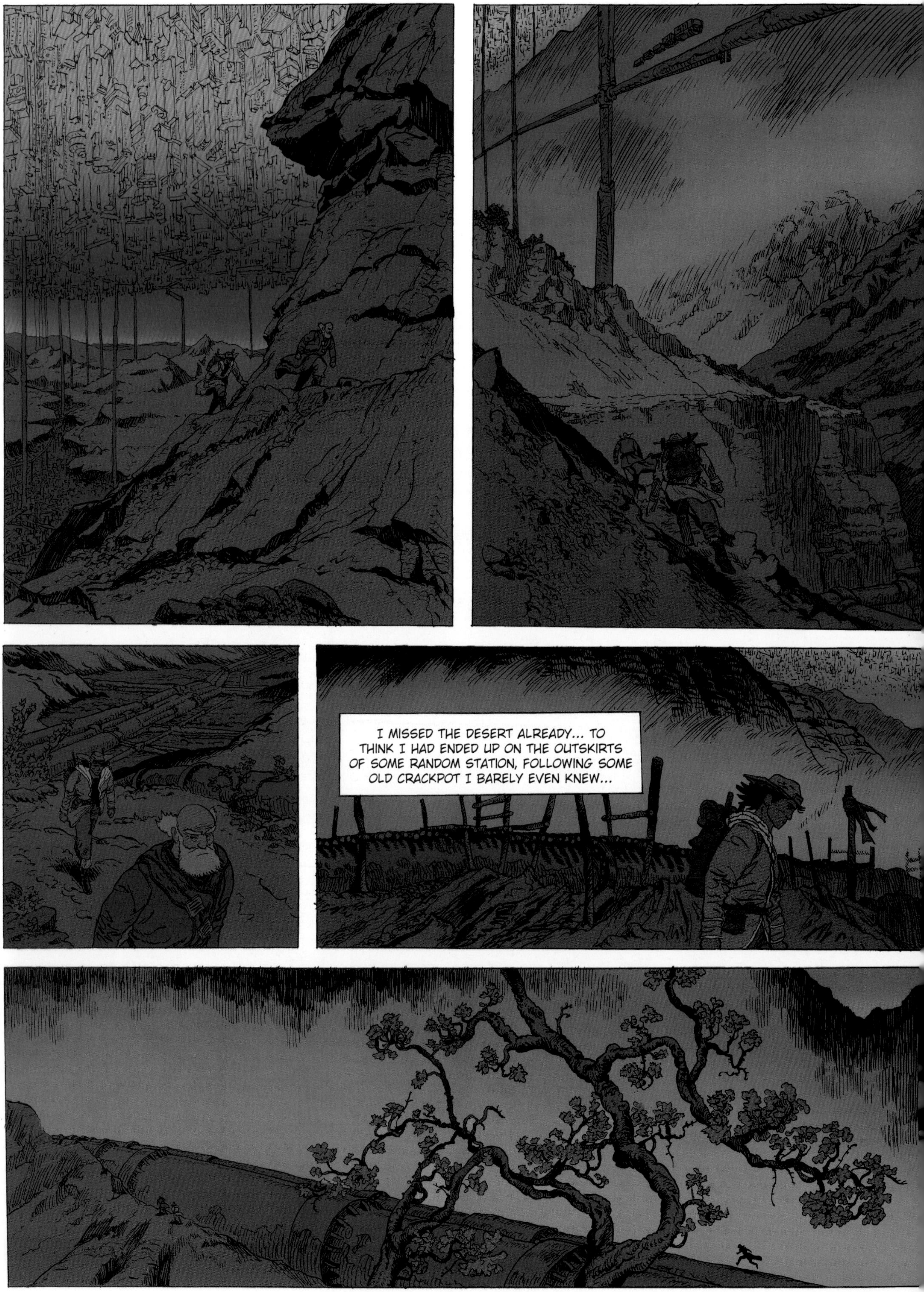
I MISSED THE DESERT ALREADY... TO THINK I HAD ENDED UP ON THE OUTSKIRTS OF SOME RANDOM STATION, FOLLOWING SOME OLD CRACKPOT I BARELY EVEN KNEW...

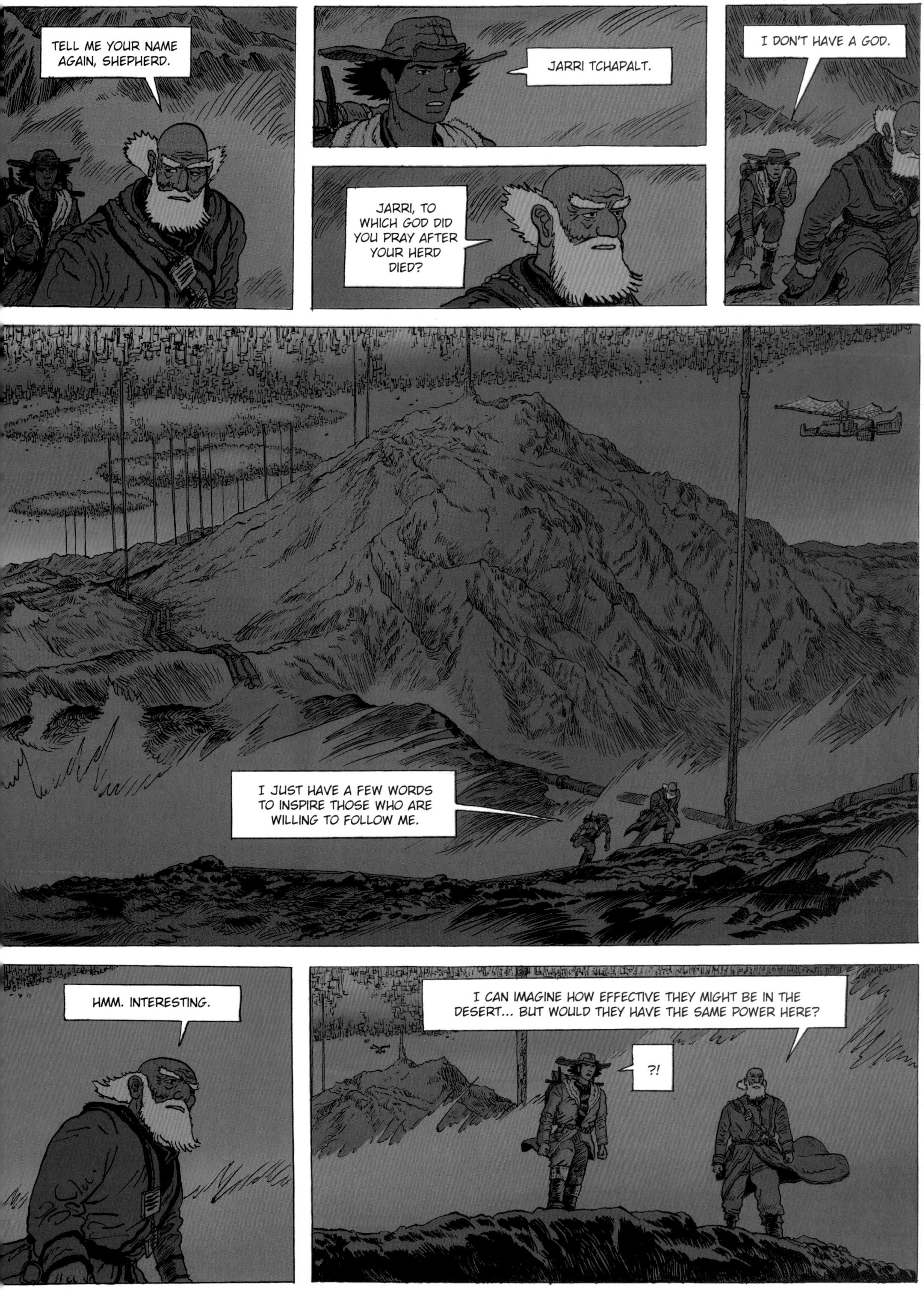

TELL ME YOUR NAME AGAIN, SHEPHERD.
JARRI TCHAPALT.
JARRI, TO WHICH GOD DID YOU PRAY AFTER YOUR HERD DIED?
I DON'T HAVE A GOD.
I JUST HAVE A FEW WORDS TO INSPIRE THOSE WHO ARE WILLING TO FOLLOW ME.
HMM. INTERESTING.
I CAN IMAGINE HOW EFFECTIVE THEY MIGHT BE IN THE DESERT... BUT WOULD THEY HAVE THE SAME POWER HERE?
?!

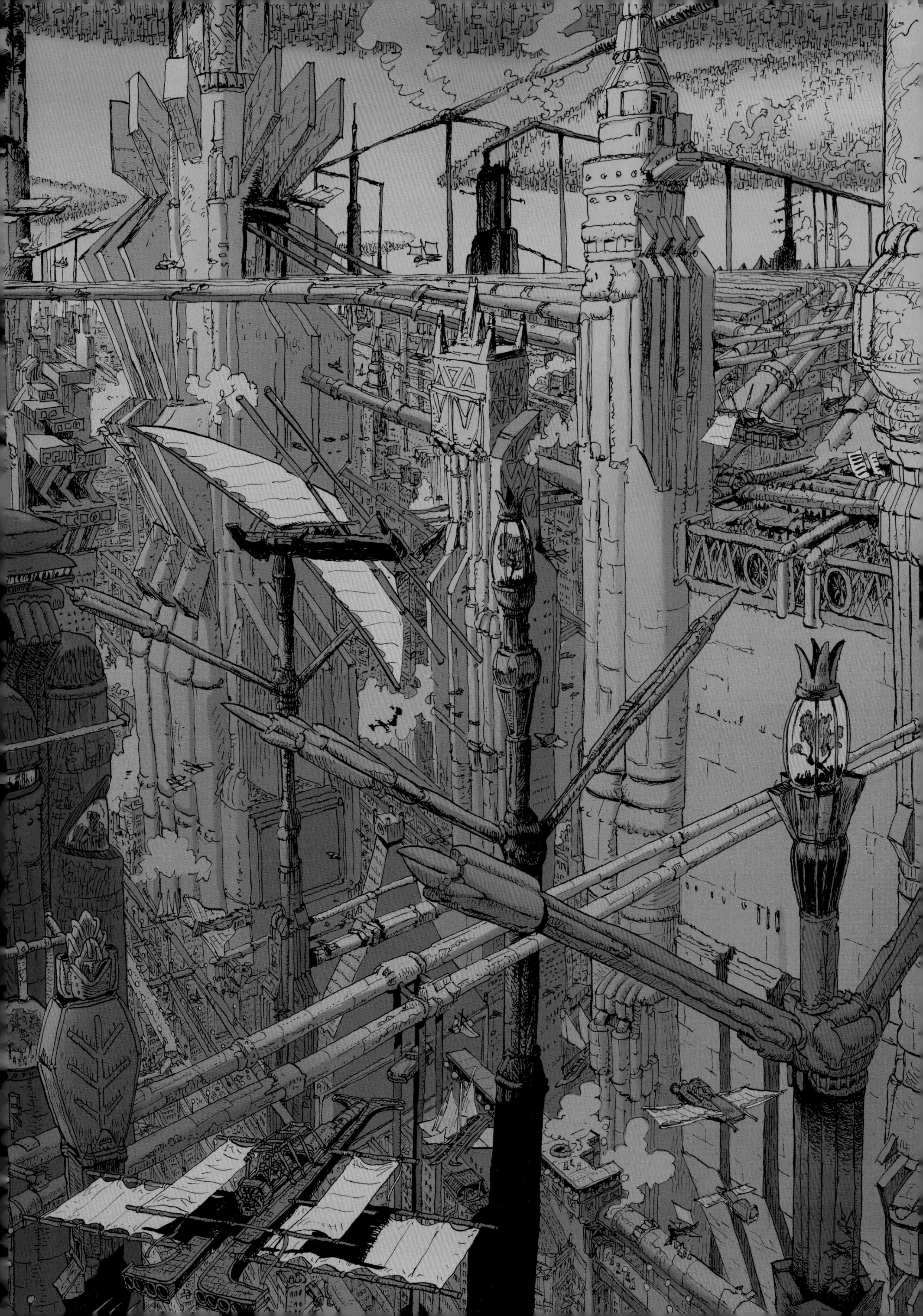

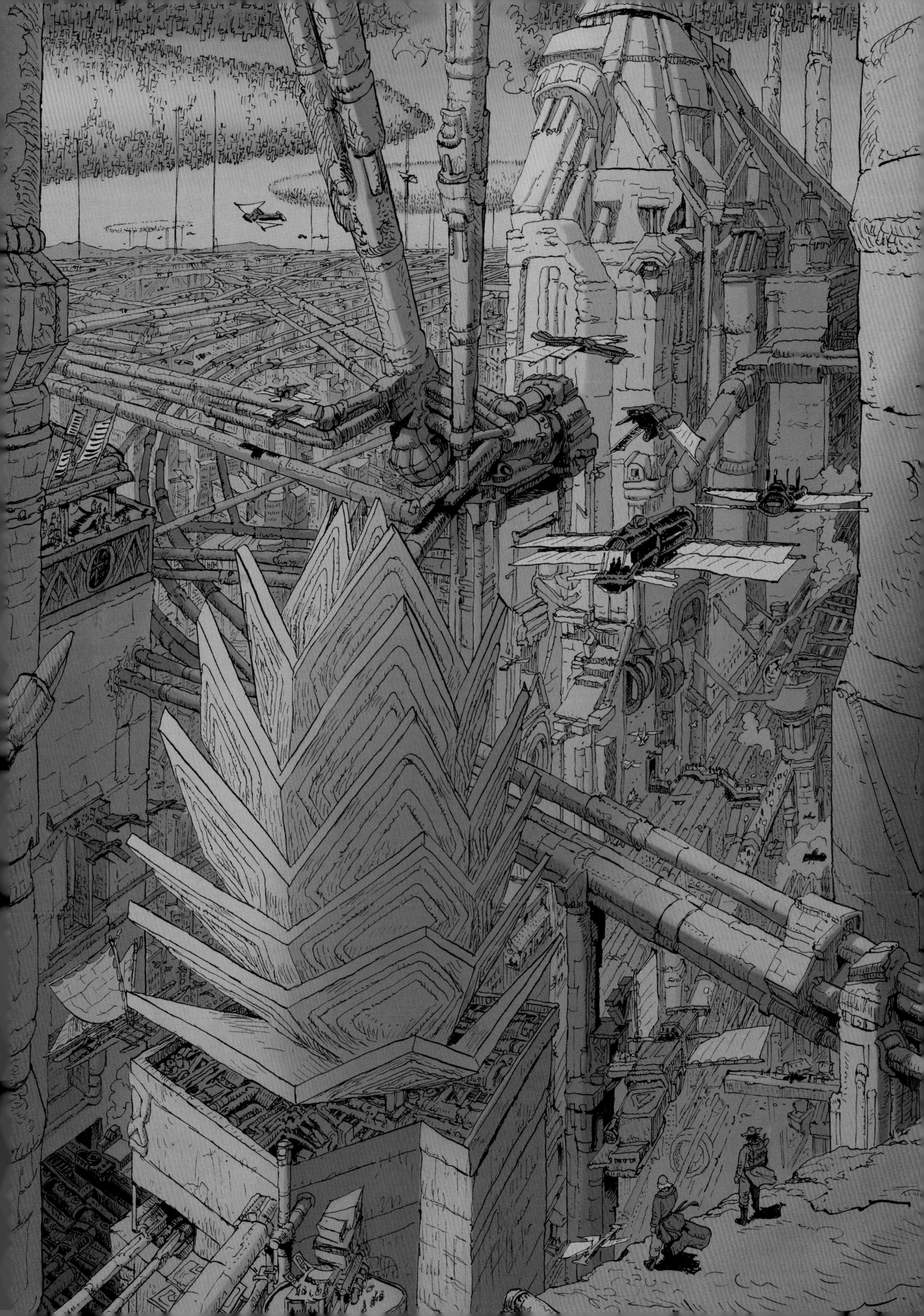

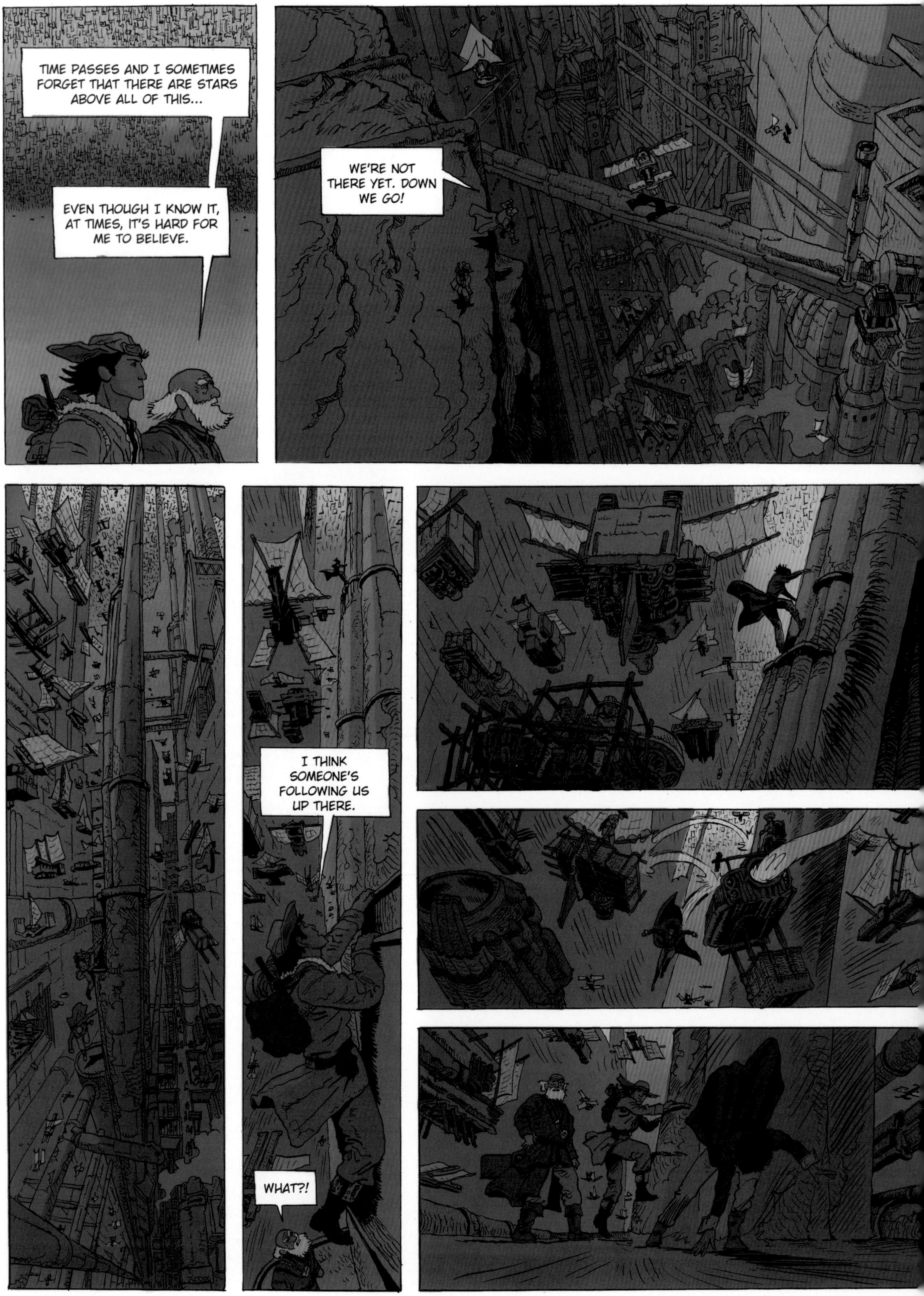
TIME PASSES AND I SOMETIMES FORGET THAT THERE ARE STARS ABOVE ALL OF THIS...
EVEN THOUGH I KNOW IT, AT TIMES, IT'S HARD FOR ME TO BELIEVE.
WE'RE NOT THERE YET. DOWN WE GO!
I THINK SOMEONE'S FOLLOWING US UP THERE.
WHAT?!

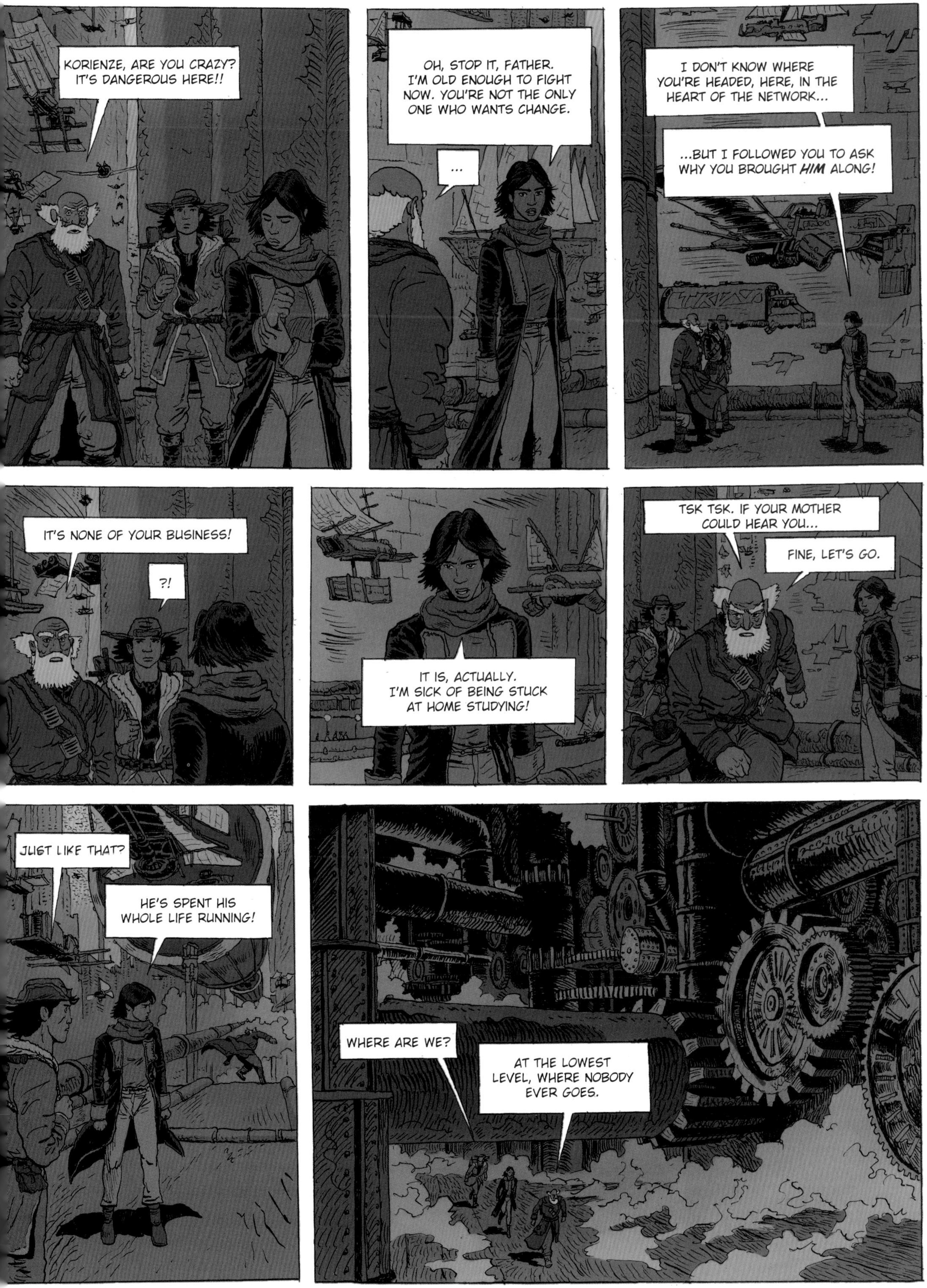
KORIENZE, ARE YOU CRAZY? IT'S DANGEROUS HERE!!
OH, STOP IT, FATHER. I'M OLD ENOUGH TO FIGHT NOW. YOU'RE NOT THE ONLY ONE WHO WANTS CHANGE.
...
I DON'T KNOW WHERE YOU'RE HEADED, HERE, IN THE HEART OF THE NETWORK...
...BUT I FOLLOWED YOU TO ASK WHY YOU BROUGHT HIM ALONG!
IT'S NONE OF YOUR BUSINESS!
?!
IT IS, ACTUALLY. I'M SICK OF BEING STUCK AT HOME STUDYING!
TSK TSK. IF YOUR MOTHER COULD HEAR YOU...
FINE, LET'S GO.
JUST LIKE THAT?
HE'S SPENT HIS WHOLE LIFE RUNNING!
WHERE ARE WE?
AT THE LOWEST LEVEL, WHERE NOBODY EVER GOES.

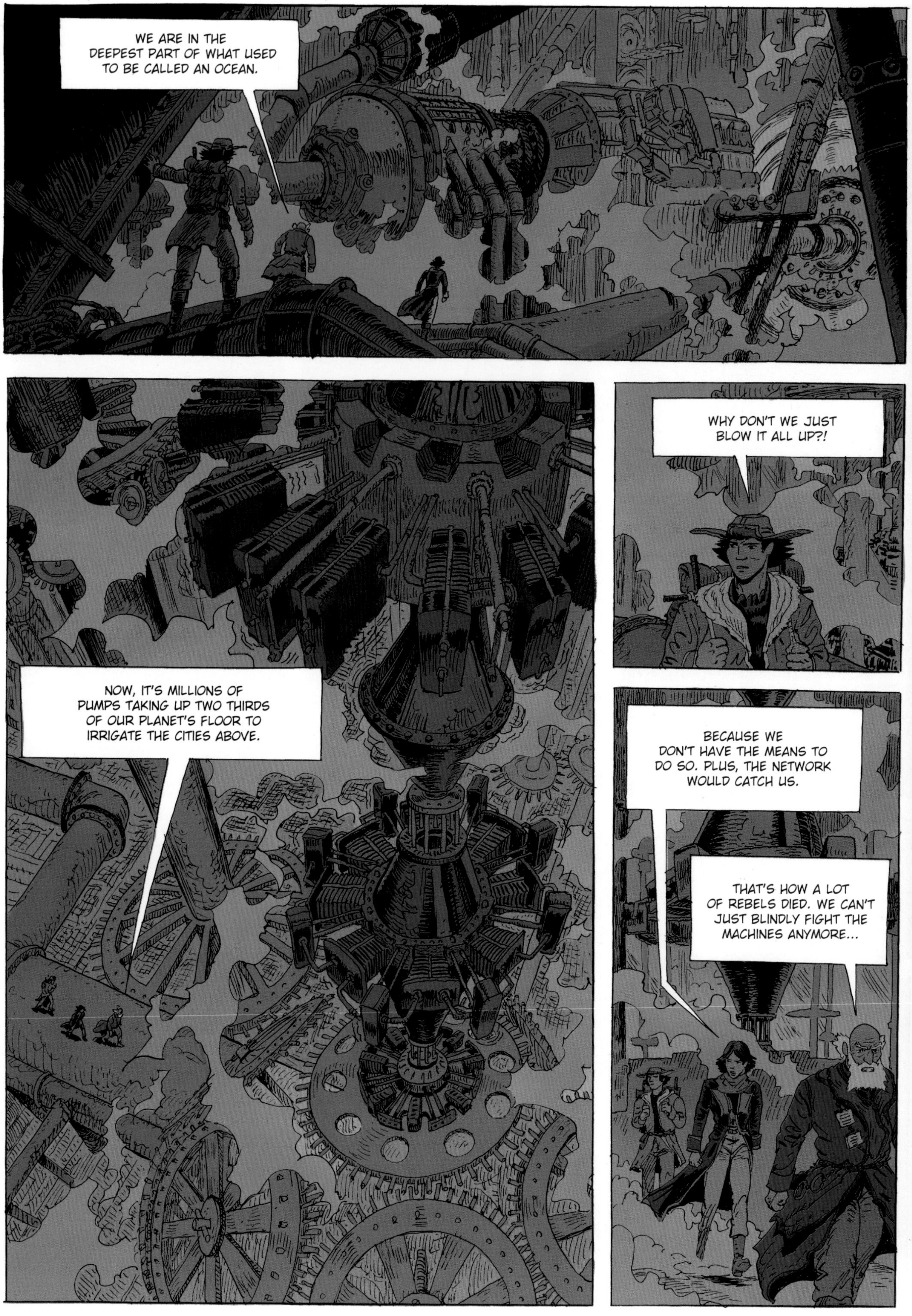
WE ARE IN THE DEEPEST PART OF WHAT USED TO BE CALLED AN OCEAN.
NOW, IT'S MILLIONS OF PUMPS TAKING UP TWO THIRDS OF OUR PLANET'S FLOOR TO IRRIGATE THE CITIES ABOVE.
WHY DON'T WE JUST BLOW IT ALL UP?!
BECAUSE WE DON'T HAVE THE MEANS TO DO SO. PLUS, THE NETWORK WOULD CATCH US.
THAT'S HOW A LOT OF REBELS DIED. WE CAN'T JUST BLINDLY FIGHT THE MACHINES ANYMORE...

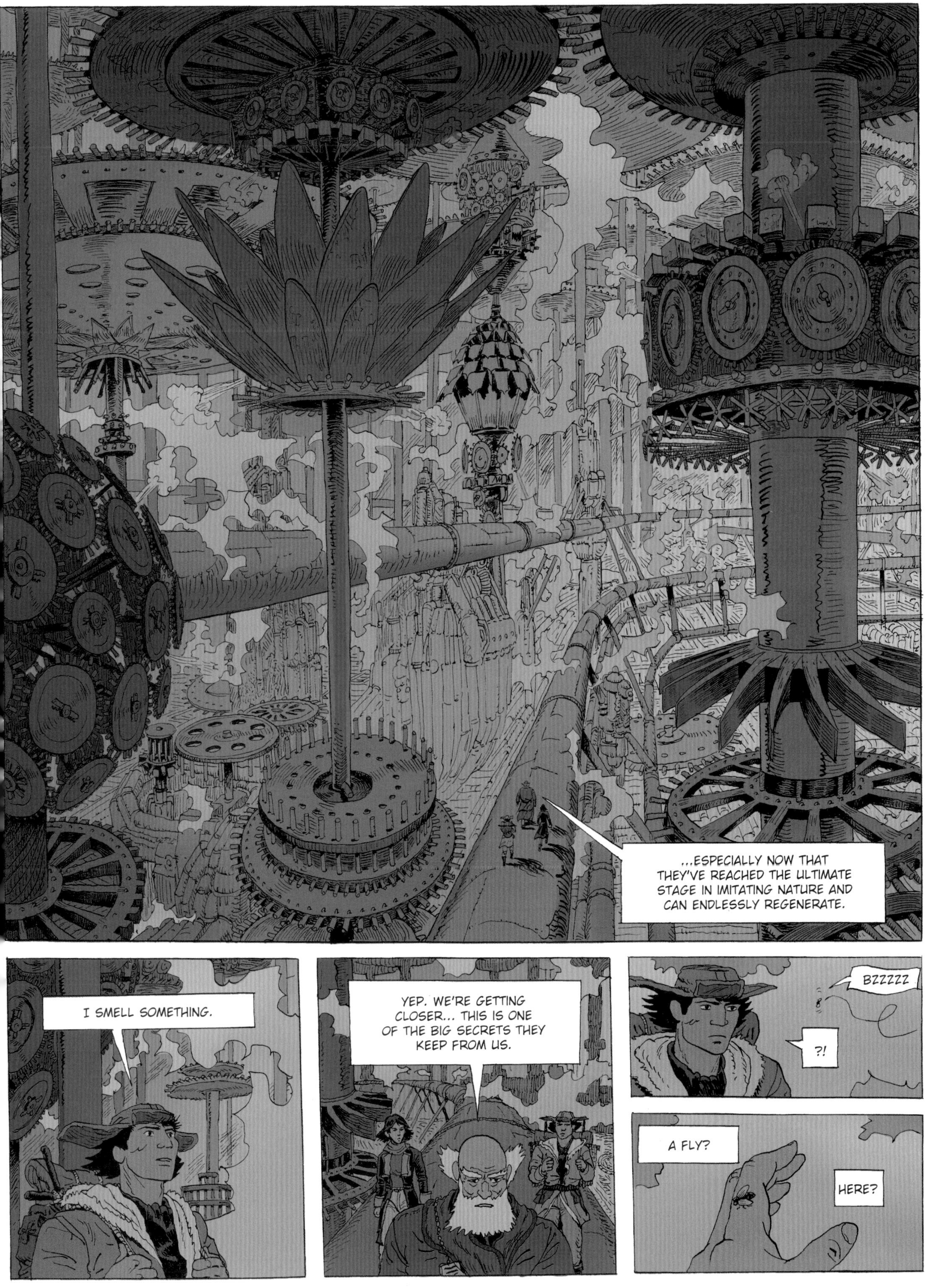
...ESPECIALLY NOW THAT THEY'VE REACHED THE ULTIMATE STAGE IN IMITATING NATURE AND CAN ENDLESSLY REGENERATE.
I SMELL SOMETHING.
YEP. WE'RE GETTING CLOSER... THIS IS ONE OF THE BIG SECRETS THEY KEEP FROM US.
BZZZZZ
?!
A FLY?
HERE?

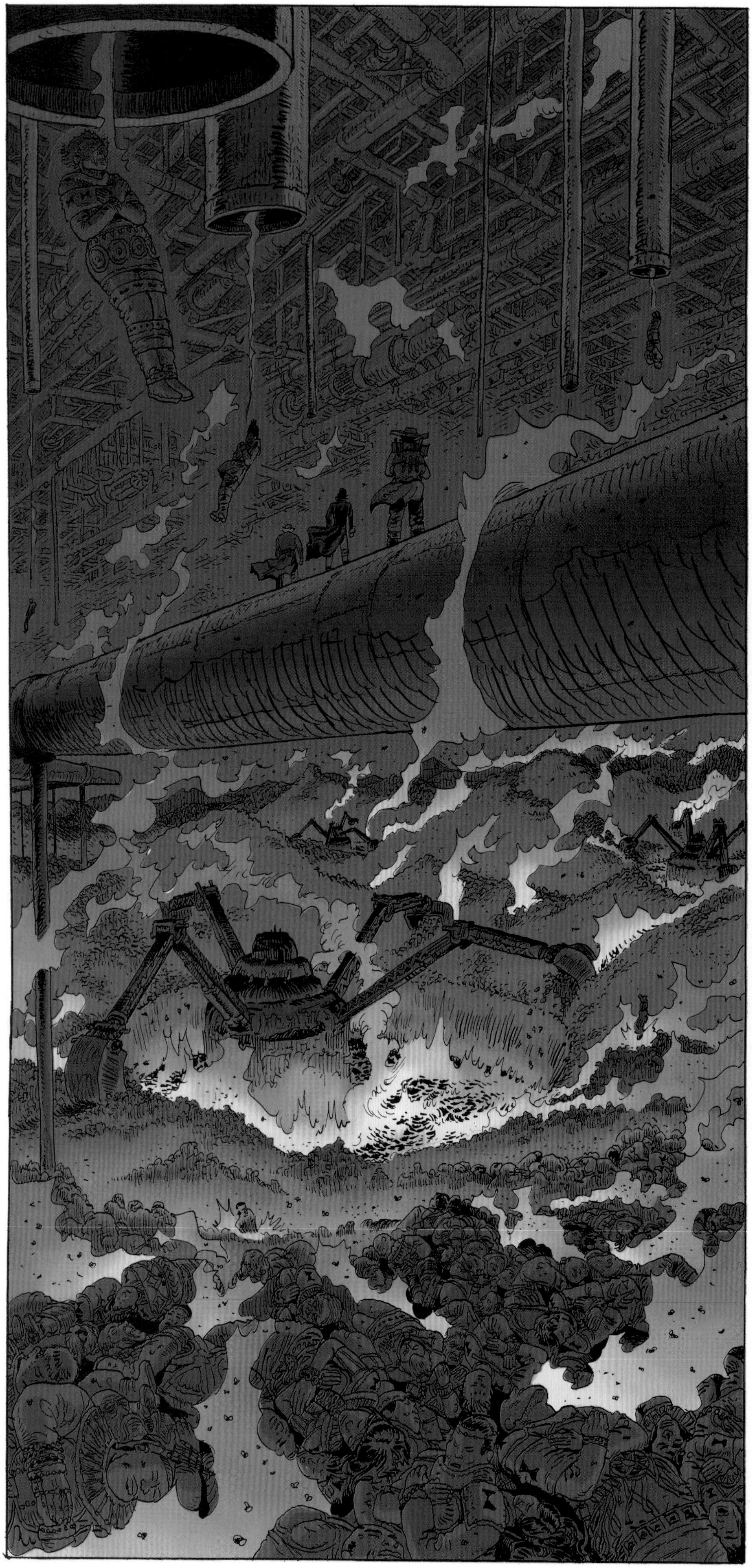

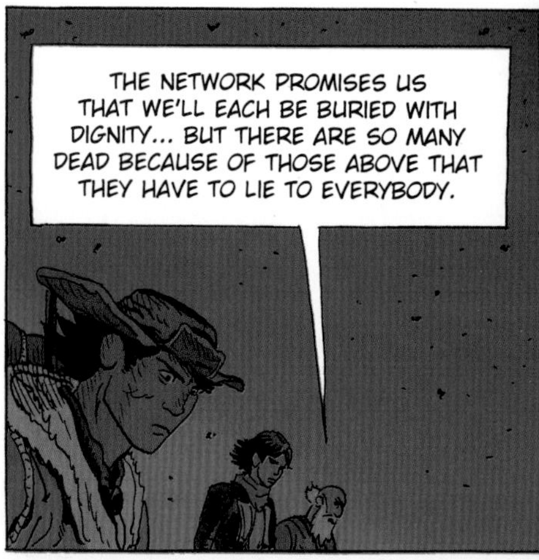
THE NETWORK PROMISES US THAT WE'LL EACH BE BURIED WITH DIGNITY... BUT THERE ARE SO MANY DEAD BECAUSE OF THOSE ABOVE THAT THEY HAVE TO LIE TO EVERYBODY.

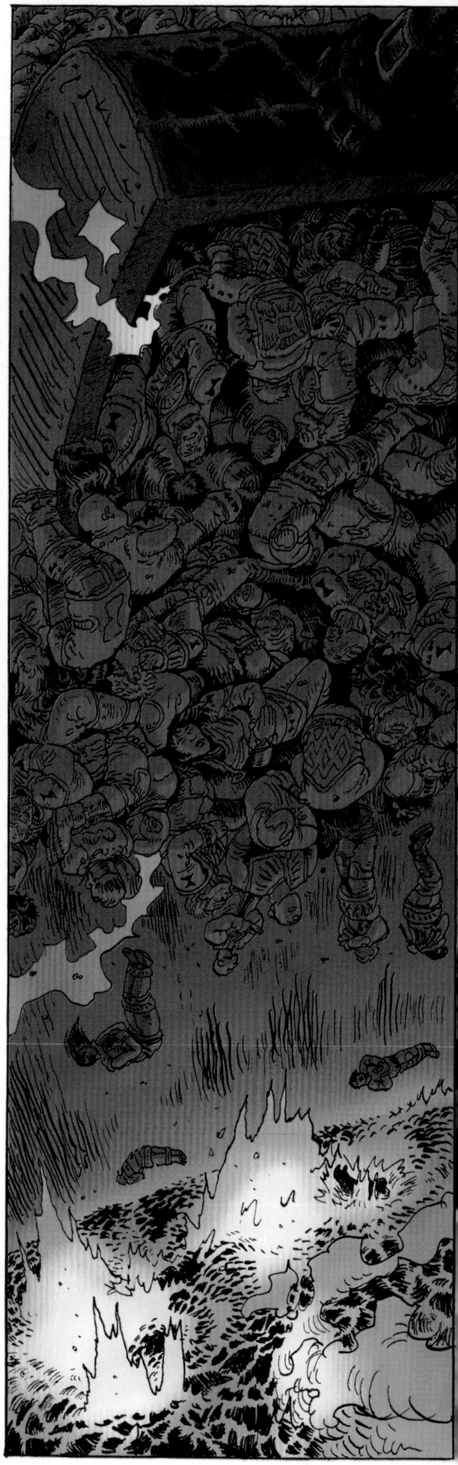

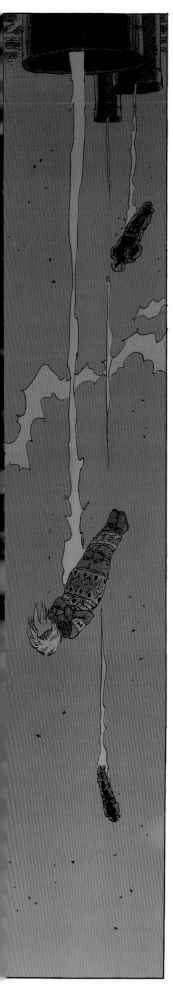

NO PRAYER COULD
POSSIBLY BRING
AN ANSWER TO ALL
THIS HORROR.

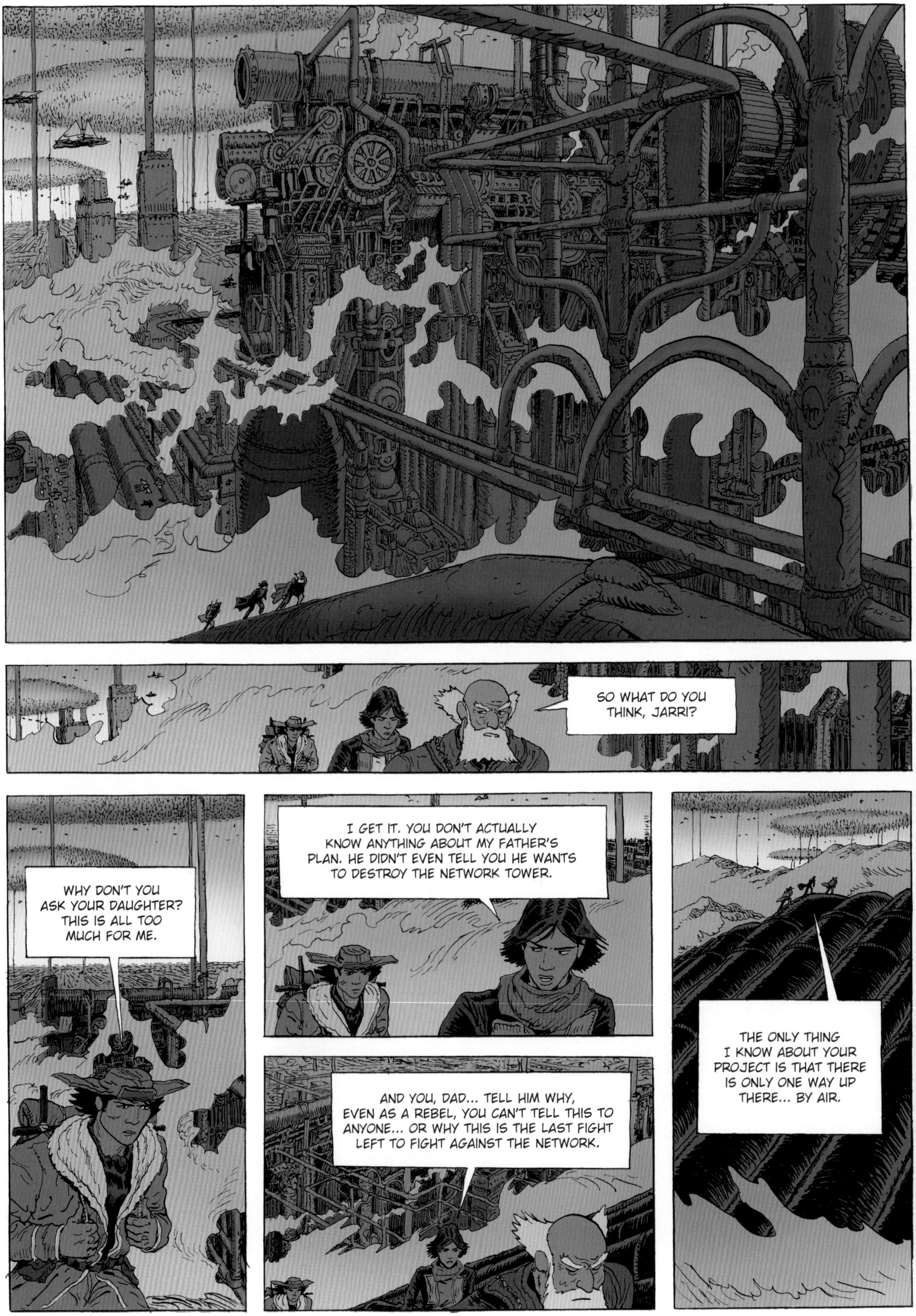
SO WHAT DO YOU THINK, JARRI?
WHY DON'T YOU ASK YOUR DAUGHTER? THIS IS ALL TOO MUCH FOR ME.
I GET IT. YOU DON'T ACTUALLY KNOW ANYTHING ABOUT MY FATHER'S PLAN. HE DIDN'T EVEN TELL YOU HE WANTS TO DESTROY THE NETWORK TOWER.
AND YOU, DAD... TELL HIM WHY, EVEN AS A REBEL, YOU CAN'T TELL THIS TO ANYONE... OR WHY THIS IS THE LAST FIGHT LEFT TO FIGHT AGAINST THE NETWORK.
THE ONLY THING I KNOW ABOUT YOUR PROJECT IS THAT THERE IS ONLY ONE WAY UP THERE... BY AIR.

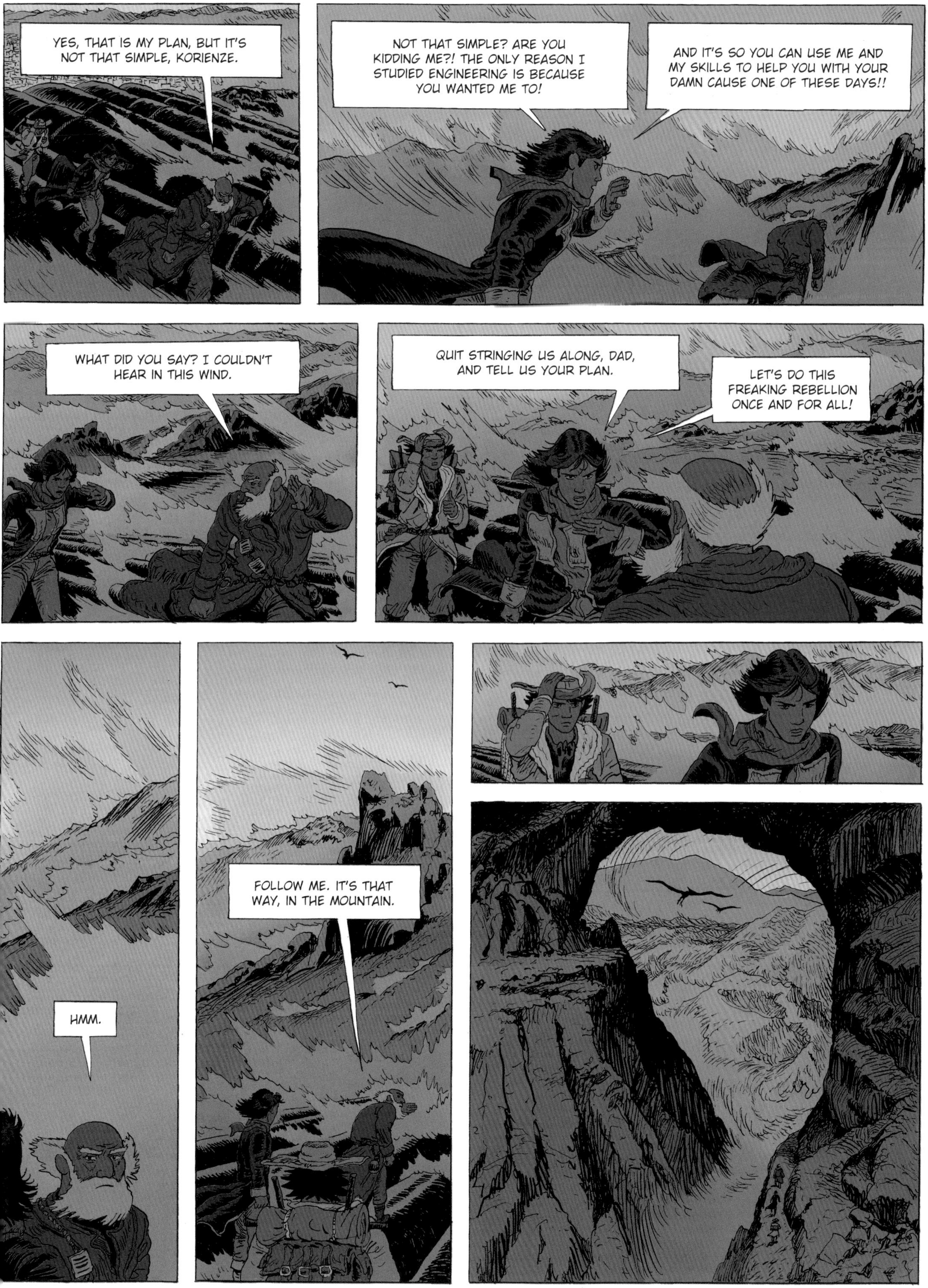
YES, THAT IS MY PLAN, BUT IT'S NOT THAT SIMPLE, KORIENZE.
NOT THAT SIMPLE? ARE YOU KIDDING ME?! THE ONLY REASON I STUDIED ENGINEERING IS BECAUSE YOU WANTED ME TO!
AND IT'S SO YOU CAN USE ME AND MY SKILLS TO HELP YOU WITH YOUR DAMN CAUSE ONE OF THESE DAYS!!
WHAT DID YOU SAY? I COULDN'T HEAR IN THIS WIND.
QUIT STRINGING US ALONG, DAD, AND TELL US YOUR PLAN.
LET'S DO THIS FREAKING REBELLION ONCE AND FOR ALL!
HMM.
FOLLOW ME. IT'S THAT WAY, IN THE MOUNTAIN.

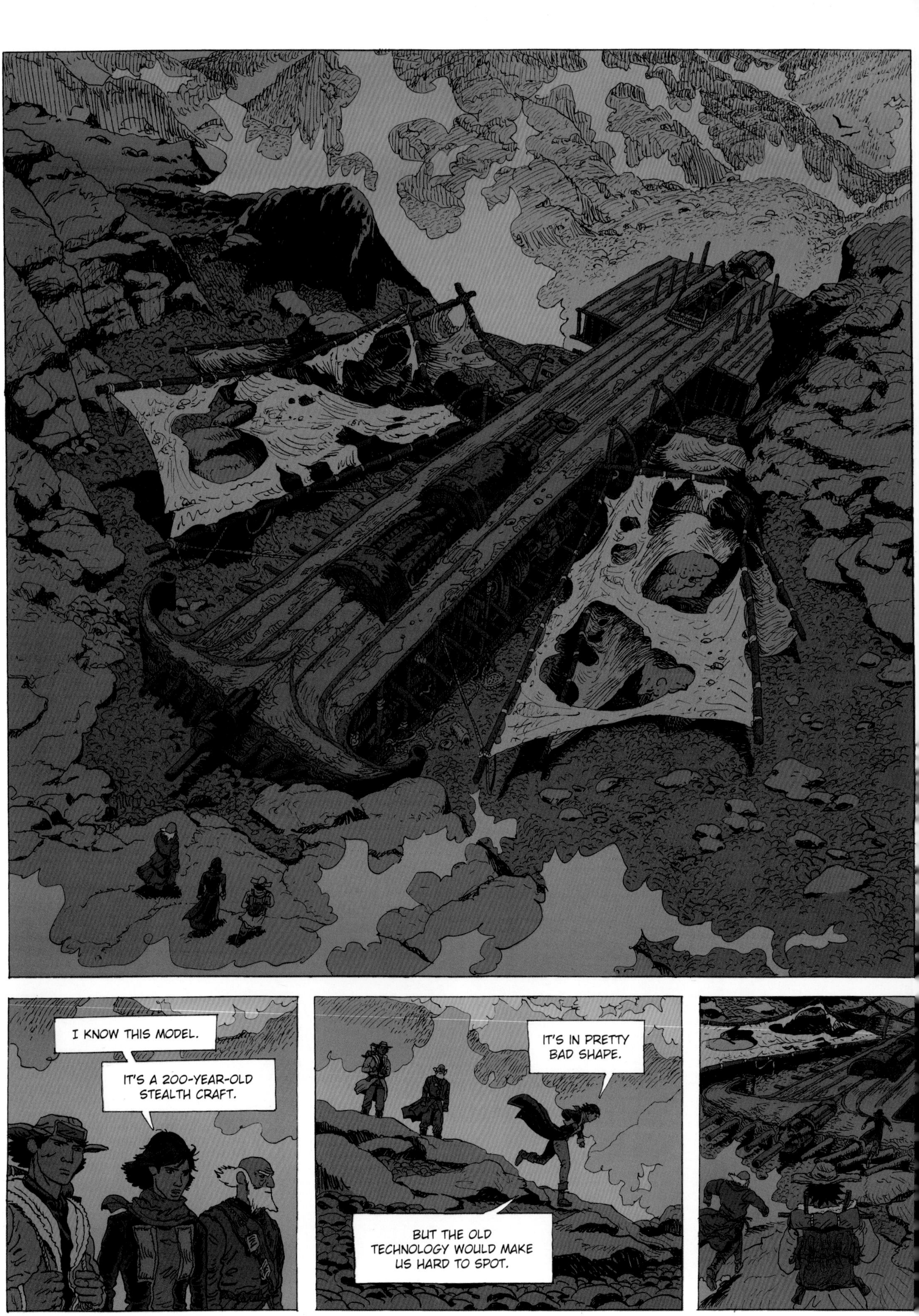
I KNOW THIS MODEL.
IT'S A 200-YEAR-OLD STEALTH CRAFT.
IT'S IN PRETTY BAD SHAPE.
BUT THE OLD TECHNOLOGY WOULD MAKE US HARD TO SPOT.

THE ARMATURE SEEMS FINE, BUT WE NEED TO CHANGE THE SAILS. DO YOU HAVE ANY TECHNICIANS?

GENERAL ALICE'S MEN ARE EXPERTS IN THE FIELD. WE CAN TRUST THEM.

WHO ELSE IS IN ON THIS, BESIDES US?

SO FAR, JUST THEM.

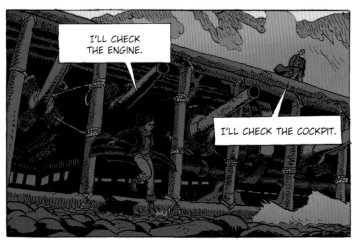

I'LL CHECK THE ENGINE.

I'LL CHECK THE COCKPIT.

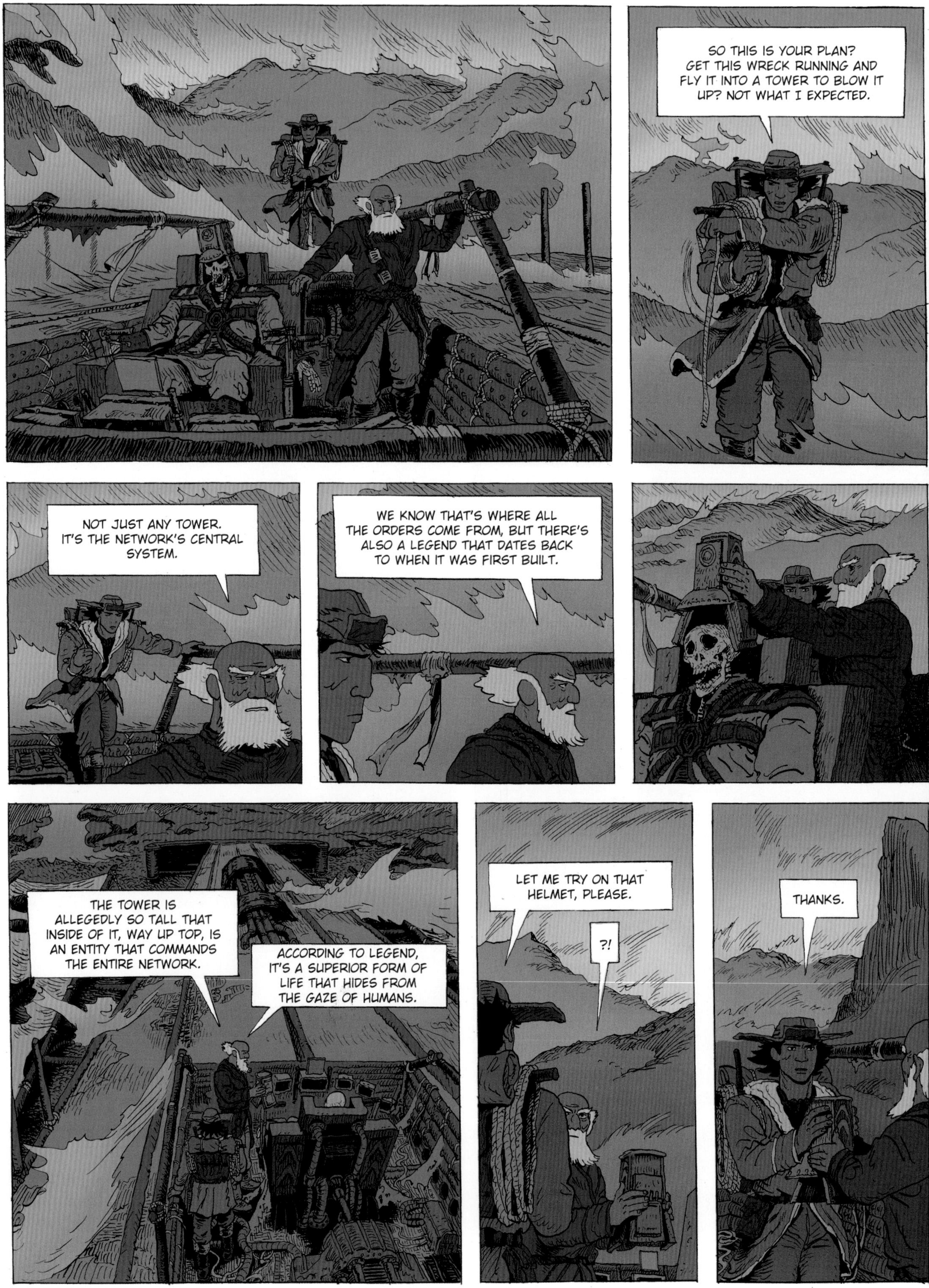
SO THIS IS YOUR PLAN? GET THIS WRECK RUNNING AND FLY IT INTO A TOWER TO BLOW IT UP? NOT WHAT I EXPECTED.
NOT JUST ANY TOWER. IT'S THE NETWORK'S CENTRAL SYSTEM.
WE KNOW THAT'S WHERE ALL THE ORDERS COME FROM, BUT THERE'S ALSO A LEGEND THAT DATES BACK TO WHEN IT WAS FIRST BUILT.
THE TOWER IS ALLEGEDLY SO TALL THAT INSIDE OF IT, WAY UP TOP, IS AN ENTITY THAT COMMANDS THE ENTIRE NETWORK.
ACCORDING TO LEGEND, IT'S A SUPERIOR FORM OF LIFE THAT HIDES FROM THE GAZE OF HUMANS.
LET ME TRY ON THAT HELMET, PLEASE.
?!
THANKS.

CAREFUL, IT'S CONNECTED. YOU HAVE NO IDEA WHAT HARM IT CAN DO.

DON'T WORRY. I KNOW WHAT I'M DOING.

...

SCRRR

VROM

?!

SCRRRR

SCRRRR

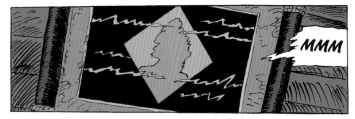

MMM

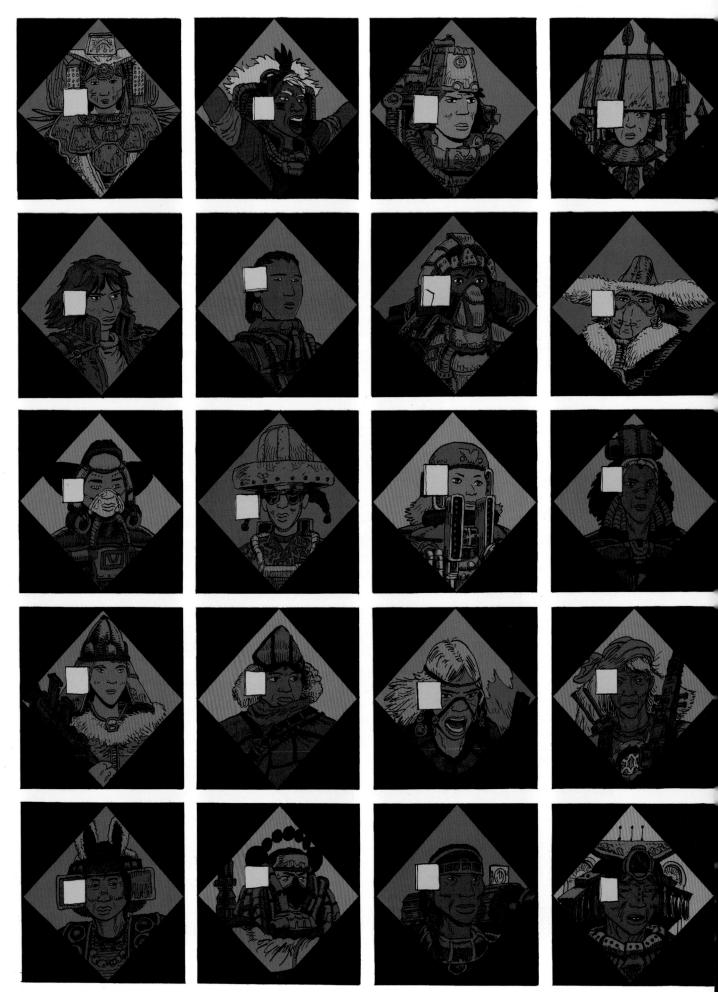

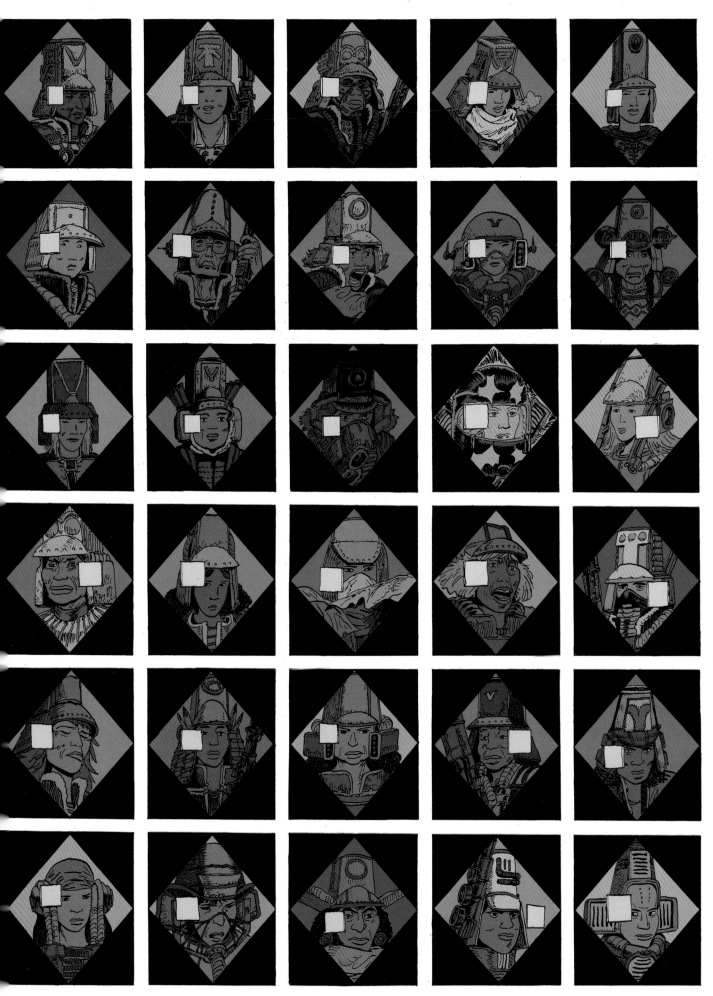

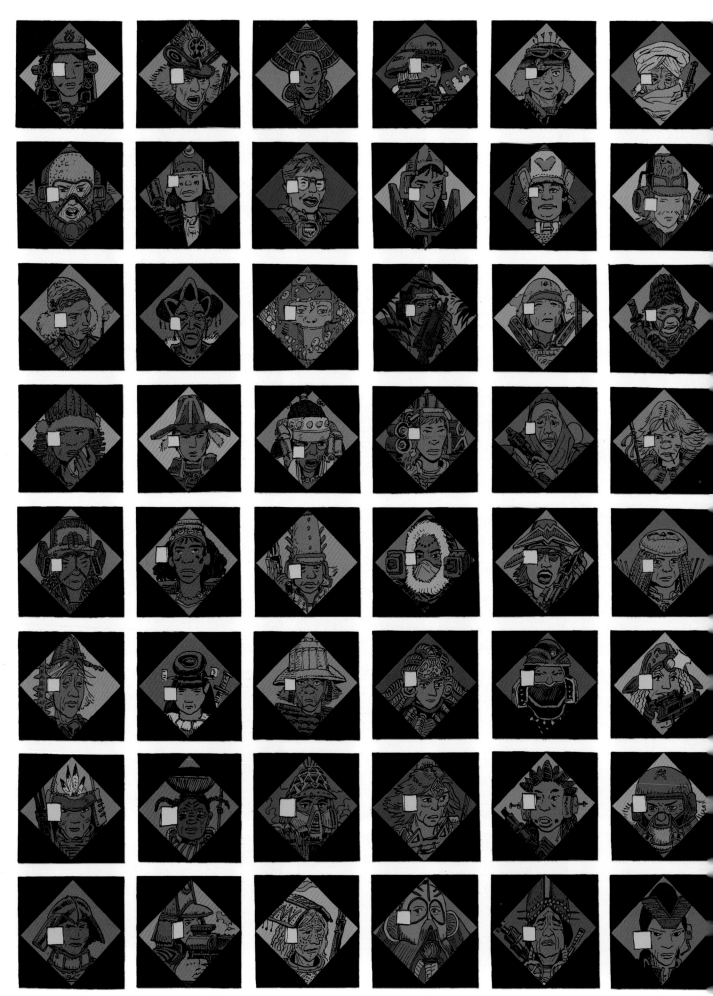

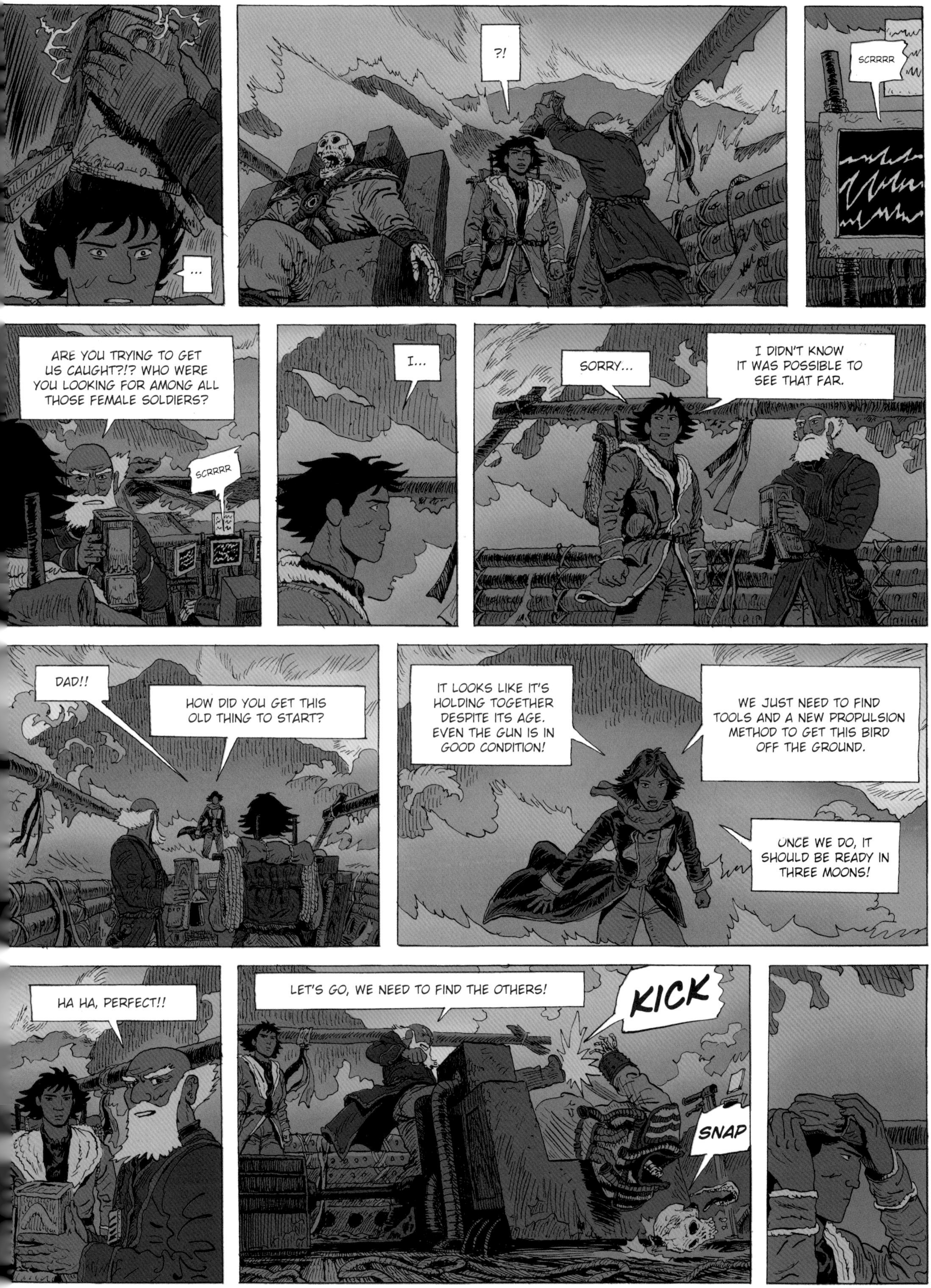
...
?!
SCRRRR
ARE YOU TRYING TO GET US CAUGHT?!? WHO WERE YOU LOOKING FOR AMONG ALL THOSE FEMALE SOLDIERS?
SCRRRR
I...
SORRY...
I DIDN'T KNOW IT WAS POSSIBLE TO SEE THAT FAR.
DAD!!
HOW DID YOU GET THIS OLD THING TO START?
IT LOOKS LIKE IT'S HOLDING TOGETHER DESPITE ITS AGE. EVEN THE GUN IS IN GOOD CONDITION!
WE JUST NEED TO FIND TOOLS AND A NEW PROPULSION METHOD TO GET THIS BIRD OFF THE GROUND.
ONCE WE DO, IT SHOULD BE READY IN THREE MOONS!
HA HA, PERFECT!!
LET'S GO, WE NEED TO FIND THE OTHERS!
KICK
SNAP

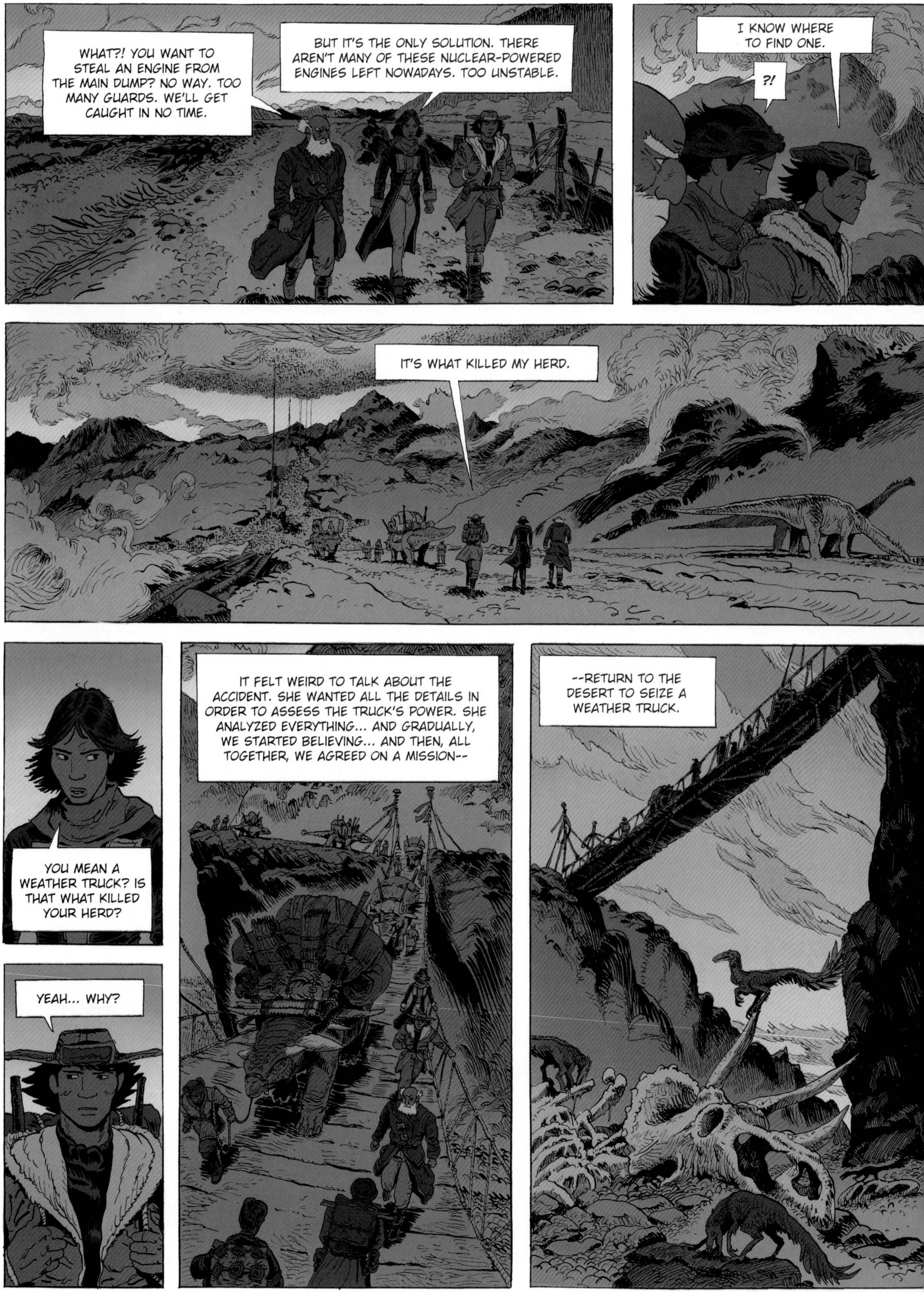

WHAT?! YOU WANT TO STEAL AN ENGINE FROM THE MAIN DUMP? NO WAY. TOO MANY GUARDS. WE'LL GET CAUGHT IN NO TIME.
BUT IT'S THE ONLY SOLUTION. THERE AREN'T MANY OF THESE NUCLEAR-POWERED ENGINES LEFT NOWADAYS. TOO UNSTABLE.
I KNOW WHERE TO FIND ONE.
?!
IT'S WHAT KILLED MY HERD.
YOU MEAN A WEATHER TRUCK? IS THAT WHAT KILLED YOUR HERD?
YEAH... WHY?
IT FELT WEIRD TO TALK ABOUT THE ACCIDENT. SHE WANTED ALL THE DETAILS IN ORDER TO ASSESS THE TRUCK'S POWER. SHE ANALYZED EVERYTHING... AND GRADUALLY, WE STARTED BELIEVING... AND THEN, ALL TOGETHER, WE AGREED ON A MISSION--
--RETURN TO THE DESERT TO SEIZE A WEATHER TRUCK.

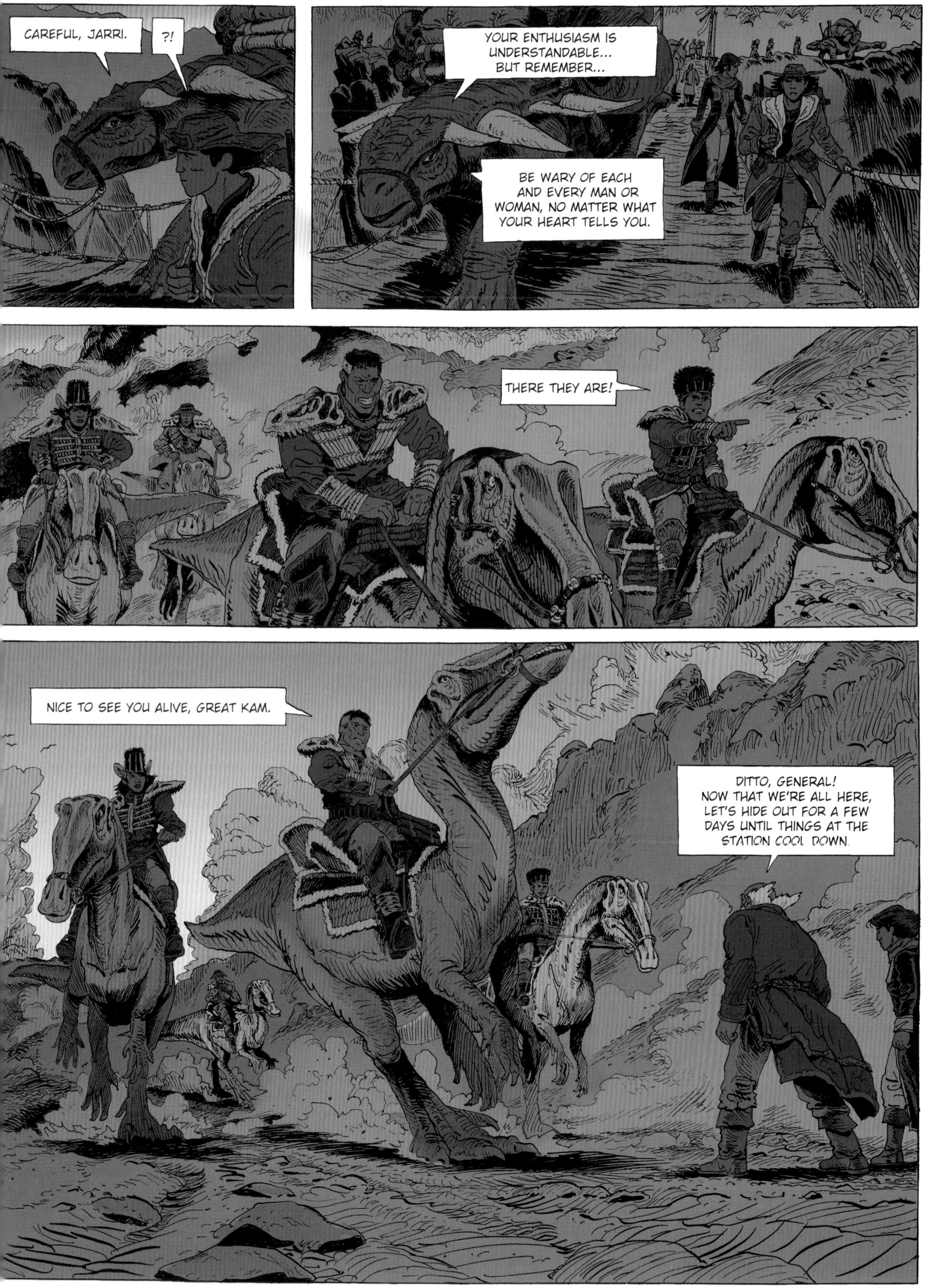
CAREFUL, JARRI.
?!
YOUR ENTHUSIASM IS UNDERSTANDABLE... BUT REMEMBER...
BE WARY OF EACH AND EVERY MAN OR WOMAN, NO MATTER WHAT YOUR HEART TELLS YOU.
THERE THEY ARE!
NICE TO SEE YOU ALIVE, GREAT KAM.
DITTO, GENERAL! NOW THAT WE'RE ALL HERE, LET'S HIDE OUT FOR A FEW DAYS UNTIL THINGS AT THE STATION COOL DOWN.

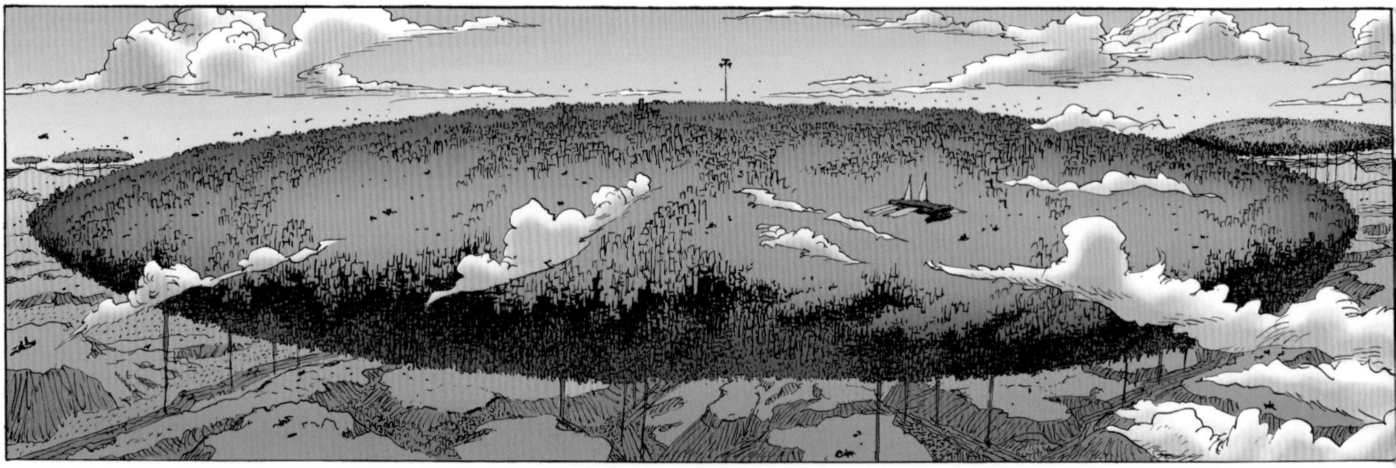
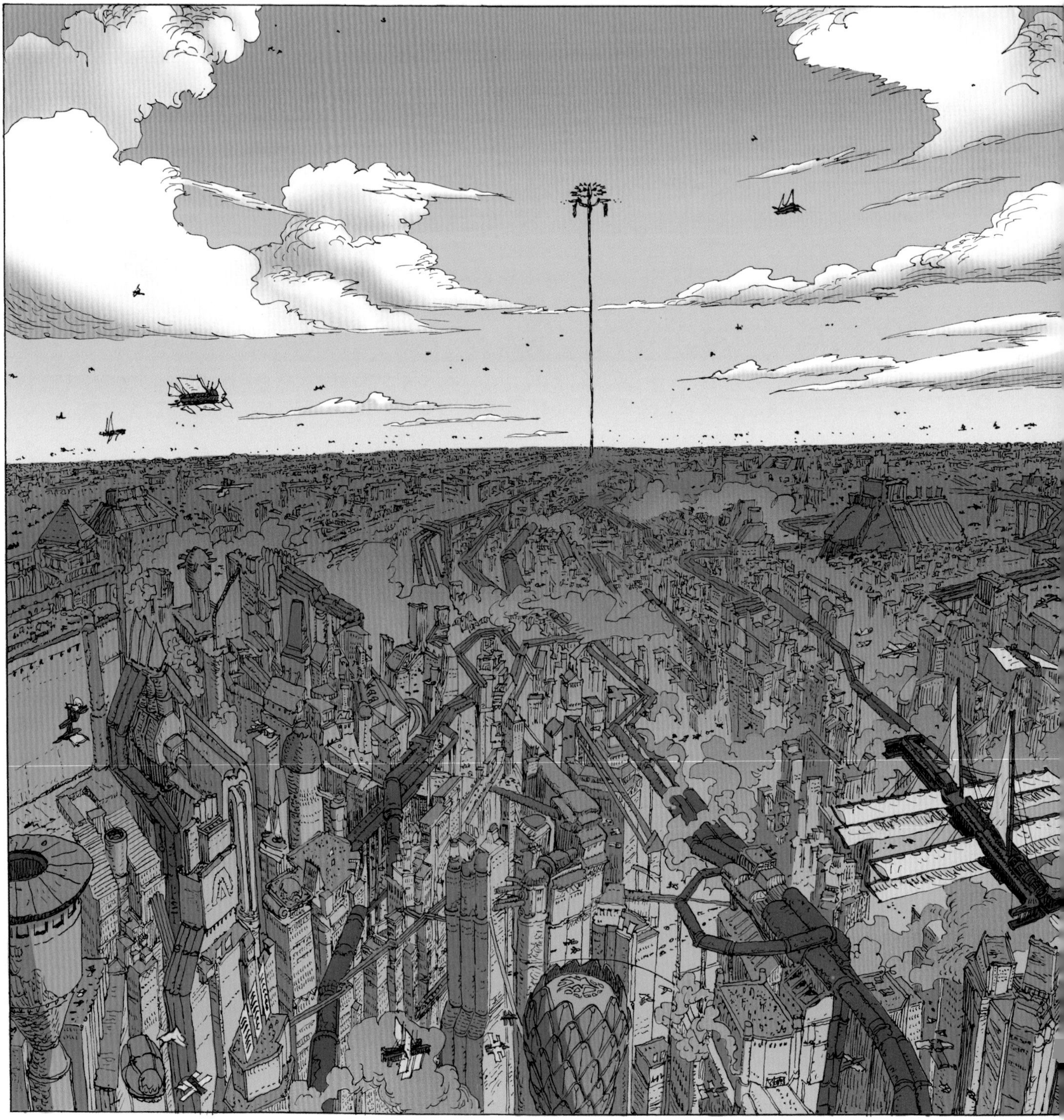

EIKO
39316
CLEAR.

NO. 7454252106
MISSION
ALL CLEAR.

GENERALIA STYA
NO.8959903279
MISSION. ALL
CLEAR.

GENERALIA DIOLA
NO.1742639841
MISSION
ALL CLEAR.

GENERAL KAMINO
NO. 5430671100
MISSION
ALL CLEAR.

GENERALIA OSUA
NO. 2035712318
MISSION
ALL CLEAR.

GENER
NO. 47
MISSIO

GENERAL
YURLUNG
NO. 5542180003
MISSION ERROR!

NO. 5542180003, YOU DID NOT
ELIMINATE THE POTENTIAL REBELS
OF STATION 3703. REPORT.

GREAT NETWORK, MY PLAN
IS TO DESTROY THEM USING
STRATEGY 798-B, INSTEAD.

95

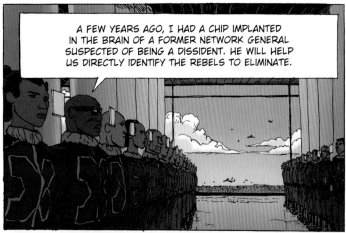

A FEW YEARS AGO, I HAD A CHIP IMPLANTED IN THE BRAIN OF A FORMER NETWORK GENERAL SUSPECTED OF BEING A DISSIDENT. HE WILL HELP US DIRECTLY IDENTIFY THE REBELS TO ELIMINATE.

YOUR STRATEGY'S SUCCESS RATE IS 31%.

THERE IS NOW ZERO TOLERANCE FOR ERROR.

IMMEDIATE EXECUTION.

DWVVV

?!!

SCHLCK

AAAAA

GENERALIA KAWONI, PLEASE LAY OUT A NEW STRATEGY FOR STATION 3703.

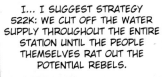

I... I SUGGEST STRATEGY 522K: WE CUT OFF THE WATER SUPPLY THROUGHOUT THE ENTIRE STATION UNTIL THE PEOPLE THEMSELVES RAT OUT THE POTENTIAL REBELS.

YOUR STRATEGY'S SUCCESS RATE IS 98%. OPERATION APPROVED.

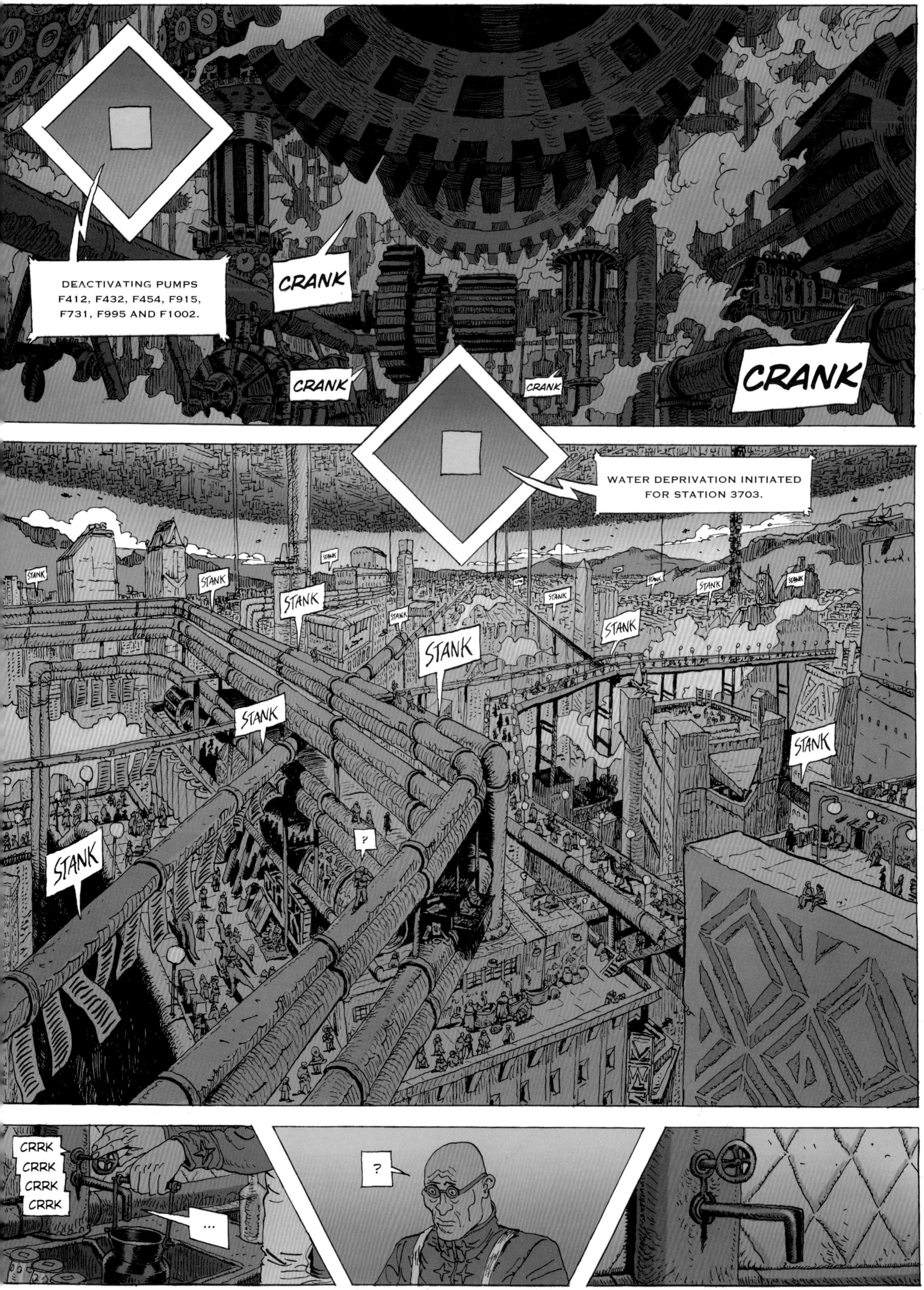
DEACTIVATING PUMPS F412, F432, F454, F915, F731, F995 AND F1002.
CRANK
CRANK
CRANK
CRANK
WATER DEPRIVATION INITIATED FOR STATION 3703.
STANK
STANK
STANK
STANK
STANK
STANK
STANK
STANK
STANK
STANK
?
CRRK
CRRK
CRRK
CRRK
...
?

FINALLY! I'M ANXIOUS TO GET BACK TO THE STATION, I DON'T LIKE GOING THIS LONG WITHOUT NEWS.

THIS IS IT!

WAIT!!

?!

I'M HEARING THE CRIES OF THOUSANDS OF ANIMALS COMING FROM THE STATION!

GOOD GODS! LOOK!!!

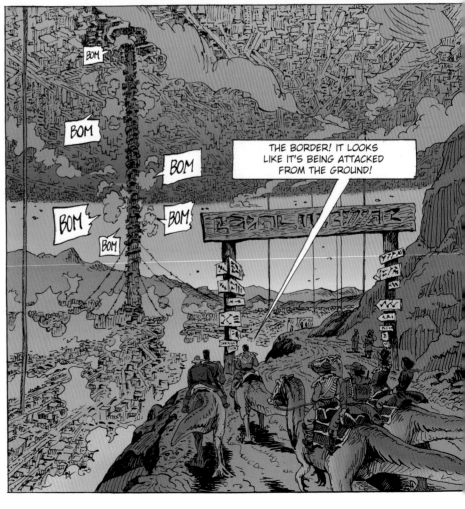

BOM

BOM

BOM

BOM

BOM

BOM

THE BORDER! IT LOOKS LIKE IT'S BEING ATTACKED FROM THE GROUND!

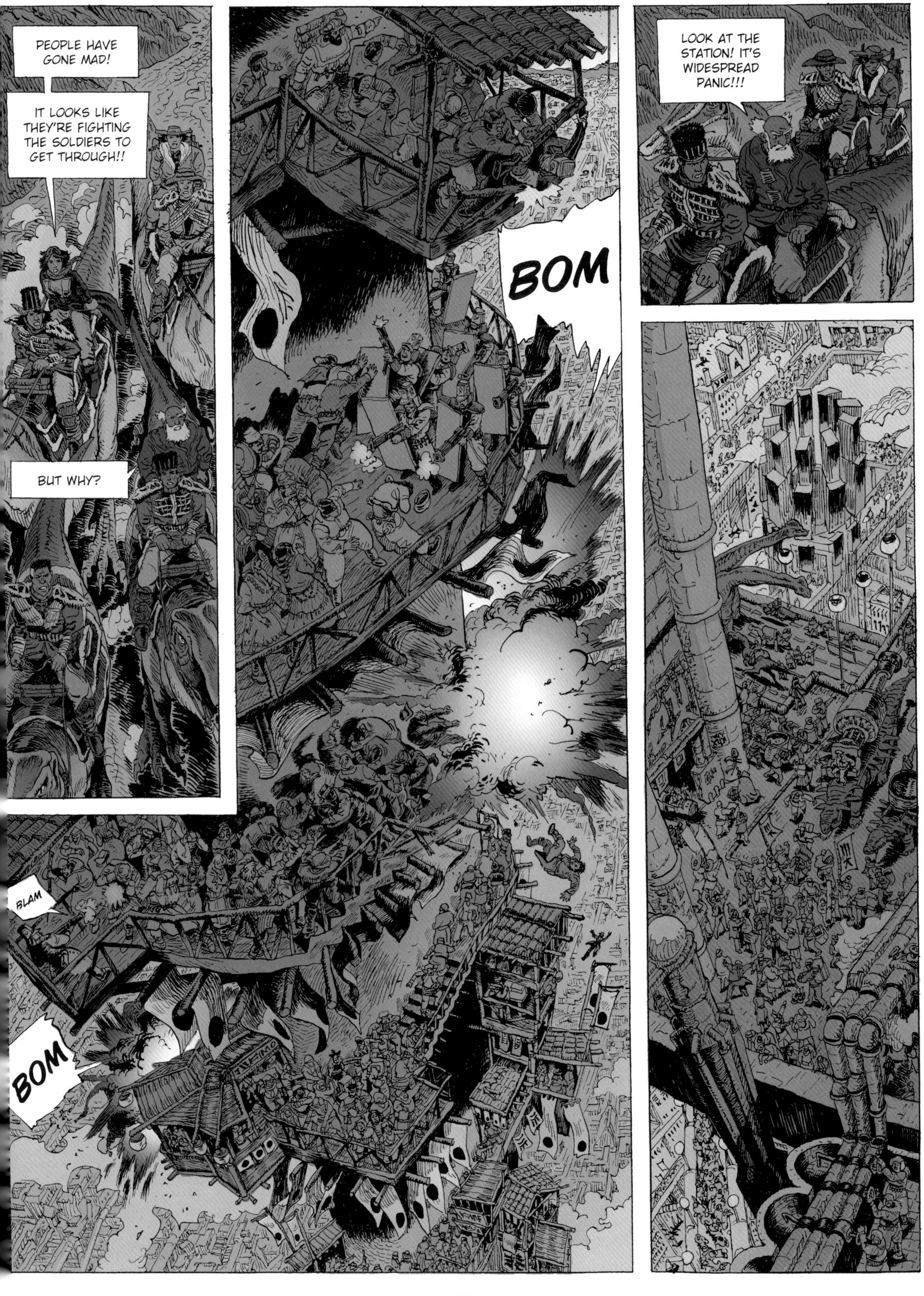
PEOPLE HAVE GONE MAD!
IT LOOKS LIKE THEY'RE FIGHTING THE SOLDIERS TO GET THROUGH!!
BUT WHY?
BOM
LOOK AT THE STATION! IT'S WIDESPREAD PANIC!!!
BLAM
BOM

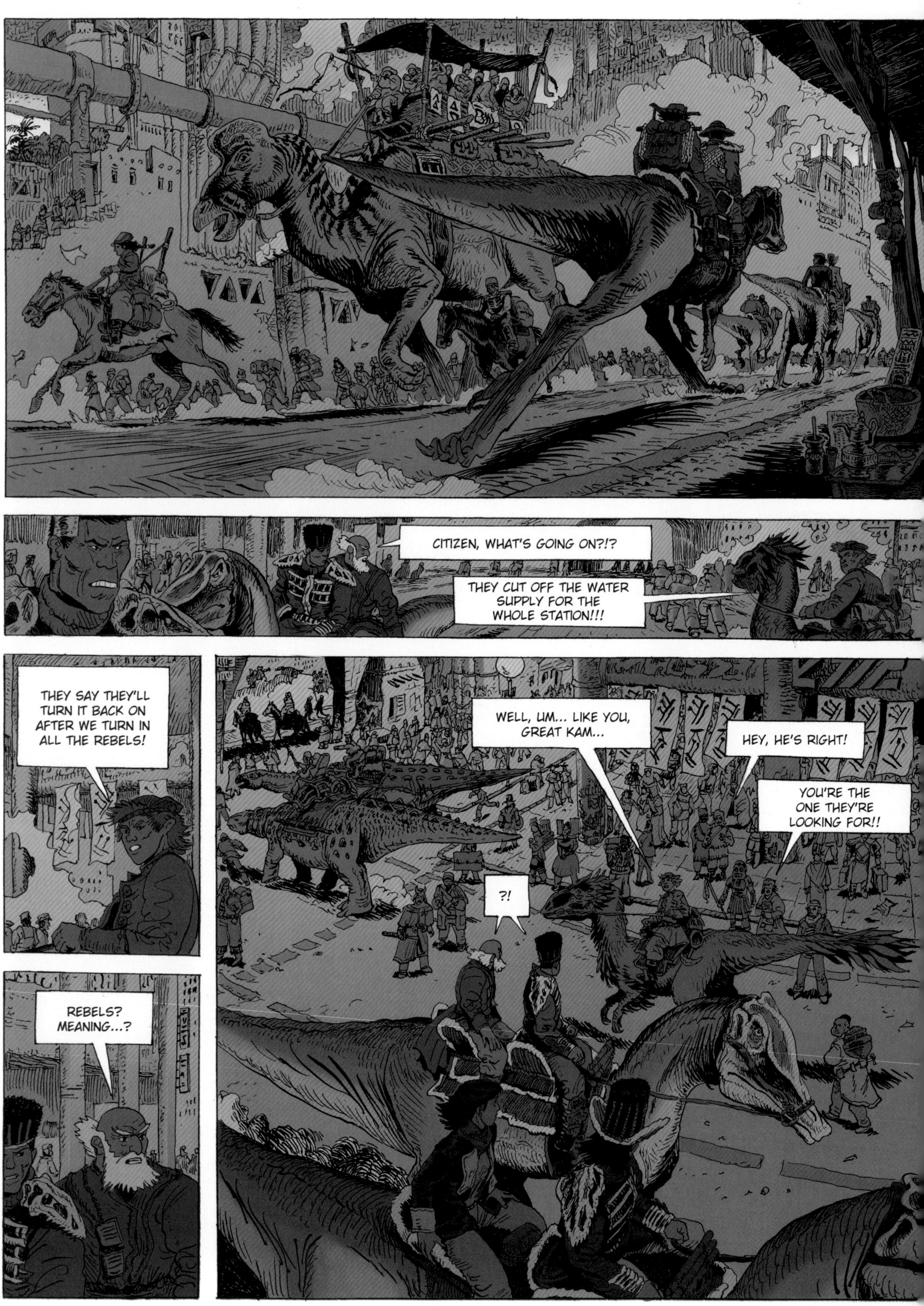
CITIZEN, WHAT'S GOING ON?!?
THEY CUT OFF THE WATER SUPPLY FOR THE WHOLE STATION!!!
THEY SAY THEY'LL TURN IT BACK ON AFTER WE TURN IN ALL THE REBELS!
REBELS? MEANING...?
WELL, UM... LIKE YOU, GREAT KAM...
HEY, HE'S RIGHT!
YOU'RE THE ONE THEY'RE LOOKING FOR!!
?!

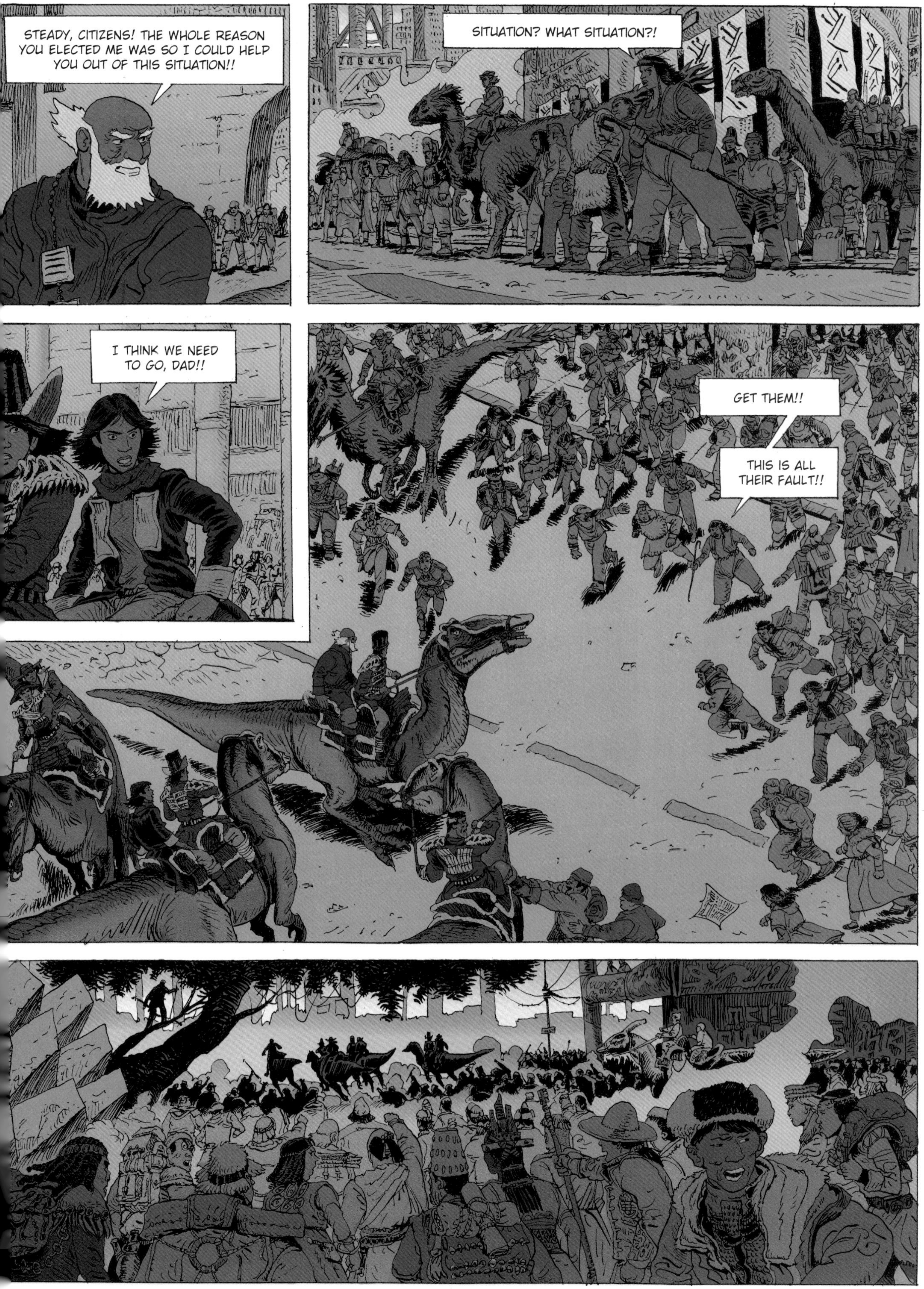

STEADY, CITIZENS! THE WHOLE REASON YOU ELECTED ME WAS SO I COULD HELP YOU OUT OF THIS SITUATION!!
SITUATION? WHAT SITUATION?!
I THINK WE NEED TO GO, DAD!!
GET THEM!!
THIS IS ALL THEIR FAULT!!

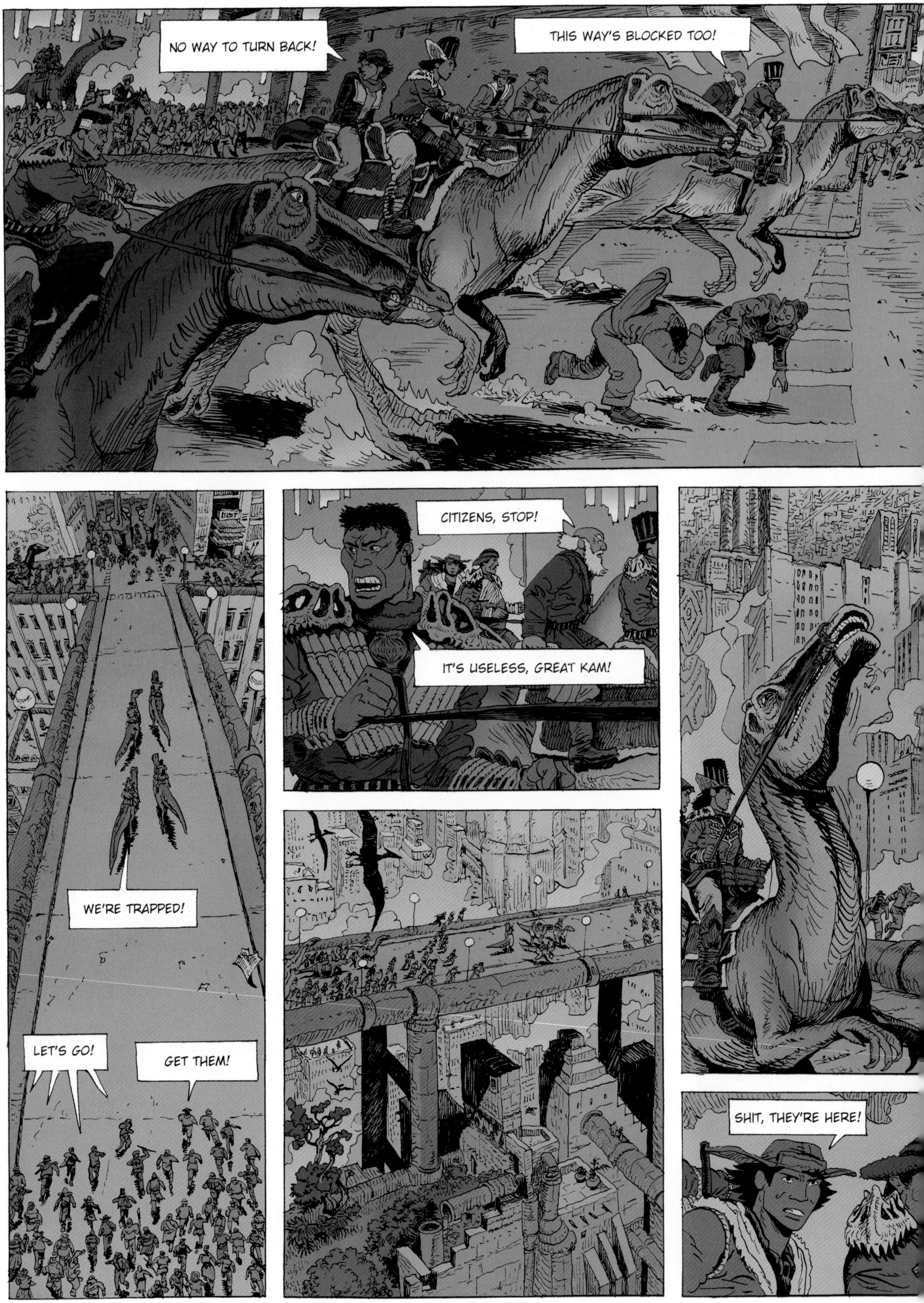
NO WAY TO TURN BACK!
THIS WAY'S BLOCKED TOO!
WE'RE TRAPPED!
LET'S GO!
GET THEM!
CITIZENS, STOP!
IT'S USELESS, GREAT KAM!
SHIT, THEY'RE HERE!

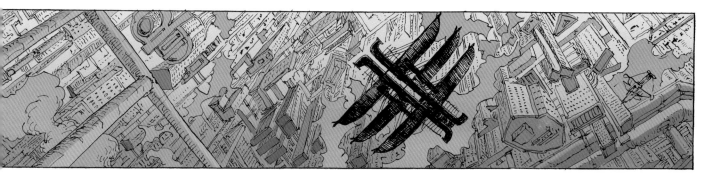

THESE KERBEROSAURUSES YOU'RE RIDING... THEY TOLD ME THEY KNOW THE CITY BETTER THAN YOU DO.

DROP YOUR REINS AND LET THEM GET US OUT OF HERE!

LISTEN, I HAVE AN IDEA!

LET'S RAM THROUGH THE CROWD INSTEAD, DAD!

WHAT DO WE DO, BOSS?

THEY'RE ALL OVER THE PLACE!

SURRENDER, GREAT KAM!!

LET GO OF YOUR REINS.

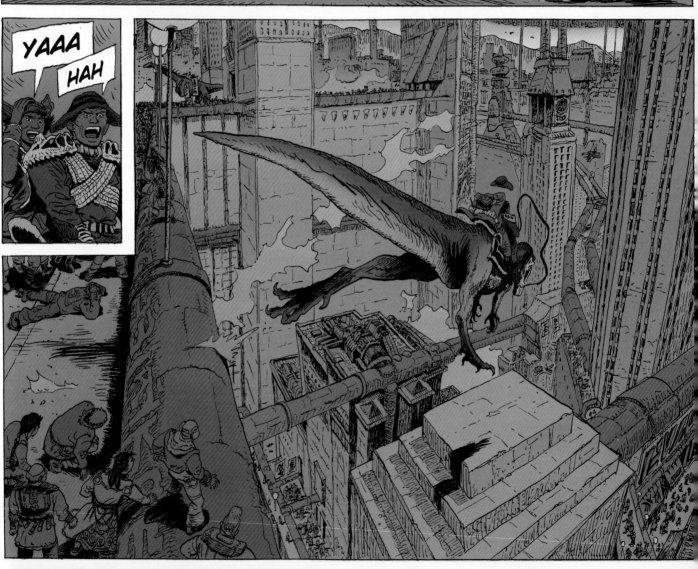

YAAA HAH

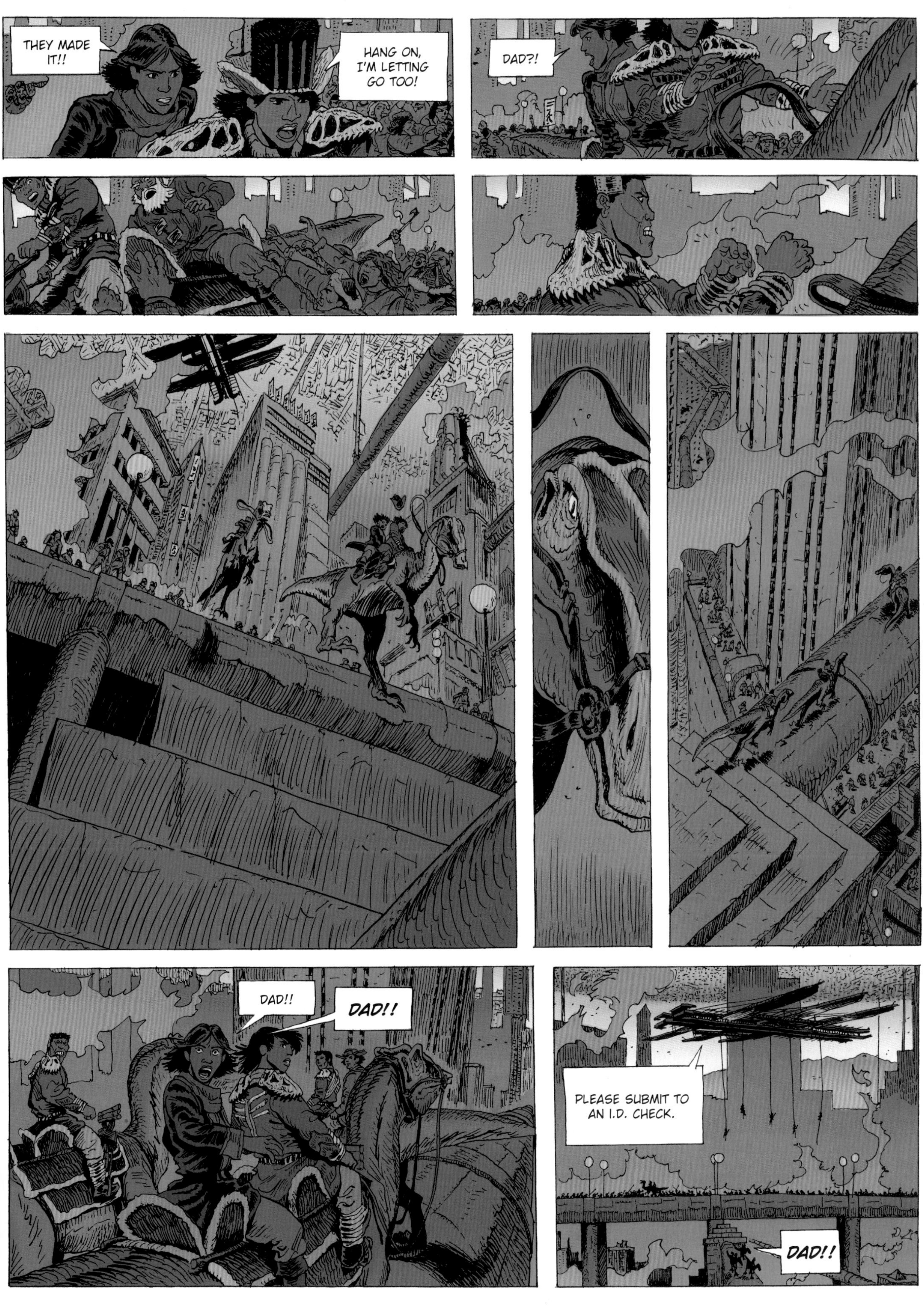
THEY MADE IT!!
HANG ON, I'M LETTING GO TOO!
DAD?!
DAD!!
DAD!!
PLEASE SUBMIT TO AN I.D. CHECK.
DAD!!

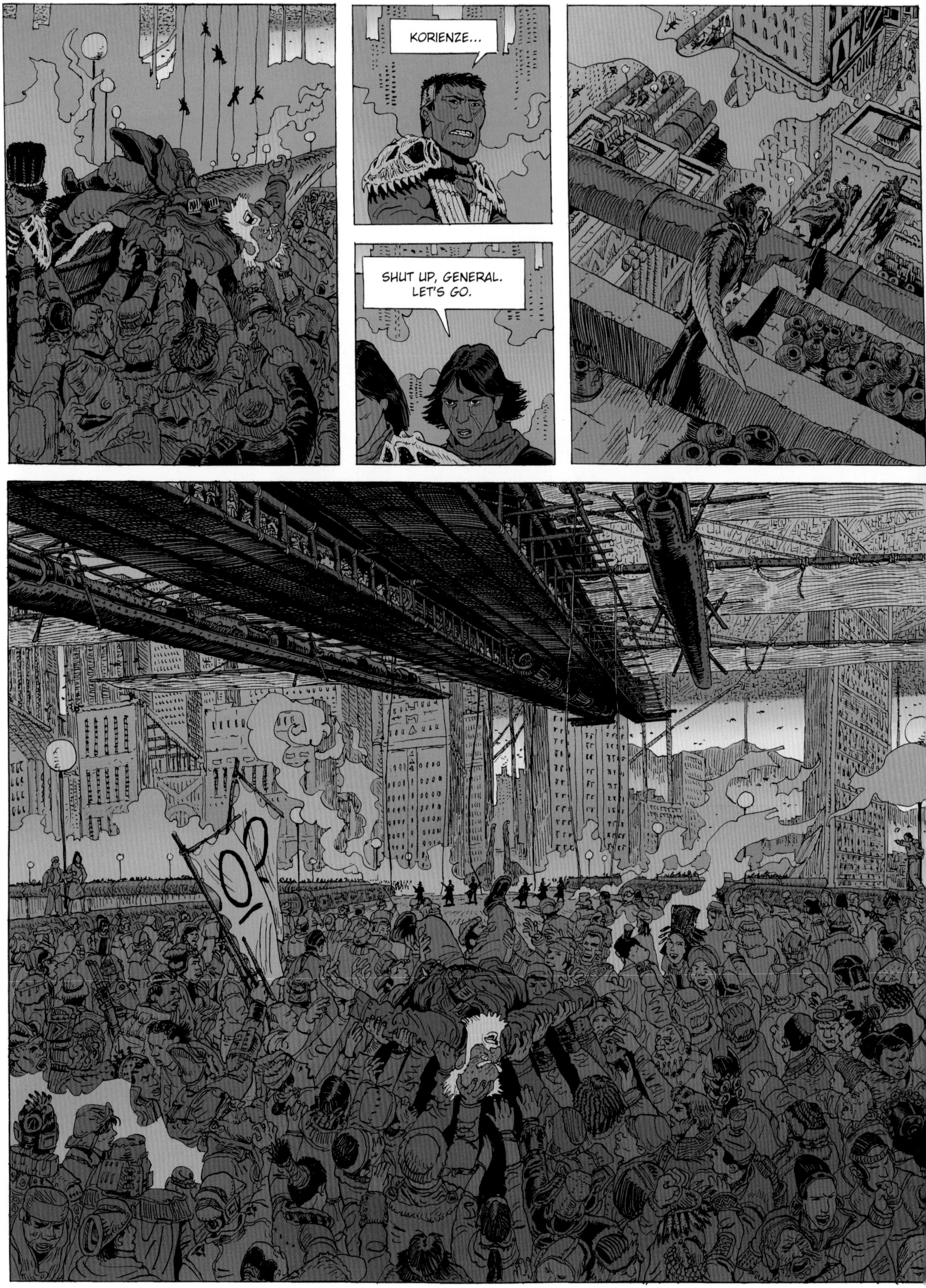
KORIENZE...
SHUT UP, GENERAL. LET'S GO.

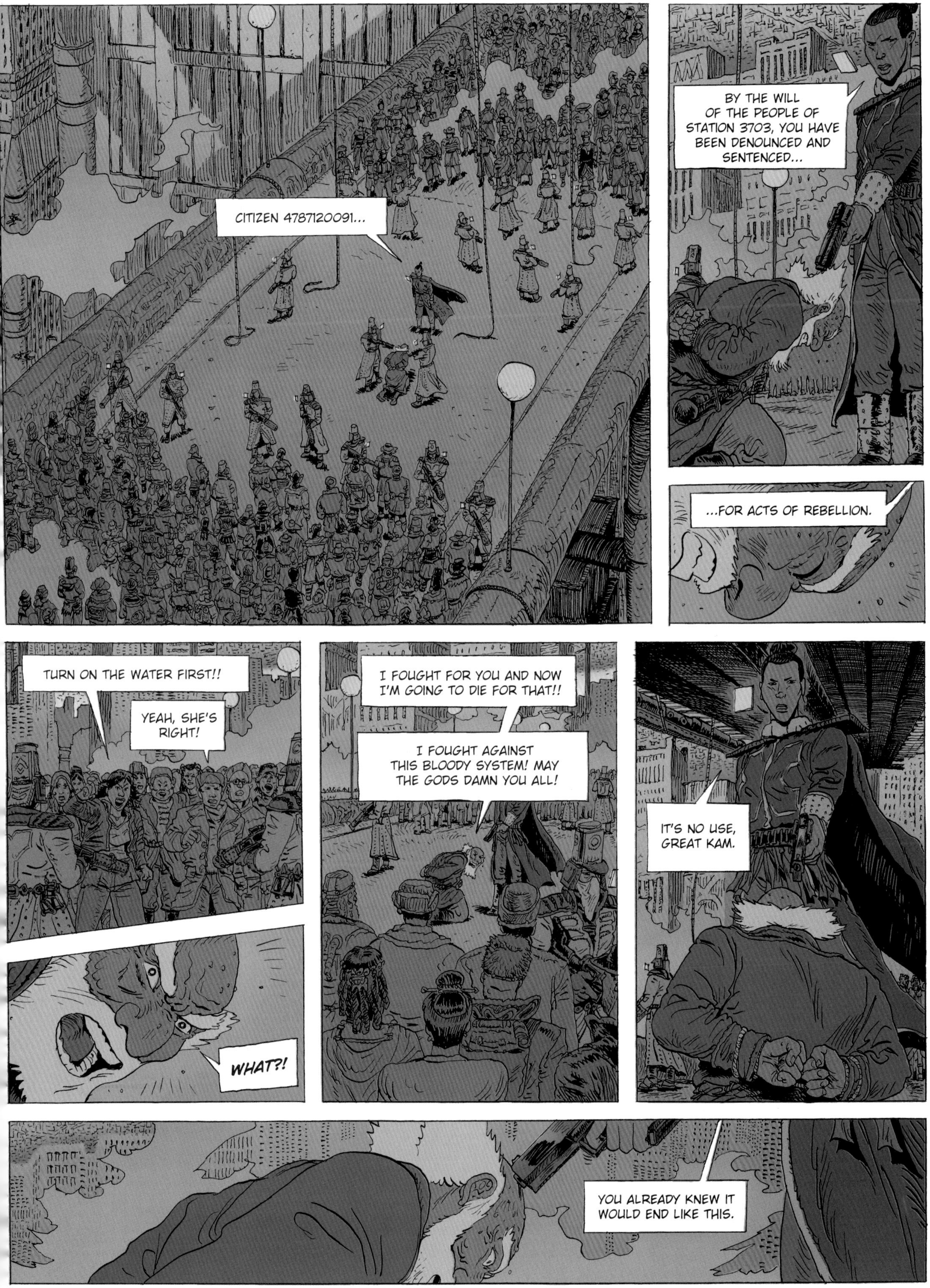
CITIZEN 4787120091...
BY THE WILL OF THE PEOPLE OF STATION 3703, YOU HAVE BEEN DENOUNCED AND SENTENCED...
...FOR ACTS OF REBELLION.
TURN ON THE WATER FIRST!!
YEAH, SHE'S RIGHT!
WHAT?!
I FOUGHT FOR YOU AND NOW I'M GOING TO DIE FOR THAT!!
I FOUGHT AGAINST THIS BLOODY SYSTEM! MAY THE GODS DAMN YOU ALL!
IT'S NO USE, GREAT KAM.
YOU ALREADY KNEW IT WOULD END LIKE THIS.

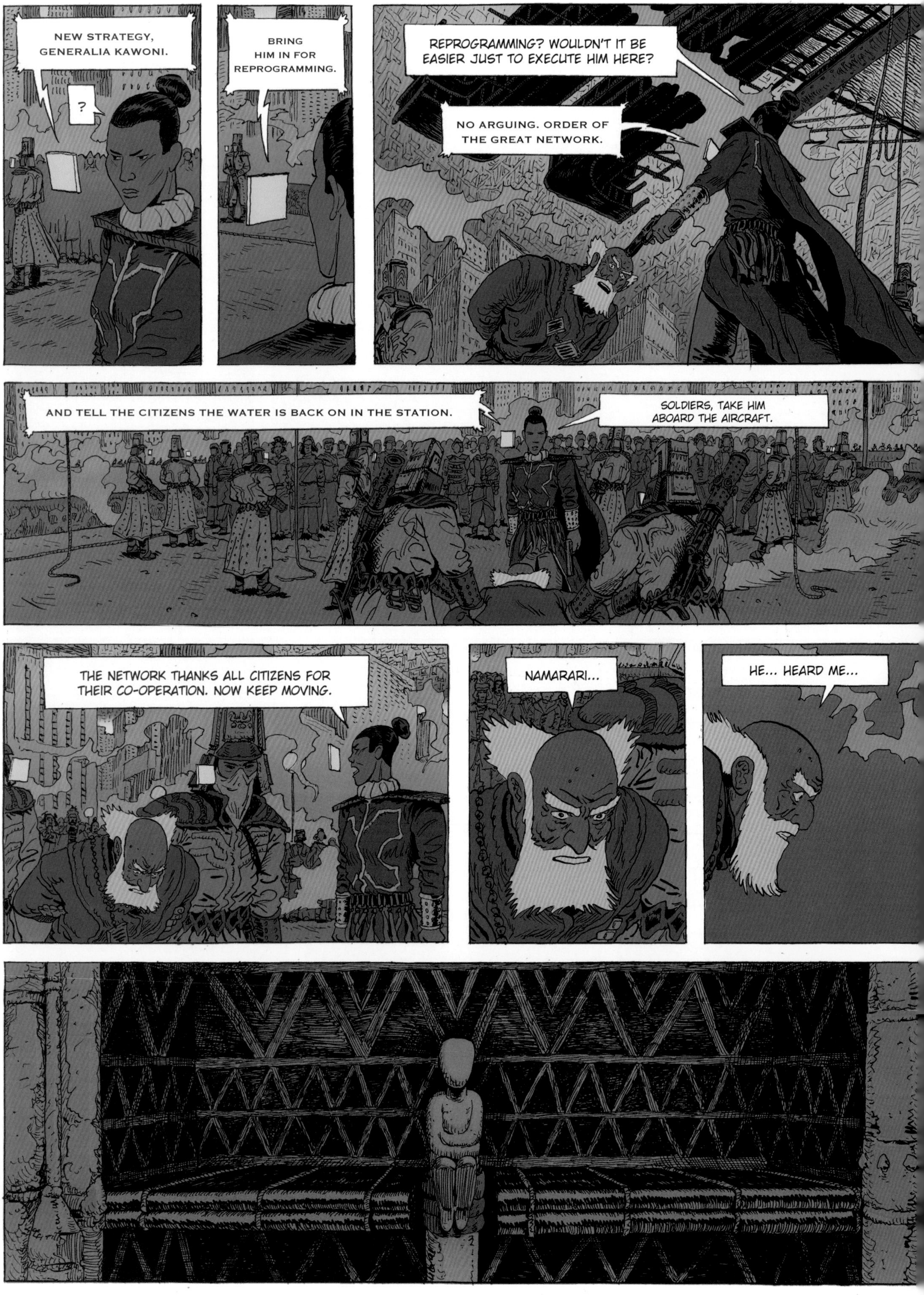
NEW STRATEGY, GENERALIA KAWONI.
?
BRING HIM IN FOR REPROGRAMMING.
REPROGRAMMING? WOULDN'T IT BE EASIER JUST TO EXECUTE HIM HERE?
NO ARGUING. ORDER OF THE GREAT NETWORK.
AND TELL THE CITIZENS THE WATER IS BACK ON IN THE STATION.
SOLDIERS, TAKE HIM ABOARD THE AIRCRAFT.
THE NETWORK THANKS ALL CITIZENS FOR THEIR CO-OPERATION. NOW KEEP MOVING.
NAMARARI...
HE... HEARD ME...

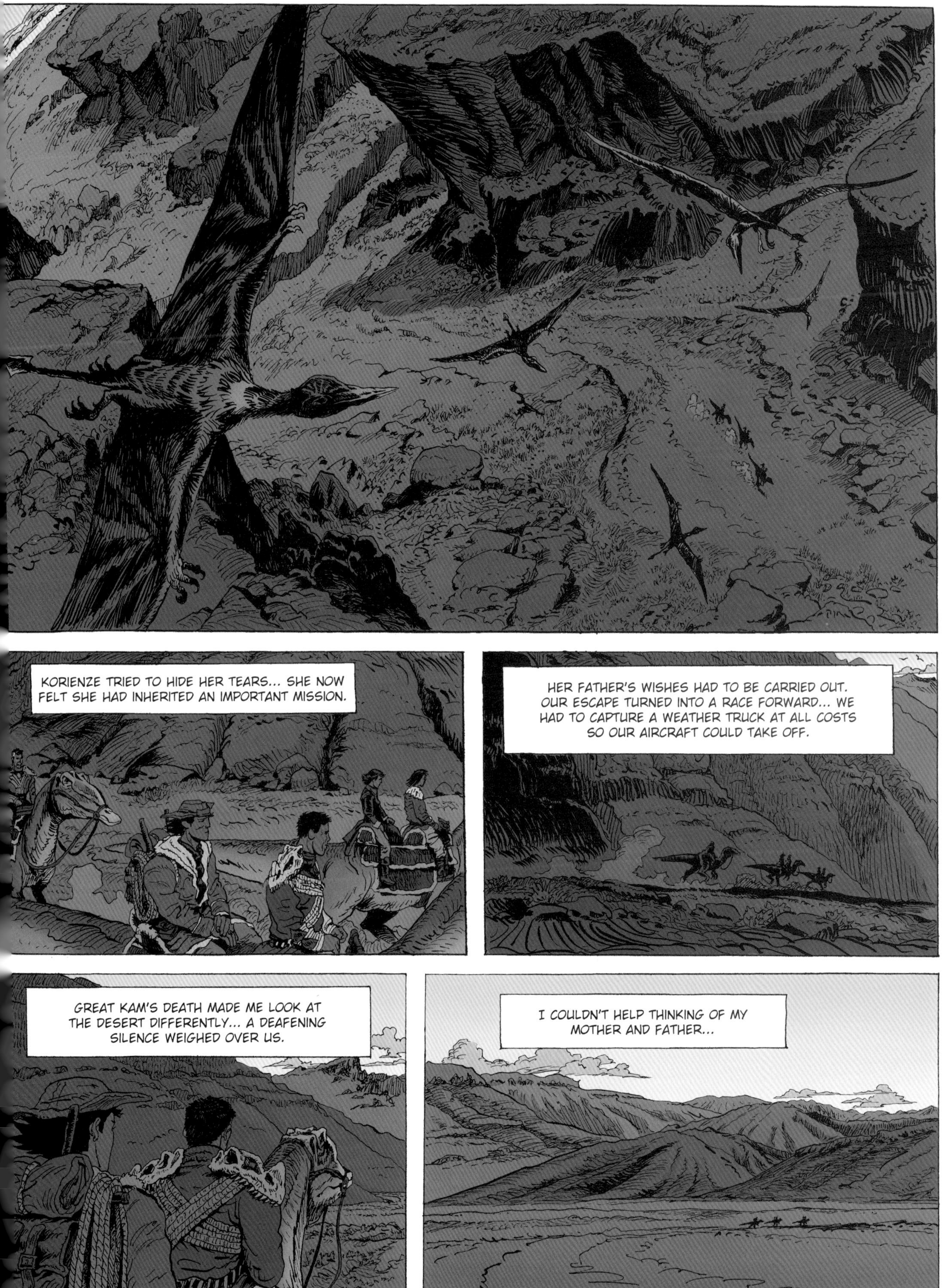

KORIENZE TRIED TO HIDE HER TEARS... SHE NOW FELT SHE HAD INHERITED AN IMPORTANT MISSION.
HER FATHER'S WISHES HAD TO BE CARRIED OUT. OUR ESCAPE TURNED INTO A RACE FORWARD... WE HAD TO CAPTURE A WEATHER TRUCK AT ALL COSTS SO OUR AIRCRAFT COULD TAKE OFF.
GREAT KAM'S DEATH MADE ME LOOK AT THE DESERT DIFFERENTLY... A DEAFENING SILENCE WEIGHED OVER US.
I COULDN'T HELP THINKING OF MY MOTHER AND FATHER...

LET ME GO! WHERE ARE YOU TAKING ME?!
TO CONVERT YOU TO YOUR NEW GOD.
??
THE NETWORK TOWER?!
YOU WILL HAVE THE PRIVILEGE OF BEING SUBJECTED TO HIGHLY SOPHISTICATED TORTURE.

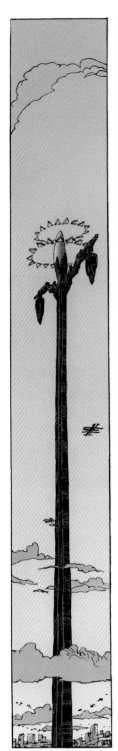

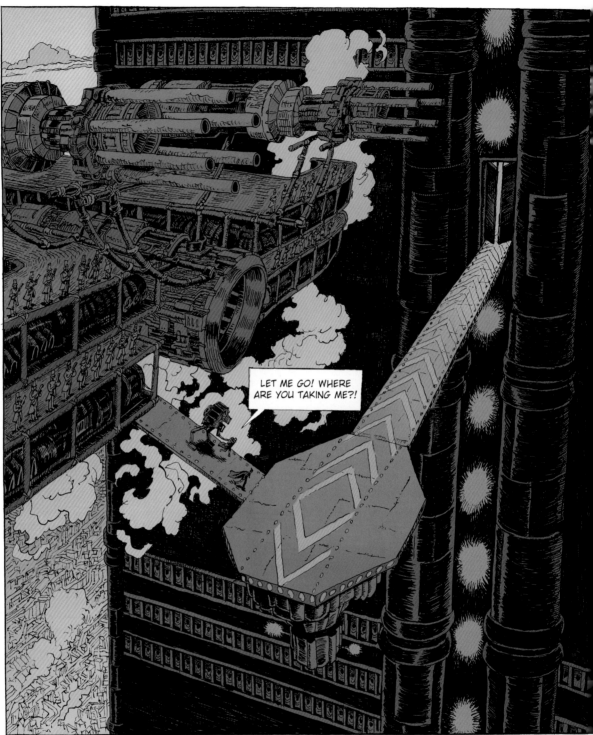

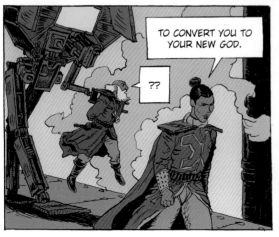

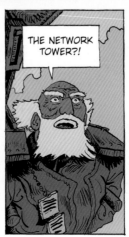

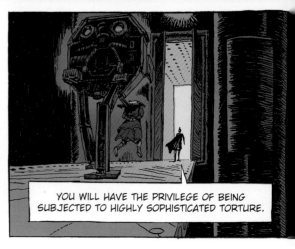

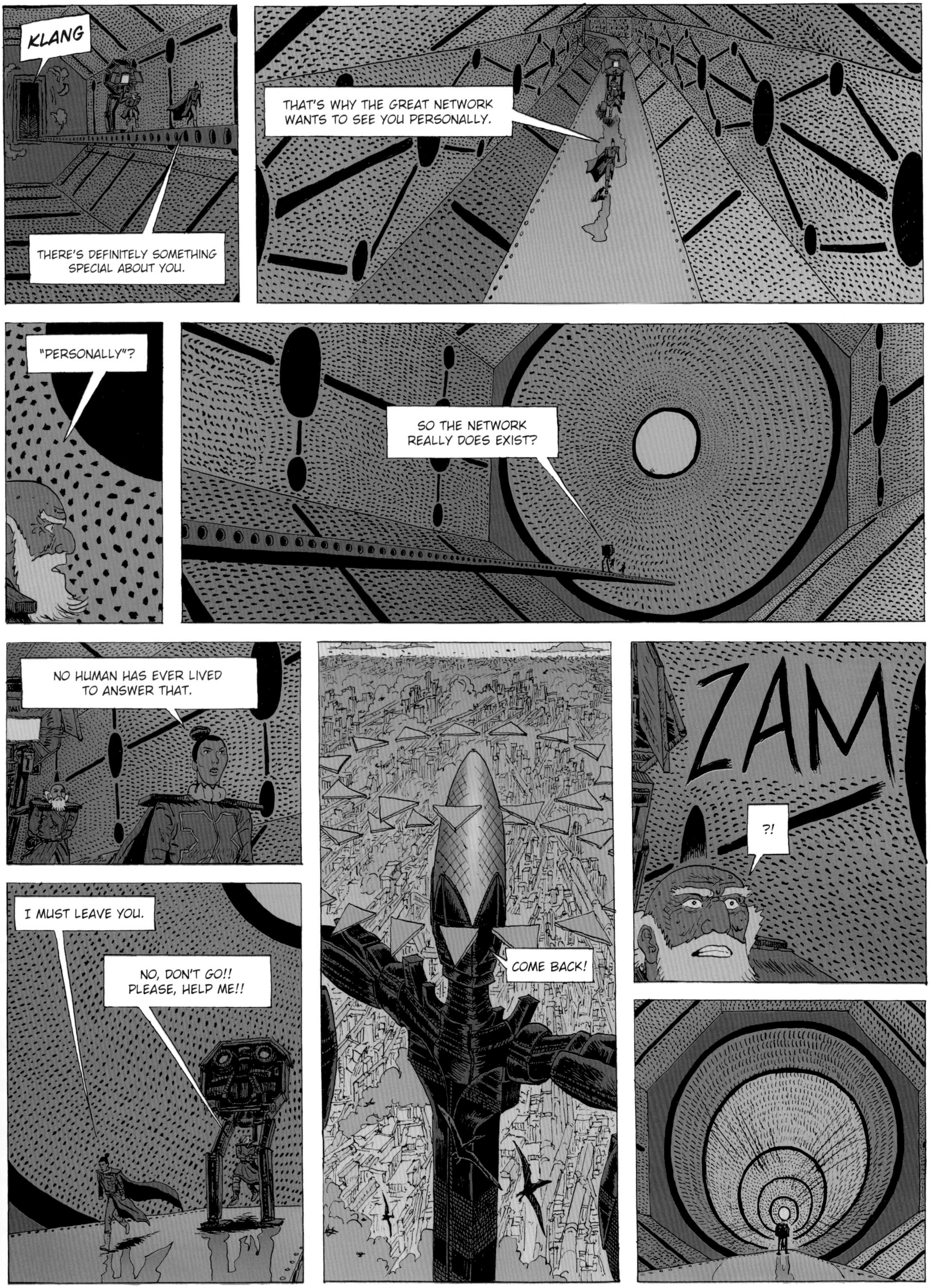
KLANG
THERE'S DEFINITELY SOMETHING SPECIAL ABOUT YOU.
THAT'S WHY THE GREAT NETWORK WANTS TO SEE YOU PERSONALLY.
"PERSONALLY"?
SO THE NETWORK REALLY DOES EXIST?
NO HUMAN HAS EVER LIVED TO ANSWER THAT.
I MUST LEAVE YOU.
NO, DON'T GO!! PLEASE, HELP ME!!
COME BACK!
ZAM
?!

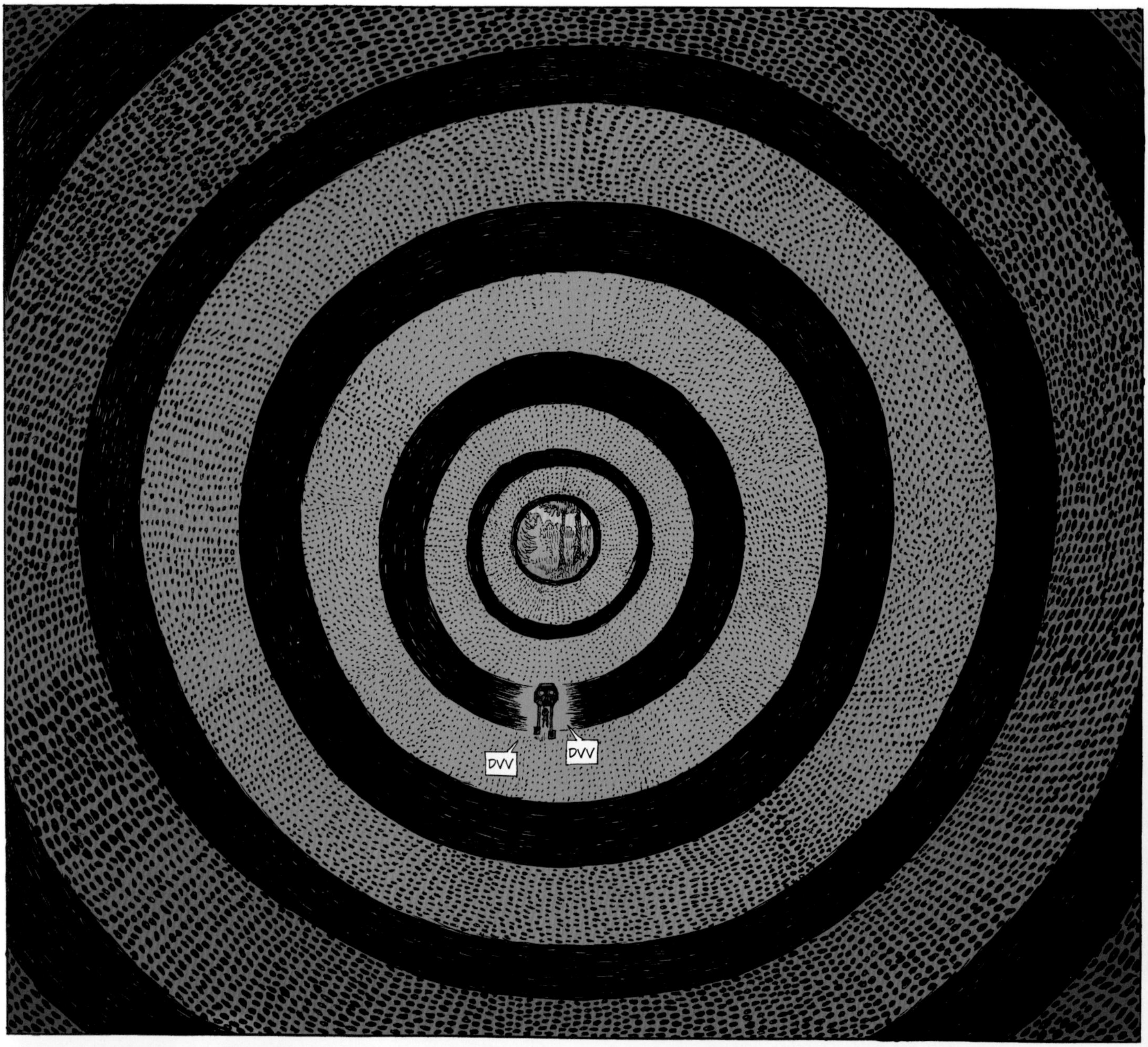
DVV
DVV

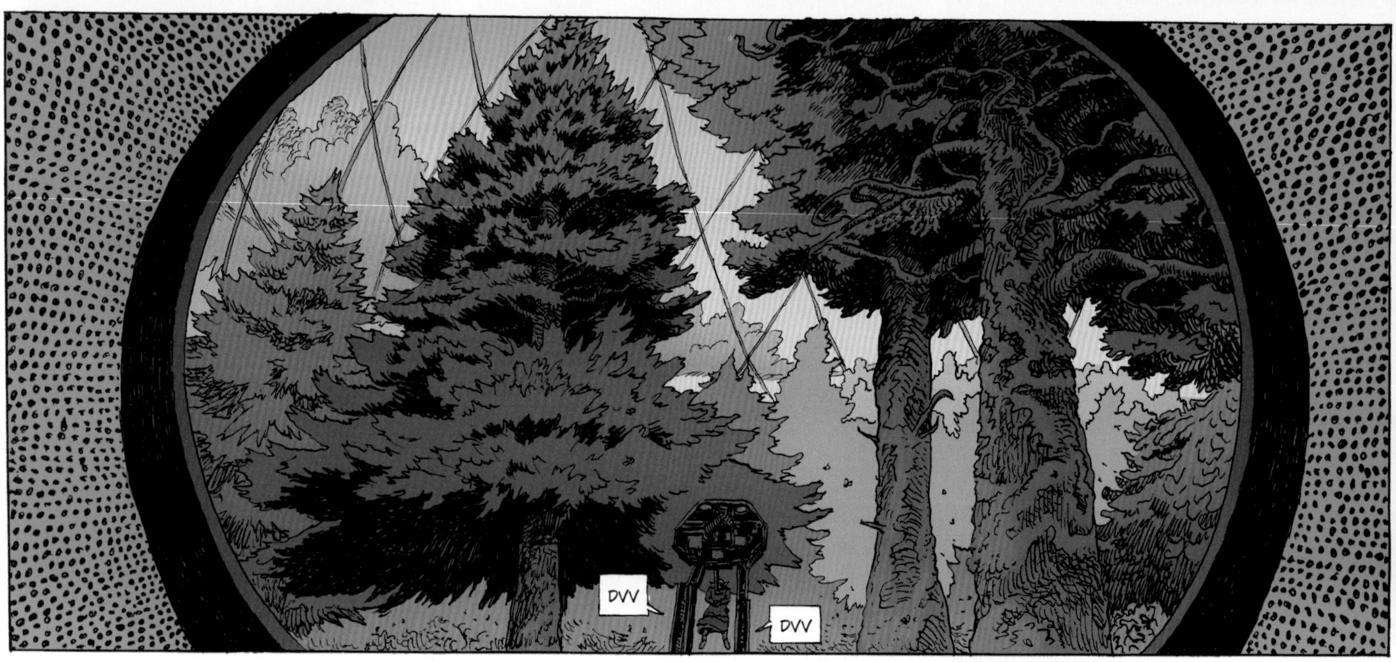
DVV
DVV

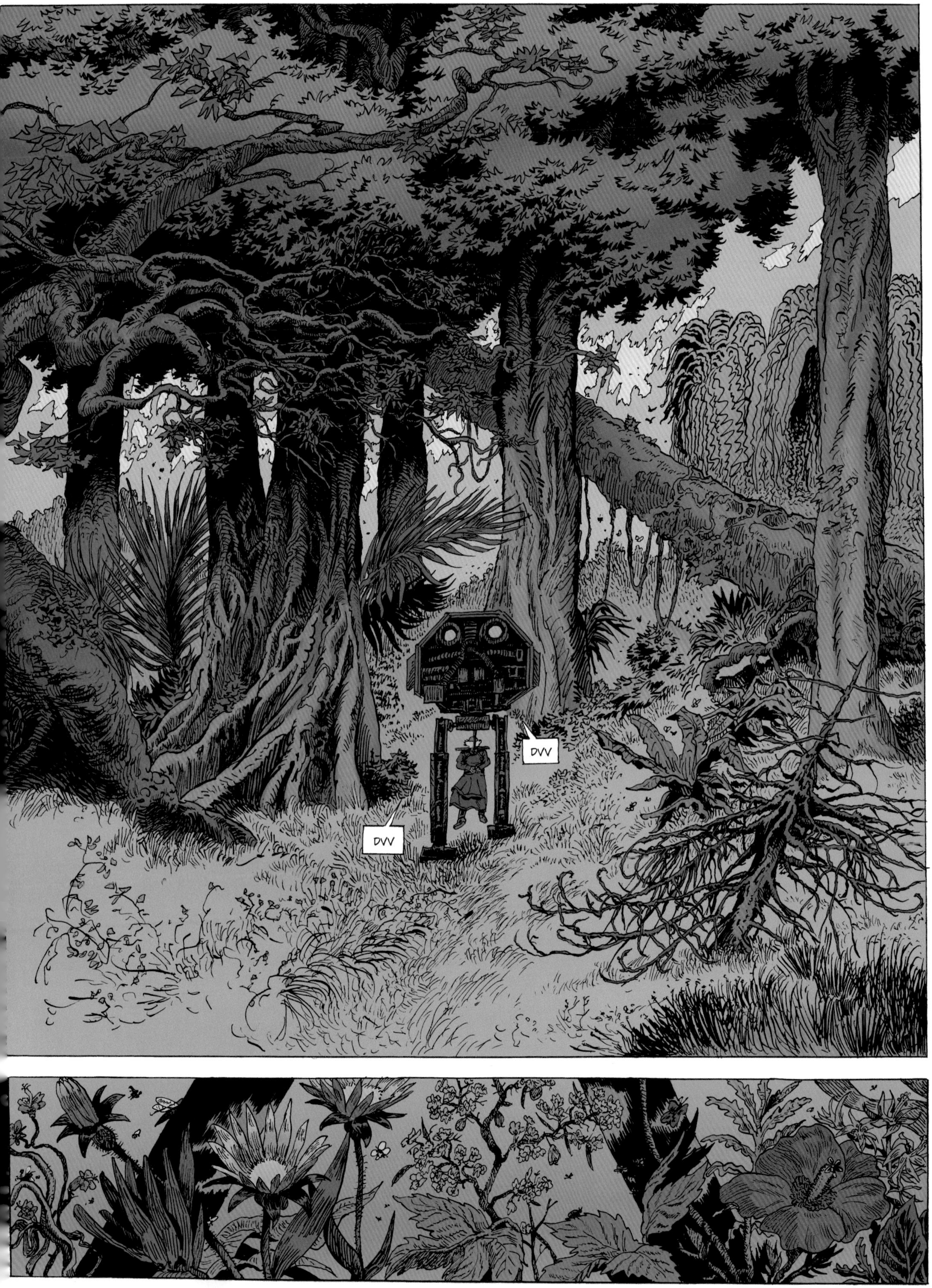
DVV
DVV

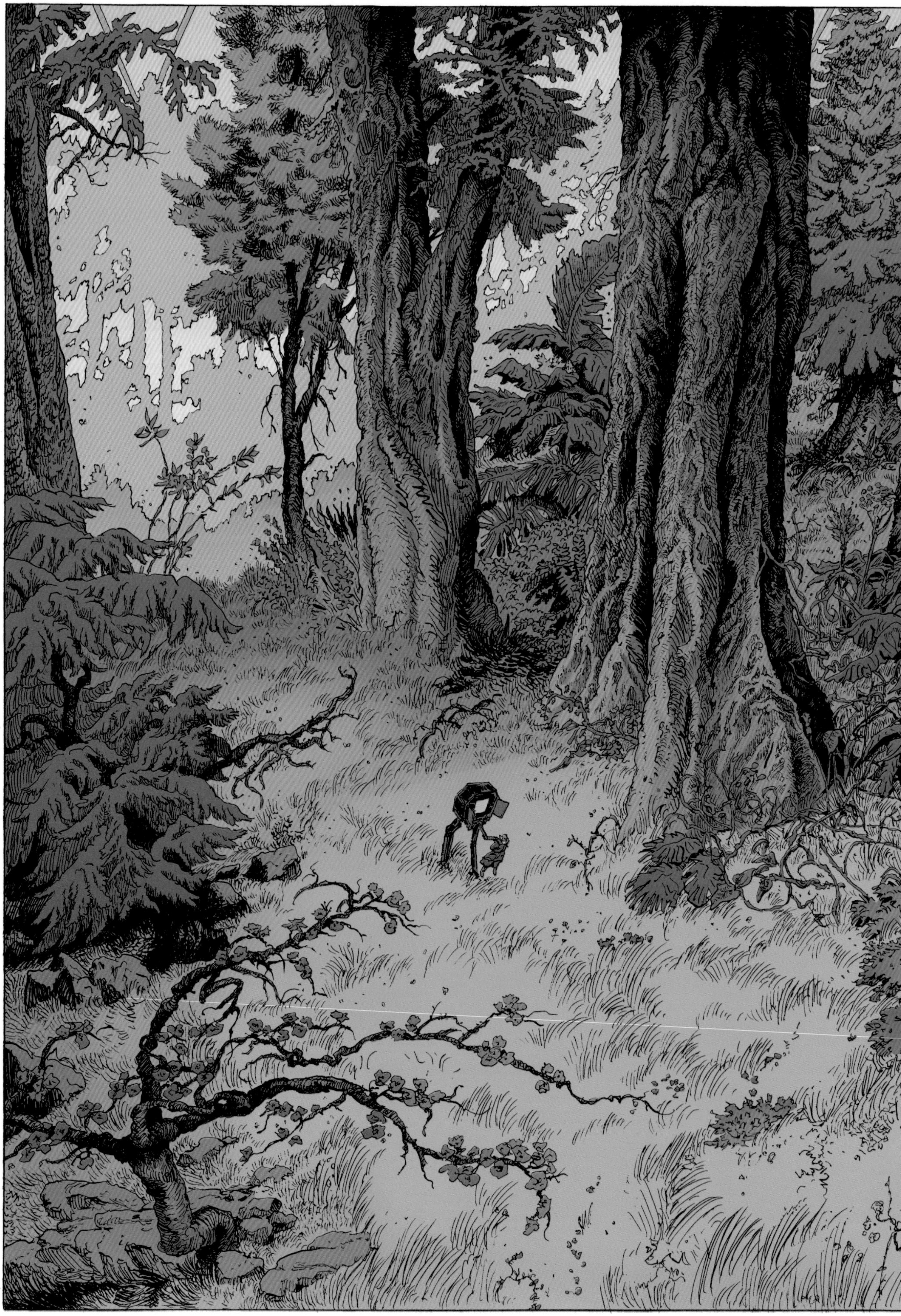

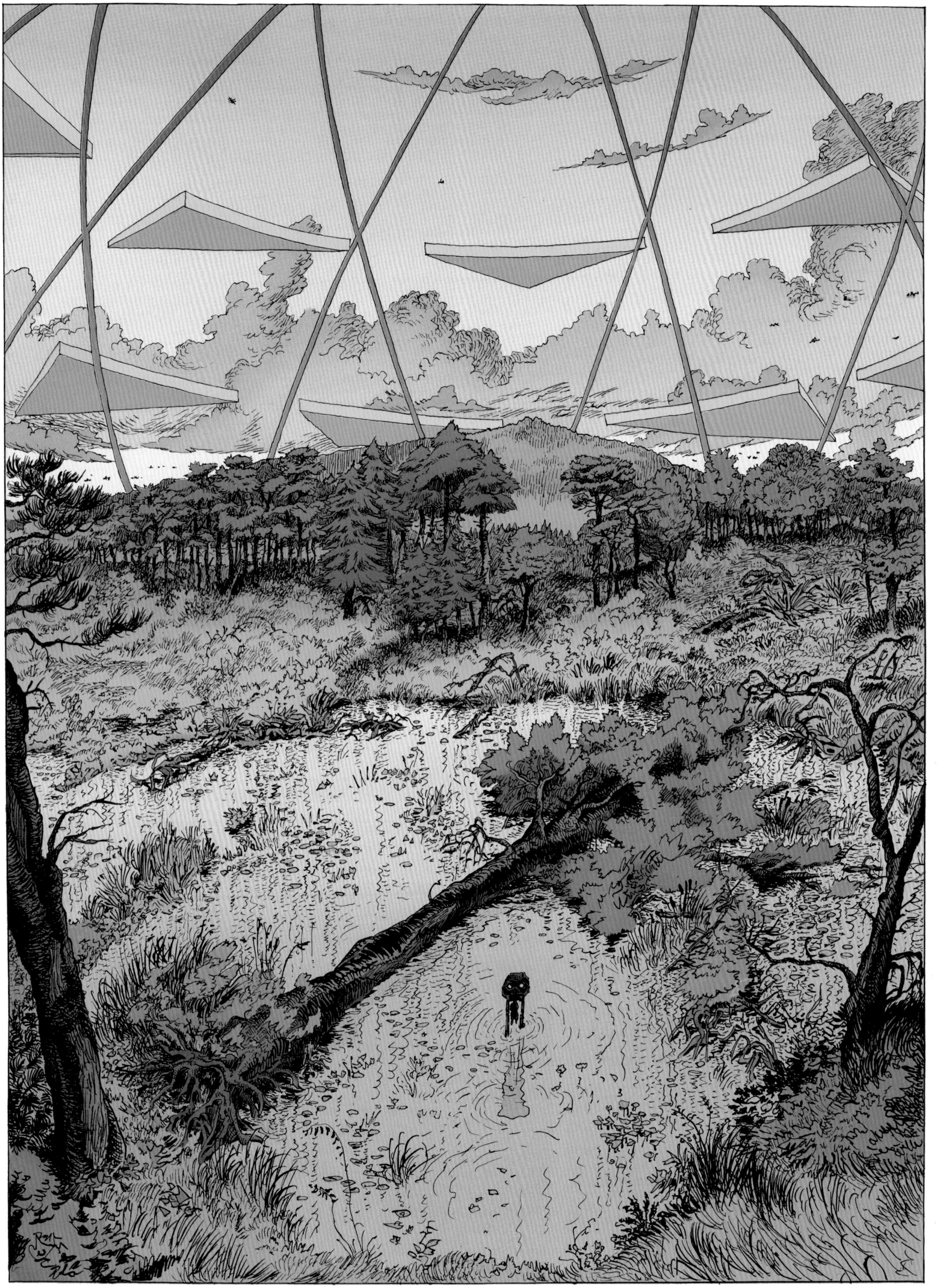

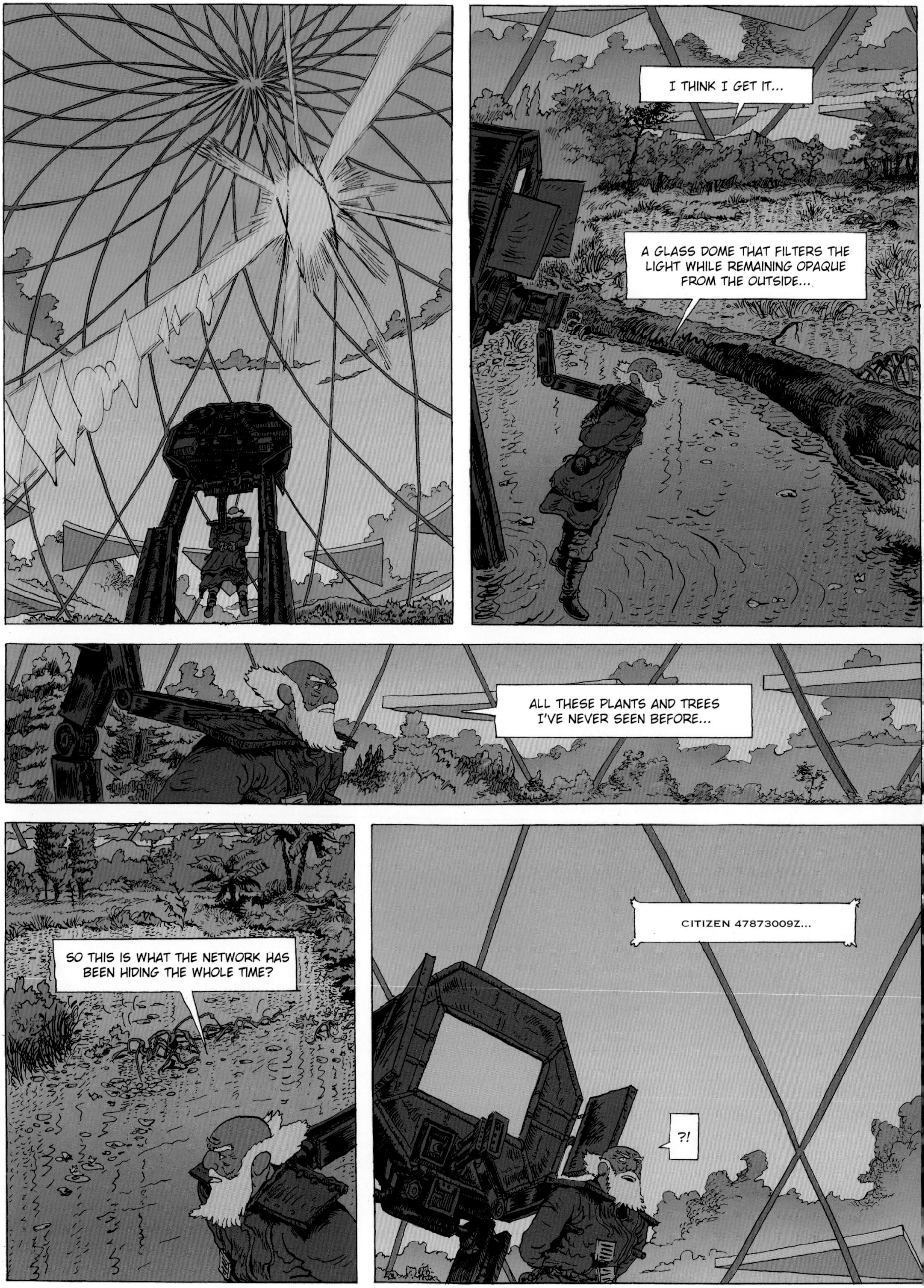
I THINK I GET IT...
A GLASS DOME THAT FILTERS THE LIGHT WHILE REMAINING OPAQUE FROM THE OUTSIDE...
ALL THESE PLANTS AND TREES I'VE NEVER SEEN BEFORE...
SO THIS IS WHAT THE NETWORK HAS BEEN HIDING THE WHOLE TIME?
CITIZEN 47873009Z...
?!

UNDER ARTICLE 245 OF THE ANTHROPO- ENGINEERING CODE, YOU WILL NOW UNDERGO REPROGRAMMING.

IN THIS PROCESS, YOUR BRAIN, WHICH HAS BEEN SINGLED OUT FOR ITS HIGH COGNITIVE POTENTIAL, WILL BE MAPPED OUT IN EIGHT POINTS.

WHY ARE YOU DOING ALL THIS?! WHO ARE YOU?!

YOUR DATA WILL BE THE SUBJECT OF FURTHER STUDIES ON THE CHARACTERISTICS OF HUMAN BEHAVIOR AIMED TO IMPROVE NETWORK PERFORMANCE.

FOR OPTIMAL RESULTS, THE PROCEDURE REQUIRES YOUR BRAIN TO BE EXPOSED TO A FORM OF ABSOLUTE TRUTH.

ABSOLUTE TRUTH?!!

DJJJJJJJJ

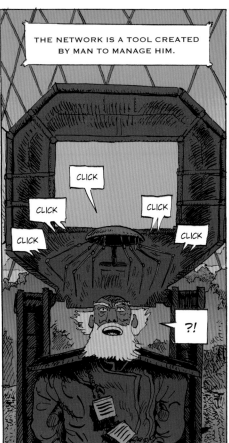

THE NETWORK IS A TOOL CREATED BY MAN TO MANAGE HIM.

CLICK

CLICK

CLICK

CLICK

CLICK

?!

HE HAS PERFECTED IT OVER THOUSANDS OF YEARS...

AAAAAAAF

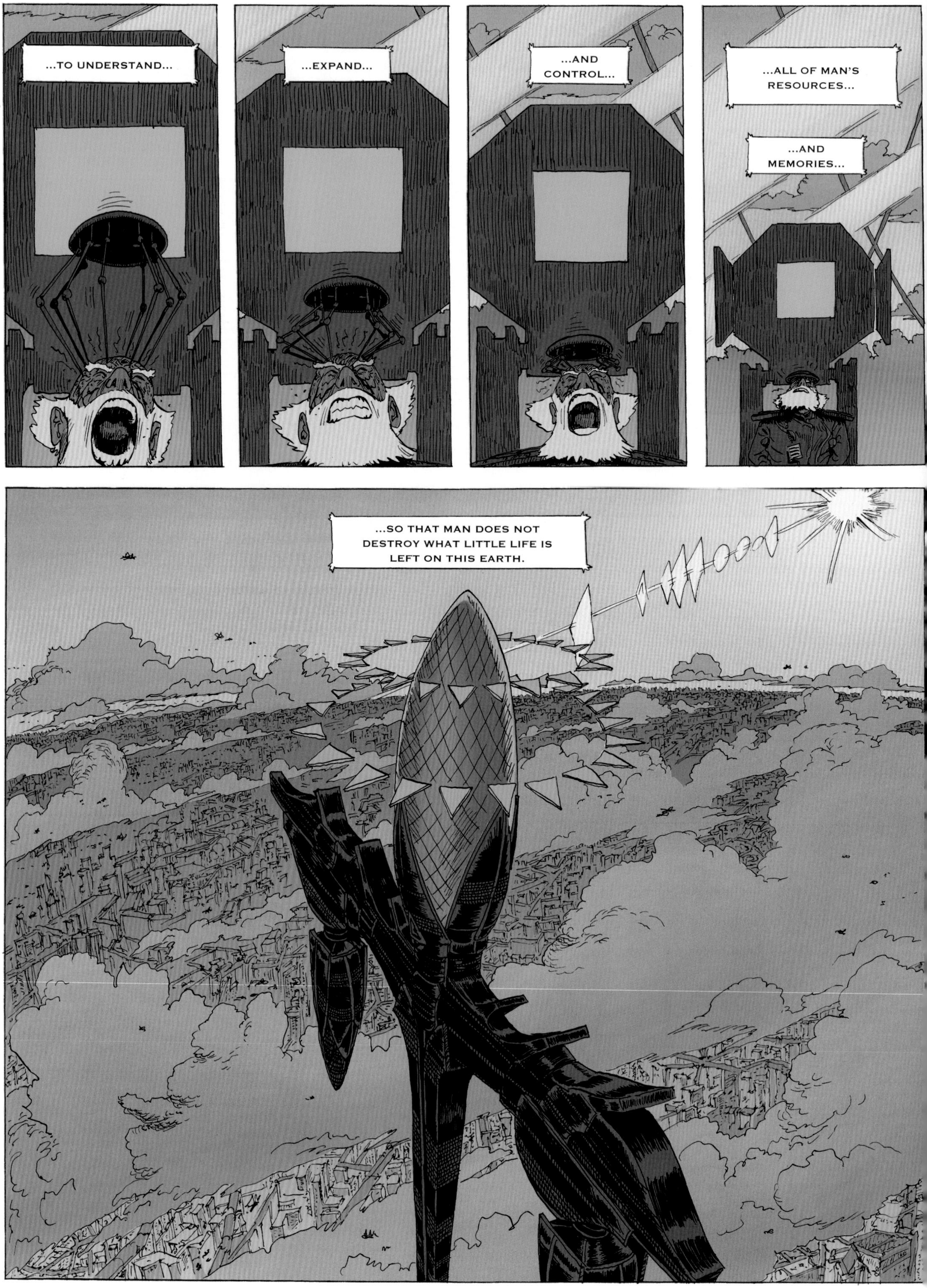
...TO UNDERSTAND...
...EXPAND...
...AND CONTROL...
...ALL OF MAN'S RESOURCES...
...AND MEMORIES...
...SO THAT MAN DOES NOT DESTROY WHAT LITTLE LIFE IS LEFT ON THIS EARTH.

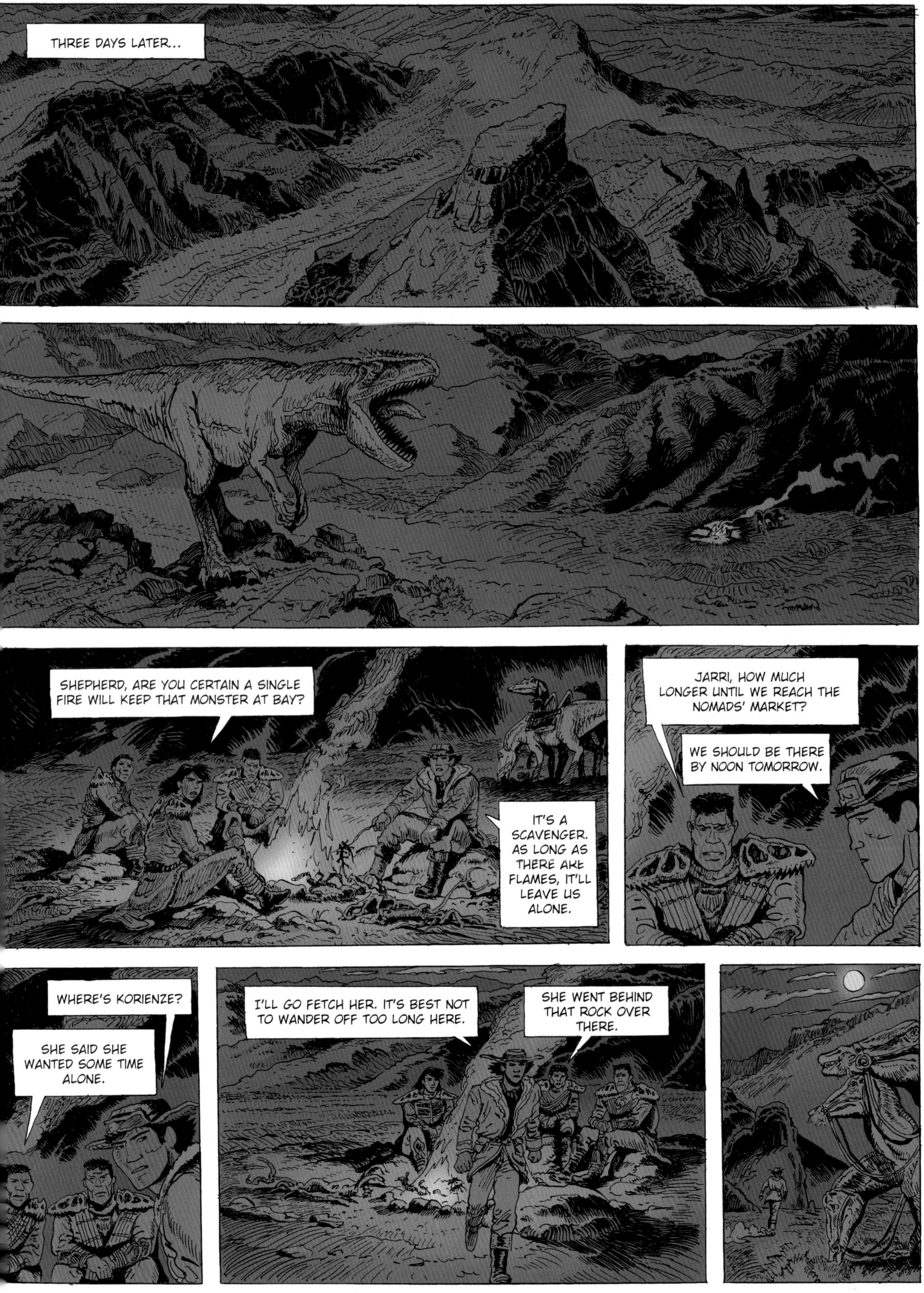
THREE DAYS LATER...
SHEPHERD, ARE YOU CERTAIN A SINGLE FIRE WILL KEEP THAT MONSTER AT BAY?
IT'S A SCAVENGER. AS LONG AS THERE ARE FLAMES, IT'LL LEAVE US ALONE.
JARRI, HOW MUCH LONGER UNTIL WE REACH THE NOMADS' MARKET?
WE SHOULD BE THERE BY NOON TOMORROW.
WHERE'S KORIENZE?
SHE SAID SHE WANTED SOME TIME ALONE.
I'LL GO FETCH HER. IT'S BEST NOT TO WANDER OFF TOO LONG HERE.
SHE WENT BEHIND THAT ROCK OVER THERE.

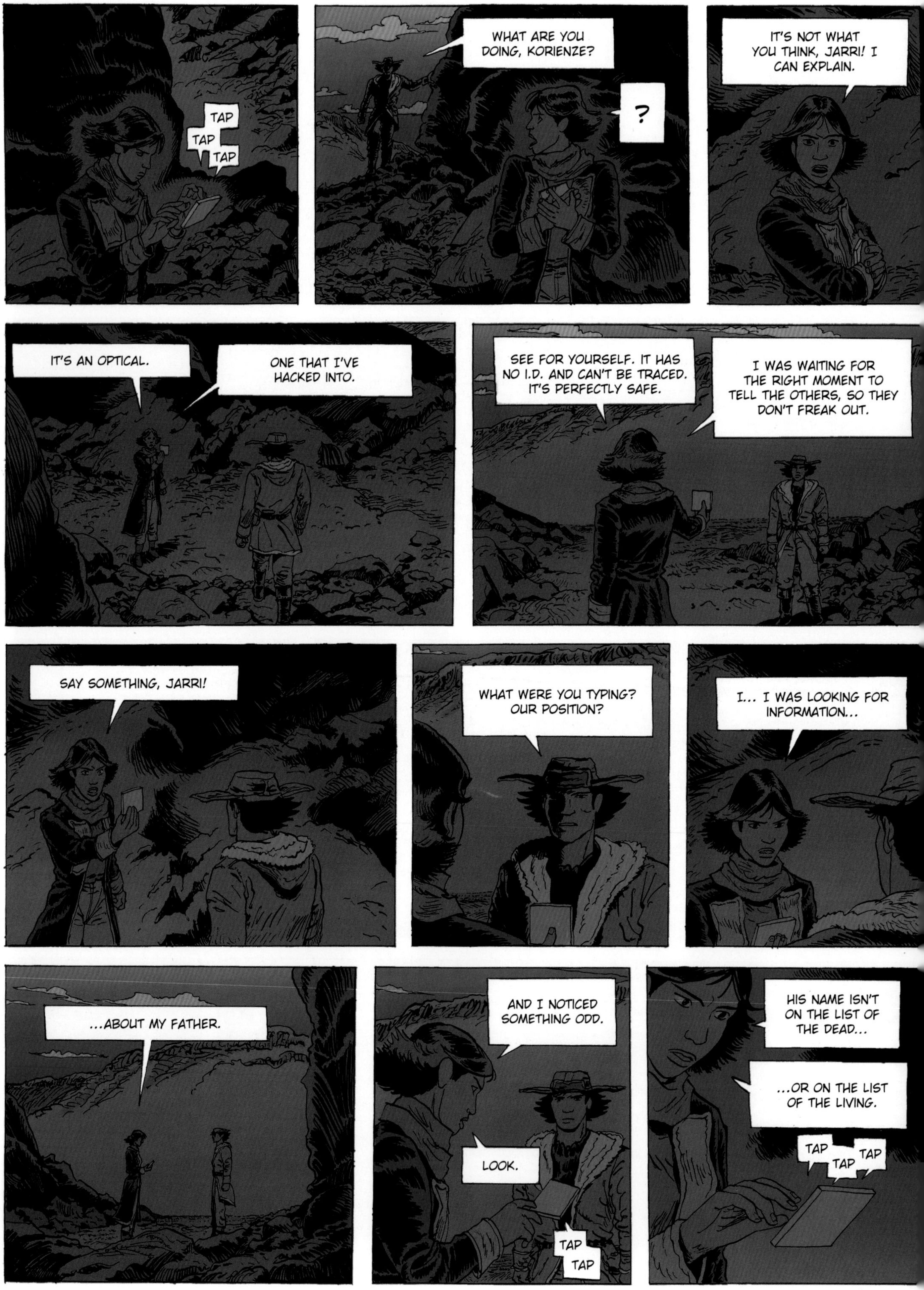
TAP
TAP
TAP
WHAT ARE YOU DOING, KORIENZE?
?
IT'S NOT WHAT YOU THINK, JARRI! I CAN EXPLAIN.
IT'S AN OPTICAL.
ONE THAT I'VE HACKED INTO.
SEE FOR YOURSELF. IT HAS NO I.D. AND CAN'T BE TRACED. IT'S PERFECTLY SAFE.
I WAS WAITING FOR THE RIGHT MOMENT TO TELL THE OTHERS, SO THEY DON'T FREAK OUT.
SAY SOMETHING, JARRI!
WHAT WERE YOU TYPING? OUR POSITION?
I... I WAS LOOKING FOR INFORMATION...
...ABOUT MY FATHER.
AND I NOTICED SOMETHING ODD.
LOOK.
TAP
TAP
HIS NAME ISN'T ON THE LIST OF THE DEAD...
...OR ON THE LIST OF THE LIVING.
TAP
TAP
TAP

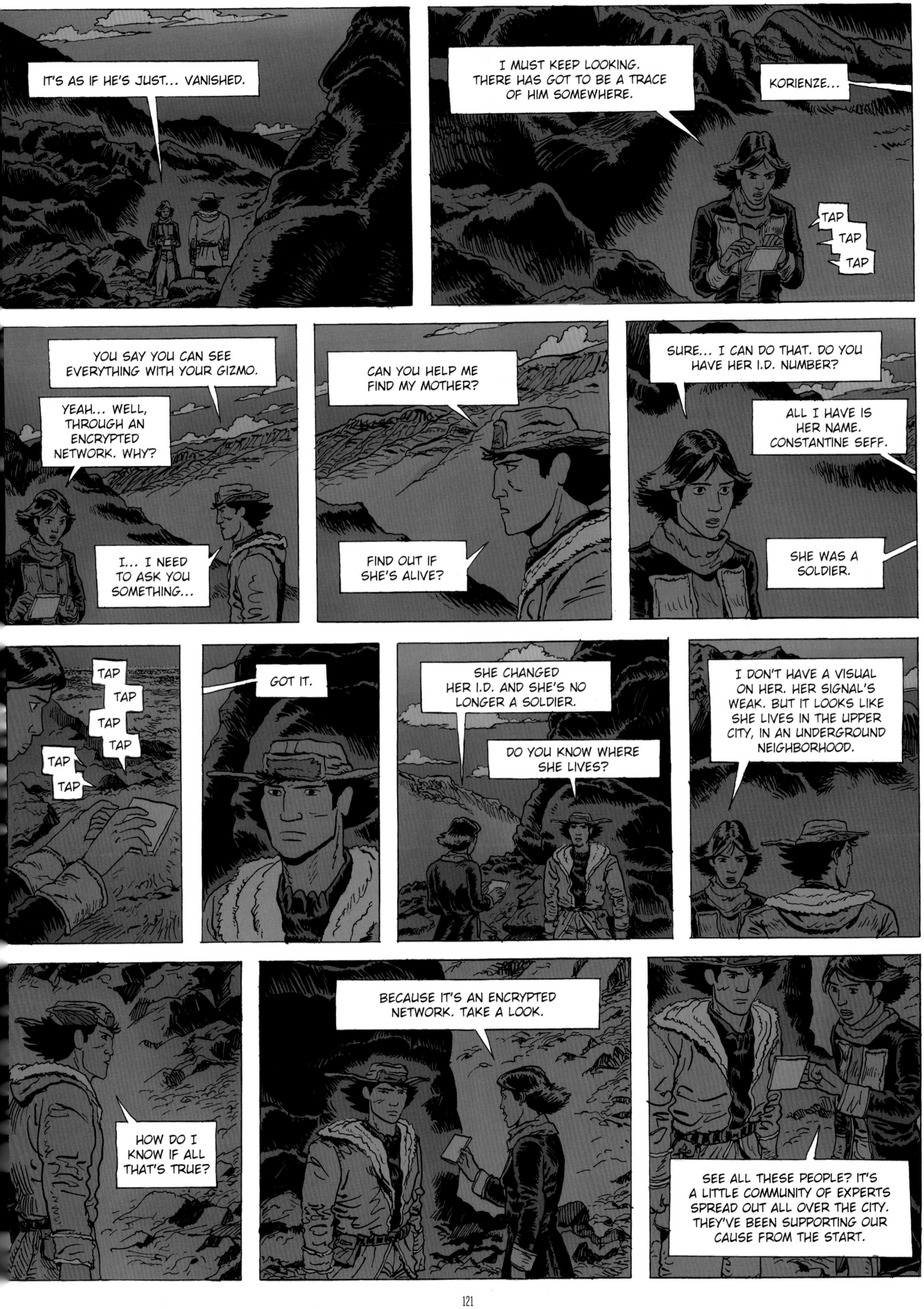

IT'S AS IF HE'S JUST... VANISHED.
I MUST KEEP LOOKING. THERE HAS GOT TO BE A TRACE OF HIM SOMEWHERE.
KORIENZE...
TAP
TAP
TAP
YOU SAY YOU CAN SEE EVERYTHING WITH YOUR GIZMO.
YEAH... WELL, THROUGH AN ENCRYPTED NETWORK. WHY?
I... I NEED TO ASK YOU SOMETHING...
CAN YOU HELP ME FIND MY MOTHER?
FIND OUT IF SHE'S ALIVE?
SURE... I CAN DO THAT. DO YOU HAVE HER I.D. NUMBER?
ALL I HAVE IS HER NAME. CONSTANTINE SEFF.
SHE WAS A SOLDIER.
TAP
TAP
TAP
TAP
TAP
TAP
GOT IT.
SHE CHANGED HER I.D. AND SHE'S NO LONGER A SOLDIER.
DO YOU KNOW WHERE SHE LIVES?
I DON'T HAVE A VISUAL ON HER. HER SIGNAL'S WEAK. BUT IT LOOKS LIKE SHE LIVES IN THE UPPER CITY, IN AN UNDERGROUND NEIGHBORHOOD.
HOW DO I KNOW IF ALL THAT'S TRUE?
BECAUSE IT'S AN ENCRYPTED NETWORK. TAKE A LOOK.
SEE ALL THESE PEOPLE? IT'S A LITTLE COMMUNITY OF EXPERTS SPREAD OUT ALL OVER THE CITY. THEY'VE BEEN SUPPORTING OUR CAUSE FROM THE START.

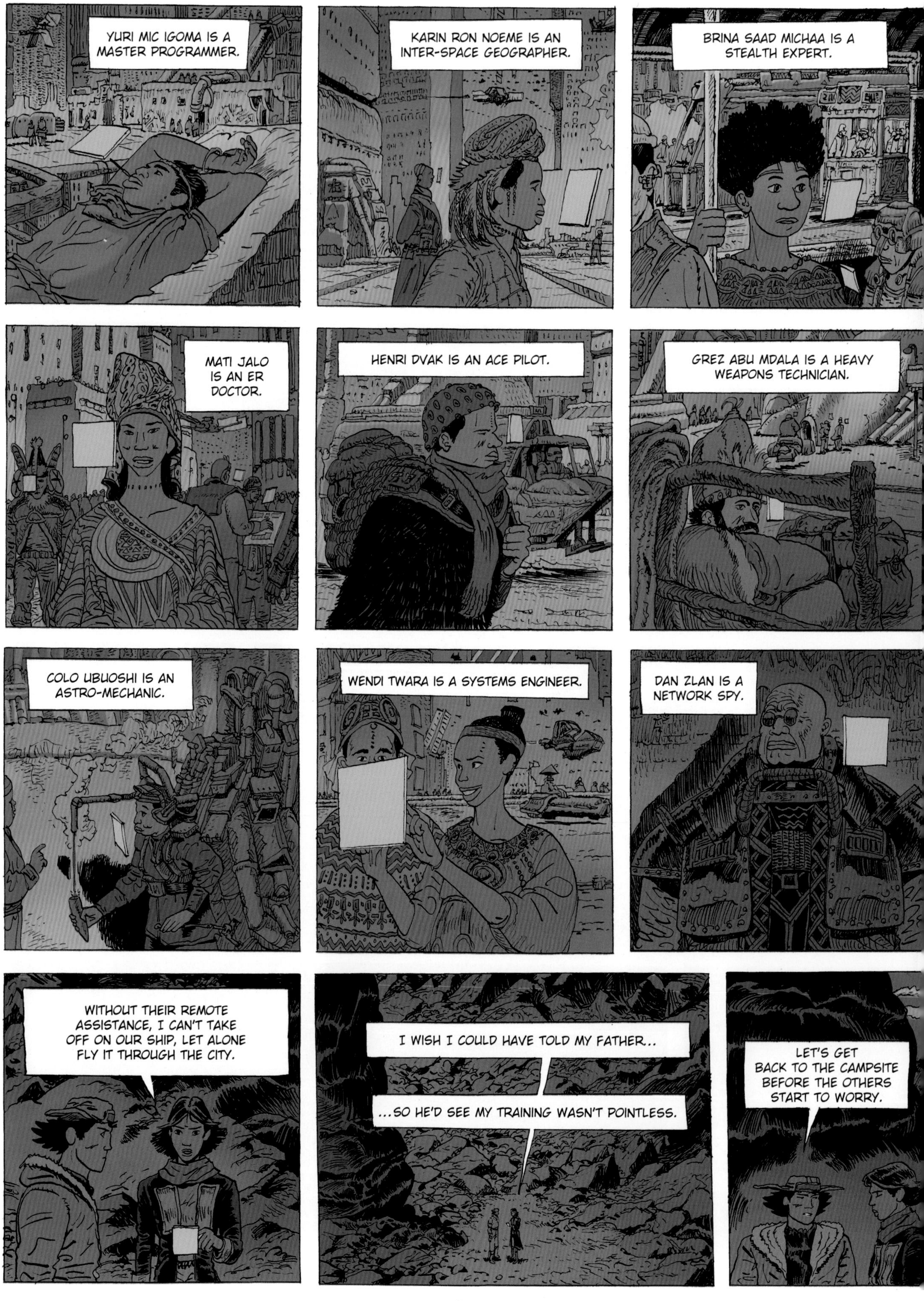
YURI MIC IGOMA IS A MASTER PROGRAMMER.
KARIN RON NOEME IS AN INTER-SPACE GEOGRAPHER.
BRINA SAAD MICHAA IS A STEALTH EXPERT.
MATI JALO IS AN ER DOCTOR.
HENRI DVAK IS AN ACE PILOT.
GREZ ABU MDALA IS A HEAVY WEAPONS TECHNICIAN.
COLO UBUOSHI IS AN ASTRO-MECHANIC.
WENDI TWARA IS A SYSTEMS ENGINEER.
DAN ZLAN IS A NETWORK SPY.
WITHOUT THEIR REMOTE ASSISTANCE, I CAN'T TAKE OFF ON OUR SHIP, LET ALONE FLY IT THROUGH THE CITY.
I WISH I COULD HAVE TOLD MY FATHER...
...SO HE'D SEE MY TRAINING WASN'T POINTLESS.
LET'S GET BACK TO THE CAMPSITE BEFORE THE OTHERS START TO WORRY.

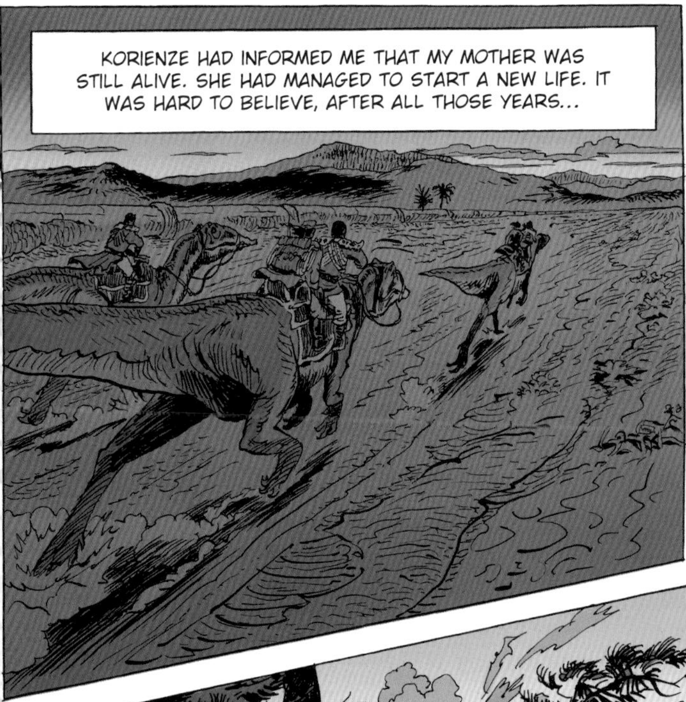
KORIENZE HAD INFORMED ME THAT MY MOTHER WAS STILL ALIVE. SHE HAD MANAGED TO START A NEW LIFE. IT WAS HARD TO BELIEVE, AFTER ALL THOSE YEARS...

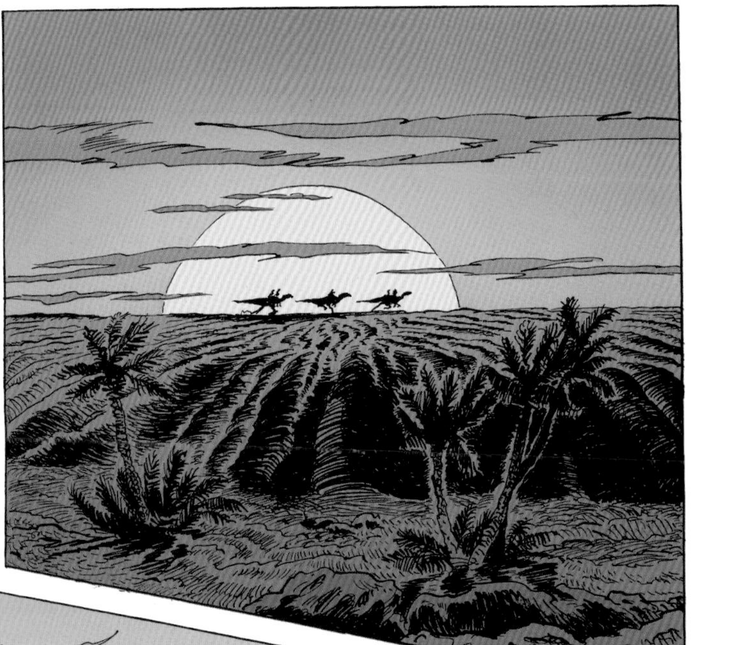

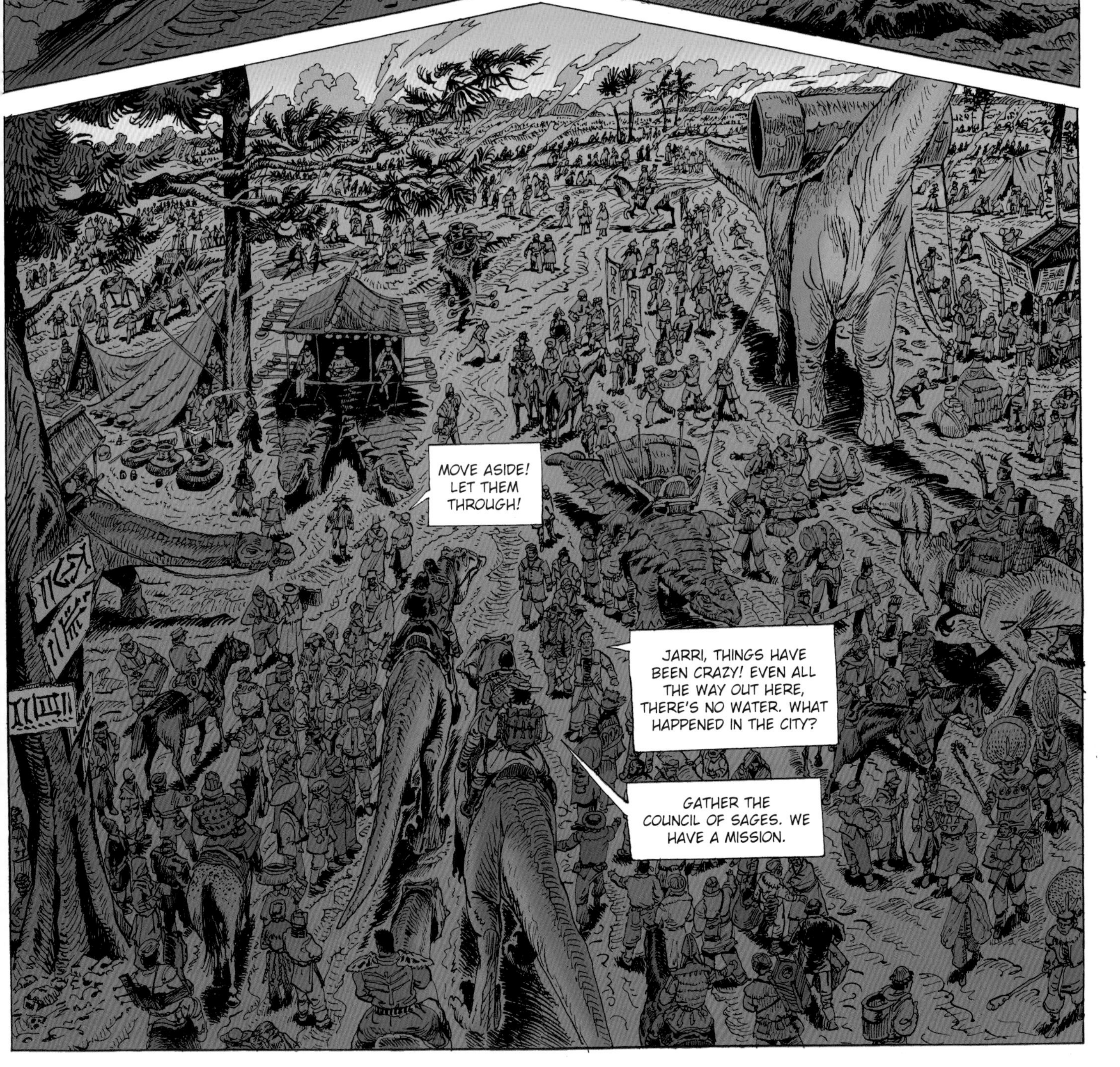
MOVE ASIDE! LET THEM THROUGH!
JARRI, THINGS HAVE BEEN CRAZY! EVEN ALL THE WAY OUT HERE, THERE'S NO WATER. WHAT HAPPENED IN THE CITY?
GATHER THE COUNCIL OF SAGES. WE HAVE A MISSION.

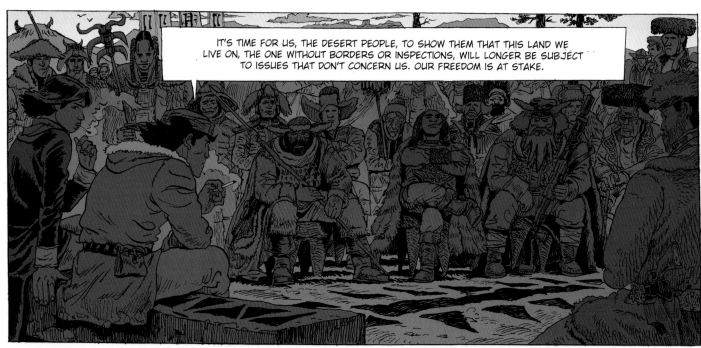

IT'S TIME FOR US, THE DESERT PEOPLE, TO SHOW THEM THAT THIS LAND WE LIVE ON, THE ONE WITHOUT BORDERS OR INSPECTIONS, WILL LONGER BE SUBJECT TO ISSUES THAT DON'T CONCERN US. OUR FREEDOM IS AT STAKE.

WE MUST THEREFORE GET A MESSAGE OUT AT ONCE TO ALL MEN AND WOMEN WHO WANT TO JOIN US ON OUR MISSION.

WOMEN? THIS ISN'T THE CITY, HERE! YOU KNOW THERE ARE NO WOMEN HERE! NEVER HAVE BEEN!

THEN AGAIN, HE PROBABLY DOESN'T EVEN KNOW WHAT THAT IS!

HAHAHA HAHAHAHA HAHAHA

I'M WITH YOU.

LATER TODAY, WE WILL TAKE THE BRAVEST AMONG YOU AND GO AFTER THE WEATHER TRUCK.

NO WEAPONS ALLOWED. A SINGLE GUNSHOT COULD ALERT THE NETWORK AND COMPROMISE THE ENTIRE OPERATION.

NO DINOS, EITHER. ONLY HORSES. THEY'RE FASTER AND MORE DOCILE.

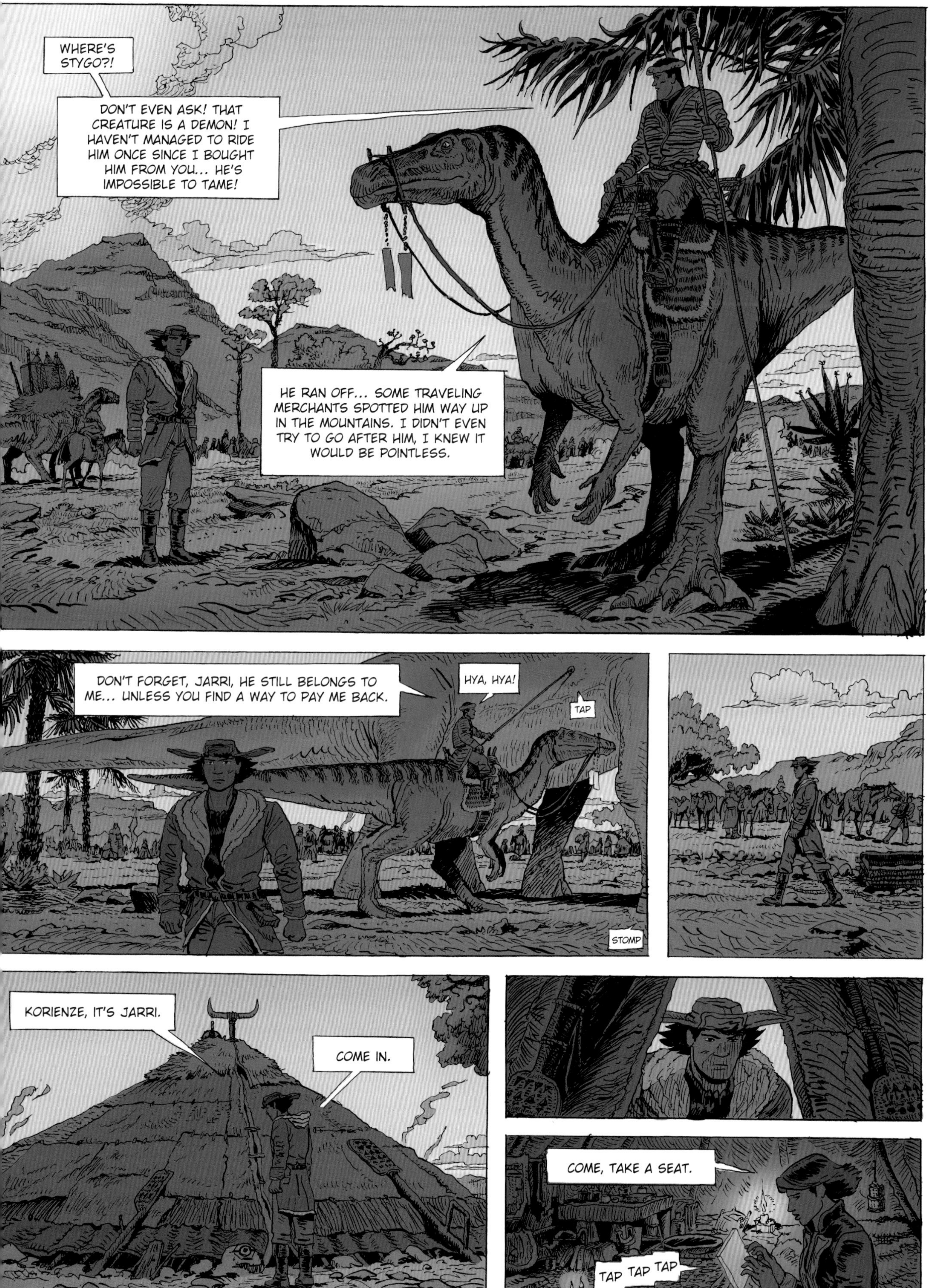
WHERE'S STYGO?!
DON'T EVEN ASK! THAT CREATURE IS A DEMON! I HAVEN'T MANAGED TO RIDE HIM ONCE SINCE I BOUGHT HIM FROM YOU... HE'S IMPOSSIBLE TO TAME!
HE RAN OFF... SOME TRAVELING MERCHANTS SPOTTED HIM WAY UP IN THE MOUNTAINS. I DIDN'T EVEN TRY TO GO AFTER HIM, I KNEW IT WOULD BE POINTLESS.
DON'T FORGET, JARRI, HE STILL BELONGS TO ME... UNLESS YOU FIND A WAY TO PAY ME BACK.
HYA, HYA!
TAP
STOMP
KORIENZE, IT'S JARRI.
COME IN.
COME, TAKE A SEAT.
TAP TAP TAP

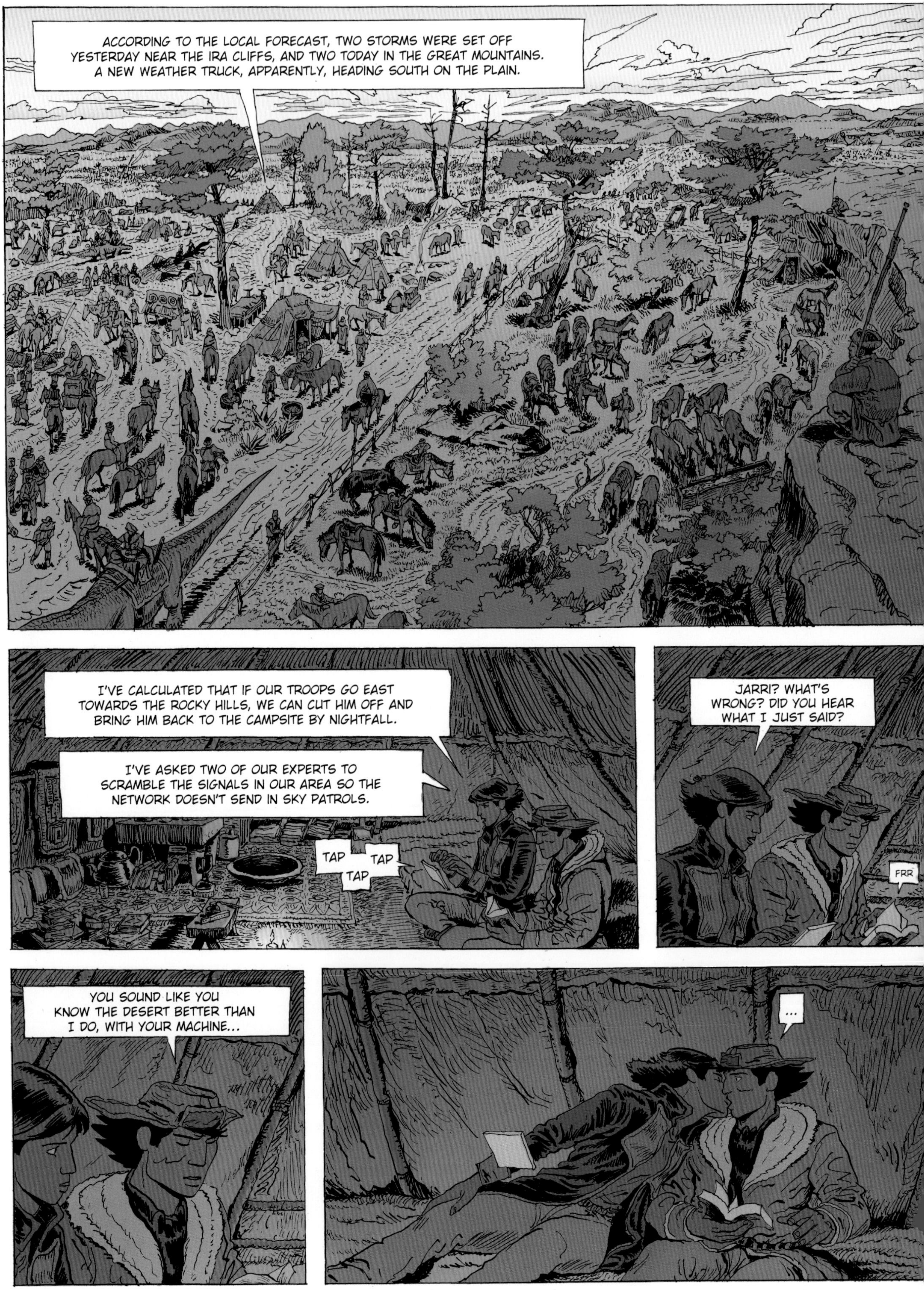
ACCORDING TO THE LOCAL FORECAST, TWO STORMS WERE SET OFF YESTERDAY NEAR THE IRA CLIFFS, AND TWO TODAY IN THE GREAT MOUNTAINS. A NEW WEATHER TRUCK, APPARENTLY, HEADING SOUTH ON THE PLAIN.
I'VE CALCULATED THAT IF OUR TROOPS GO EAST TOWARDS THE ROCKY HILLS, WE CAN CUT HIM OFF AND BRING HIM BACK TO THE CAMPSITE BY NIGHTFALL.
I'VE ASKED TWO OF OUR EXPERTS TO SCRAMBLE THE SIGNALS IN OUR AREA SO THE NETWORK DOESN'T SEND IN SKY PATROLS.
TAP
TAP
TAP
JARRI? WHAT'S WRONG? DID YOU HEAR WHAT I JUST SAID?
FRR
YOU SOUND LIKE YOU KNOW THE DESERT BETTER THAN I DO, WITH YOUR MACHINE...
...

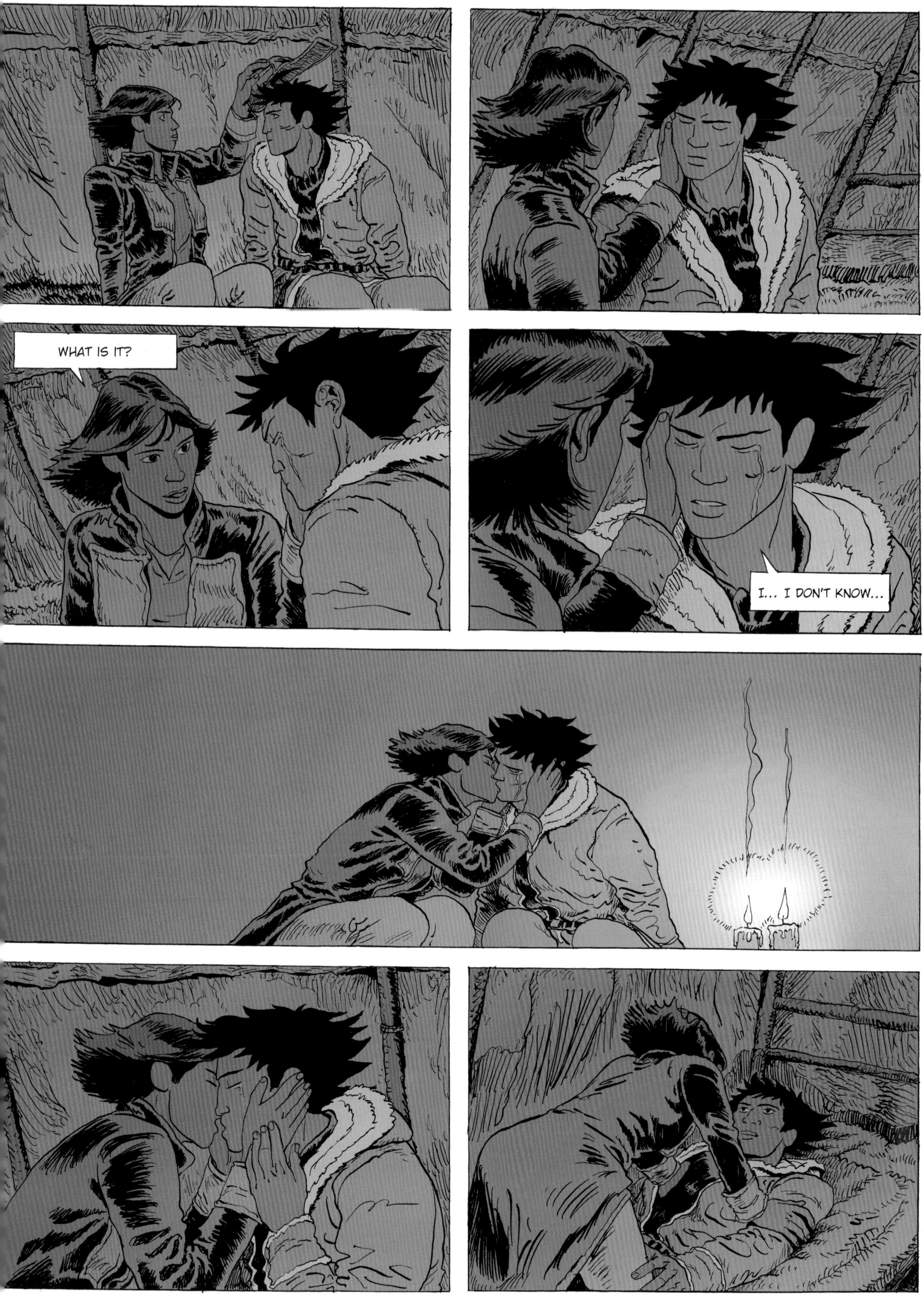
WHAT IS IT?
I... I DON'T KNOW...

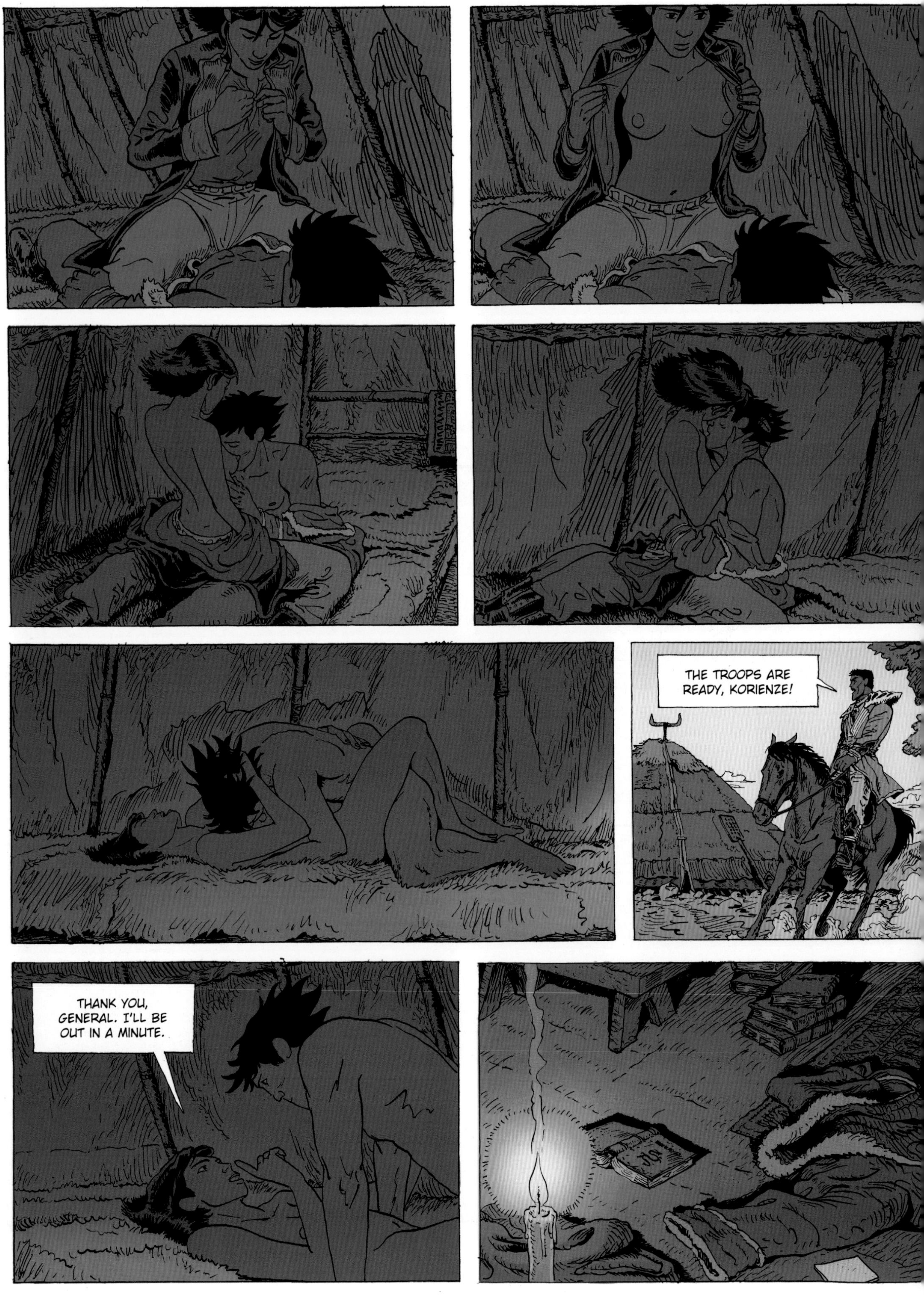
THE TROOPS ARE READY, KORIENZE!
THANK YOU, GENERAL. I'LL BE OUT IN A MINUTE.

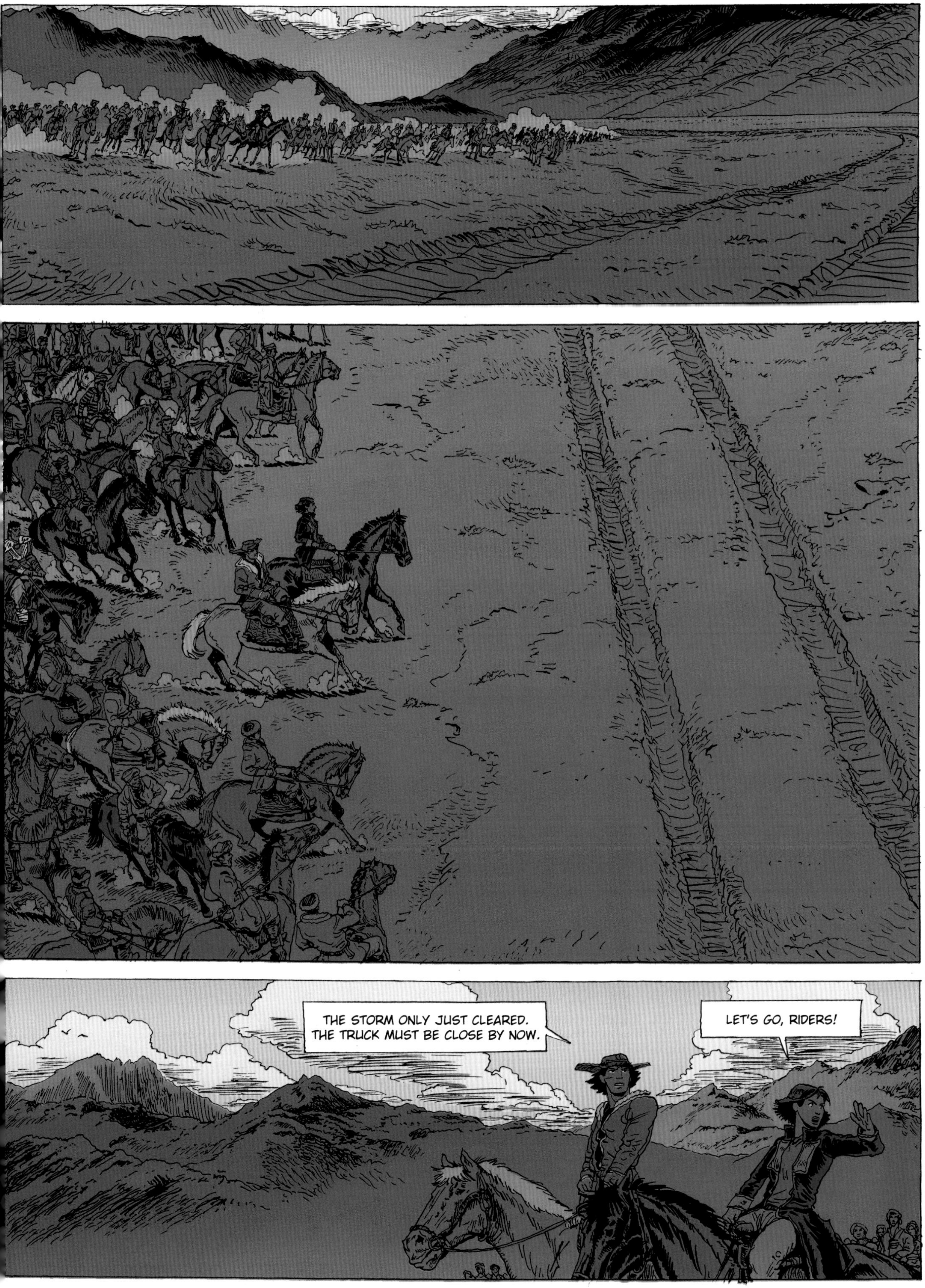
THE STORM ONLY JUST CLEARED. THE TRUCK MUST BE CLOSE BY NOW.
LET'S GO, RIDERS!

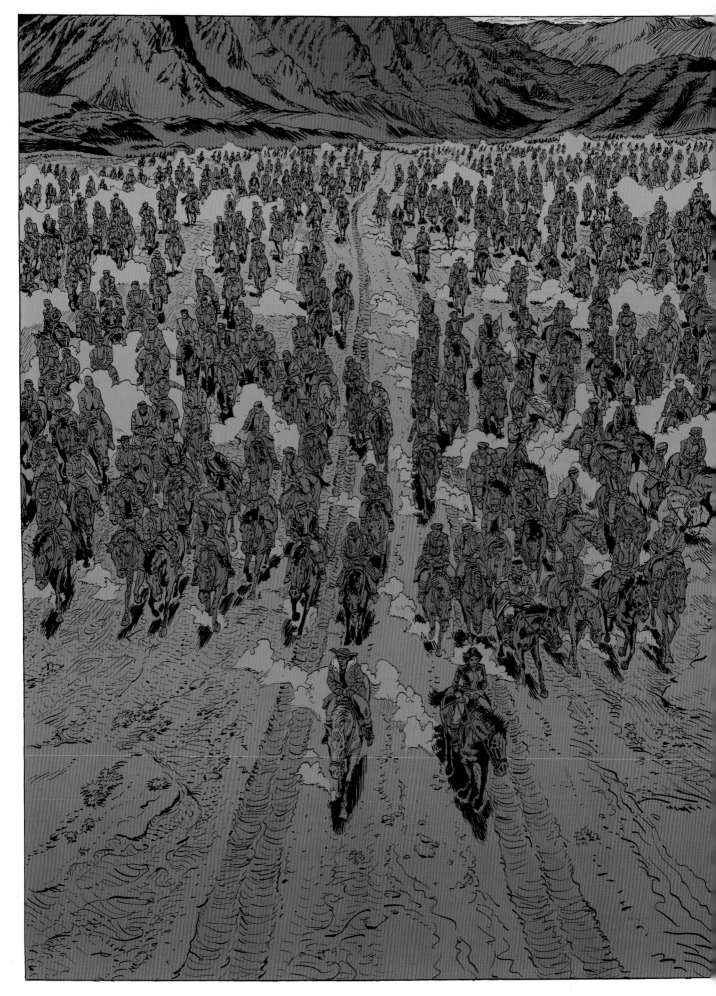

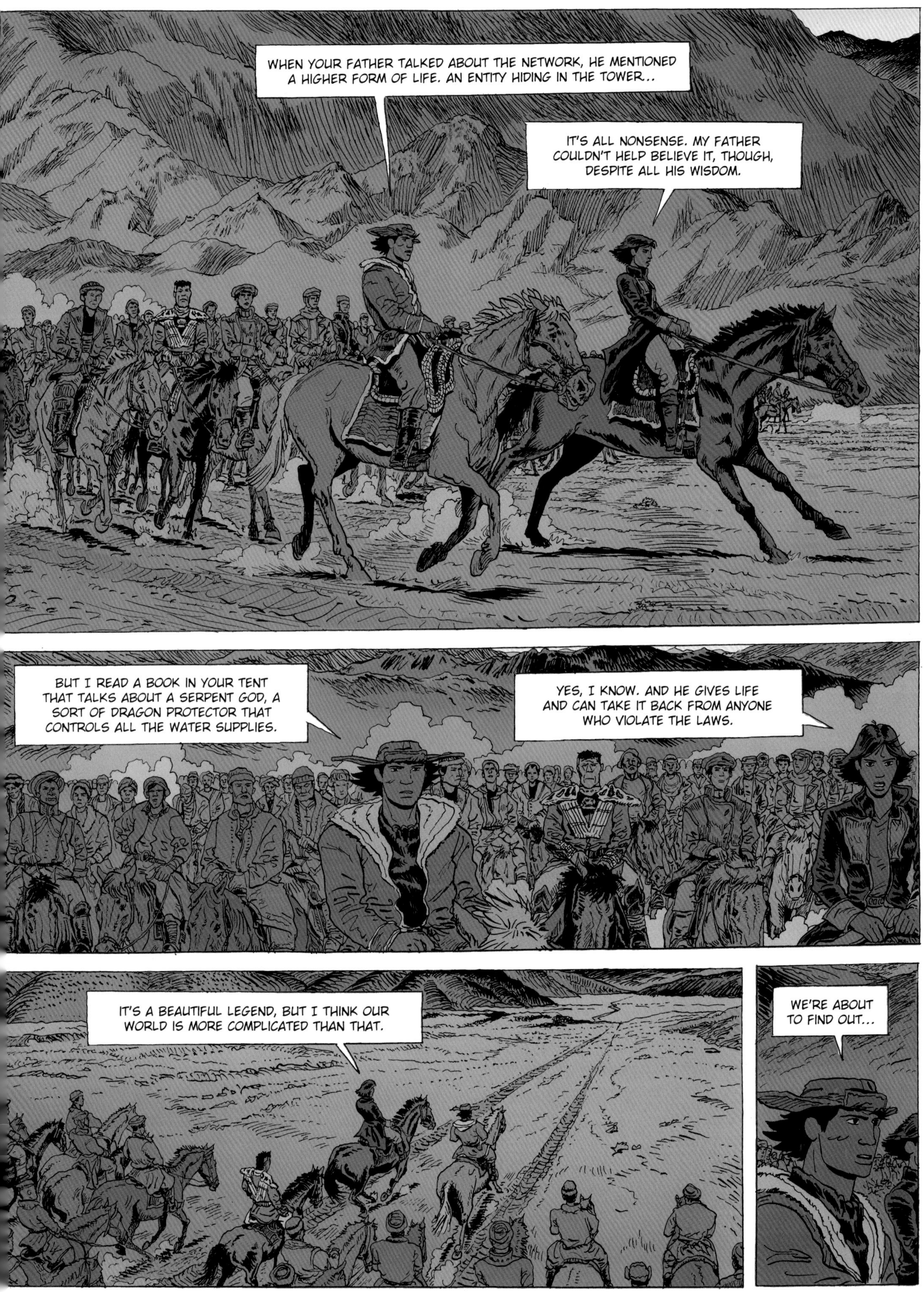
WHEN YOUR FATHER TALKED ABOUT THE NETWORK, HE MENTIONED A HIGHER FORM OF LIFE. AN ENTITY HIDING IN THE TOWER...
IT'S ALL NONSENSE. MY FATHER COULDN'T HELP BELIEVE IT, THOUGH, DESPITE ALL HIS WISDOM.
BUT I READ A BOOK IN YOUR TENT THAT TALKS ABOUT A SERPENT GOD, A SORT OF DRAGON PROTECTOR THAT CONTROLS ALL THE WATER SUPPLIES.
YES, I KNOW. AND HE GIVES LIFE AND CAN TAKE IT BACK FROM ANYONE WHO VIOLATE THE LAWS.
IT'S A BEAUTIFUL LEGEND, BUT I THINK OUR WORLD IS MORE COMPLICATED THAN THAT.
WE'RE ABOUT TO FIND OUT...

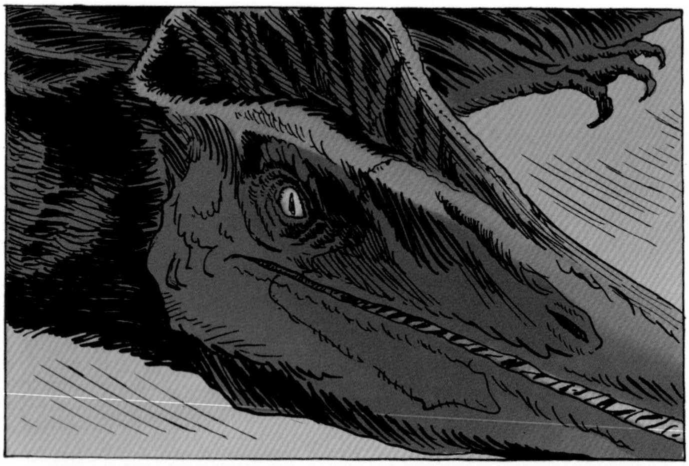

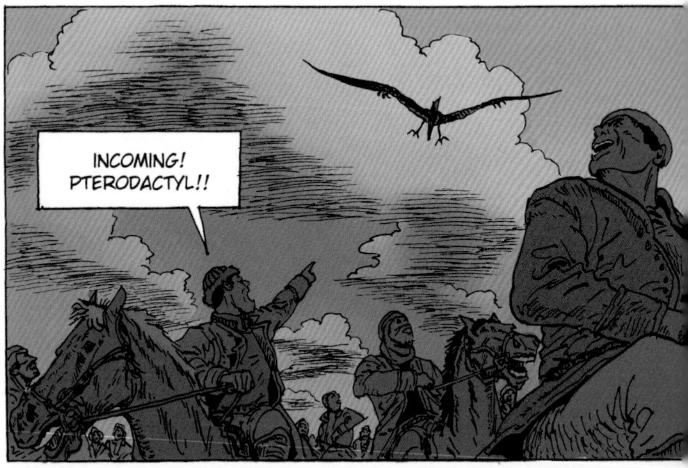
INCOMING! PTERODACTYL!!

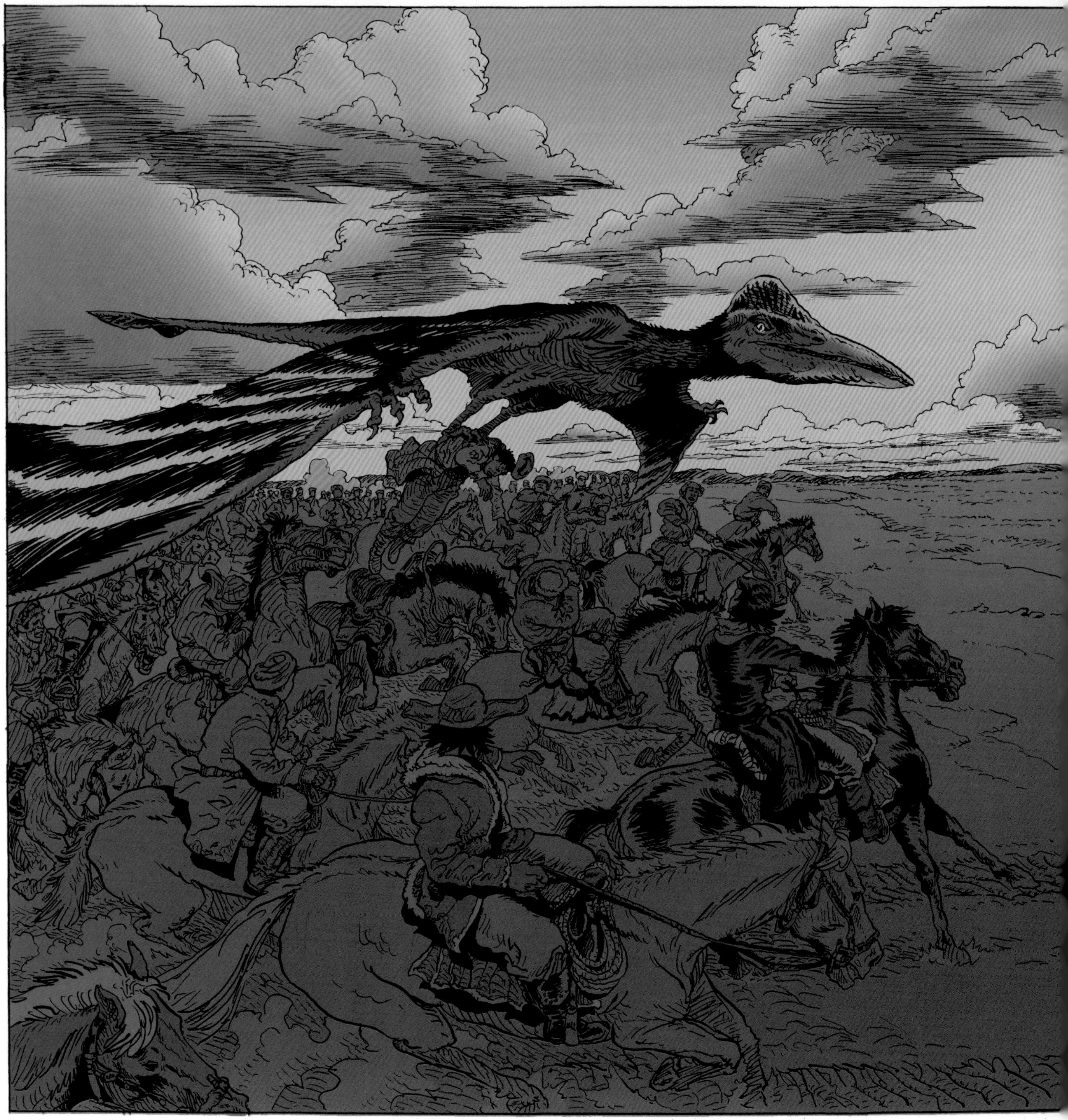

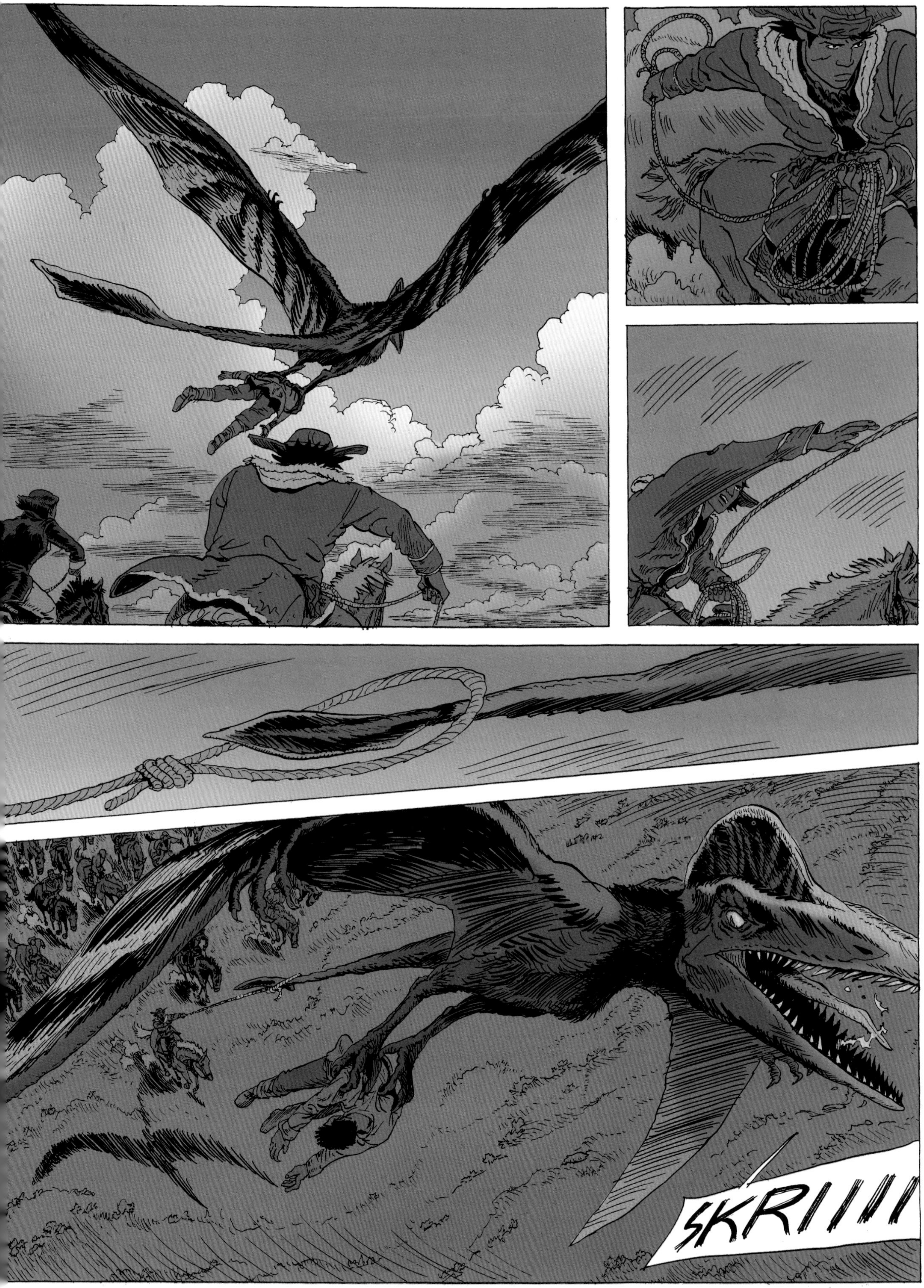
SKRIIIII

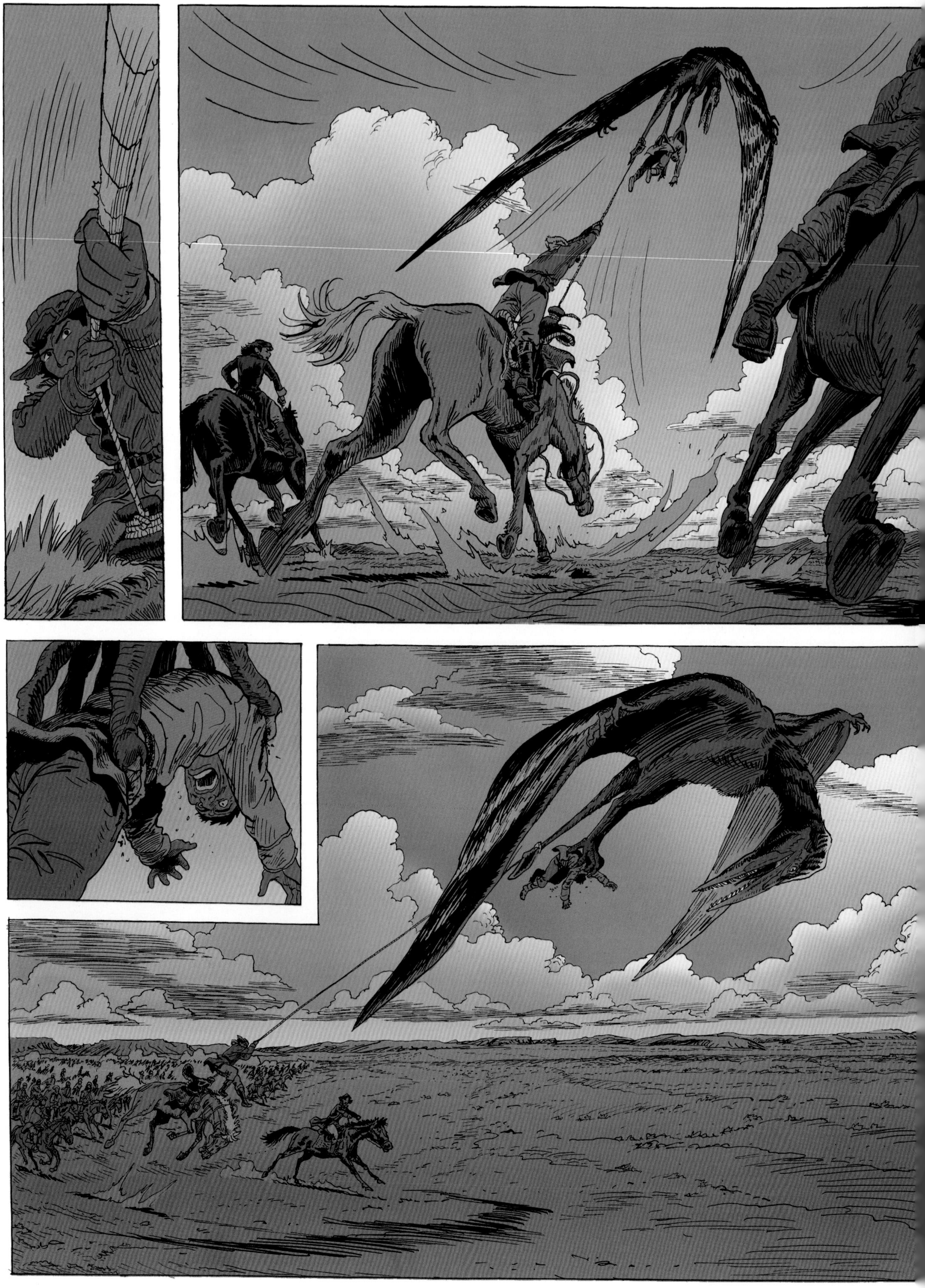

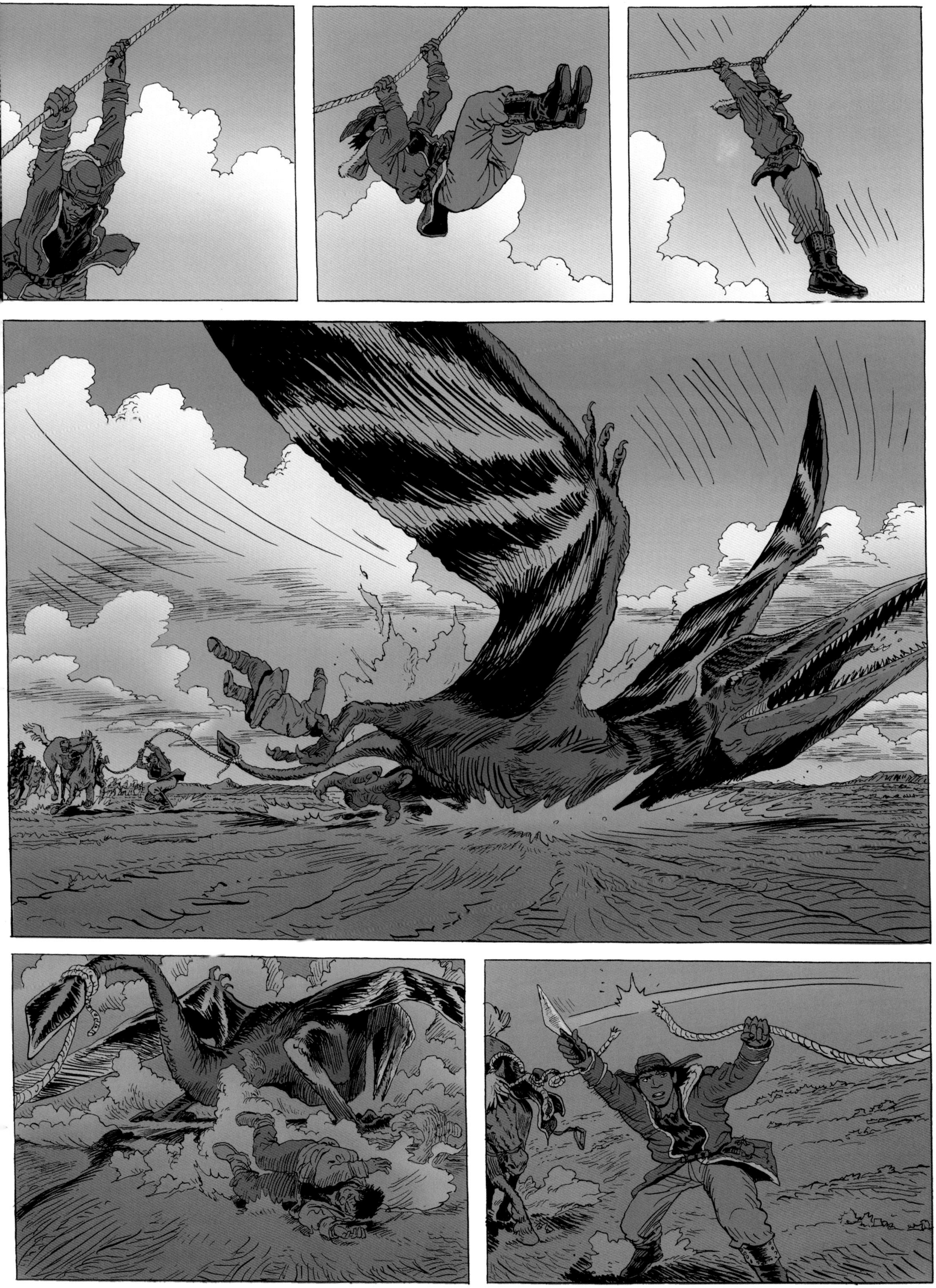

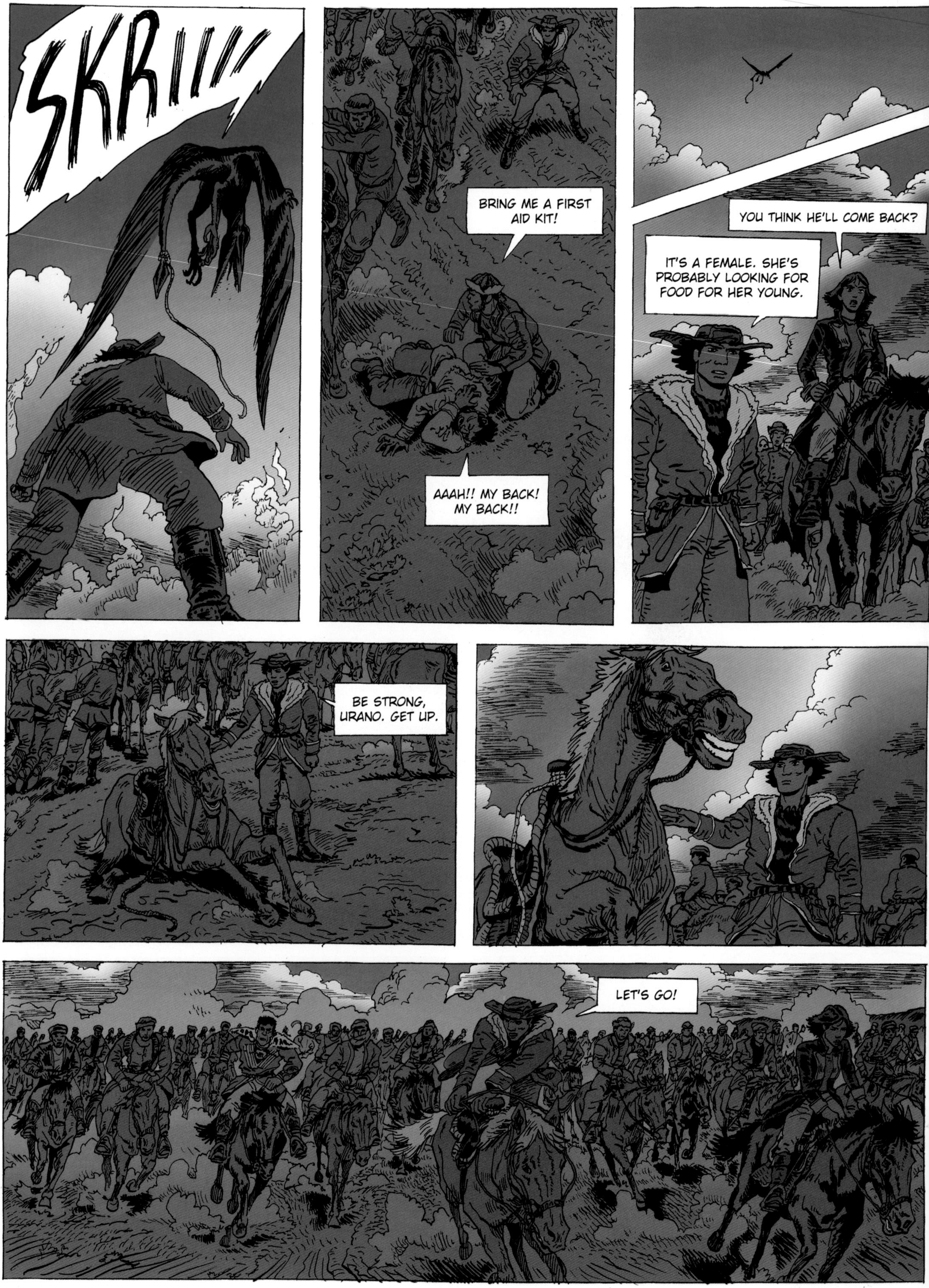
SKRIII
BRING ME A FIRST AID KIT!
AAAH!! MY BACK! MY BACK!!
YOU THINK HE'LL COME BACK?
IT'S A FEMALE. SHE'S PROBABLY LOOKING FOR FOOD FOR HER YOUNG.
BE STRONG, URANO. GET UP.
LET'S GO!

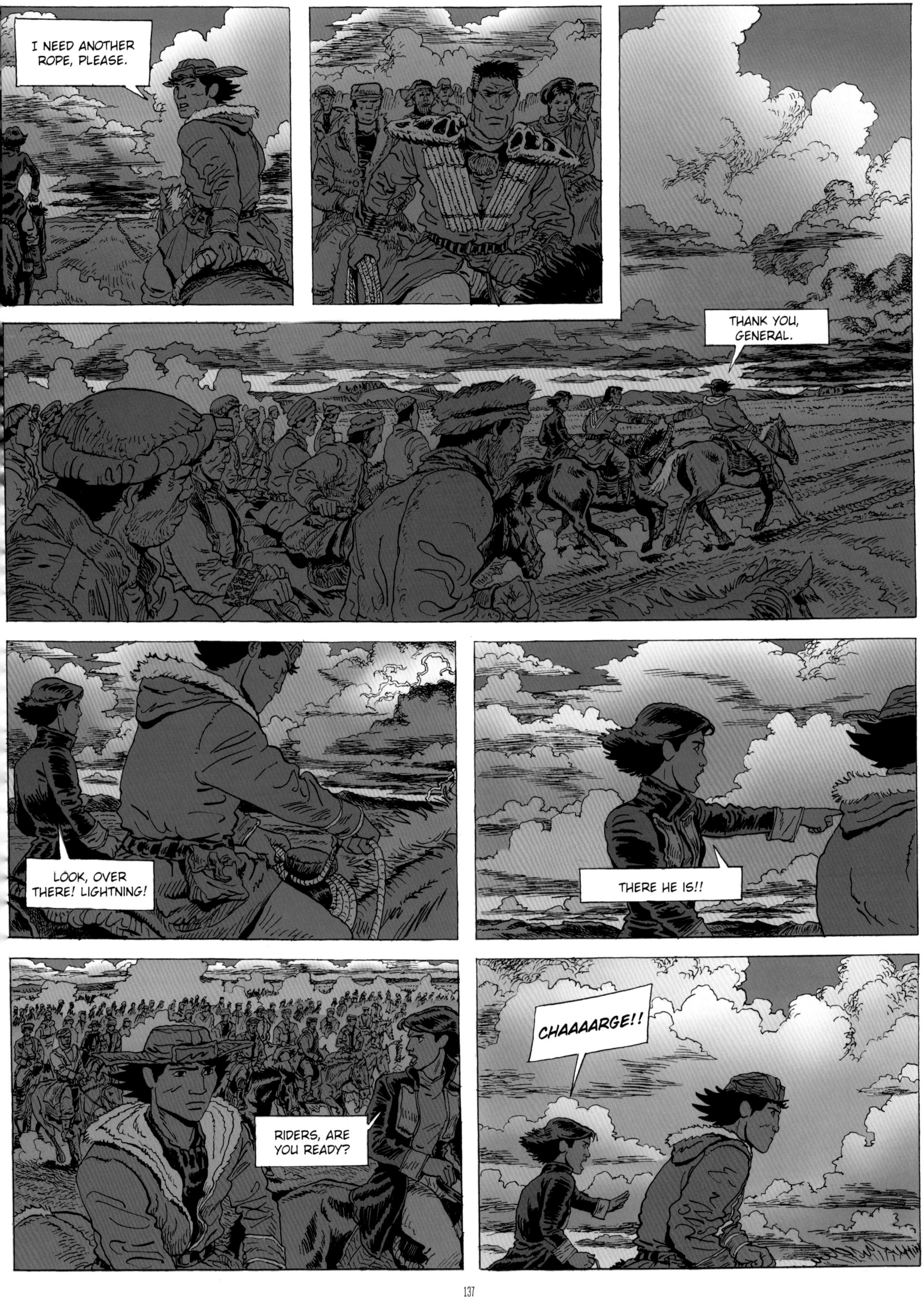

I NEED ANOTHER ROPE, PLEASE.
THANK YOU, GENERAL.
LOOK, OVER THERE! LIGHTNING!
THERE HE IS!!
RIDERS, ARE YOU READY?
CHAAAARGE!!

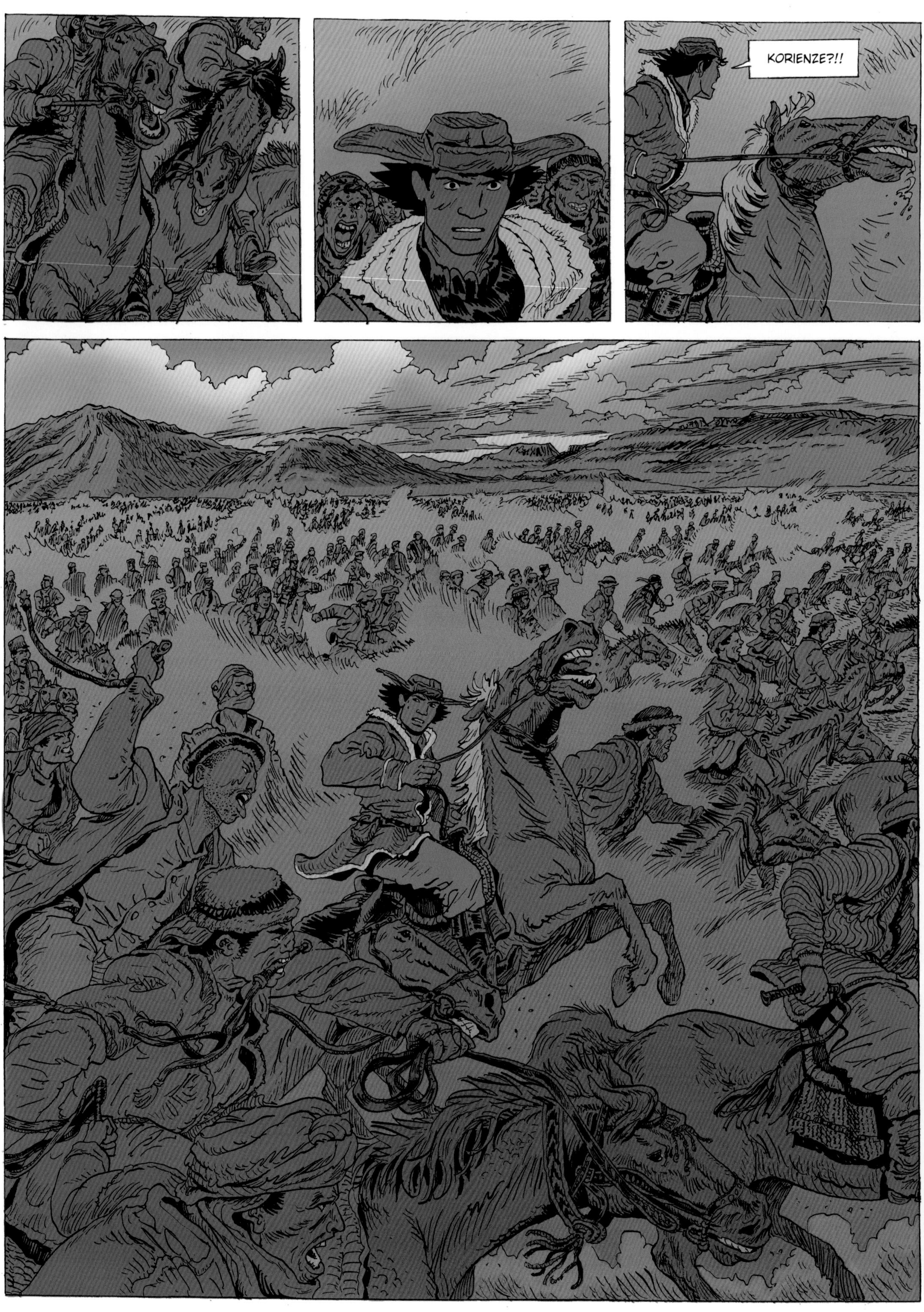
KORIENZE?!!

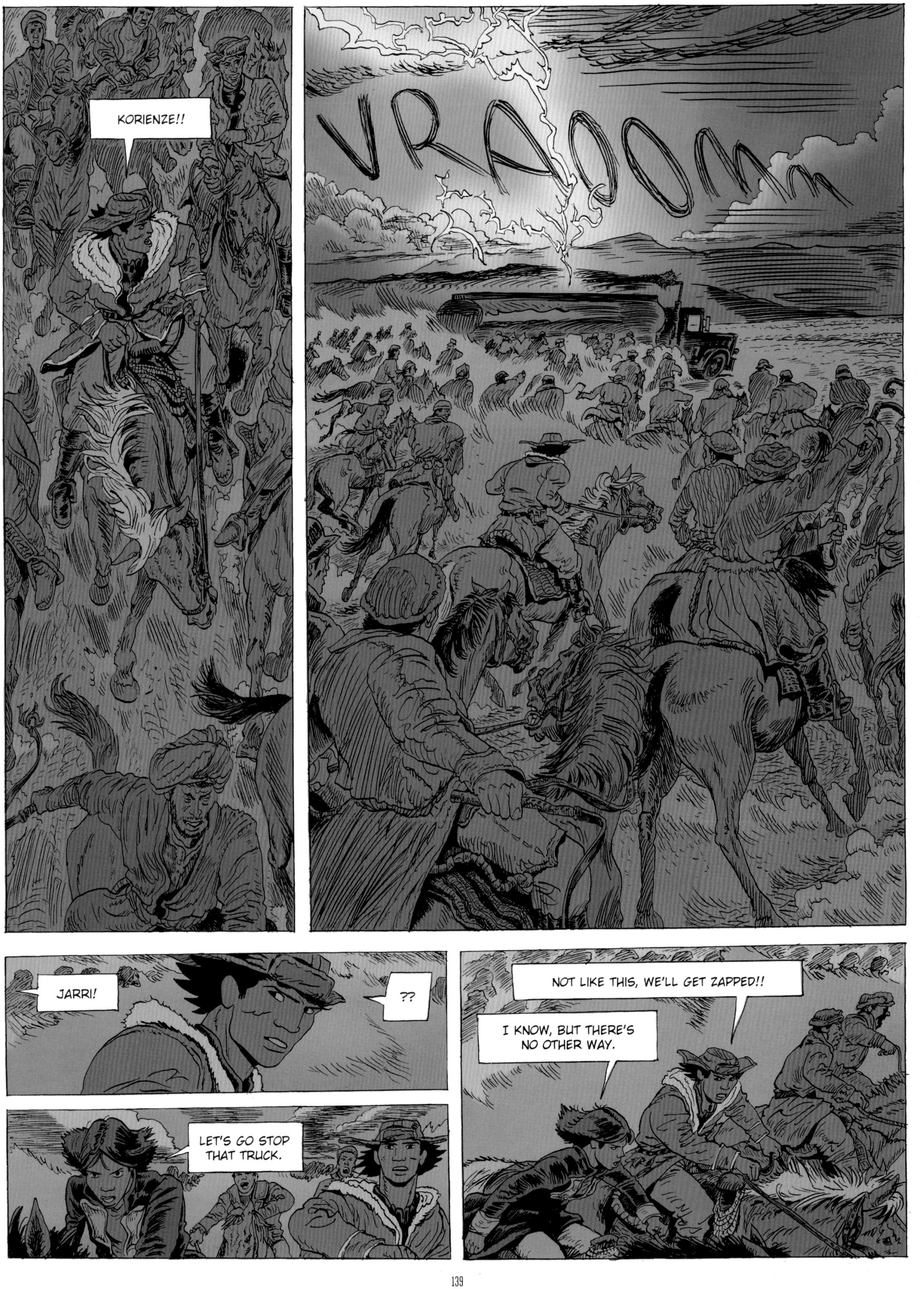
KORIENZE!!
VRAOOMM
JARRI!
??
LET'S GO STOP THAT TRUCK.
NOT LIKE THIS, WE'LL GET ZAPPED!!
I KNOW, BUT THERE'S NO OTHER WAY.

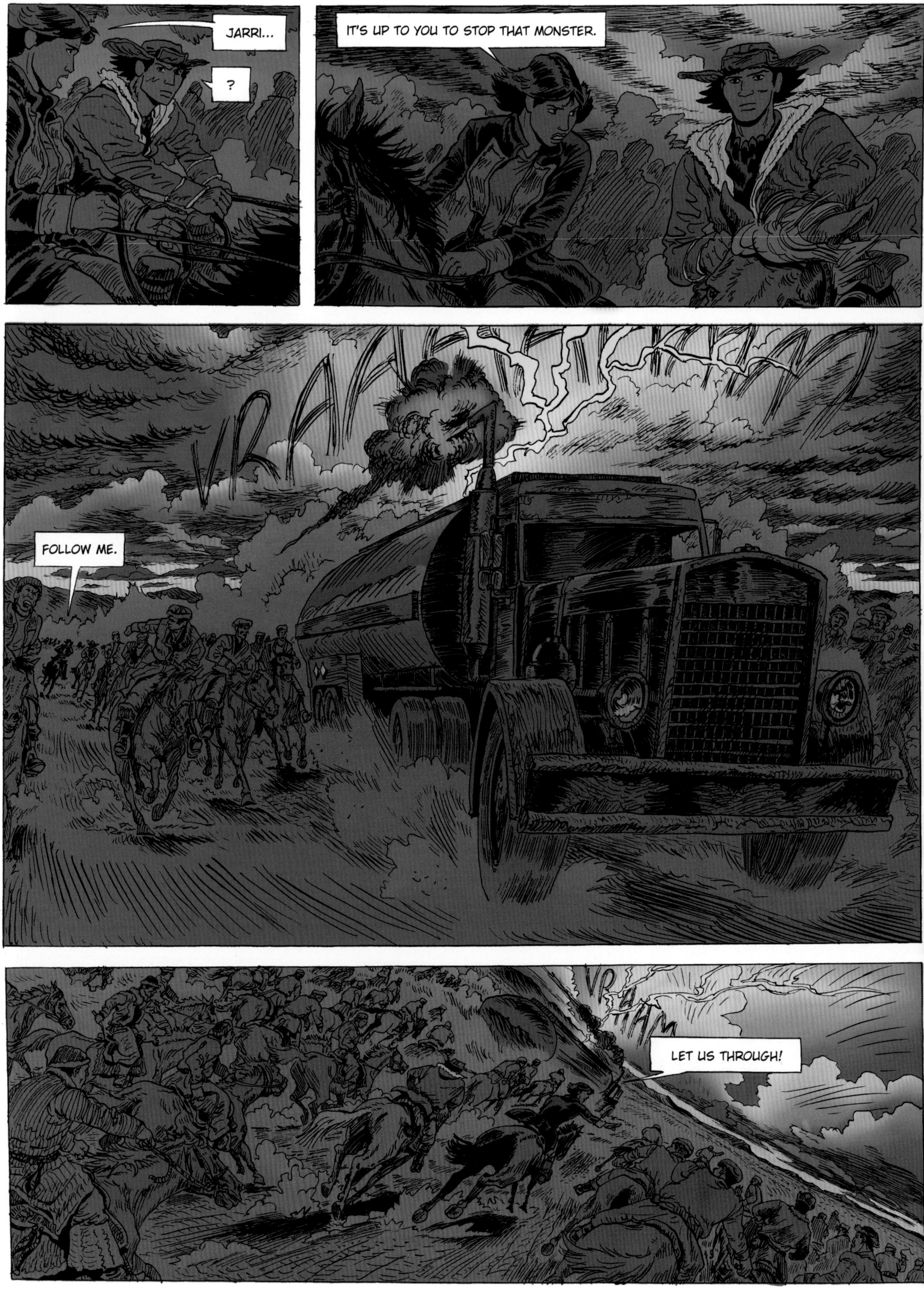
JARRI...
?
IT'S UP TO YOU TO STOP THAT MONSTER.
VRAAAAAAAAAAAAM
FOLLOW ME.
VRAAAM
LET US THROUGH!

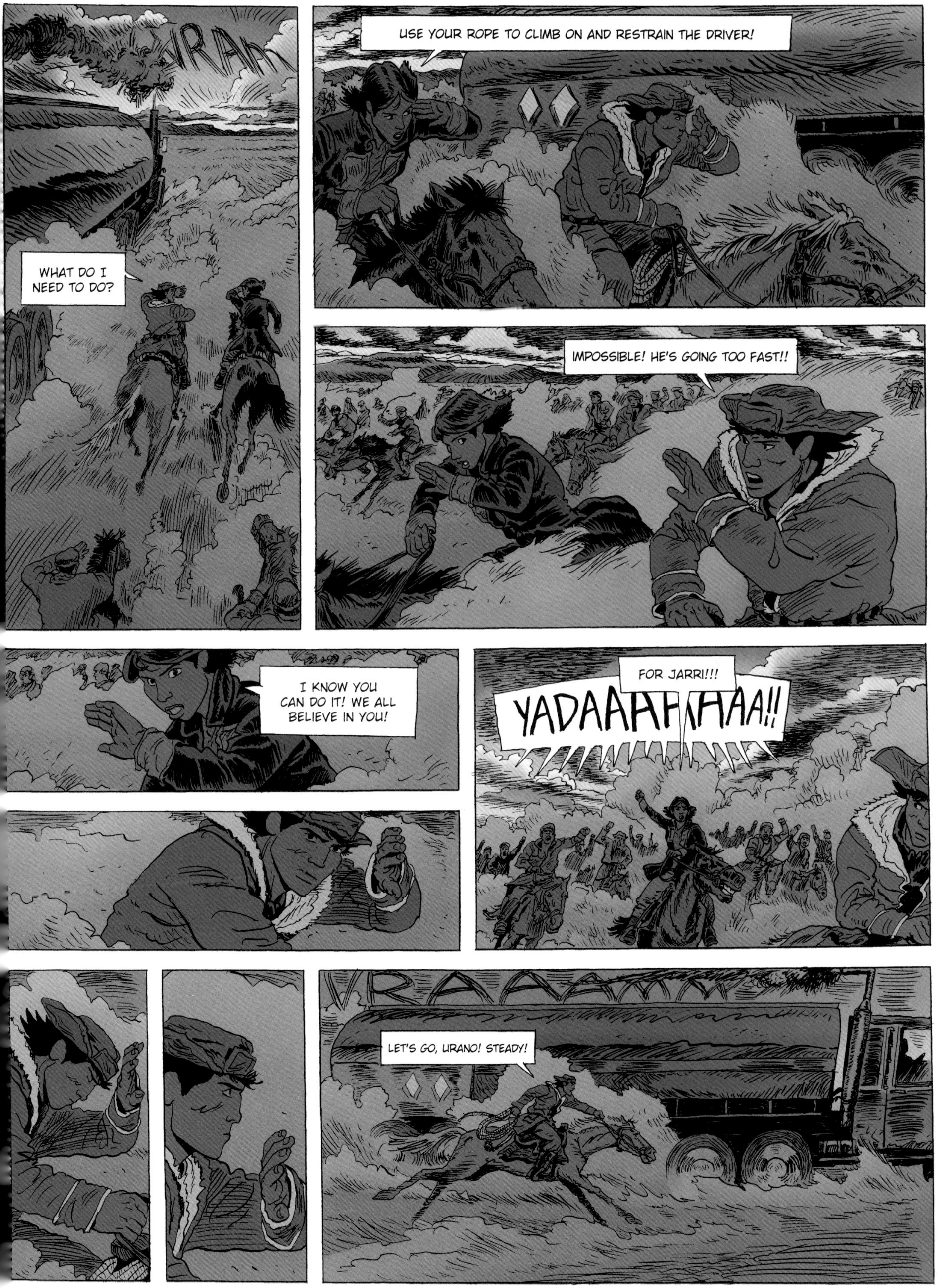
VRAM
WHAT DO I NEED TO DO?
USE YOUR ROPE TO CLIMB ON AND RESTRAIN THE DRIVER!
IMPOSSIBLE! HE'S GOING TOO FAST!!
I KNOW YOU CAN DO IT! WE ALL BELIEVE IN YOU!
FOR JARRI!!!
YADAAAHHHAA!!
VRAAAAMM
LET'S GO, URANO! STEADY!

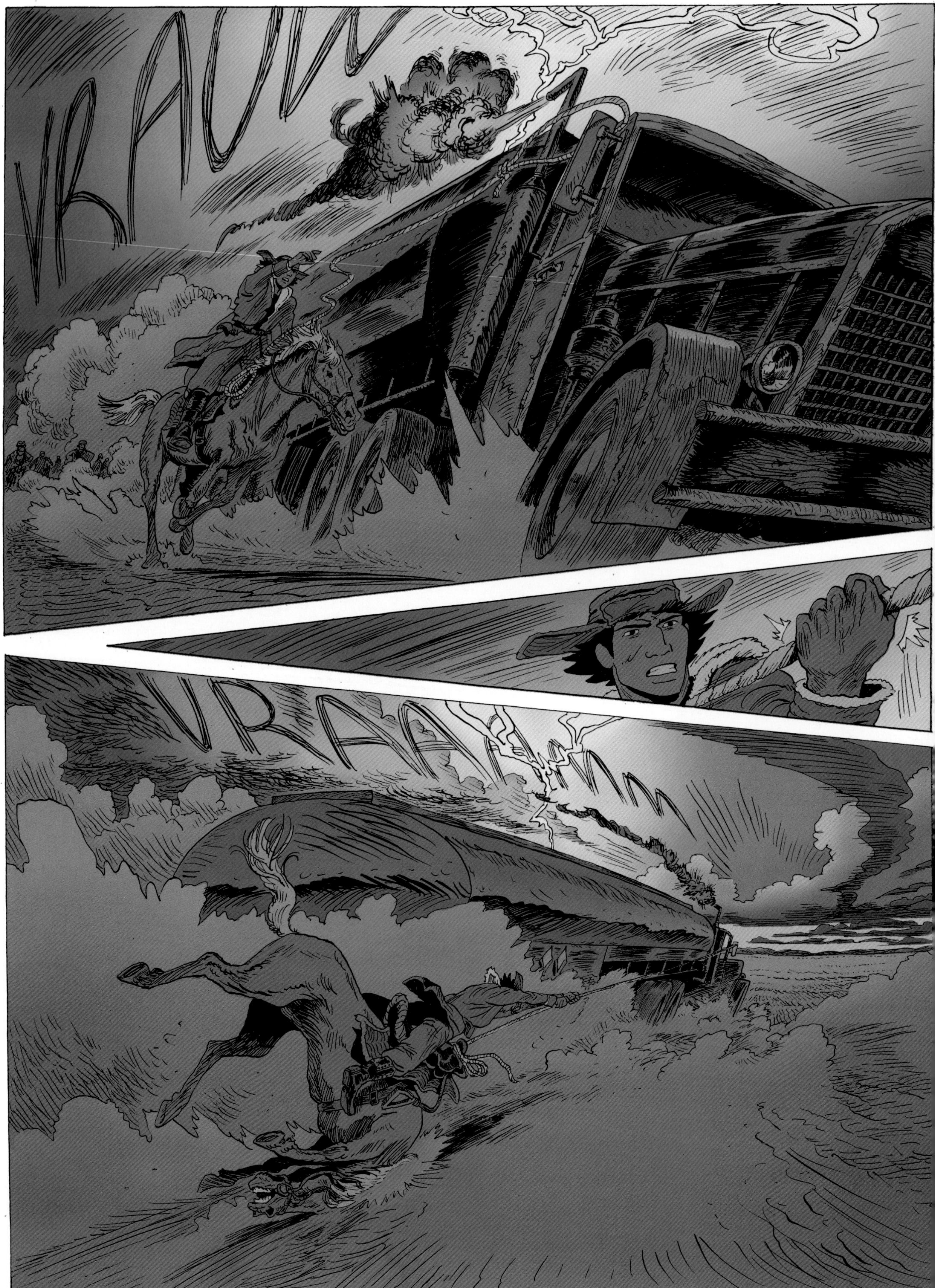
VRAUM
VRAAAMMM

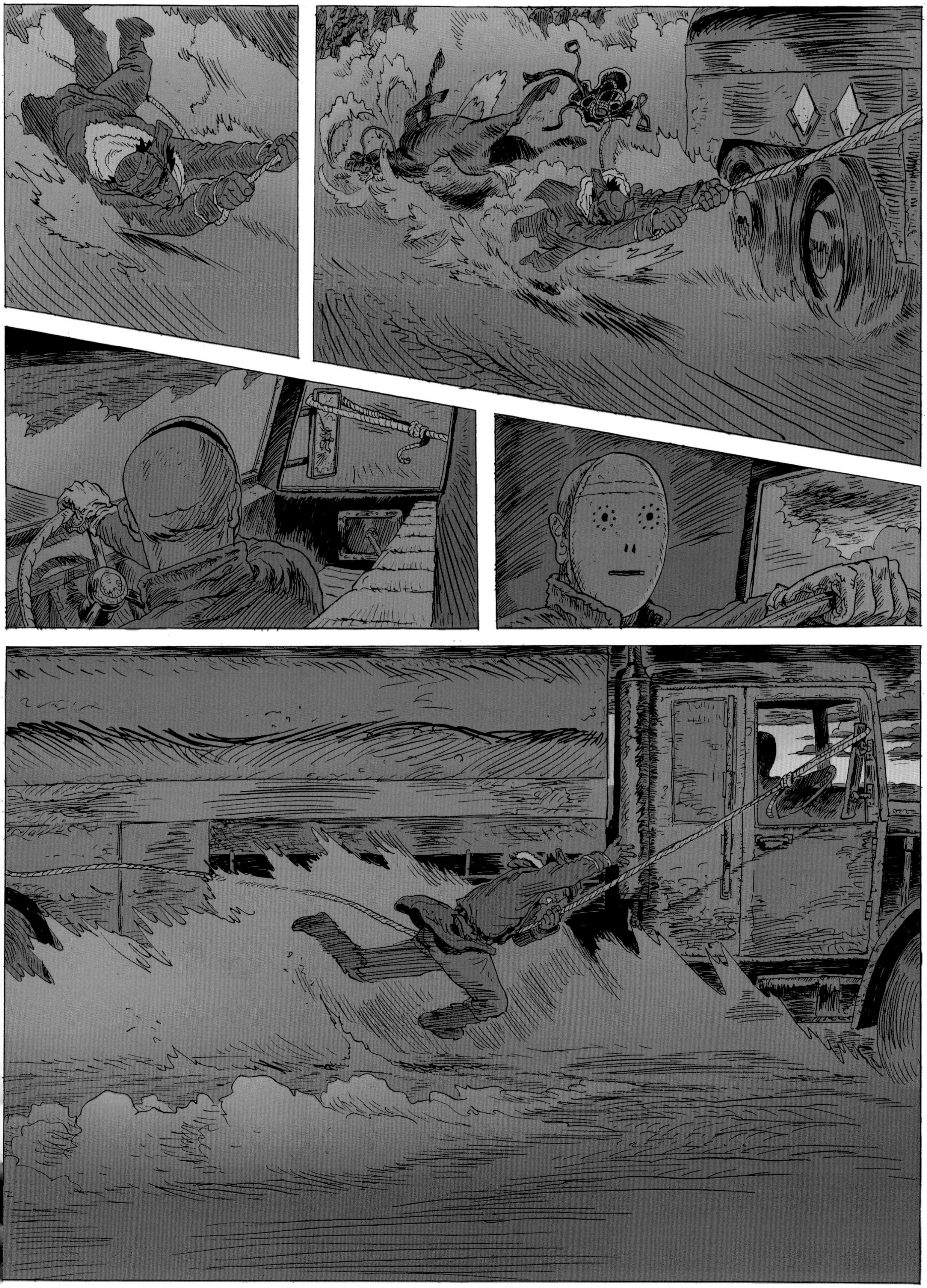

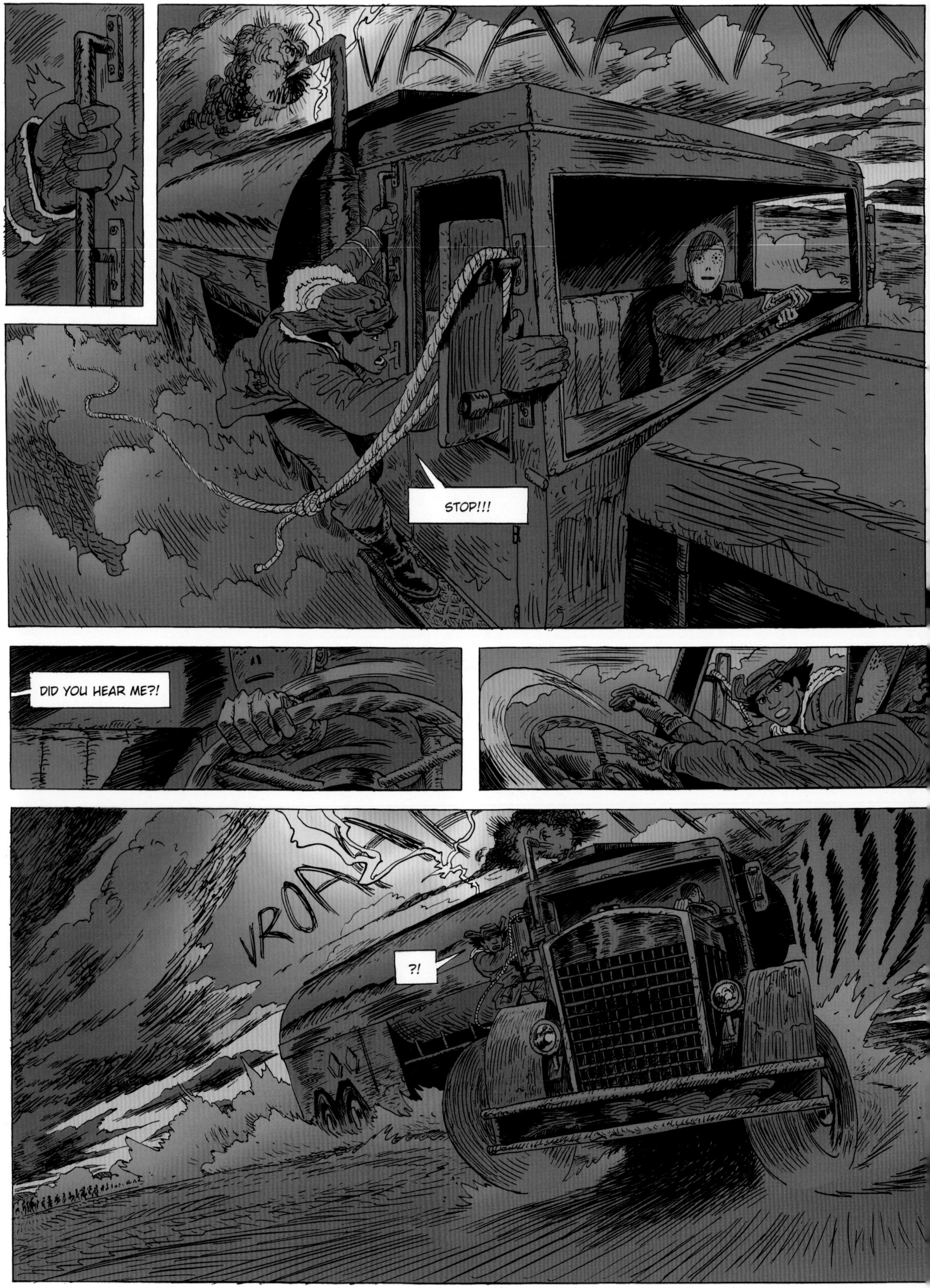
VRAAM
STOP!!!
DID YOU HEAR ME?!
VROA
?!

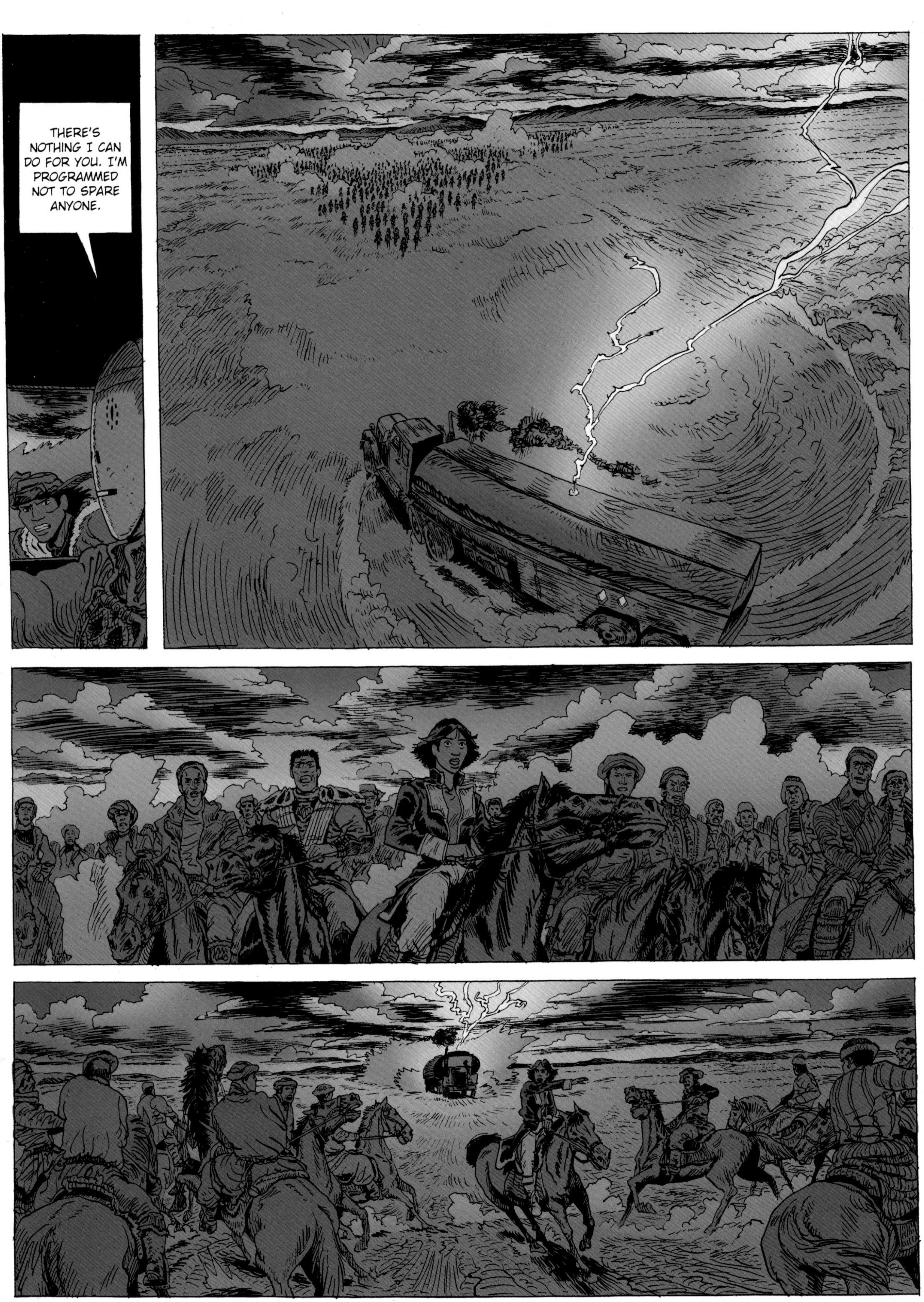
THERE'S NOTHING I CAN DO FOR YOU. I'M PROGRAMMED NOT TO SPARE ANYONE.

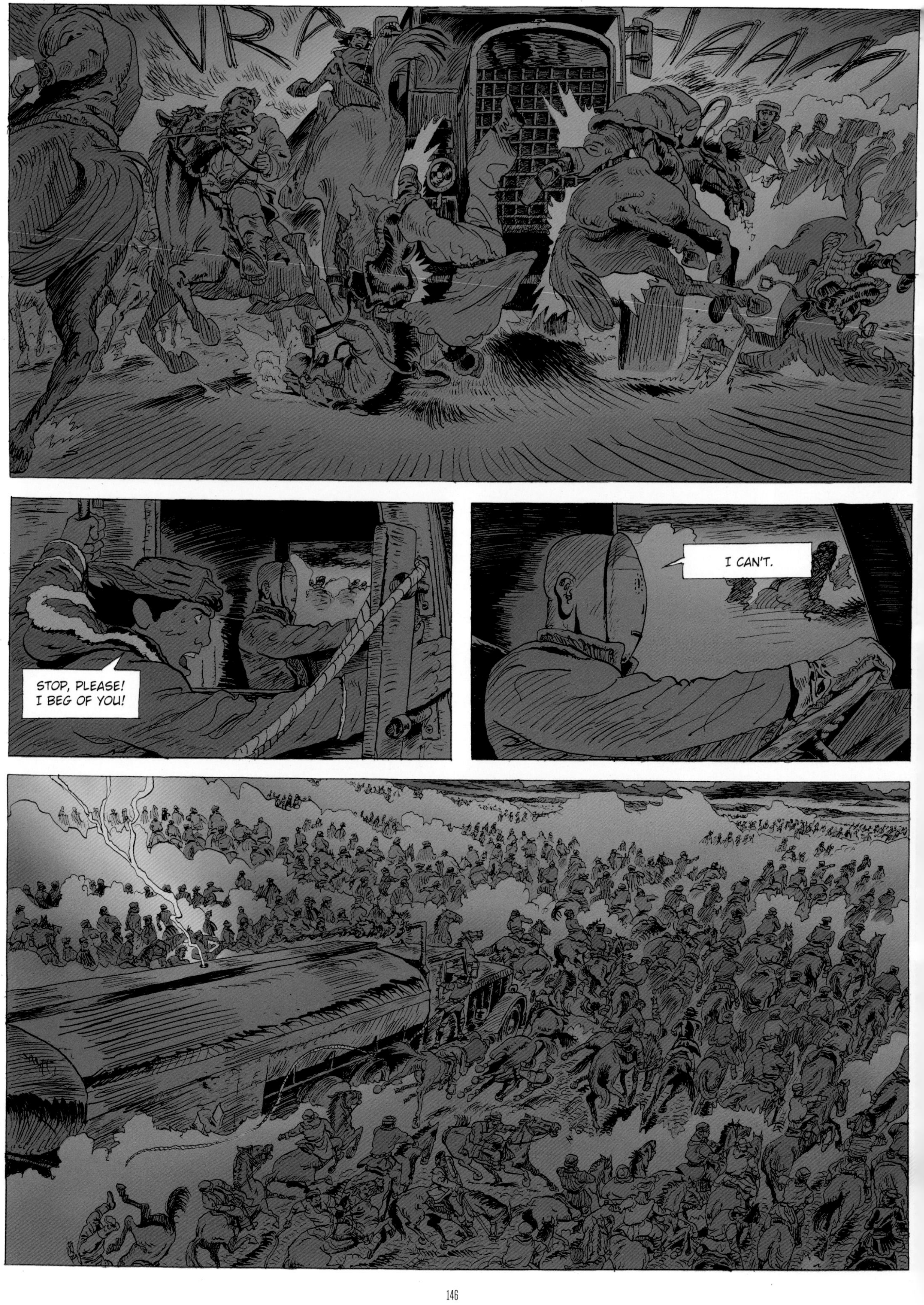
VRA HAAM
STOP, PLEASE! I BEG OF YOU!
I CAN'T.

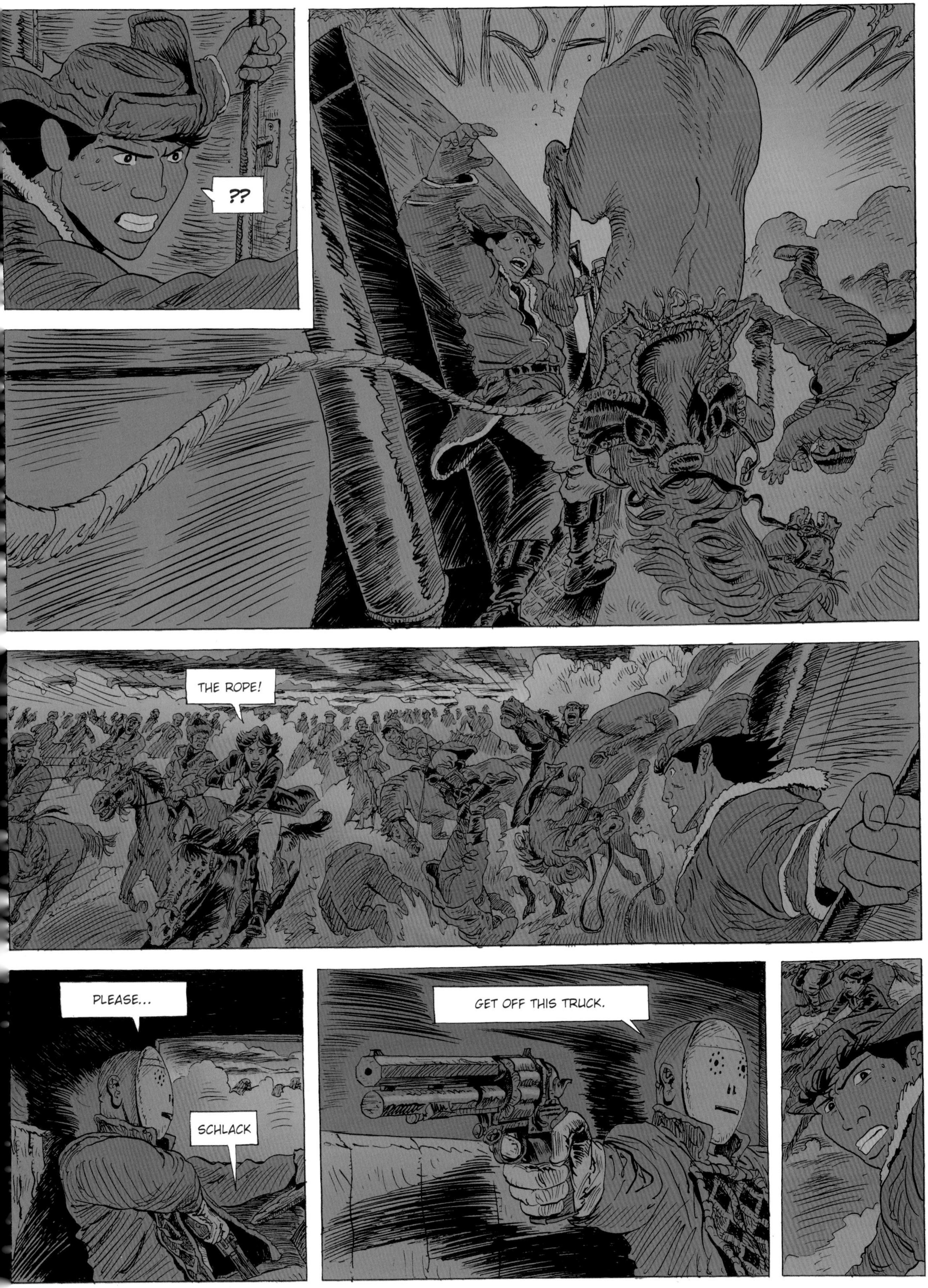
??
VRAM
THE ROPE!
PLEASE...
SCHLACK
GET OFF THIS TRUCK.

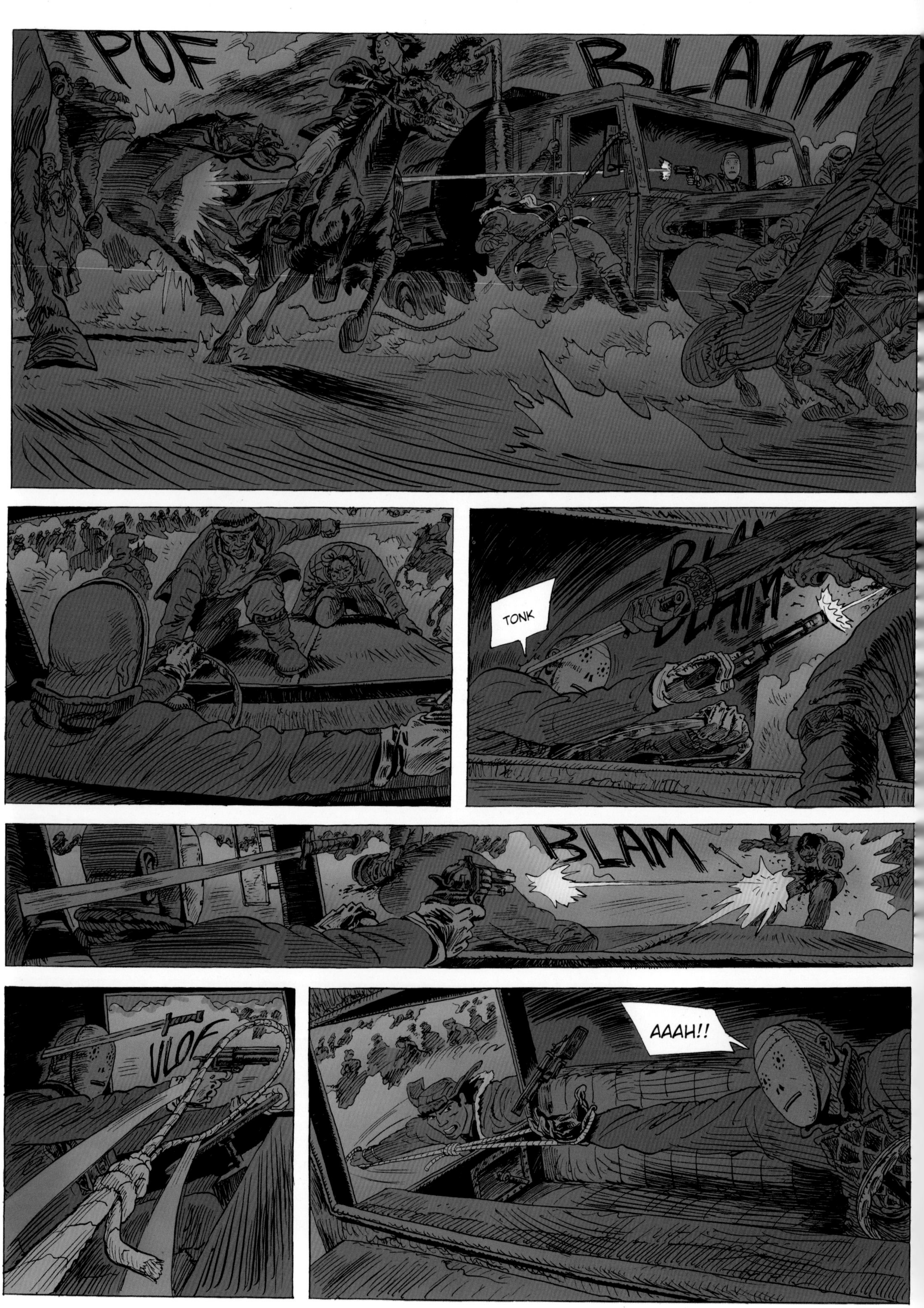
POF
BLAM
TONK
BLAM
BLAM
VLOF
AAAH!!

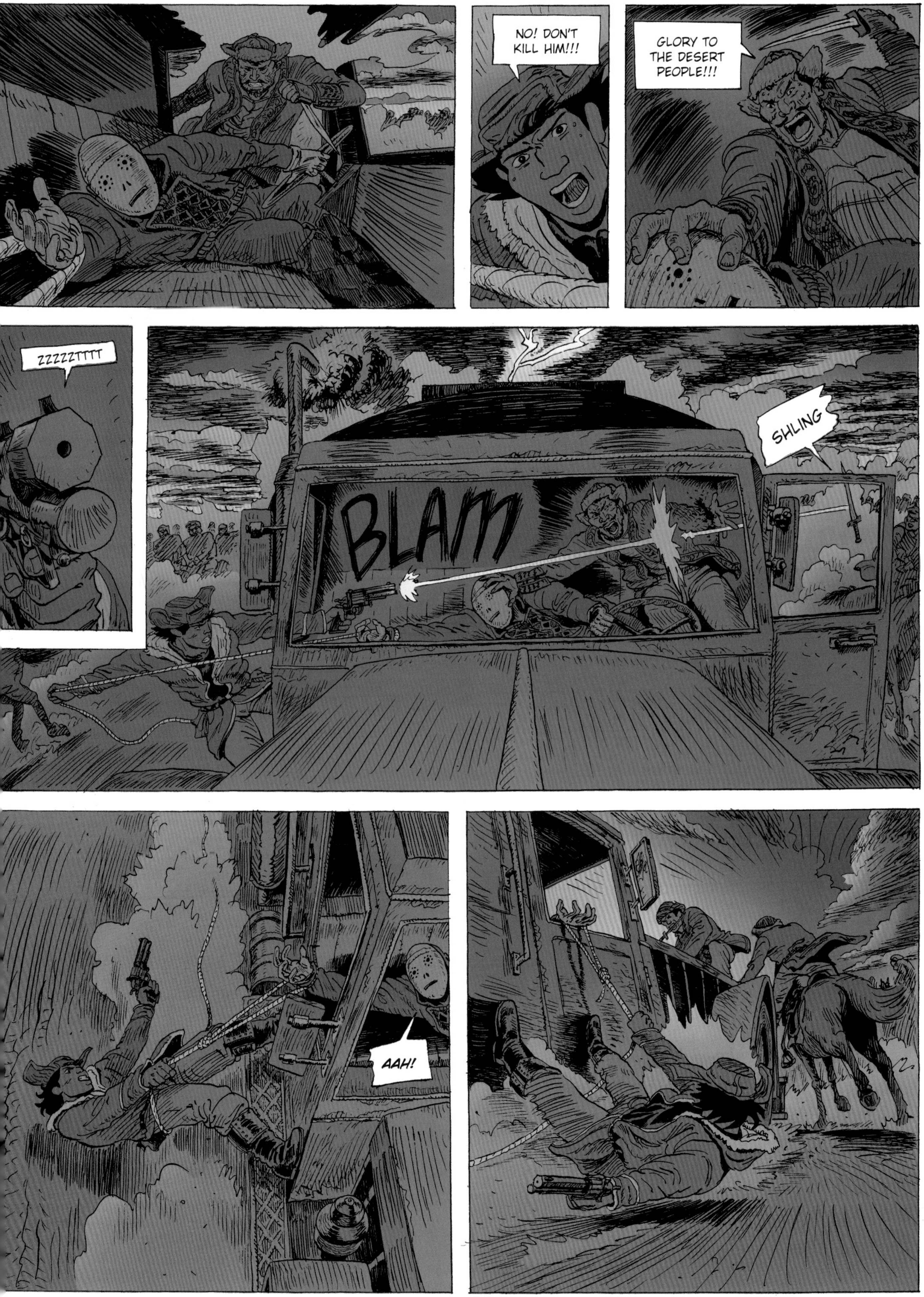
NO! DON'T KILL HIM!!!
GLORY TO THE DESERT PEOPLE!!!
ZZZZZTTTT
SHLING
BLAM
AAH!

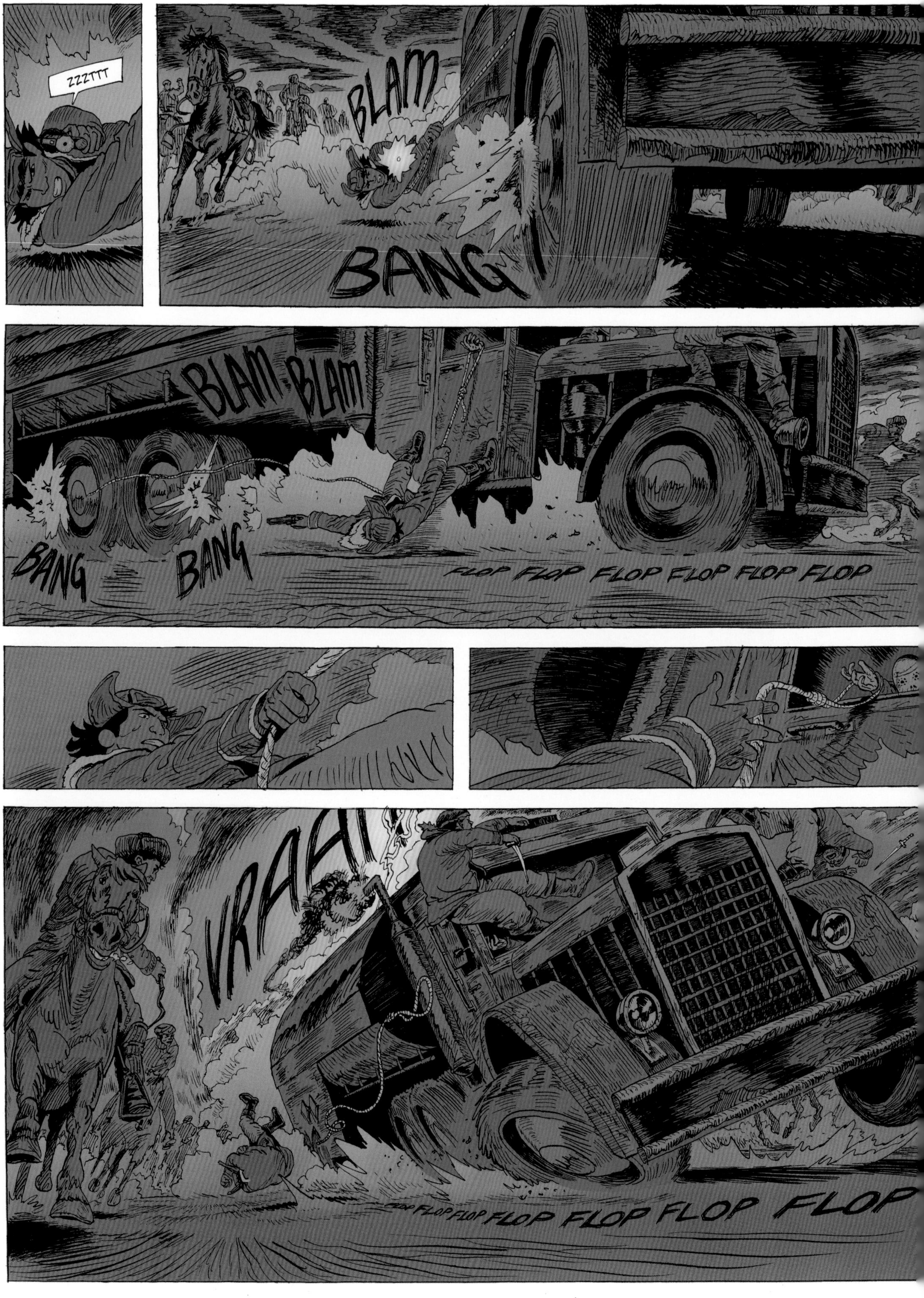
ZZZTTT
BLAM
BANG
BLAM BLAM
BANG
BANG
FLOP FLOP FLOP FLOP FLOP FLOP
VRAAA
FLOP FLOP FLOP FLOP FLOP FLOP FLOP

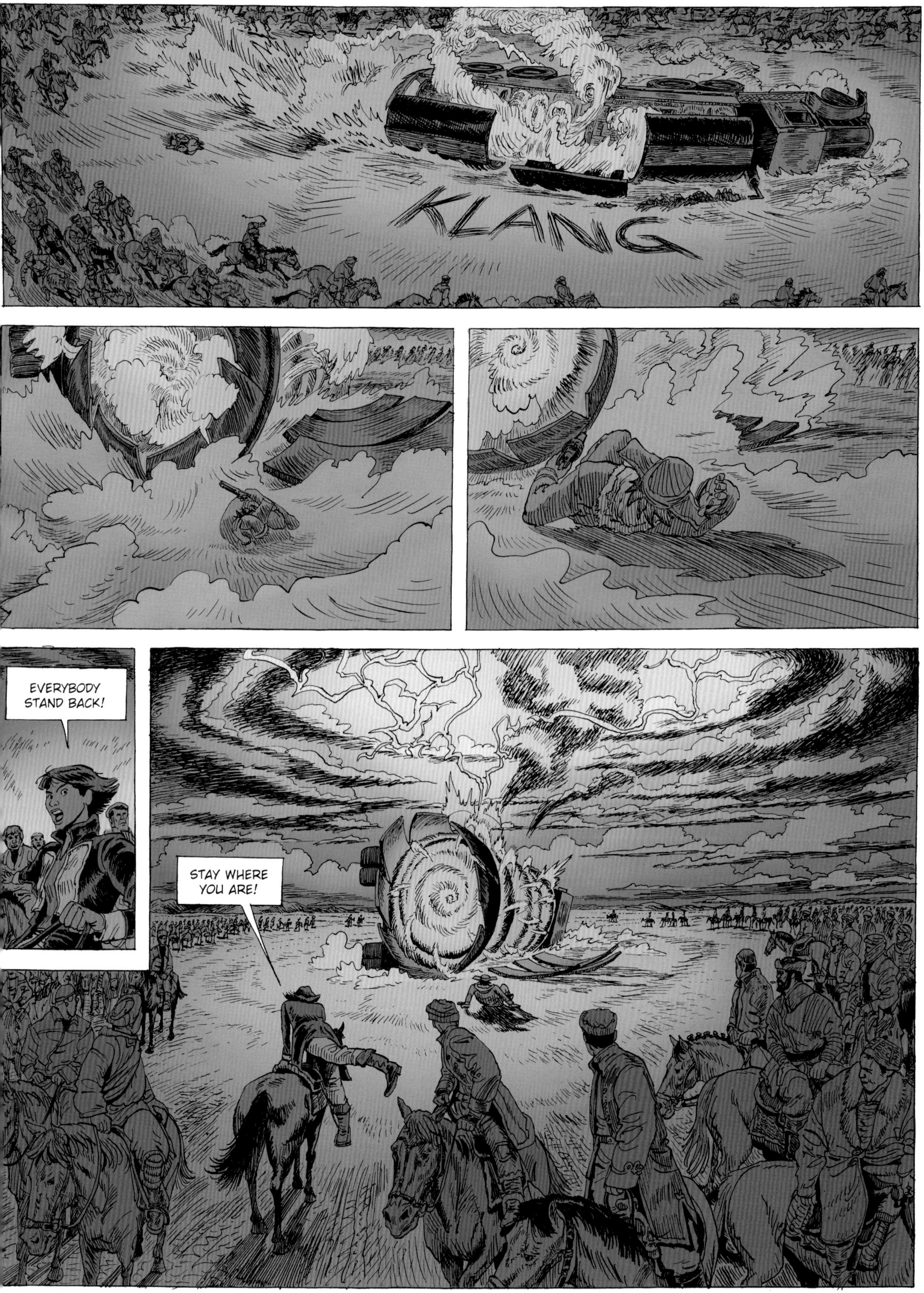
KLANG
EVERYBODY STAND BACK!
STAY WHERE YOU ARE!

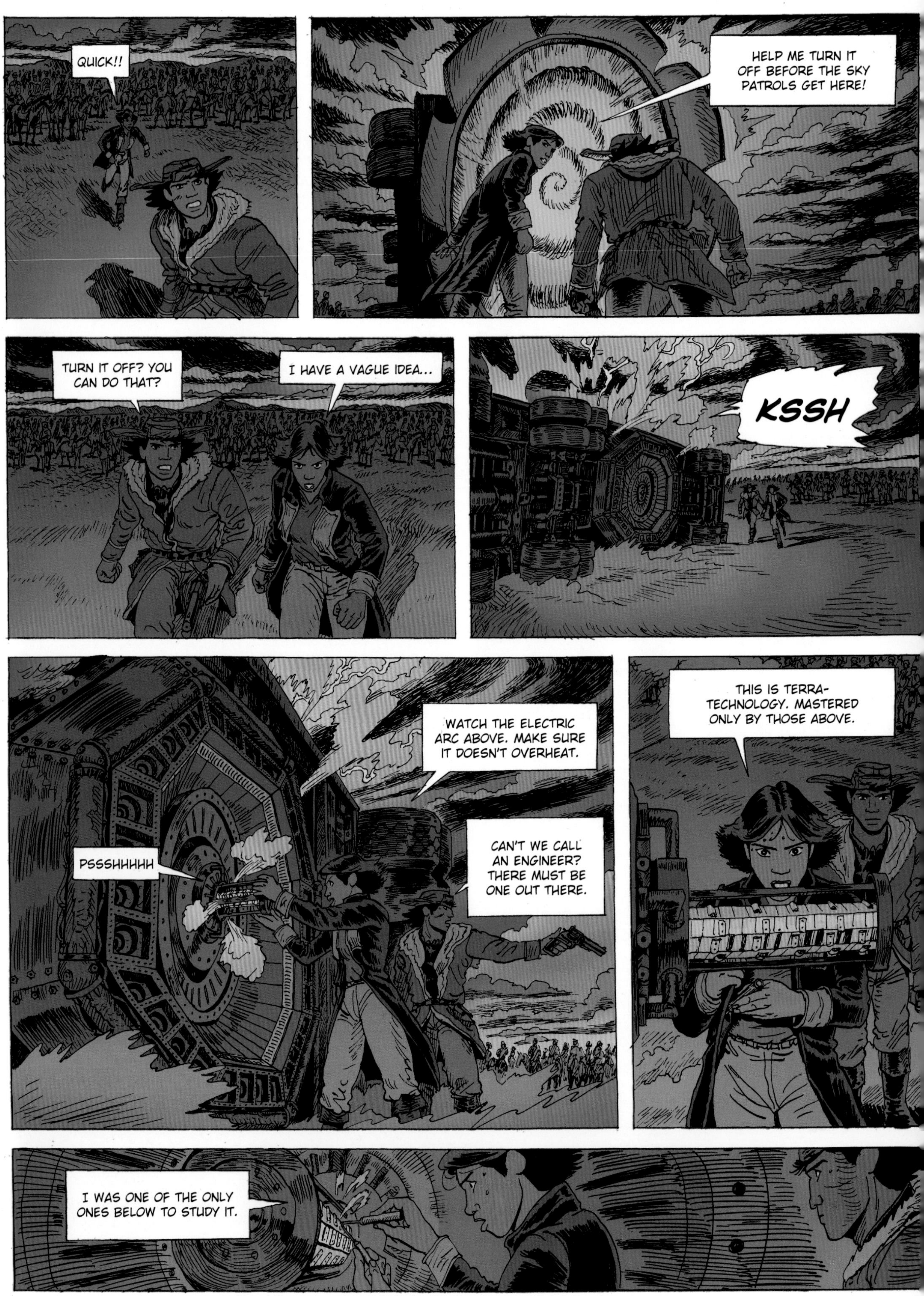
QUICK!!
HELP ME TURN IT OFF BEFORE THE SKY PATROLS GET HERE!
TURN IT OFF? YOU CAN DO THAT?
I HAVE A VAGUE IDEA...
KSSH
WATCH THE ELECTRIC ARC ABOVE. MAKE SURE IT DOESN'T OVERHEAT.
PSSSHHHHH
CAN'T WE CALL AN ENGINEER? THERE MUST BE ONE OUT THERE.
THIS IS TERRA-TECHNOLOGY. MASTERED ONLY BY THOSE ABOVE.
I WAS ONE OF THE ONLY ONES BELOW TO STUDY IT.

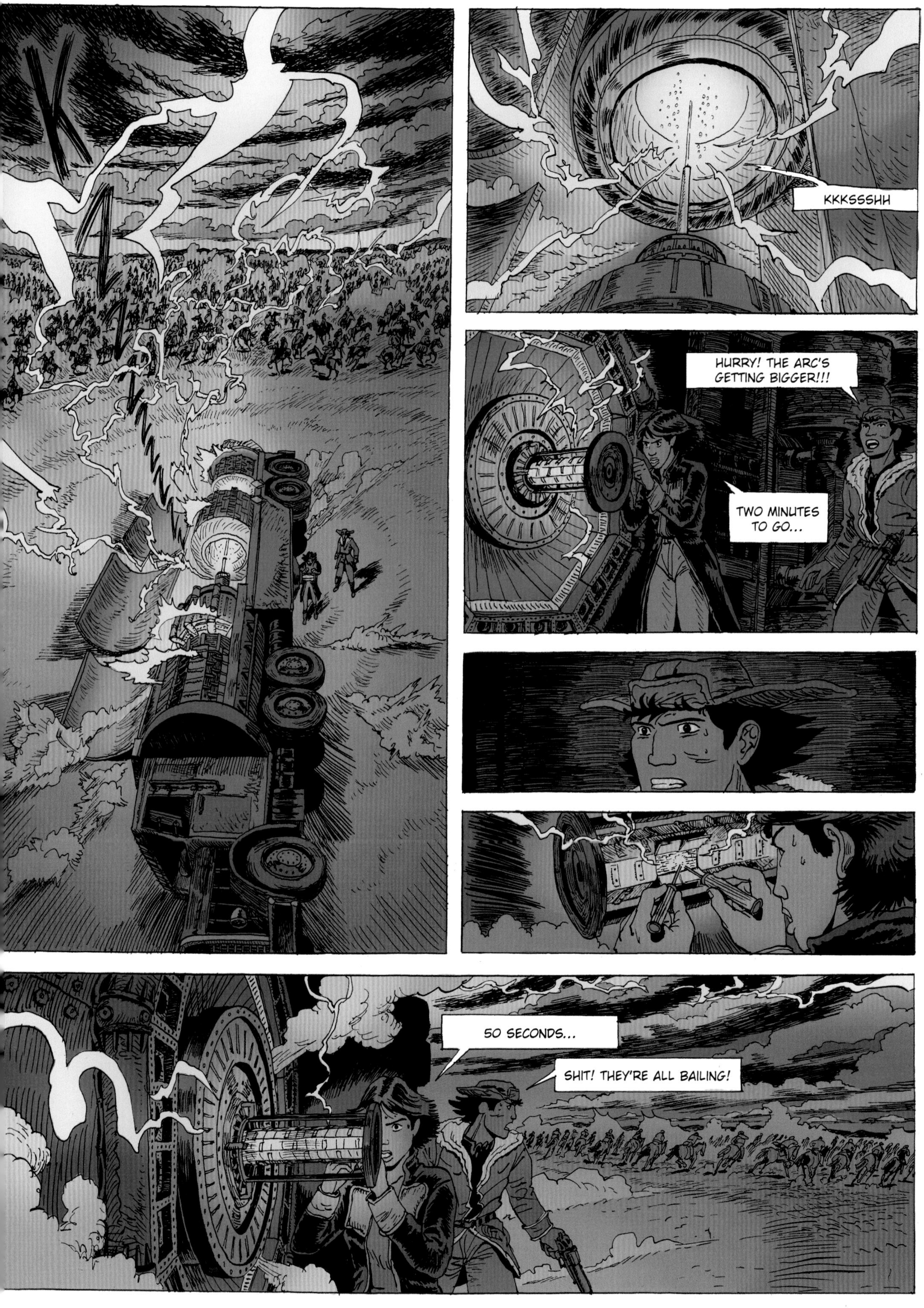

KKKSSSHH
HURRY! THE ARC'S GETTING BIGGER!!!
TWO MINUTES TO GO...
50 SECONDS...
SHIT! THEY'RE ALL BAILING!

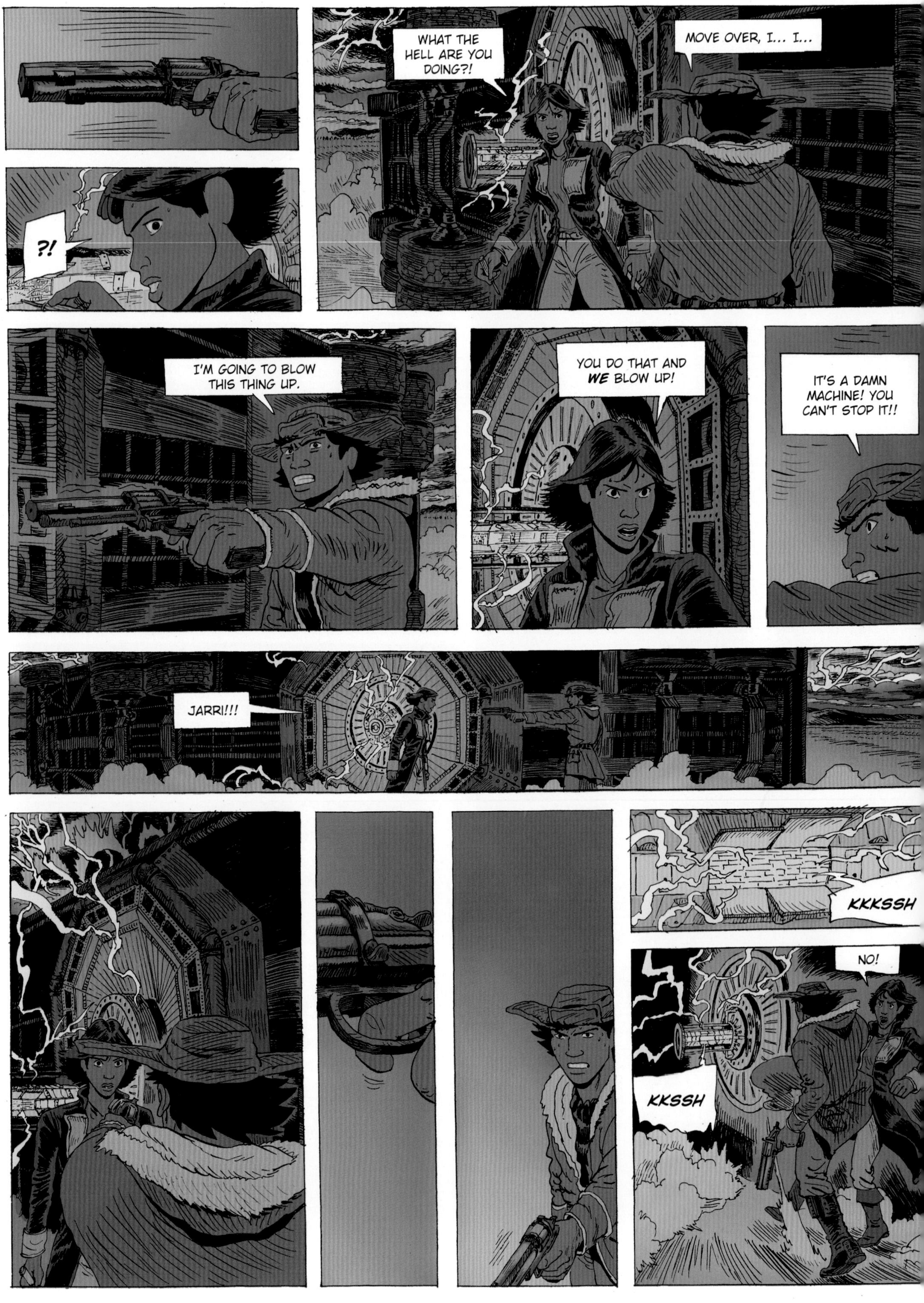
?!
WHAT THE HELL ARE YOU DOING?!
MOVE OVER, I... I...
I'M GOING TO BLOW THIS THING UP.
YOU DO THAT AND WE BLOW UP!
IT'S A DAMN MACHINE! YOU CAN'T STOP IT!!
JARRI!!!
KKKSSH
NO!
KKSSH

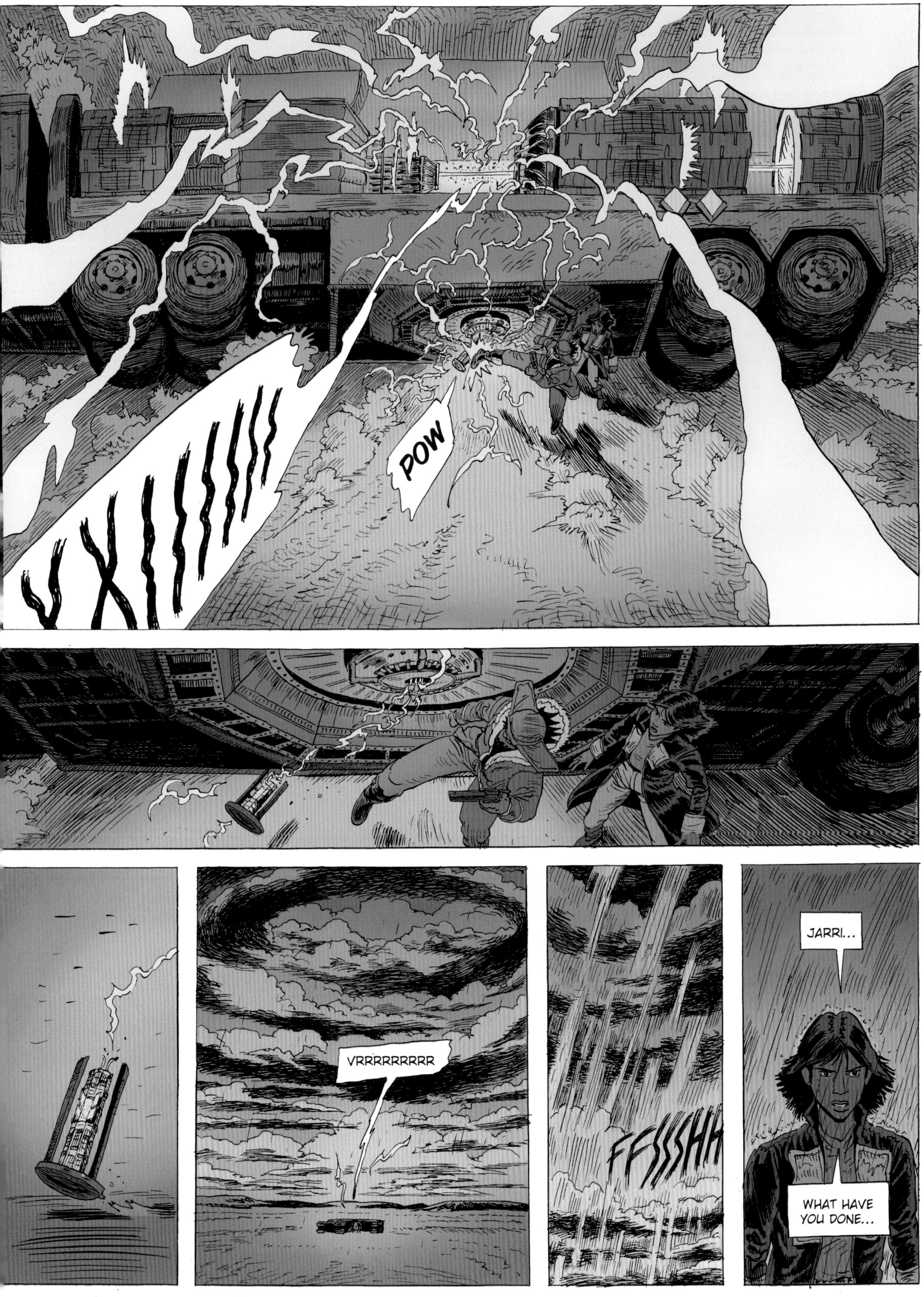
VXIIIIIII
POW
VRRRRRRRRR
FFSSSHH
JARRI...
WHAT HAVE YOU DONE...

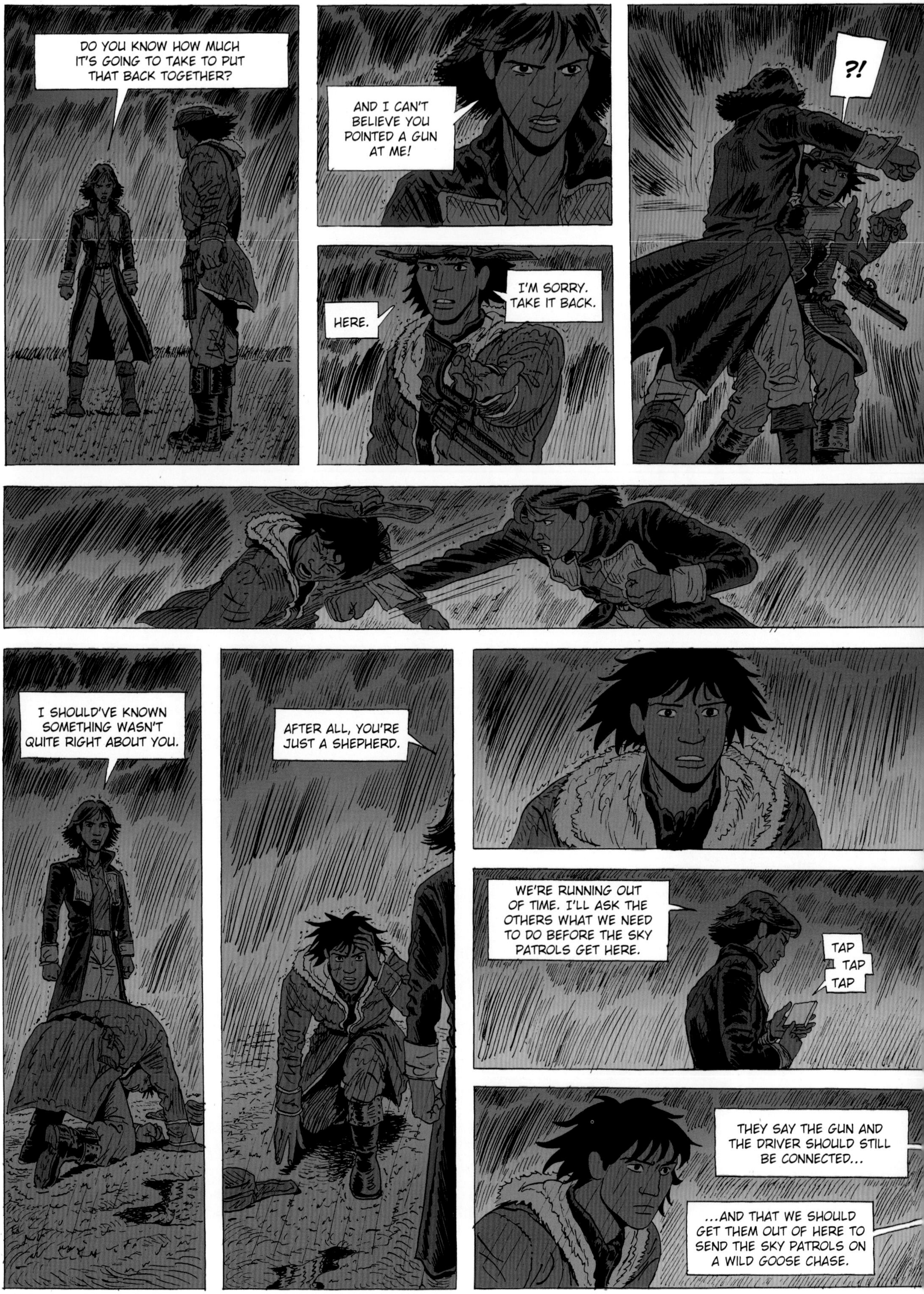
DO YOU KNOW HOW MUCH IT'S GOING TO TAKE TO PUT THAT BACK TOGETHER?
AND I CAN'T BELIEVE YOU POINTED A GUN AT ME!
HERE.
I'M SORRY. TAKE IT BACK.
?!
I SHOULD'VE KNOWN SOMETHING WASN'T QUITE RIGHT ABOUT YOU.
AFTER ALL, YOU'RE JUST A SHEPHERD.
WE'RE RUNNING OUT OF TIME. I'LL ASK THE OTHERS WHAT WE NEED TO DO BEFORE THE SKY PATROLS GET HERE.
TAP
TAP
TAP
THEY SAY THE GUN AND THE DRIVER SHOULD STILL BE CONNECTED...
...AND THAT WE SHOULD GET THEM OUT OF HERE TO SEND THE SKY PATROLS ON A WILD GOOSE CHASE.

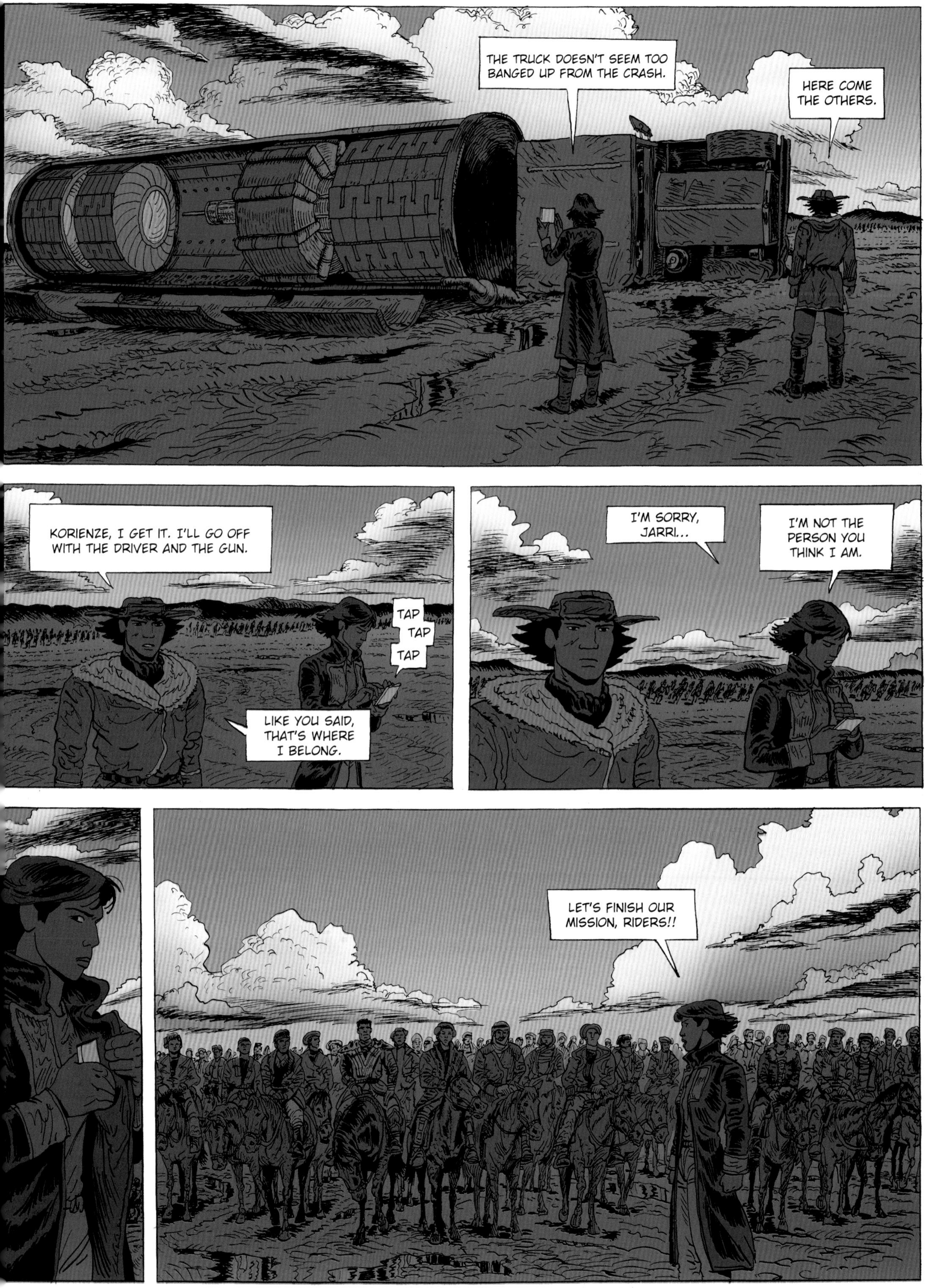

THE TRUCK DOESN'T SEEM TOO BANGED UP FROM THE CRASH.
HERE COME THE OTHERS.
KORIENZE, I GET IT. I'LL GO OFF WITH THE DRIVER AND THE GUN.
TAP
TAP
TAP
LIKE YOU SAID, THAT'S WHERE I BELONG.
I'M SORRY, JARRI...
I'M NOT THE PERSON YOU THINK I AM.
LET'S FINISH OUR MISSION, RIDERS!!

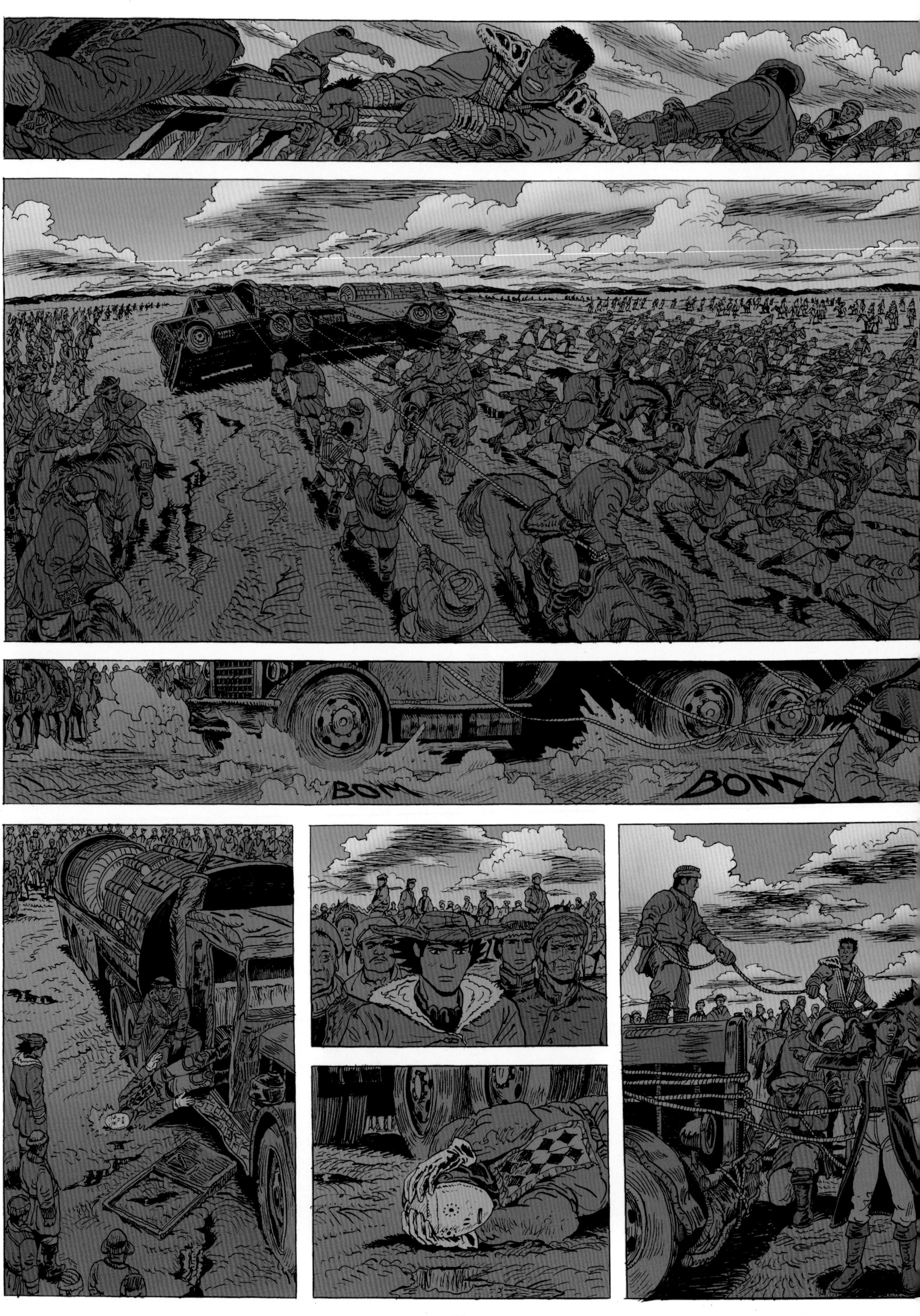
BOM
BOM

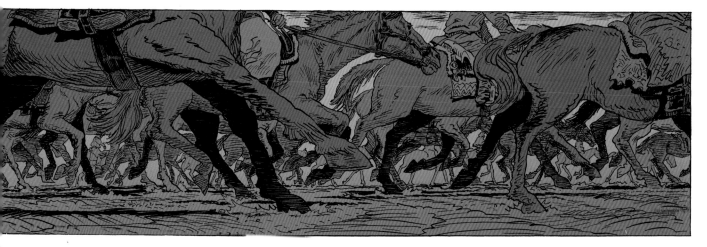

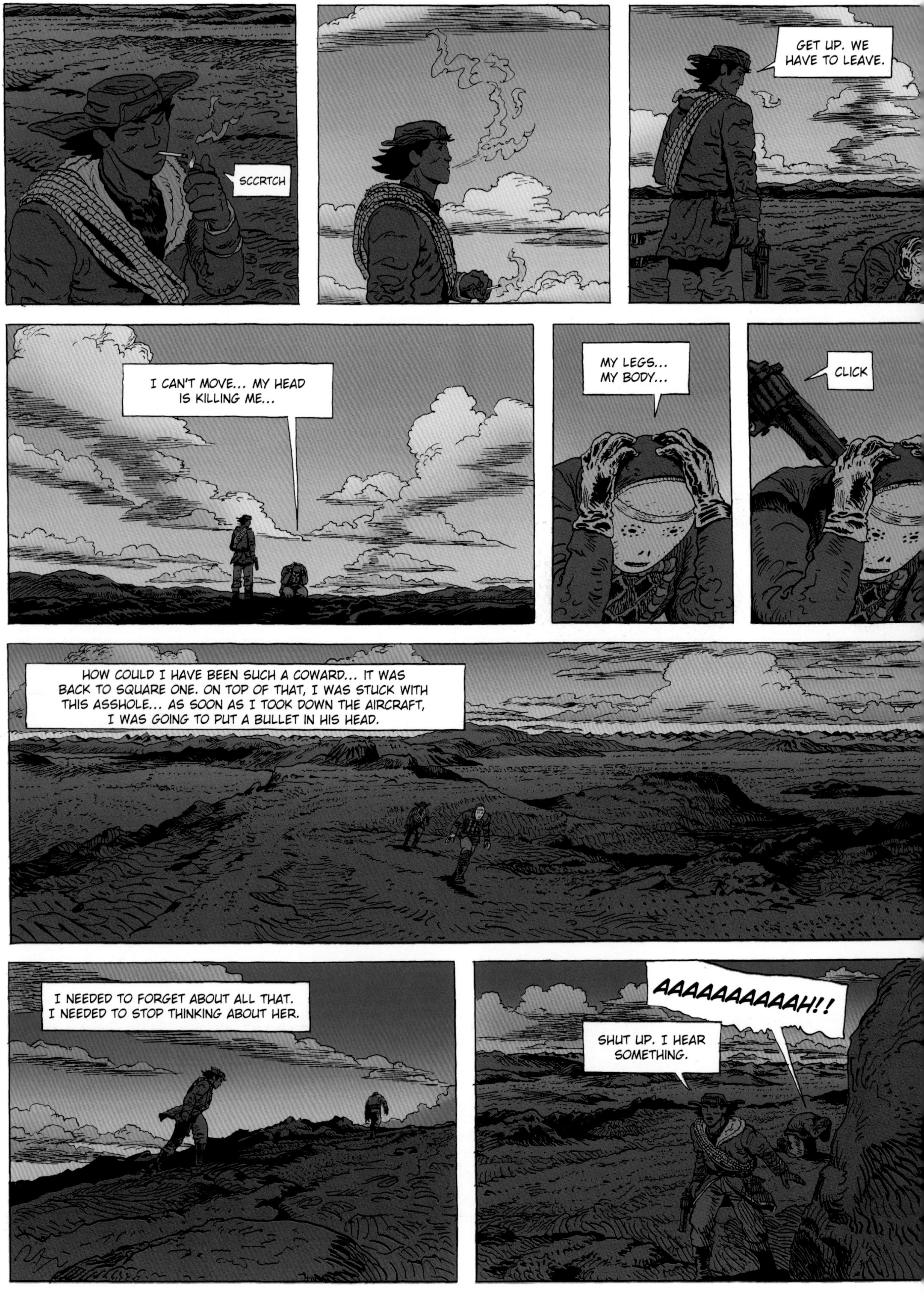
SCCRTCH
GET UP. WE HAVE TO LEAVE.
I CAN'T MOVE... MY HEAD IS KILLING ME...
MY LEGS... MY BODY...
CLICK
HOW COULD I HAVE BEEN SUCH A COWARD... IT WAS BACK TO SQUARE ONE. ON TOP OF THAT, I WAS STUCK WITH THIS ASSHOLE... AS SOON AS I TOOK DOWN THE AIRCRAFT, I WAS GOING TO PUT A BULLET IN HIS HEAD.
I NEEDED TO FORGET ABOUT ALL THAT. I NEEDED TO STOP THINKING ABOUT HER.
AAAAAAAAAAH!!
SHUT UP. I HEAR SOMETHING.

THE SIGNAL'S GETTING CLOSER. STILL NO VISUAL ON THE TRUCK THOUGH.
OVER HERE, GUYS.
DOWN THERE!!
NEXT TO THE BIG ROCK!!
BLAM
BLAM
BLAM
BOM
BOM
BLAM
BLAM

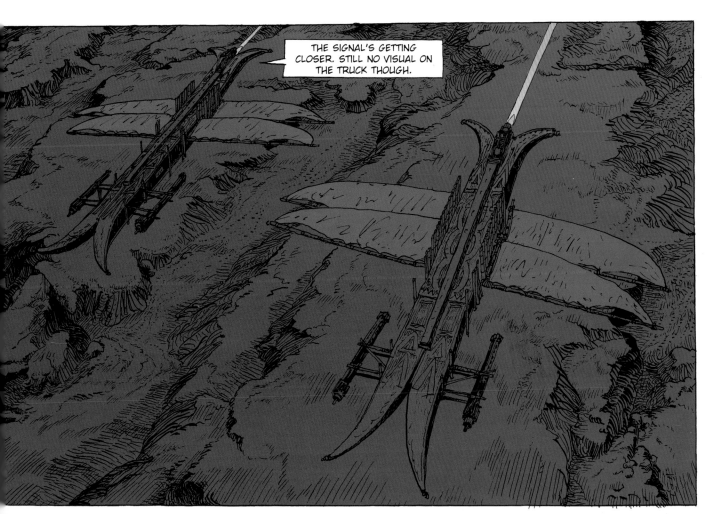

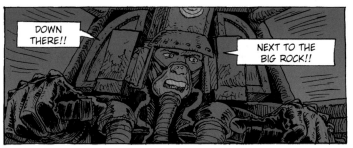

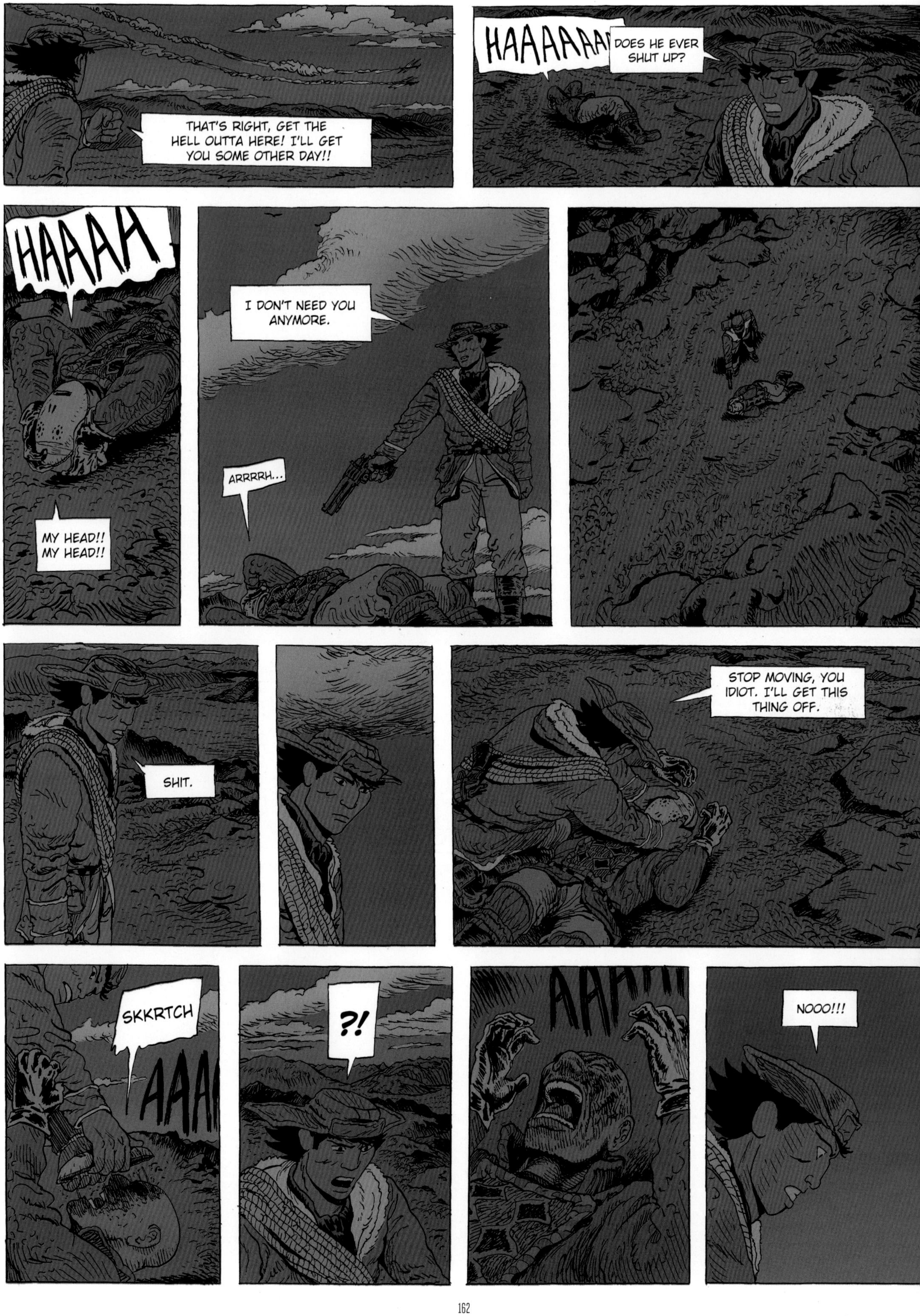

THAT'S RIGHT, GET THE HELL OUTTA HERE! I'LL GET YOU SOME OTHER DAY!!
HAAAAAA
DOES HE EVER SHUT UP?
HAAAH
MY HEAD!! MY HEAD!!
I DON'T NEED YOU ANYMORE.
ARRRRH...
SHIT.
STOP MOVING, YOU IDIOT. I'LL GET THIS THING OFF.
SKKRTCH
AAA
?!
AAH
NOOO!!!

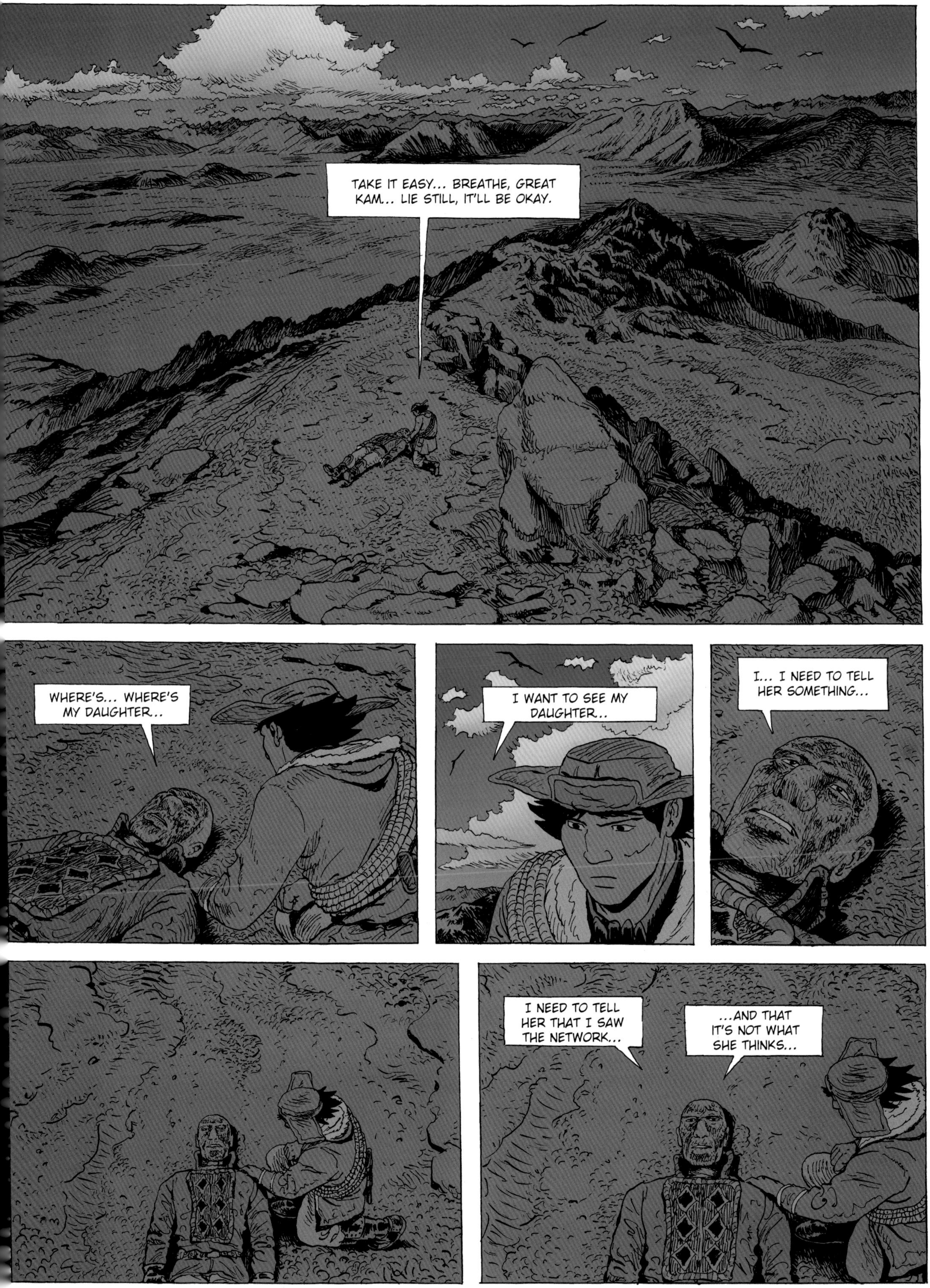
TAKE IT EASY... BREATHE, GREAT KAM... LIE STILL, IT'LL BE OKAY.
WHERE'S... WHERE'S MY DAUGHTER..
I WANT TO SEE MY DAUGHTER..
I... I NEED TO TELL HER SOMETHING...
I NEED TO TELL HER THAT I SAW THE NETWORK...
...AND THAT IT'S NOT WHAT SHE THINKS...

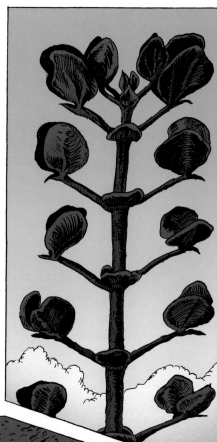

UP THERE IN THE NETWORK TOWER... THERE ARE PLANTS... THOUSANDS... OF BEAUTIFUL PLANTS...

AND DESPITE THE TORTURE... BEFORE I WAS ERASED... I UNDERSTOOD SOMETHING...

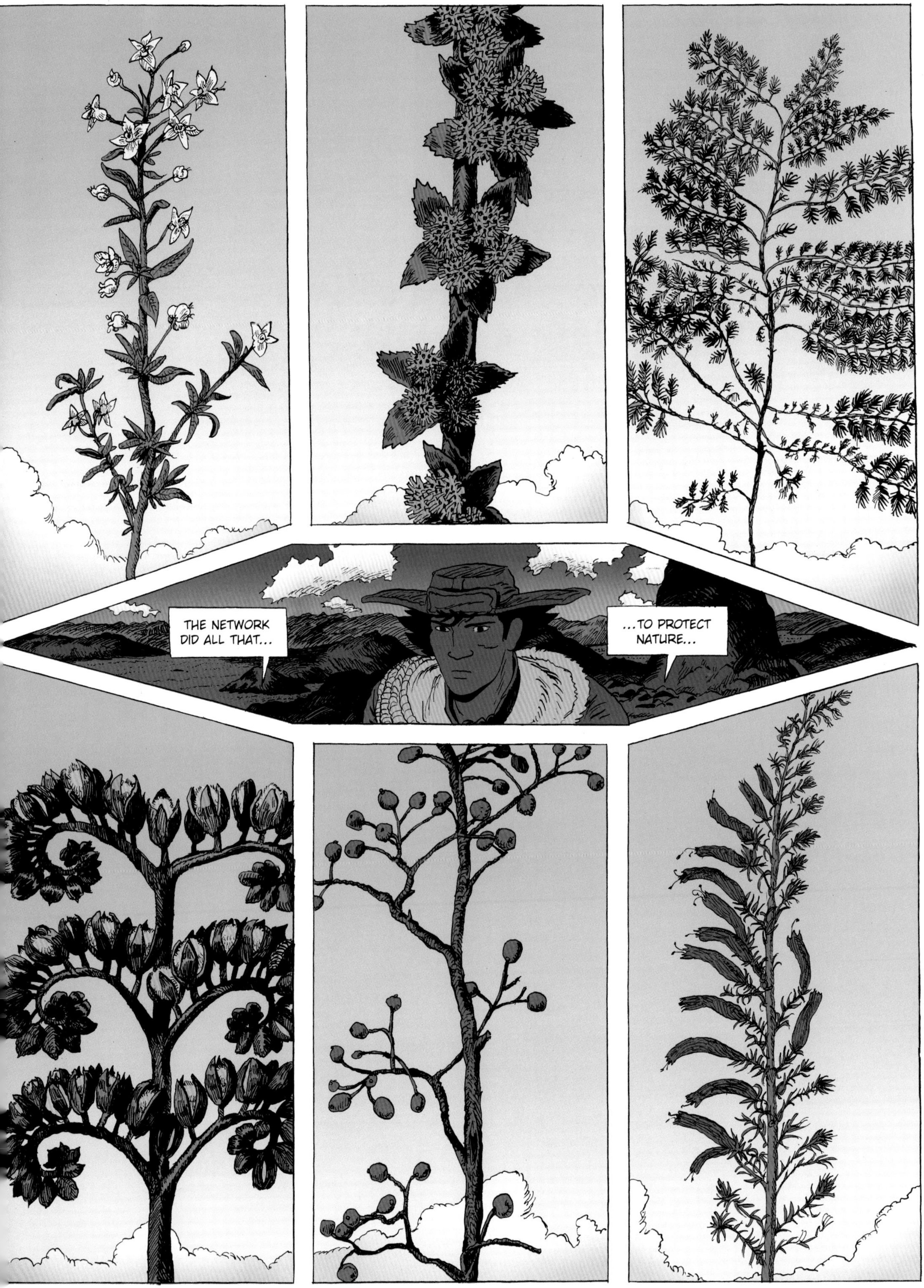

THE NETWORK DID ALL THAT...
...TO PROTECT NATURE...

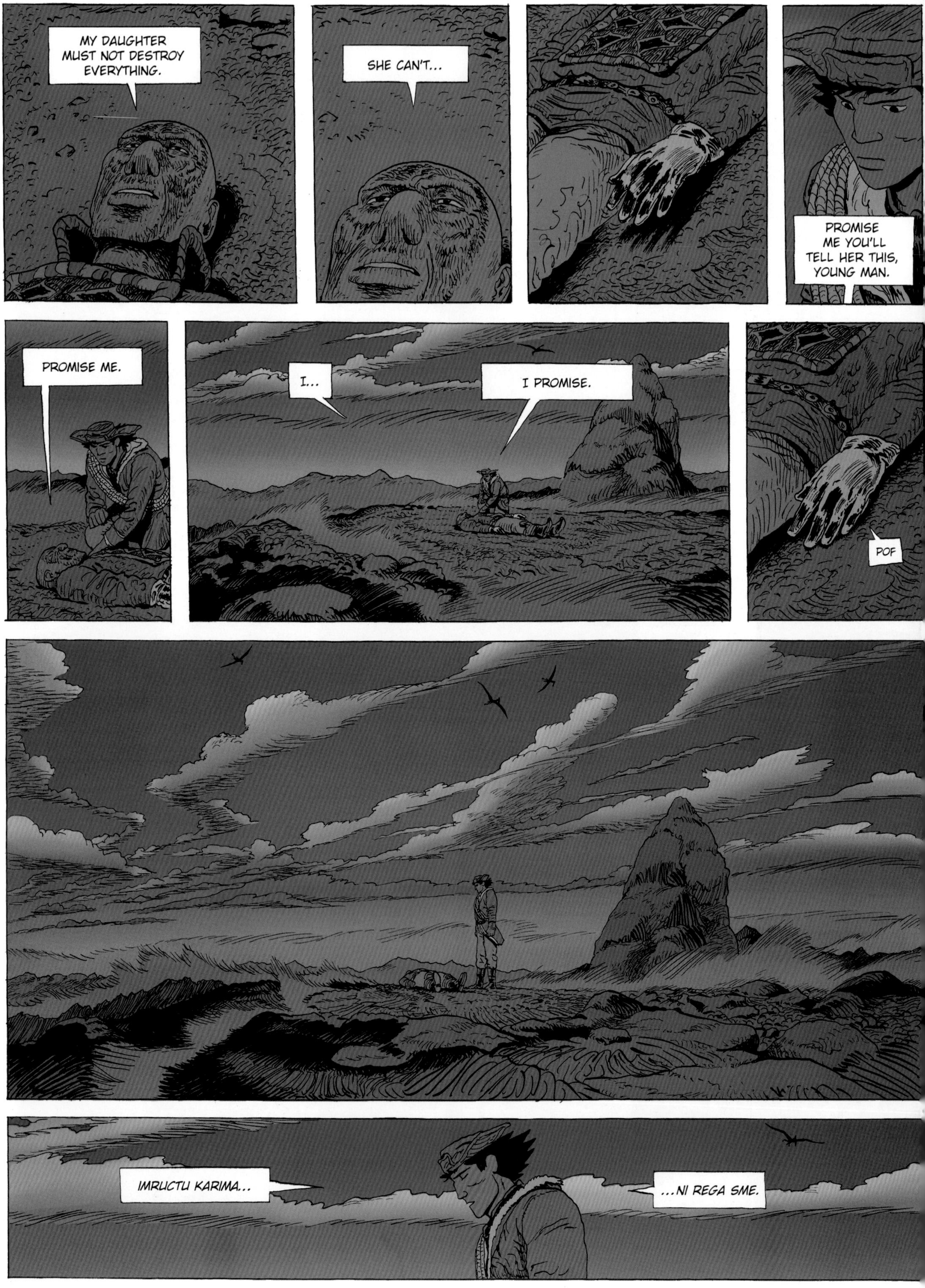
MY DAUGHTER MUST NOT DESTROY EVERYTHING.
SHE CAN'T...
PROMISE ME YOU'LL TELL HER THIS, YOUNG MAN.
PROMISE ME.
I...
I PROMISE.
POF
IMRUCTU KARIMA...
...NI REGA SME.

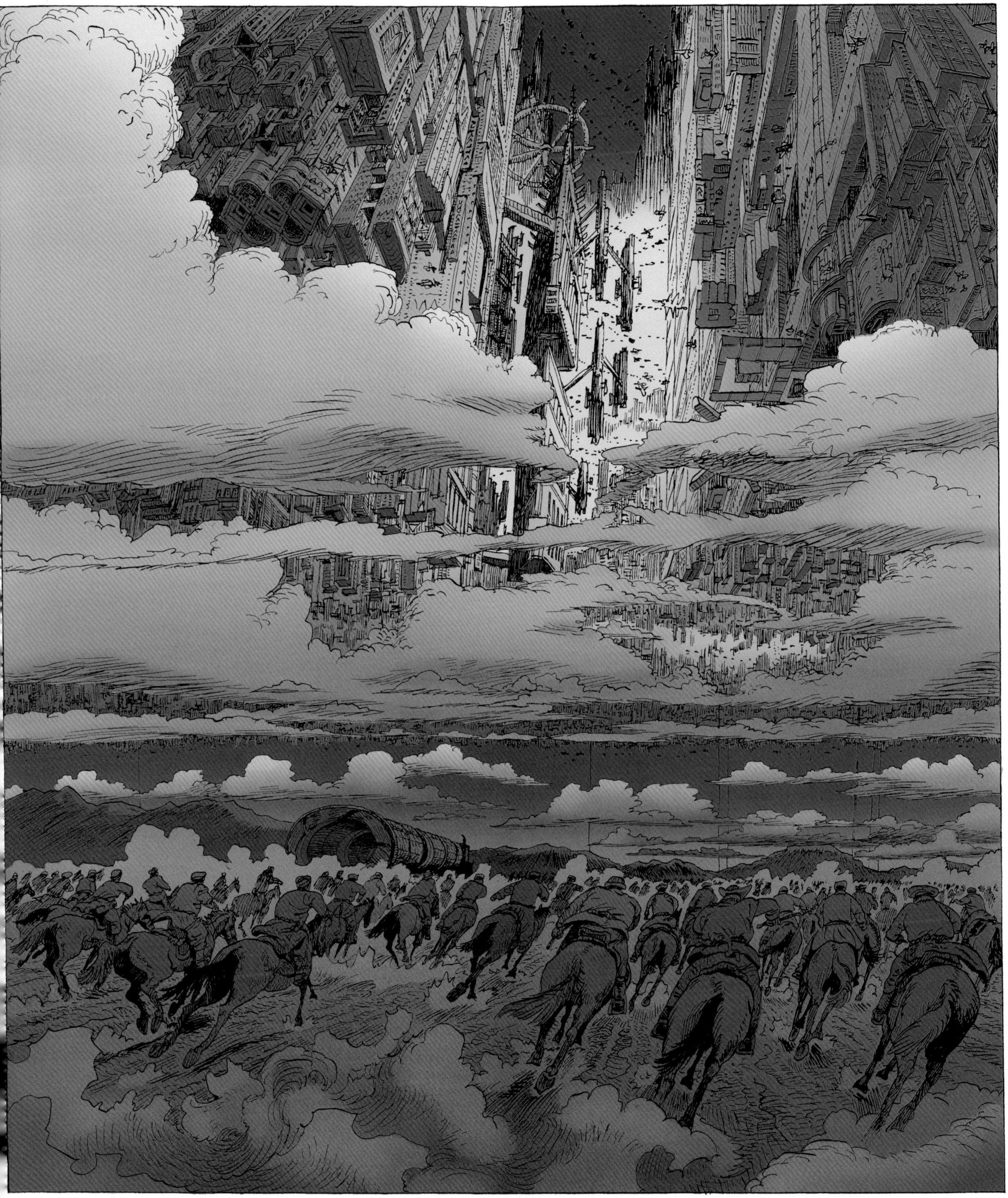

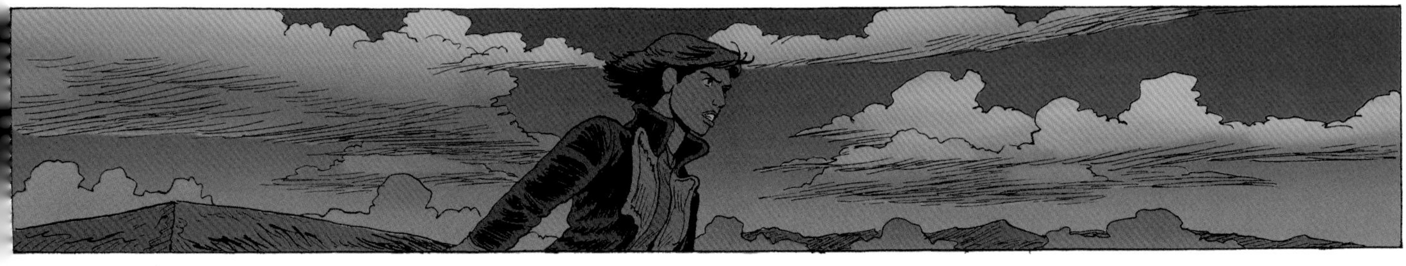

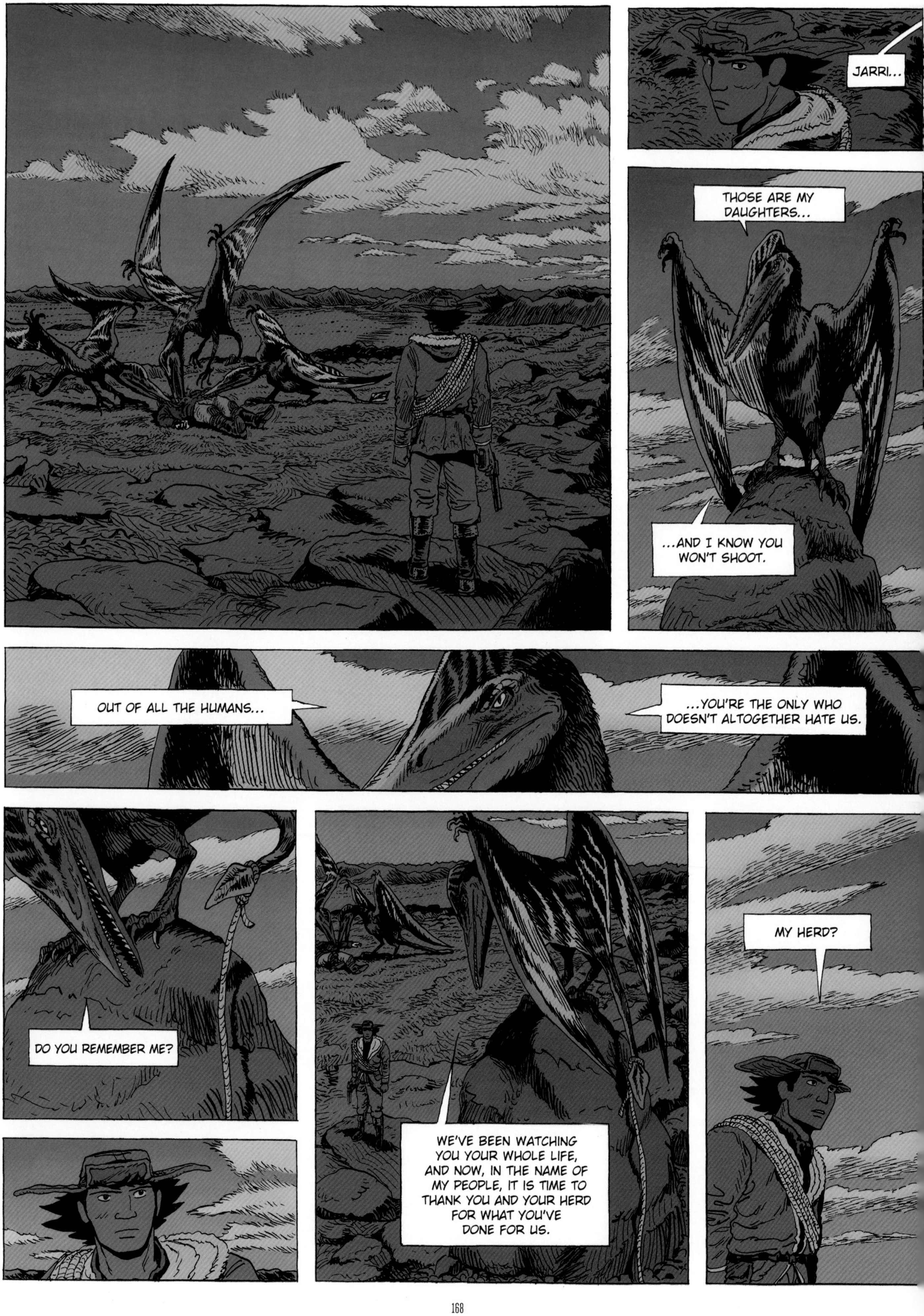
JARRI...
THOSE ARE MY DAUGHTERS...
...AND I KNOW YOU WON'T SHOOT.
OUT OF ALL THE HUMANS...
...YOU'RE THE ONLY WHO DOESN'T ALTOGETHER HATE US.
DO YOU REMEMBER ME?
WE'VE BEEN WATCHING YOU YOUR WHOLE LIFE, AND NOW, IN THE NAME OF MY PEOPLE, IT IS TIME TO THANK YOU AND YOUR HERD FOR WHAT YOU'VE DONE FOR US.
MY HERD?

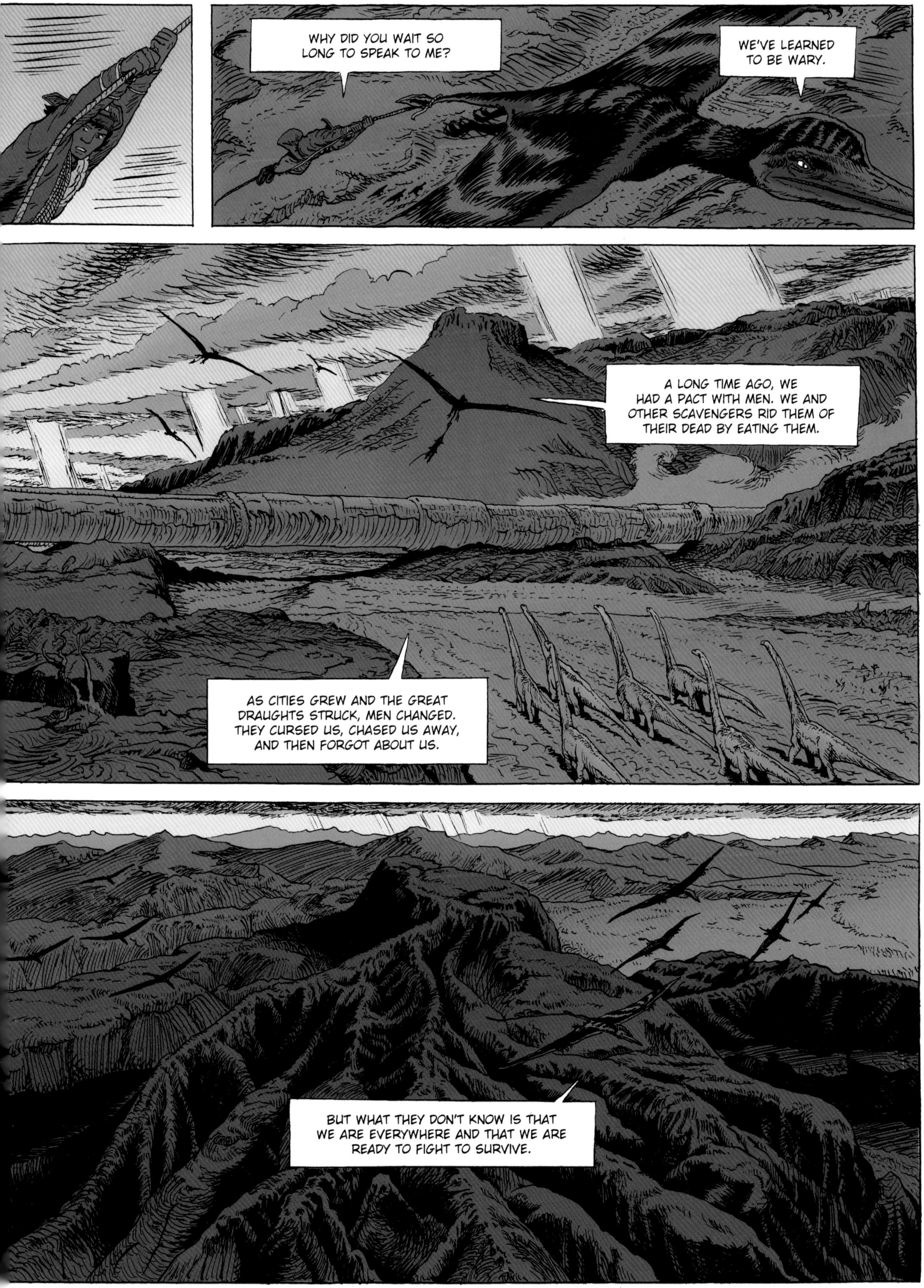
WHY DID YOU WAIT SO LONG TO SPEAK TO ME?
WE'VE LEARNED TO BE WARY.
A LONG TIME AGO, WE HAD A PACT WITH MEN. WE AND OTHER SCAVENGERS RID THEM OF THEIR DEAD BY EATING THEM.
AS CITIES GREW AND THE GREAT DRAUGHTS STRUCK, MEN CHANGED. THEY CURSED US, CHASED US AWAY, AND THEN FORGOT ABOUT US.
BUT WHAT THEY DON'T KNOW IS THAT WE ARE EVERYWHERE AND THAT WE ARE READY TO FIGHT TO SURVIVE.

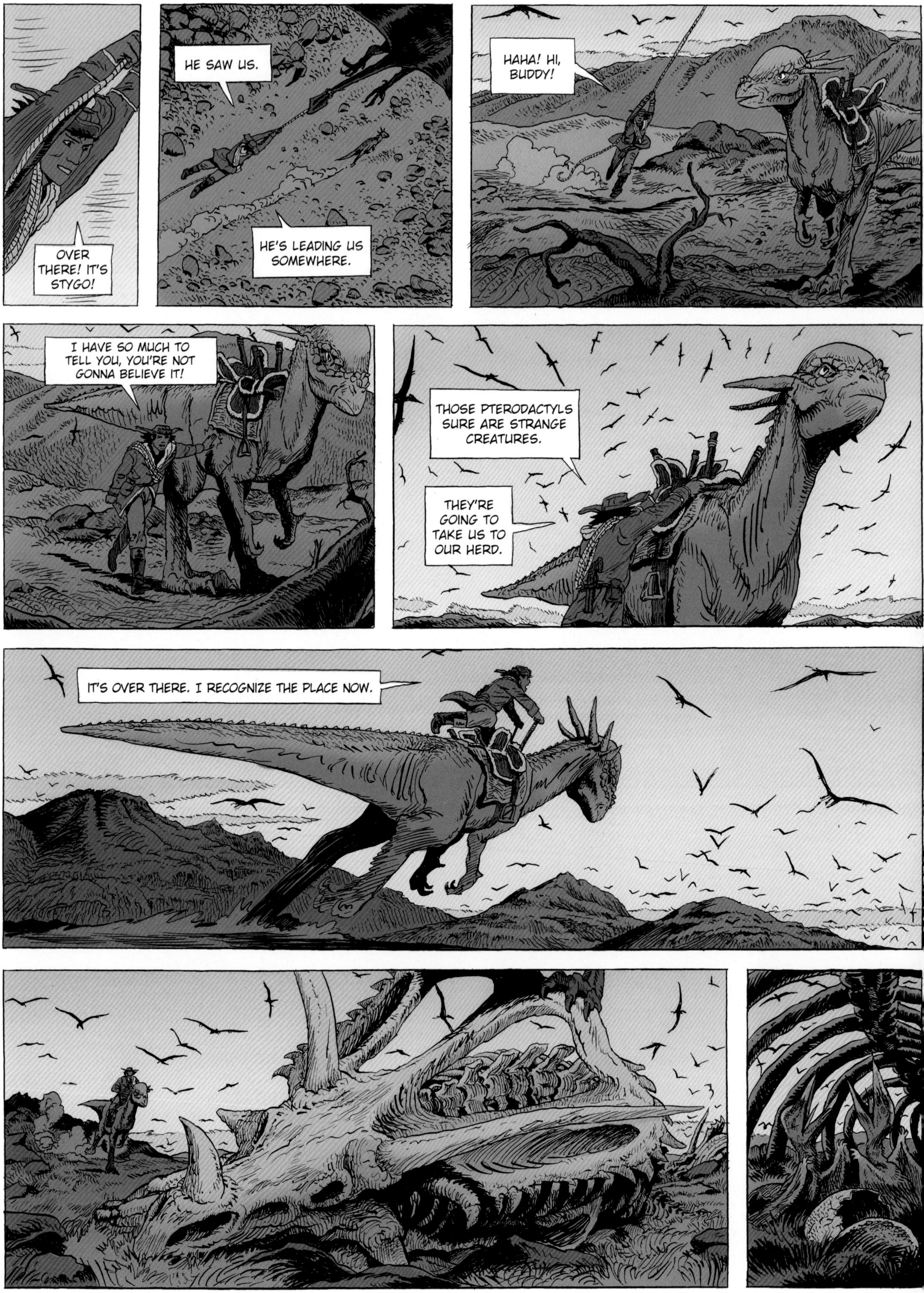

OVER THERE! IT'S STYGO!
HE SAW US.
HE'S LEADING US SOMEWHERE.
HAHA! HI, BUDDY!
I HAVE SO MUCH TO TELL YOU, YOU'RE NOT GONNA BELIEVE IT!
THOSE PTERODACTYLS SURE ARE STRANGE CREATURES.
THEY'RE GOING TO TAKE US TO OUR HERD.
IT'S OVER THERE. I RECOGNIZE THE PLACE NOW.

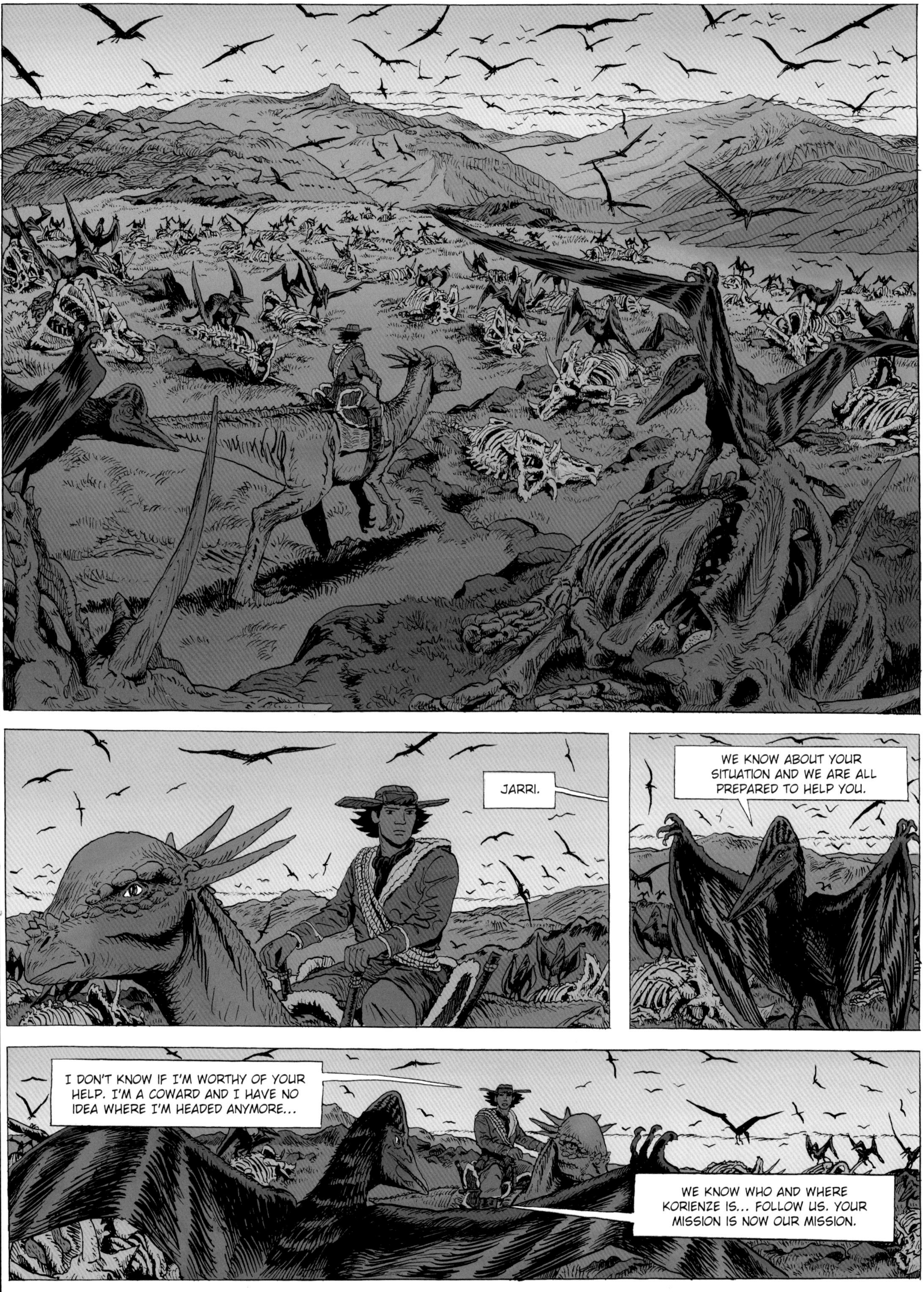
JARRI.
WE KNOW ABOUT YOUR SITUATION AND WE ARE ALL PREPARED TO HELP YOU.
I DON'T KNOW IF I'M WORTHY OF YOUR HELP. I'M A COWARD AND I HAVE NO IDEA WHERE I'M HEADED ANYMORE...
WE KNOW WHO AND WHERE KORIENZE IS... FOLLOW US. YOUR MISSION IS NOW OUR MISSION.

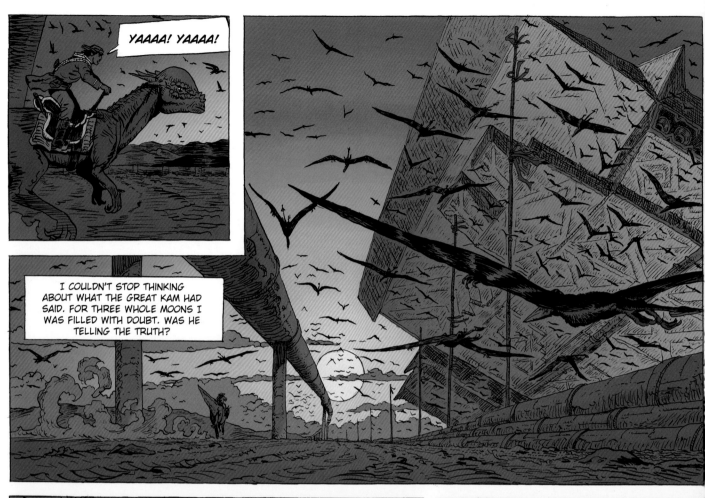

YAAAA! YAAAA!

I COULDN'T STOP THINKING ABOUT WHAT THE GREAT KAM HAD SAID. FOR THREE WHOLE MOONS I WAS FILLED WITH DOUBT. WAS HE TELLING THE TRUTH?

JARRI, CAN I ASK YOU A QUESTION?

MMH.

IT'S JUST THAT SOME OF US STILL NEED CONVINCING.

THAT KORIENZE GIRL... YOU LOVE HER, DON'T YOU?

LOVE IS THE DRIVING FORCE OF LIFE!

WE STILL HAVE A LONG WAY TO GO. I DON'T WANT TO TALK ABOUT IT.

I HAVE MY ANSWER... AND WITH IT, ENOUGH TO RALLY THE ENTIRE CONTINENT!

THE PTERODACTYLS KNEW WHAT KORIENZE WAS DOING DOZENS OF VALLEYS FROM THERE.

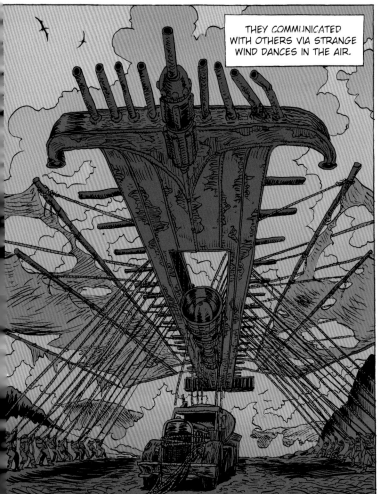

THEY COMMUNICATED WITH OTHERS VIA STRANGE WIND DANCES IN THE AIR.

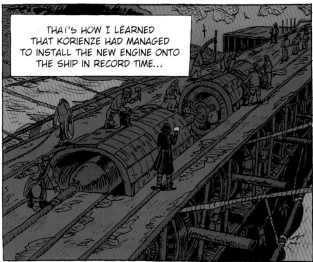

THAT'S HOW I LEARNED THAT KORIENZE HAD MANAGED TO INSTALL THE NEW ENGINE ONTO THE SHIP IN RECORD TIME...

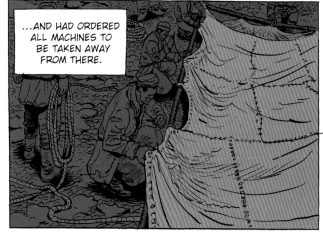

...AND HAD ORDERED ALL MACHINES TO BE TAKEN AWAY FROM THERE.

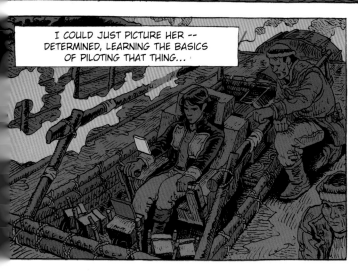

I COULD JUST PICTURE HER -- DETERMINED, LEARNING THE BASICS OF PILOTING THAT THING...

BLAM BLAM

...AND BLASTING HER WAY THROUGH THE ROCK TO MAKE AN AIRSTRIP FOR HERSELF.

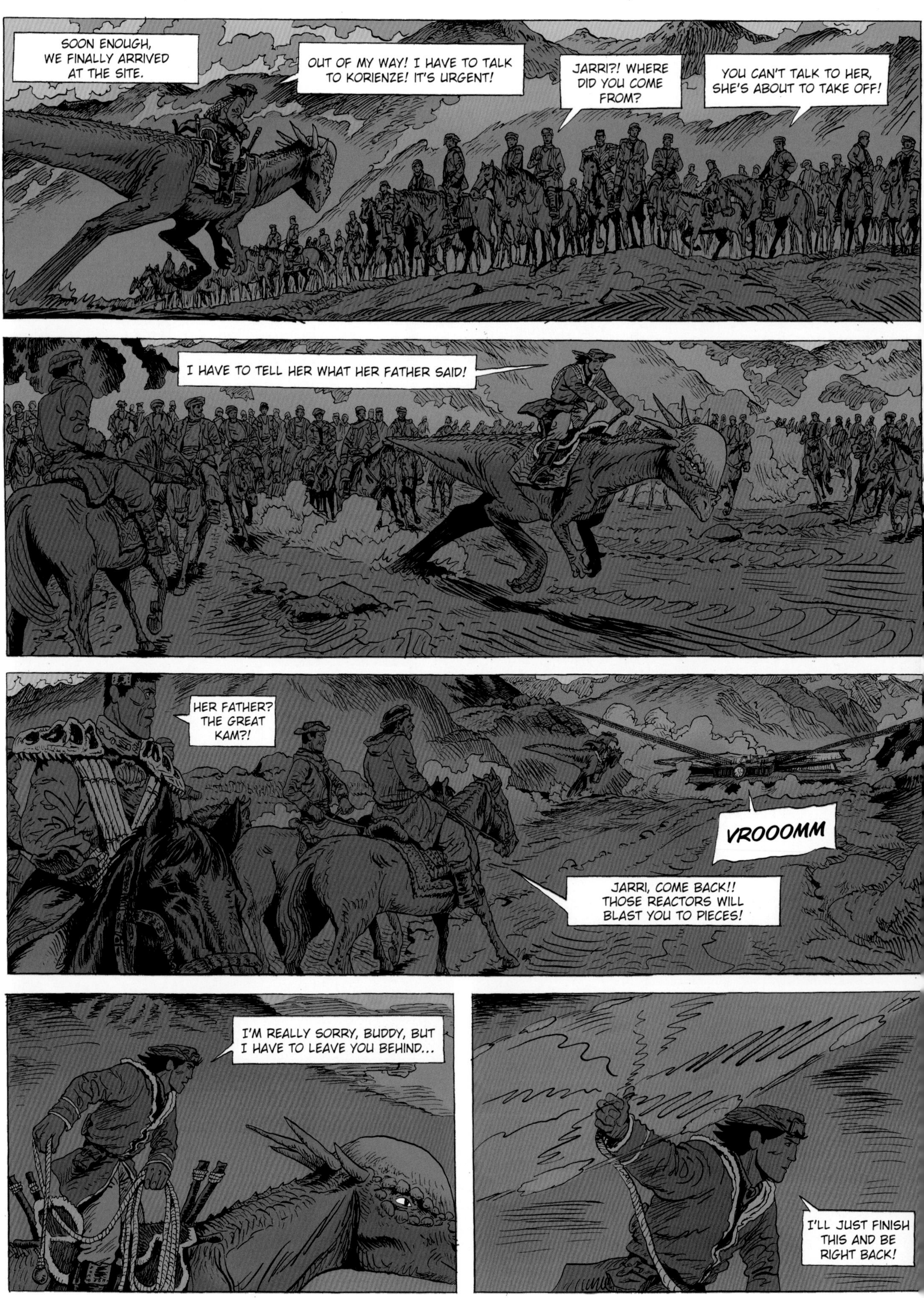
SOON ENOUGH, WE FINALLY ARRIVED AT THE SITE.
OUT OF MY WAY! I HAVE TO TALK TO KORIENZE! IT'S URGENT!
JARRI?! WHERE DID YOU COME FROM?
YOU CAN'T TALK TO HER, SHE'S ABOUT TO TAKE OFF!
I HAVE TO TELL HER WHAT HER FATHER SAID!
HER FATHER? THE GREAT KAM?!
VROOOMM
JARRI, COME BACK!! THOSE REACTORS WILL BLAST YOU TO PIECES!
I'M REALLY SORRY, BUDDY, BUT I HAVE TO LEAVE YOU BEHIND...
I'LL JUST FINISH THIS AND BE RIGHT BACK!

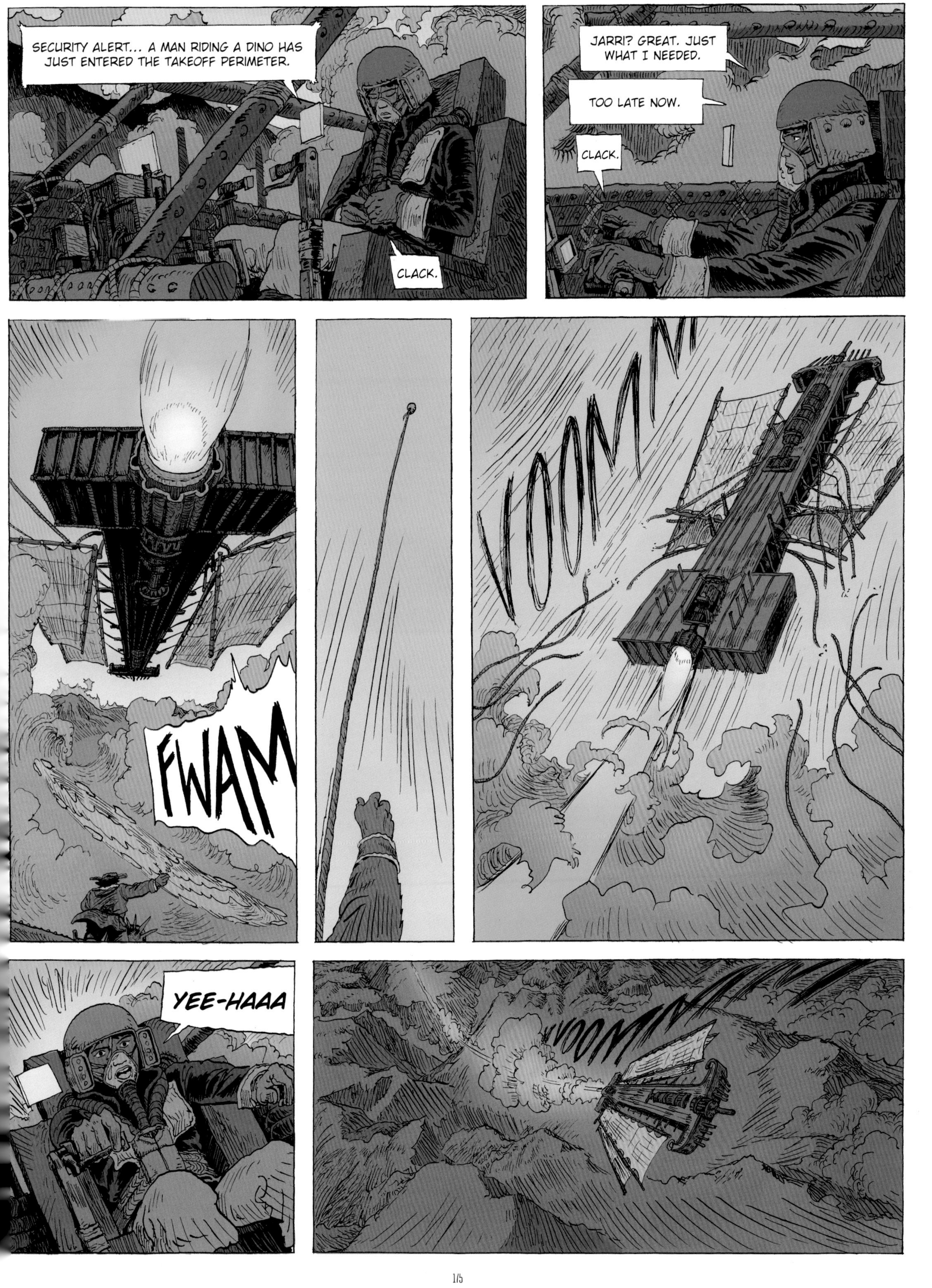
SECURITY ALERT... A MAN RIDING A DINO HAS JUST ENTERED THE TAKEOFF PERIMETER.
CLACK.
JARRI? GREAT. JUST WHAT I NEEDED.
TOO LATE NOW.
CLACK.
FWAM
VOOMM
YEE-HAAA

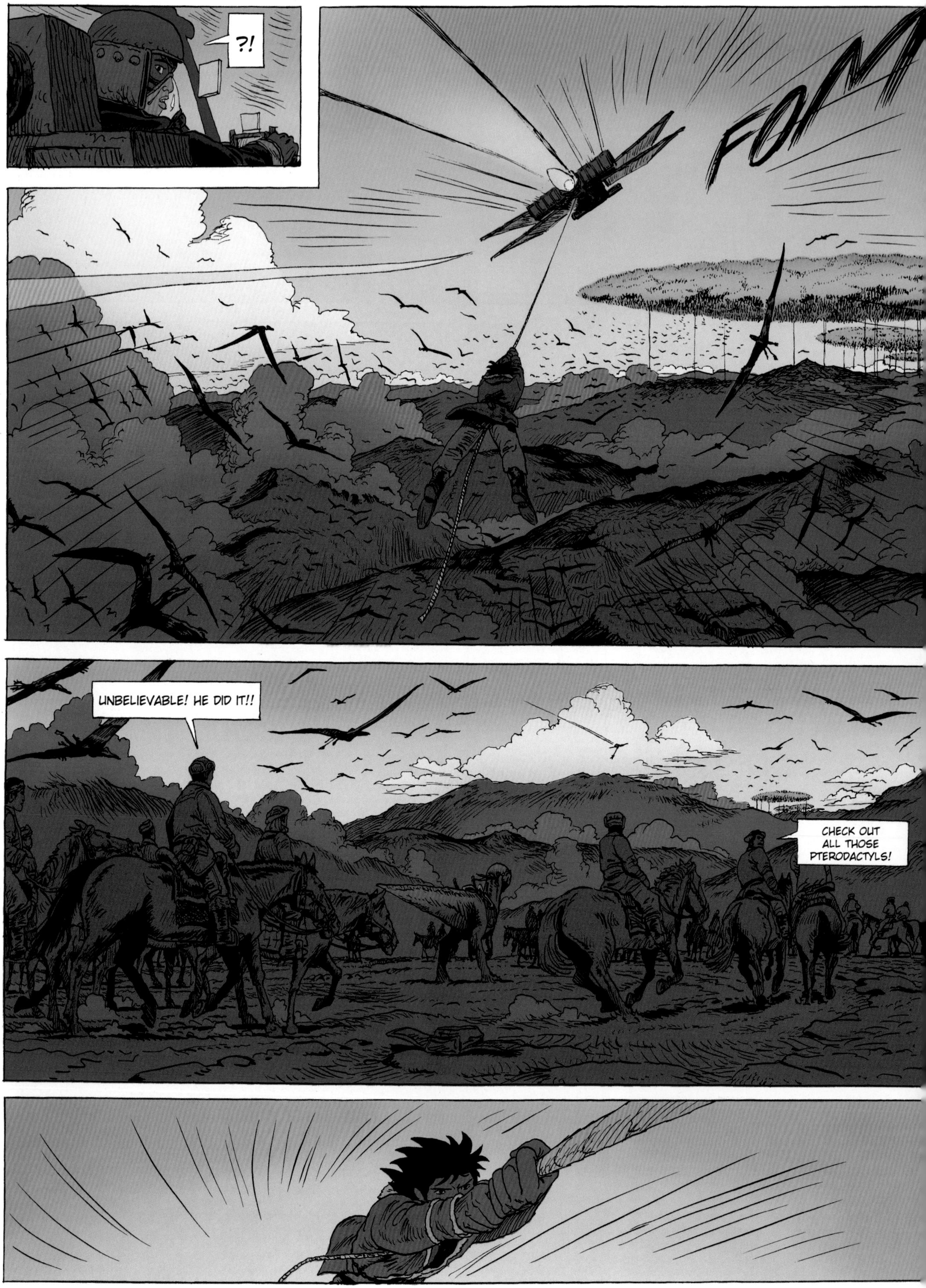

?!
FOM
UNBELIEVABLE! HE DID IT!!
CHECK OUT ALL THOSE PTERODACTYLS!

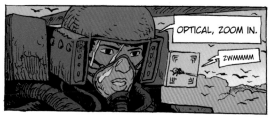

OPTICAL, ZOOM IN.

ZWMMMM

DAMN IT! WHAT THE HELL IS HE DOING? HE'LL RUIN EVERYTHING!

YOU CAN SCREAM ALL YOU WANT, JARRI, I CAN'T HEAR YOU IN HERE.

ALL THOSE PTERODACTYLS...

IT'S LIKE THEY'RE FOLLOWING US...

DO THEY ACTUALLY THINK THEY CAN STOP ME?

SORRY, JARRI, BUT I CAN'T TURN BACK NOW... I HOPE YOU'RE STRONG ENOUGH TO HOLD ON TILL THE END...

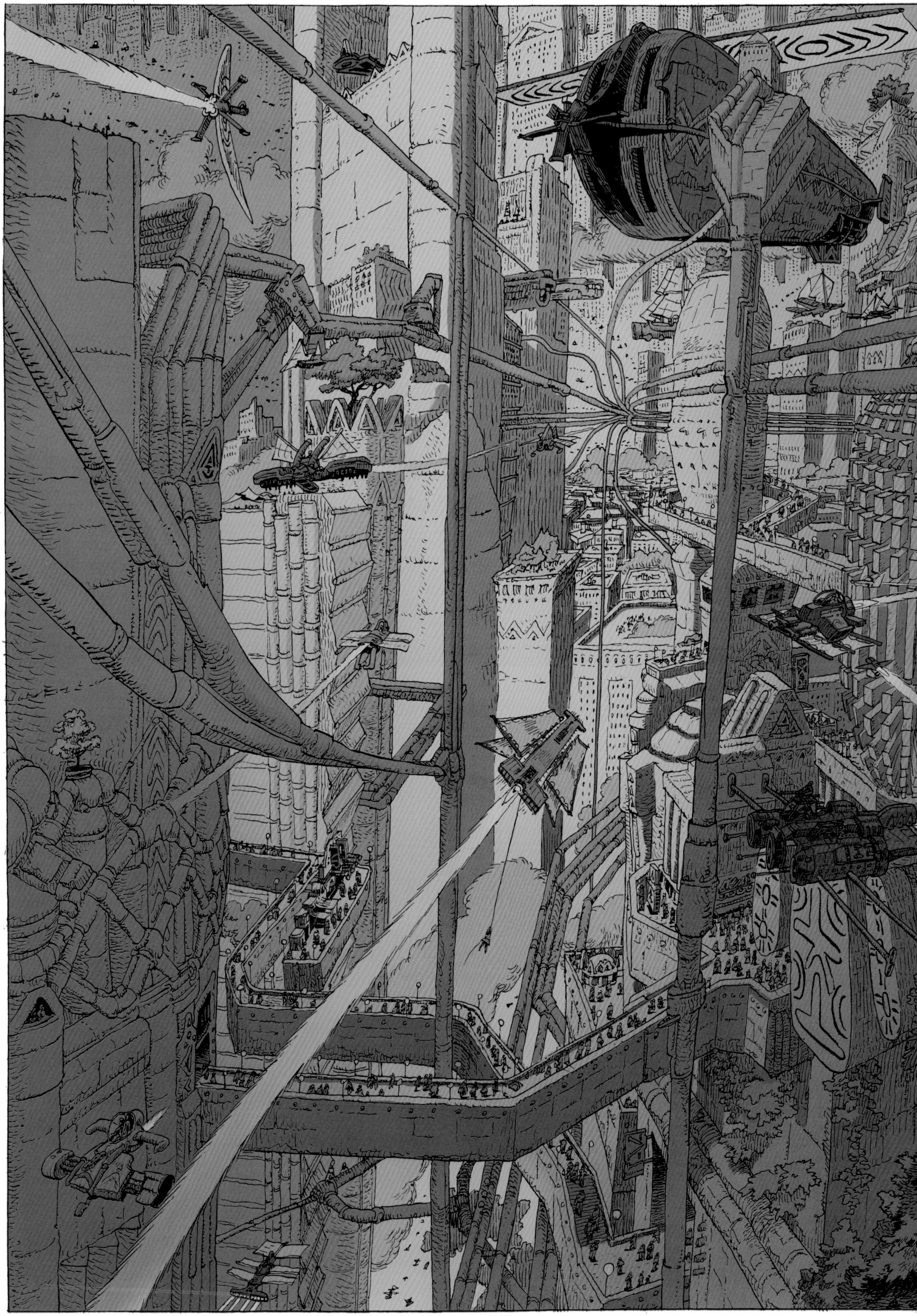

CAREFUL, KORIENZE, THEY'VE SPOTTED YOU!!
WHAT? ALREADY?!
DAMN! THOSE ARE FIGHTER-CRAFTS!
THE MOST DANGEROUS ONES, TOO. BUILT FOR SPEED.
IT'S HARD TO SAY IF YOUR BIRD CAN TAKE IT, ESPECIALLY IN TOWN!
WE'RE ABOUT TO FIND OUT.
YOU ARE FLYING A NON-LISTED SHIP. PLEASE STOP AND IDENTIFY YOURSELF IMMEDIATELY.
THIS IS OUR LAST WARNING BEFORE WE OPEN FIRE.

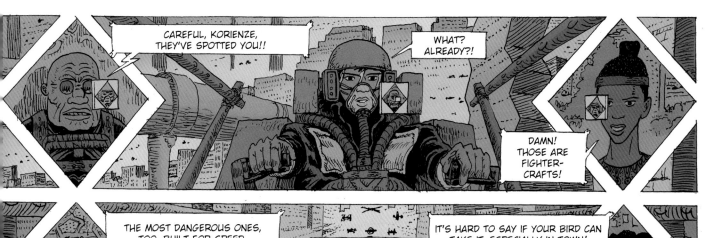

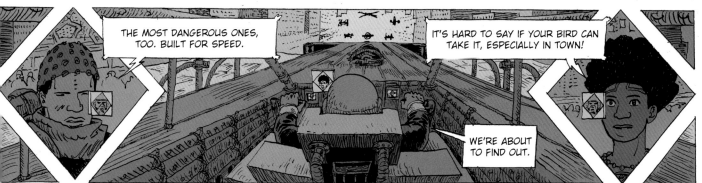

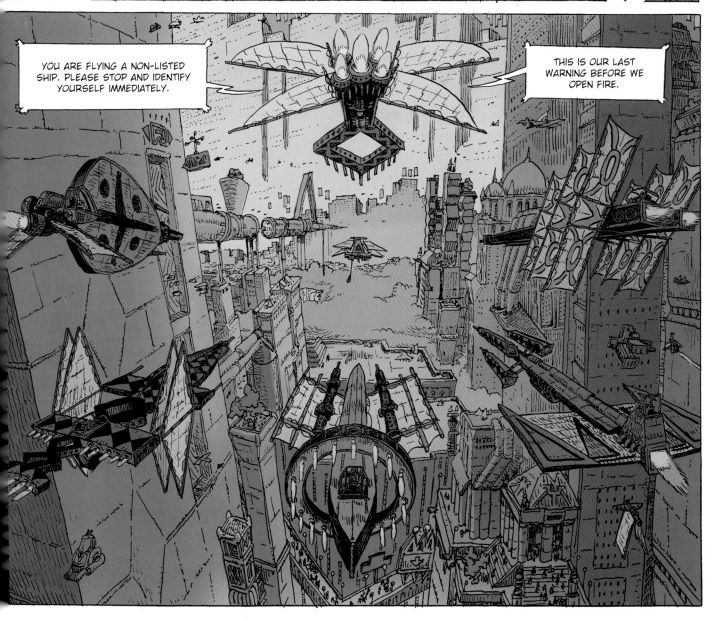

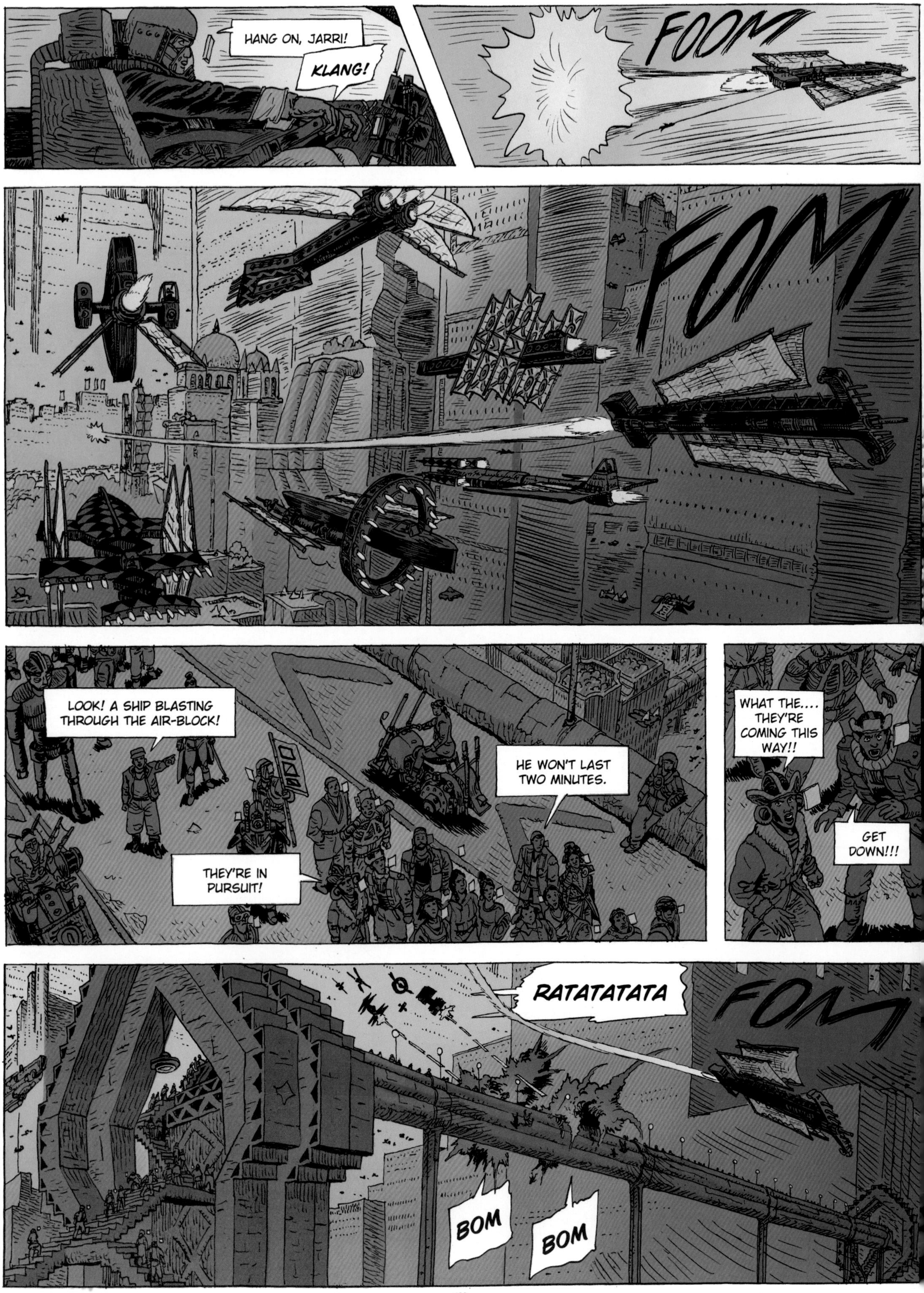

HANG ON, JARRI!
KLANG!
FOOM
FOM
LOOK! A SHIP BLASTING THROUGH THE AIR-BLOCK!
HE WON'T LAST TWO MINUTES.
THEY'RE IN PURSUIT!
WHAT THE.... THEY'RE COMING THIS WAY!!
GET DOWN!!!
RATATATATA
FOM
BOM
BOM

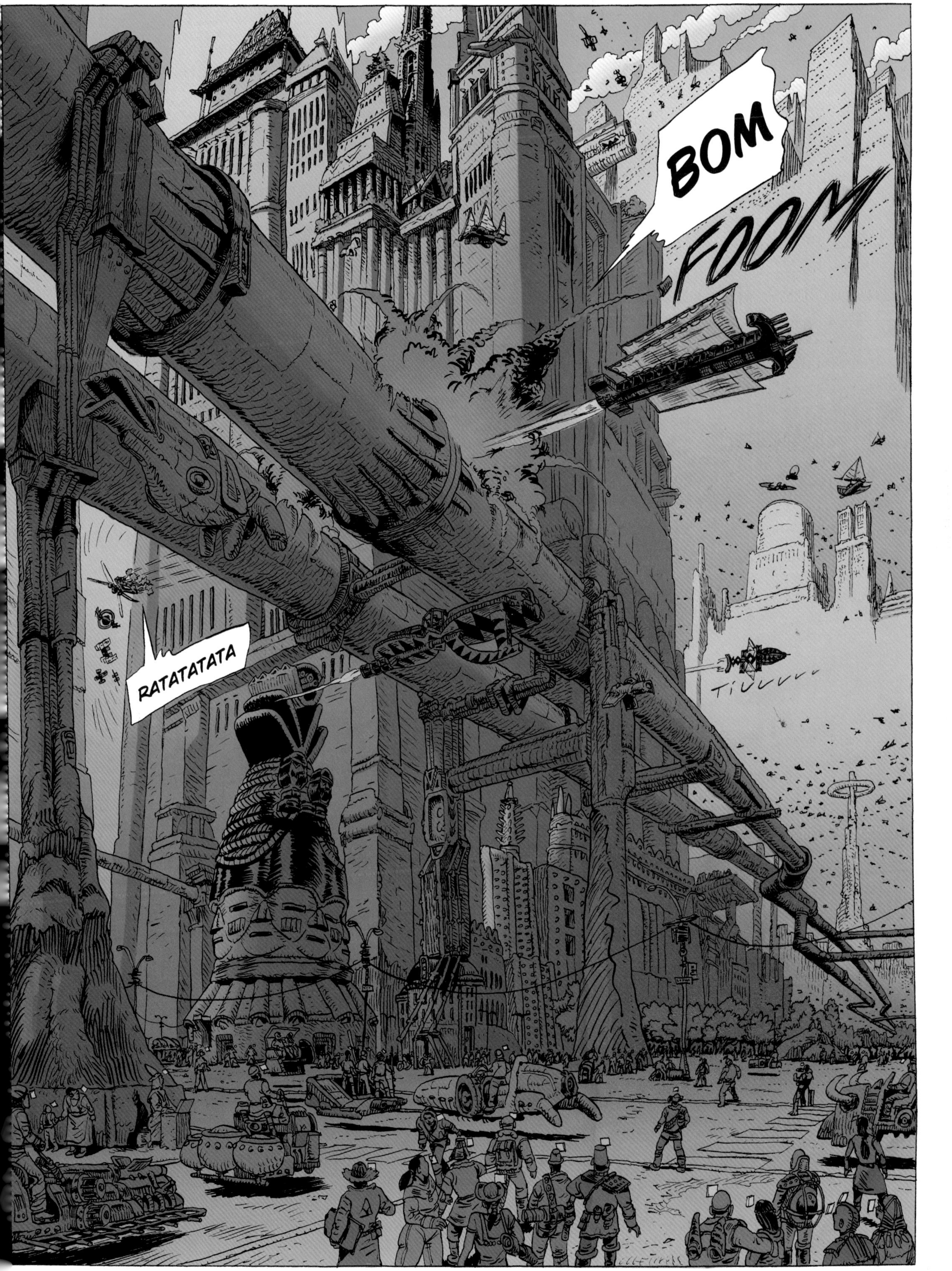
BOM
FOOM
RATATATATA
TIUUUUU

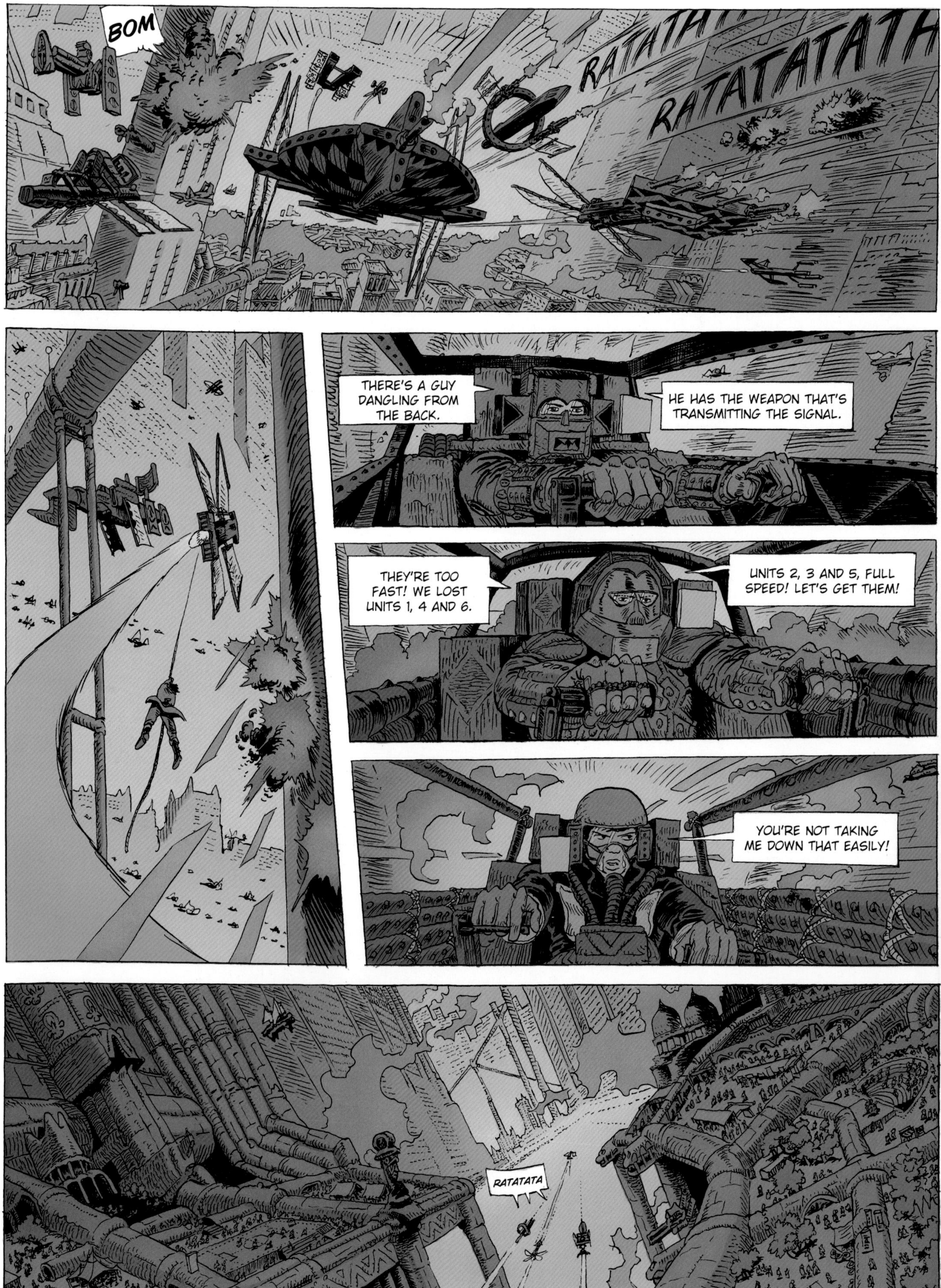
BOM
RATATH
RATATATATH
THERE'S A GUY DANGLING FROM THE BACK.
HE HAS THE WEAPON THAT'S TRANSMITTING THE SIGNAL.
THEY'RE TOO FAST! WE LOST UNITS 1, 4 AND 6.
UNITS 2, 3 AND 5, FULL SPEED! LET'S GET THEM!
YOU'RE NOT TAKING ME DOWN THAT EASILY!
RATATATA

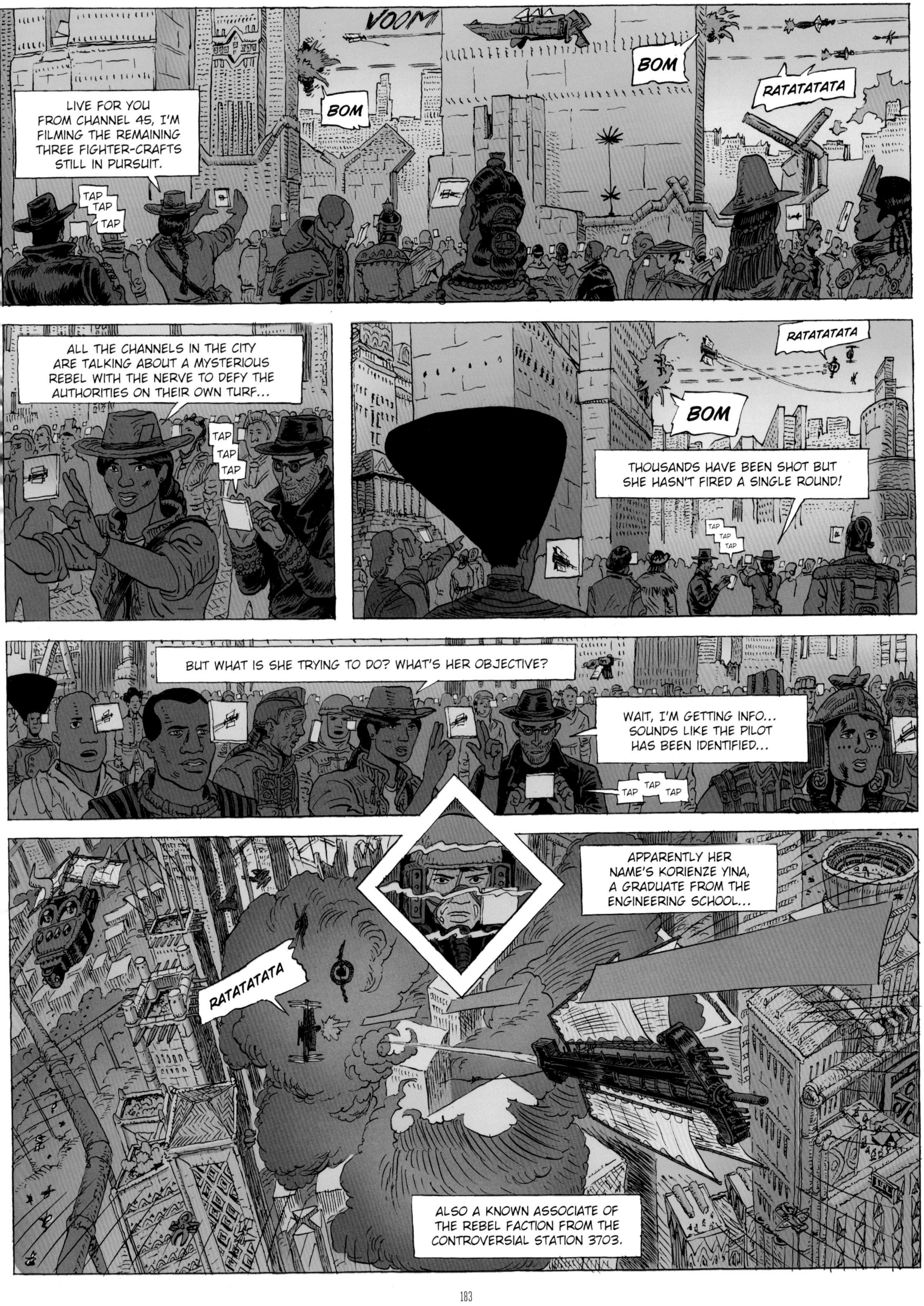
VOOM
BOM
BOM
RATATATATA
LIVE FOR YOU FROM CHANNEL 45, I'M FILMING THE REMAINING THREE FIGHTER-CRAFTS STILL IN PURSUIT.
TAP TAP TAP
ALL THE CHANNELS IN THE CITY ARE TALKING ABOUT A MYSTERIOUS REBEL WITH THE NERVE TO DEFY THE AUTHORITIES ON THEIR OWN TURF...
TAP TAP TAP
RATATATATA
BOM
THOUSANDS HAVE BEEN SHOT BUT SHE HASN'T FIRED A SINGLE ROUND!
TAP TAP TAP
BUT WHAT IS SHE TRYING TO DO? WHAT'S HER OBJECTIVE?
WAIT, I'M GETTING INFO... SOUNDS LIKE THE PILOT HAS BEEN IDENTIFIED...
TAP TAP TAP
APPARENTLY HER NAME'S KORIENZE YINA, A GRADUATE FROM THE ENGINEERING SCHOOL...
RATATATATA
ALSO A KNOWN ASSOCIATE OF THE REBEL FACTION FROM THE CONTROVERSIAL STATION 3703.

TARGET IN THE CROSSHAIRS.

RATATA

RATATATATA

TAK

TAK TAK TAK

?!

SHIT, MY SAILS!!

YOU'LL REGRET THIS!

FOLLOW ME, YOU AMATEURS.

A TUBULAR? AGAINST TRAFFIC! IT'S A TRAP!

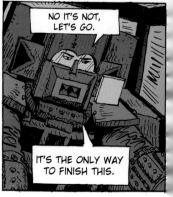

NO IT'S NOT, LET'S GO.

IT'S THE ONLY WAY TO FINISH THIS.

RATATATATA
BOM
TOOT
TOOT
VRAMM
FOOM
?!
BOM
WE SHOULDN'T HAVE FOLLOWED HER IN HERE, IT'S TOO DANGEROUS!
KEEP SHOOTING, WE'LL GET HER!
HEY, WHAT'S THAT BOZO DOING?
KKCCHHH
WATCH OUT!!!
BLAM
BLAM
BLAM
BLAM

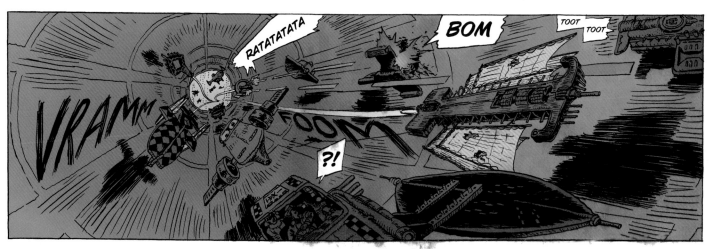

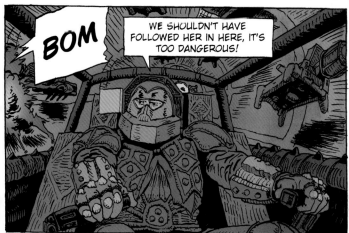

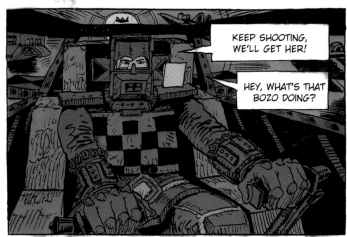

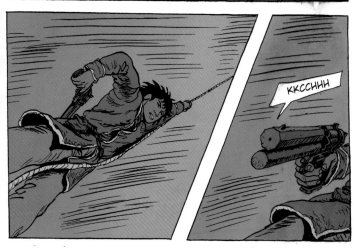

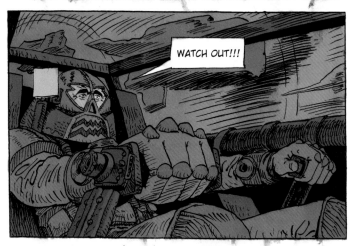

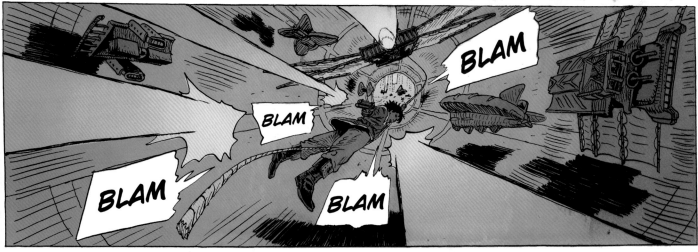

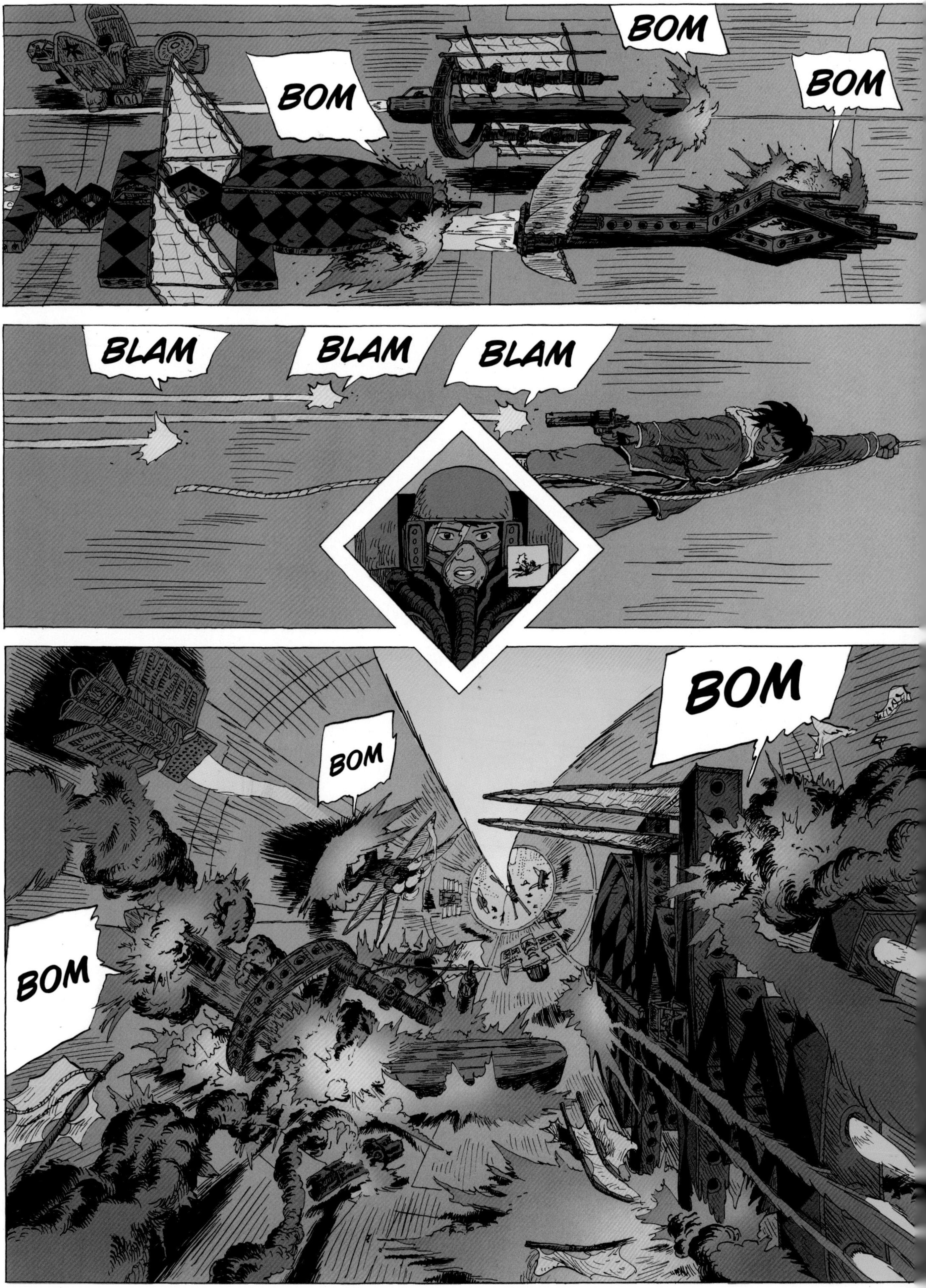
BOM
BOM
BOM
BLAM
BLAM
BLAM
BOM
BOM
BOM

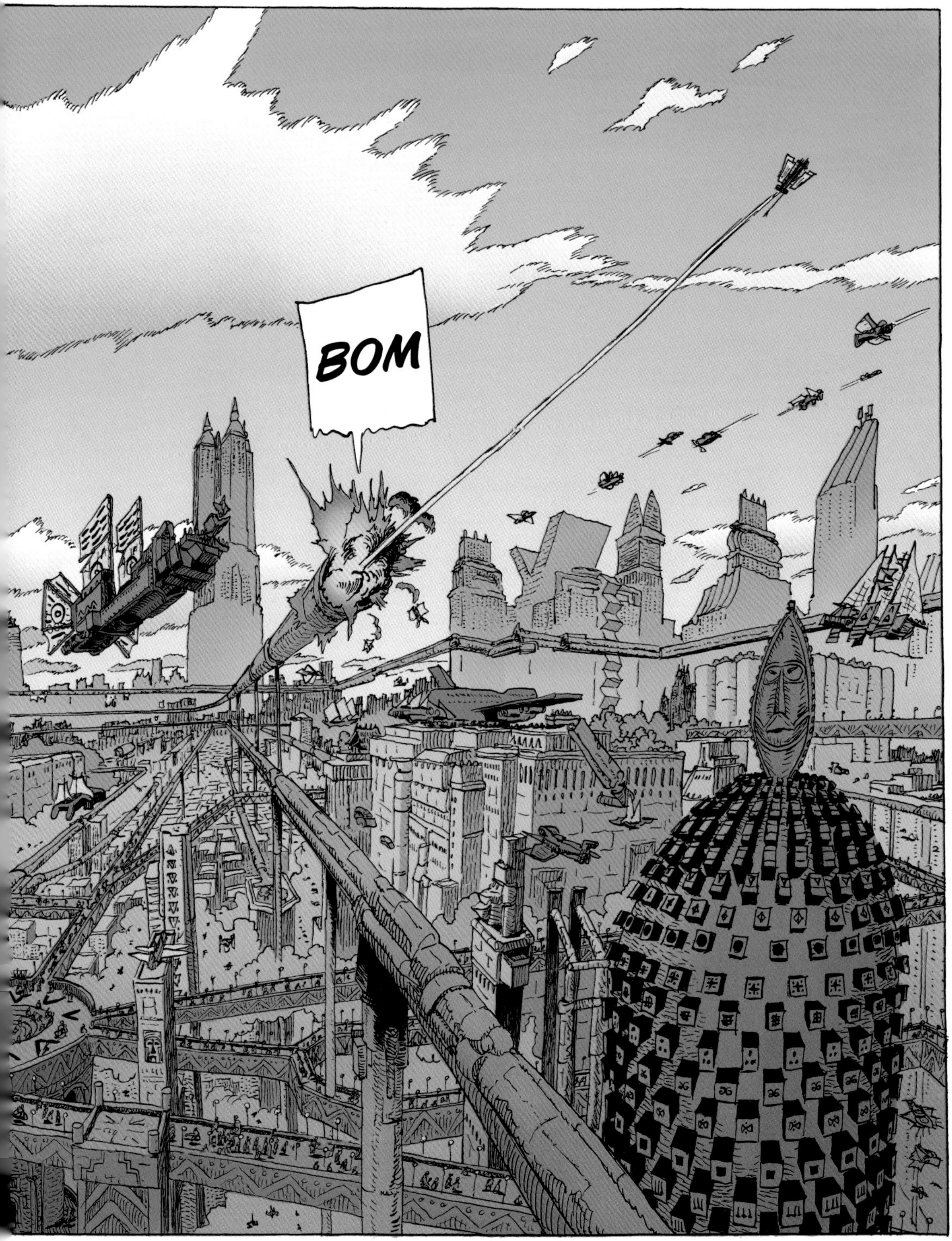
BOM
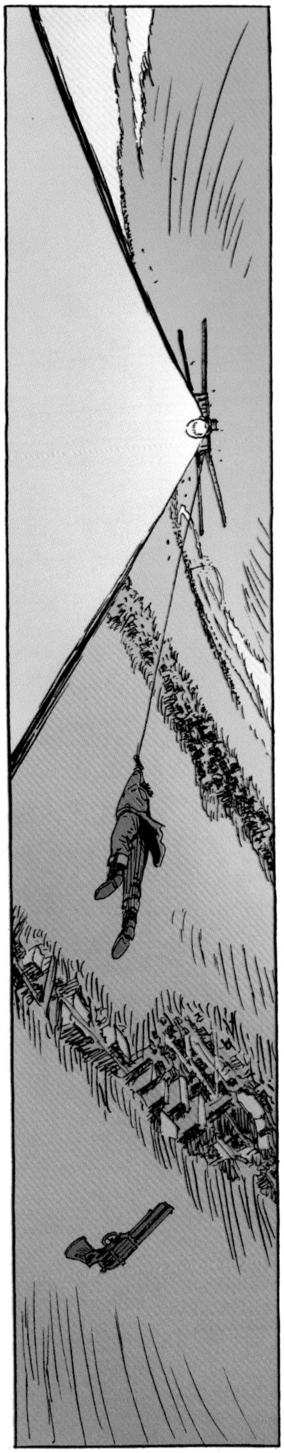
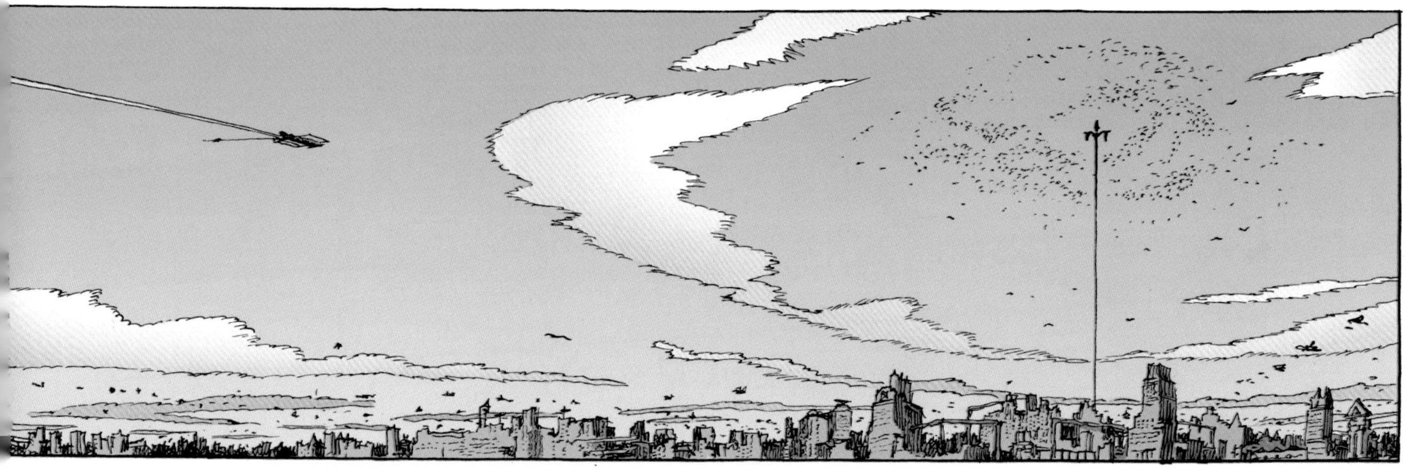

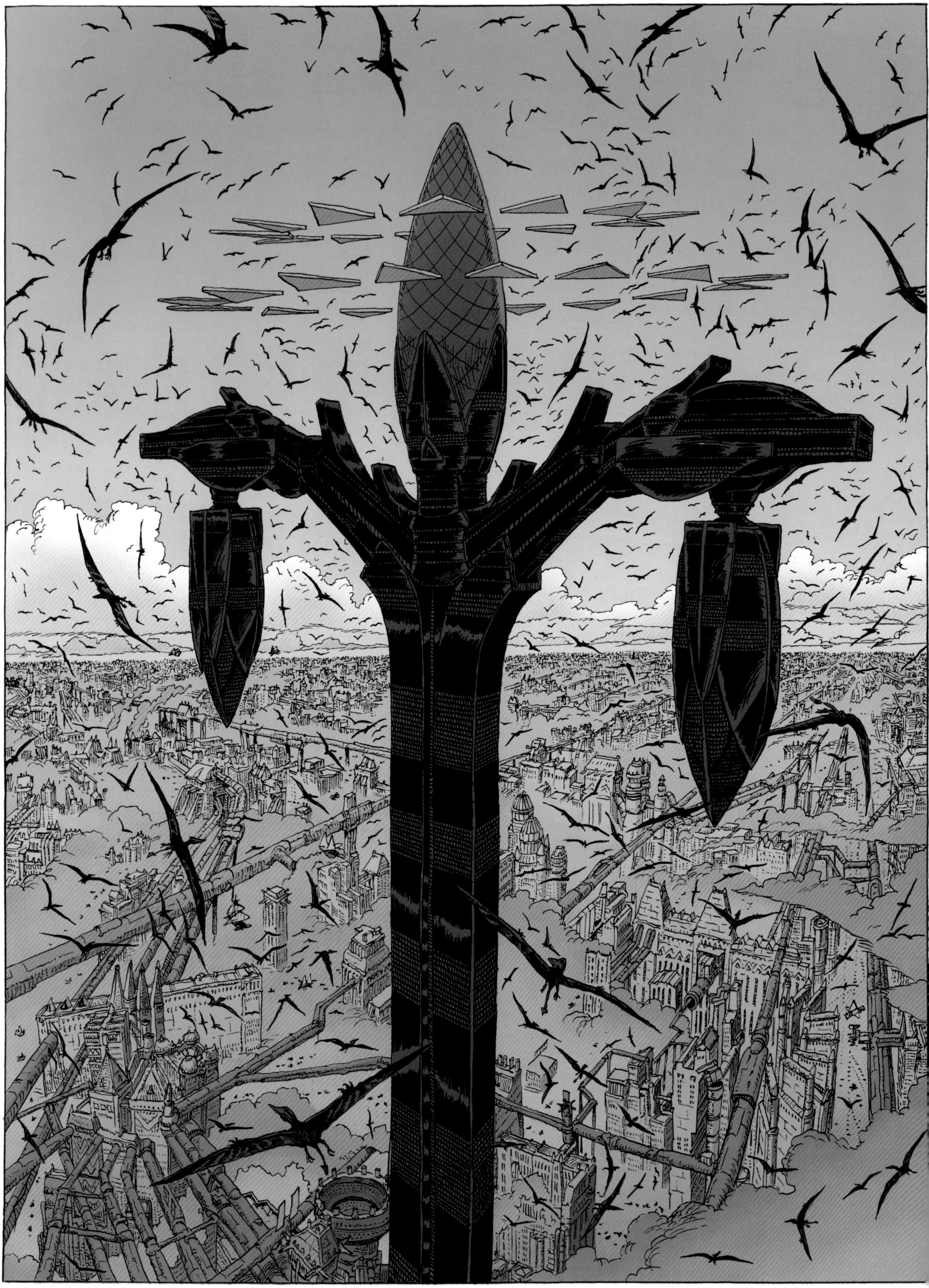

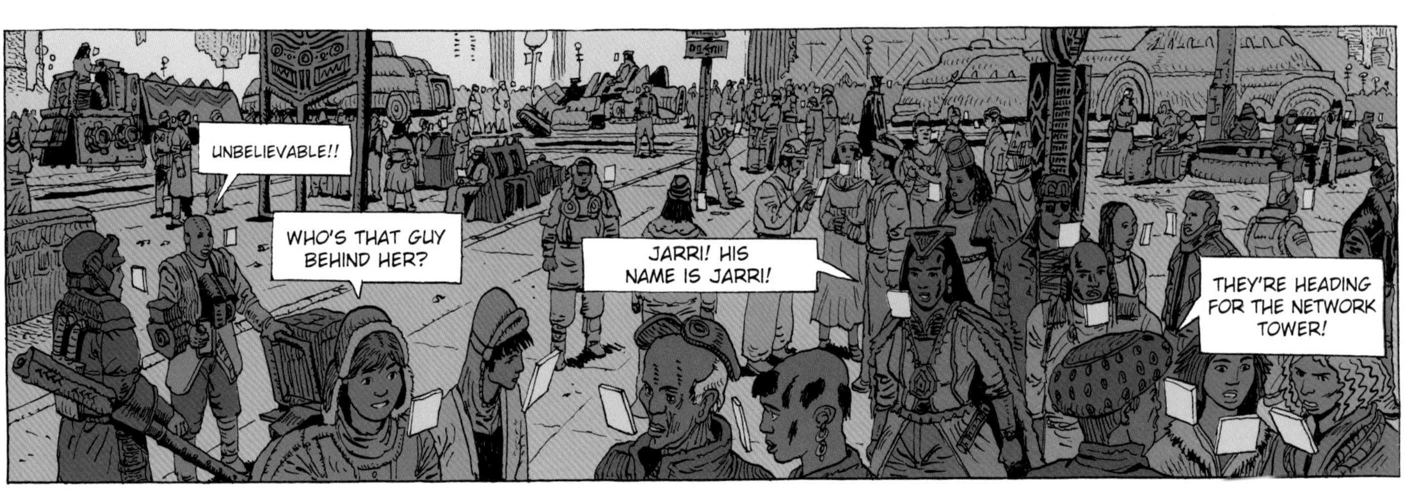
UNBELIEVABLE!!
WHO'S THAT GUY BEHIND HER?
JARRI! HIS NAME IS JARRI!
THEY'RE HEADING FOR THE NETWORK TOWER!
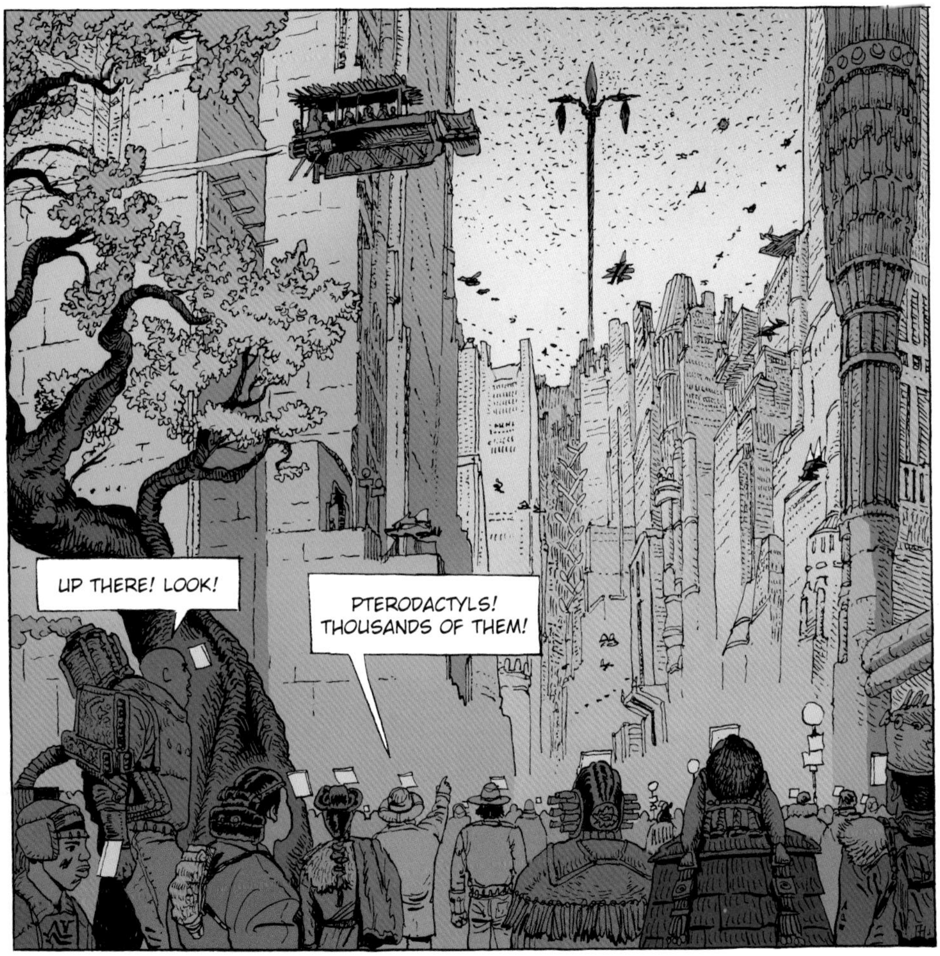
UP THERE! LOOK!
PTERODACTYLS! THOUSANDS OF THEM!
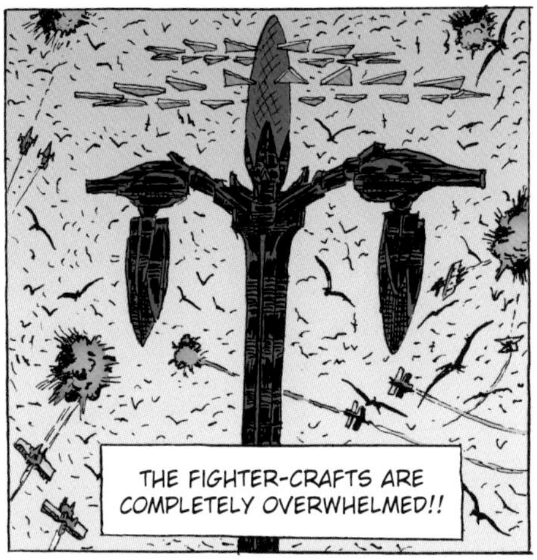
THE FIGHTER-CRAFTS ARE COMPLETELY OVERWHELMED!!
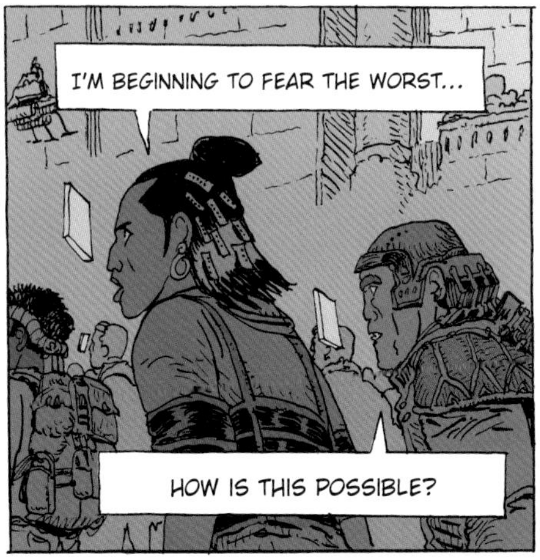
I'M BEGINNING TO FEAR THE WORST...
HOW IS THIS POSSIBLE?
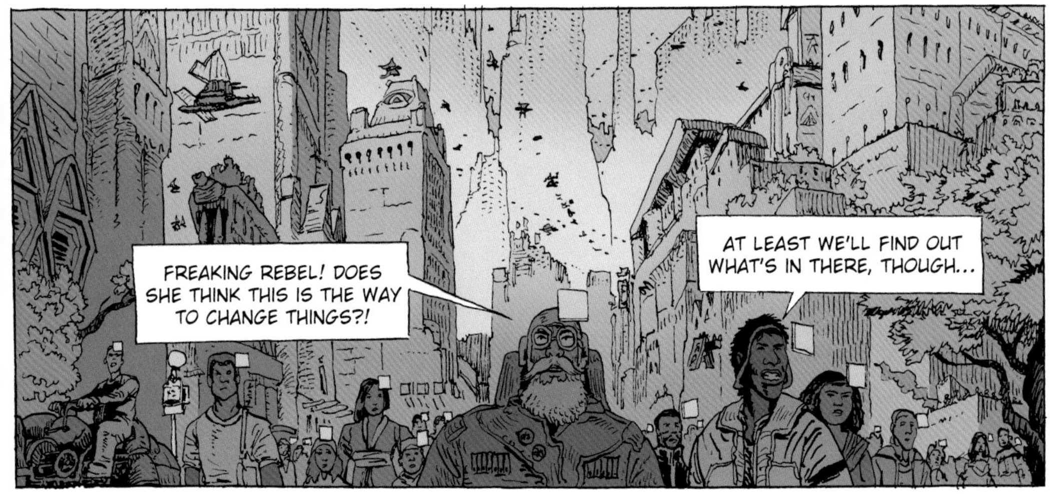
FREAKING REBEL! DOES SHE THINK THIS IS THE WAY TO CHANGE THINGS?!
AT LEAST WE'LL FIND OUT WHAT'S IN THERE, THOUGH...
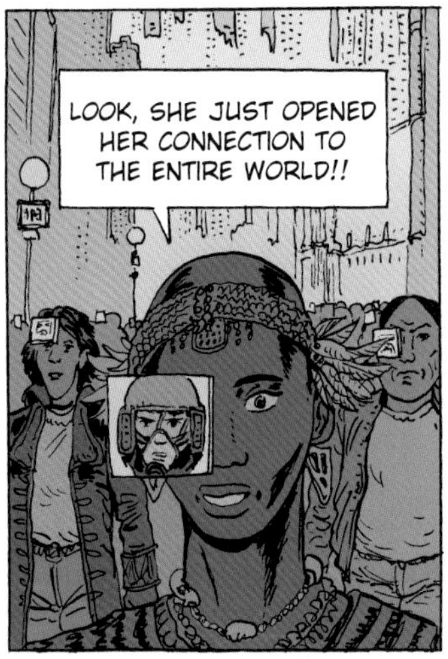
LOOK, SHE JUST OPENED HER CONNECTION TO THE ENTIRE WORLD!!

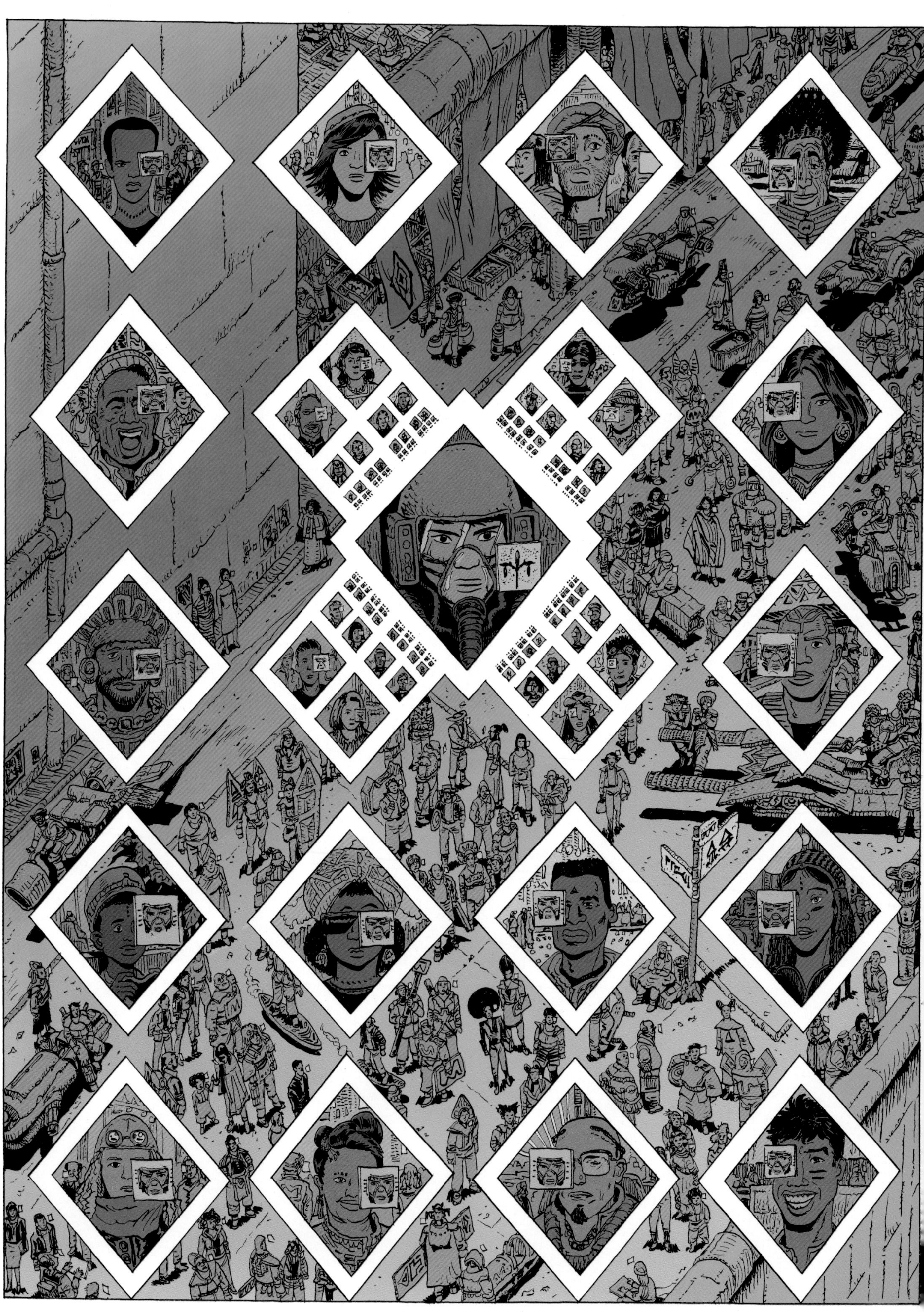

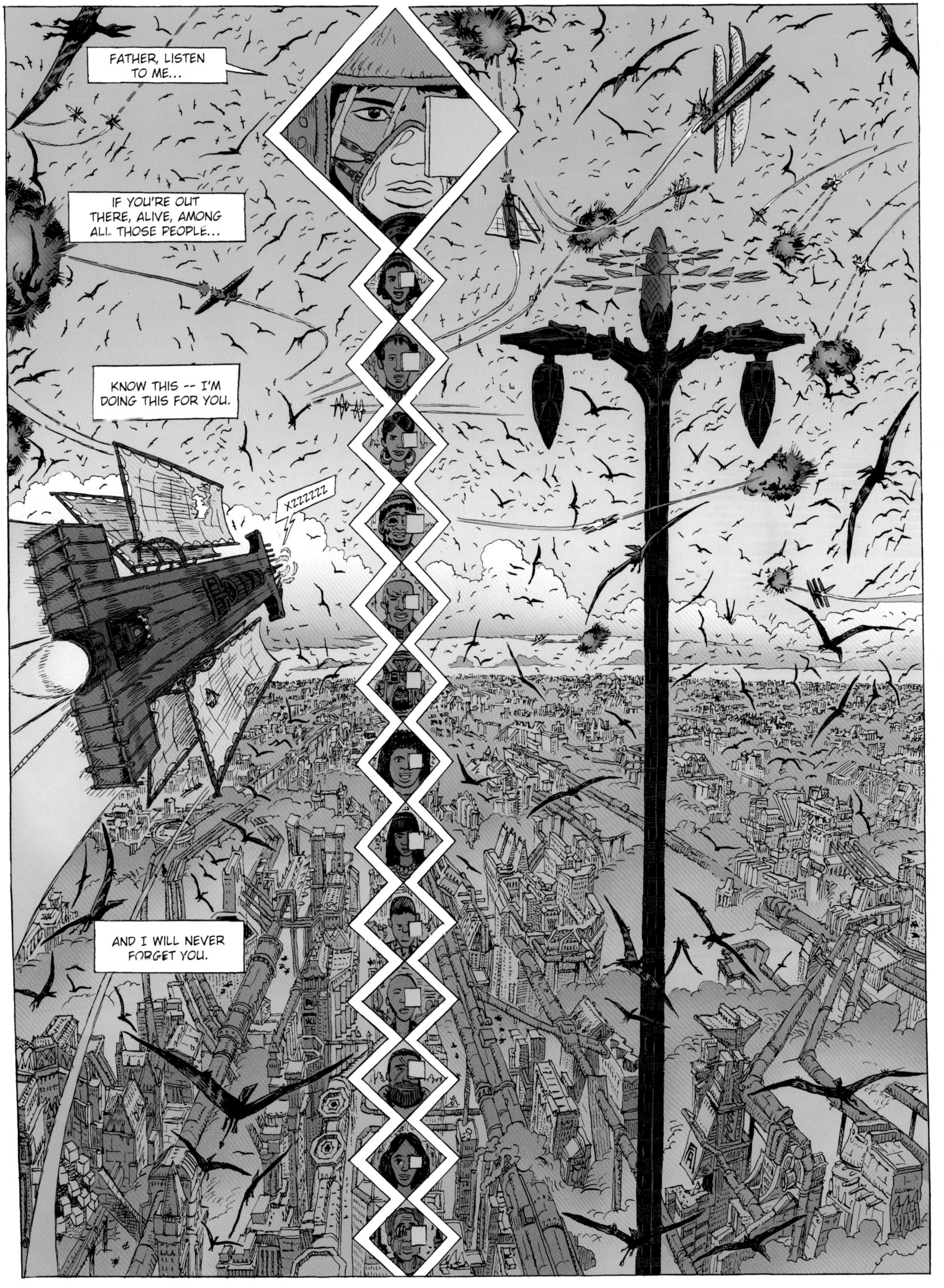
FATHER, LISTEN TO ME...
IF YOU'RE OUT THERE, ALIVE, AMONG ALL THOSE PEOPLE...
KNOW THIS -- I'M DOING THIS FOR YOU.
XZZZZZZ
AND I WILL NEVER FORGET YOU.

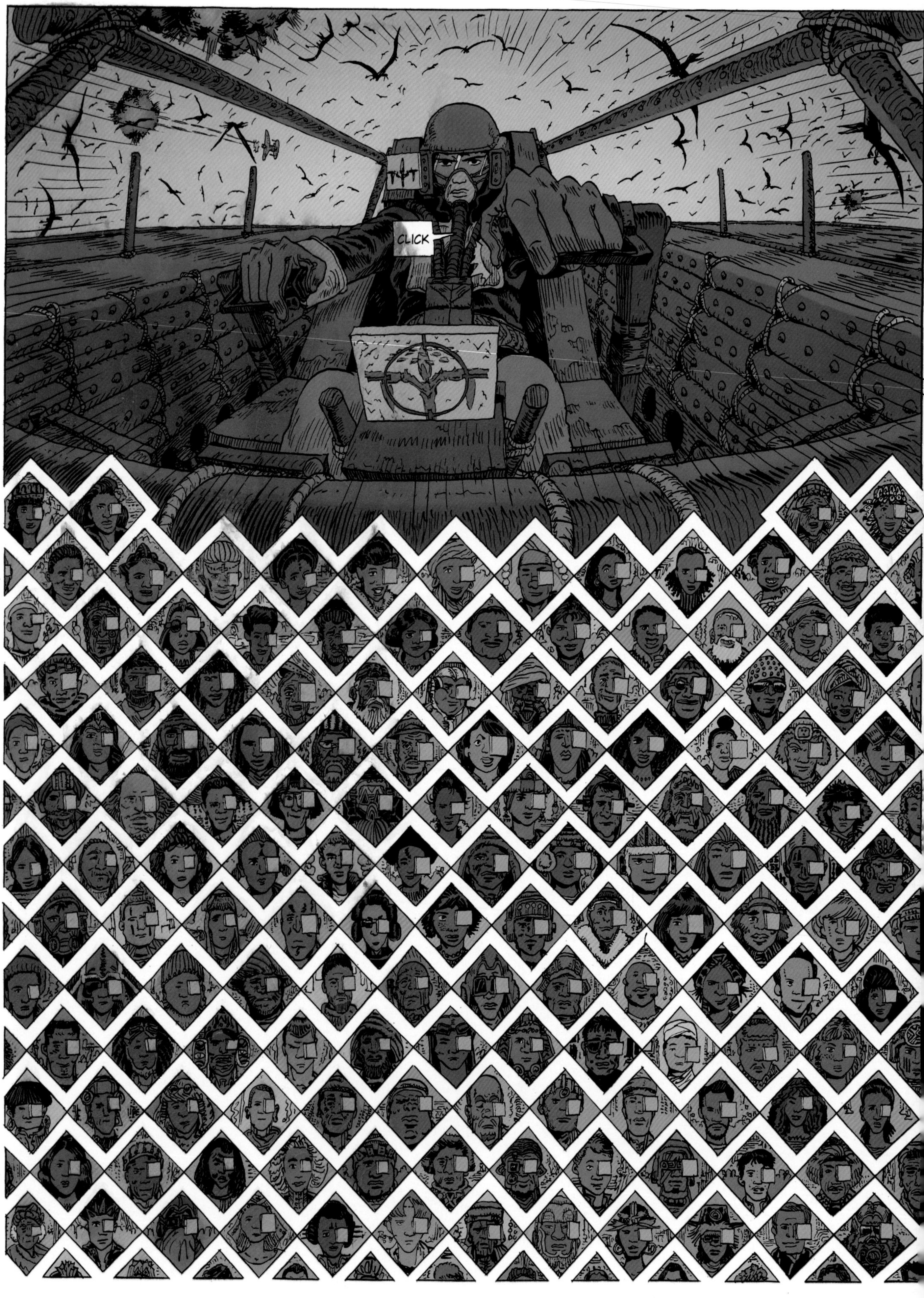
CLICK

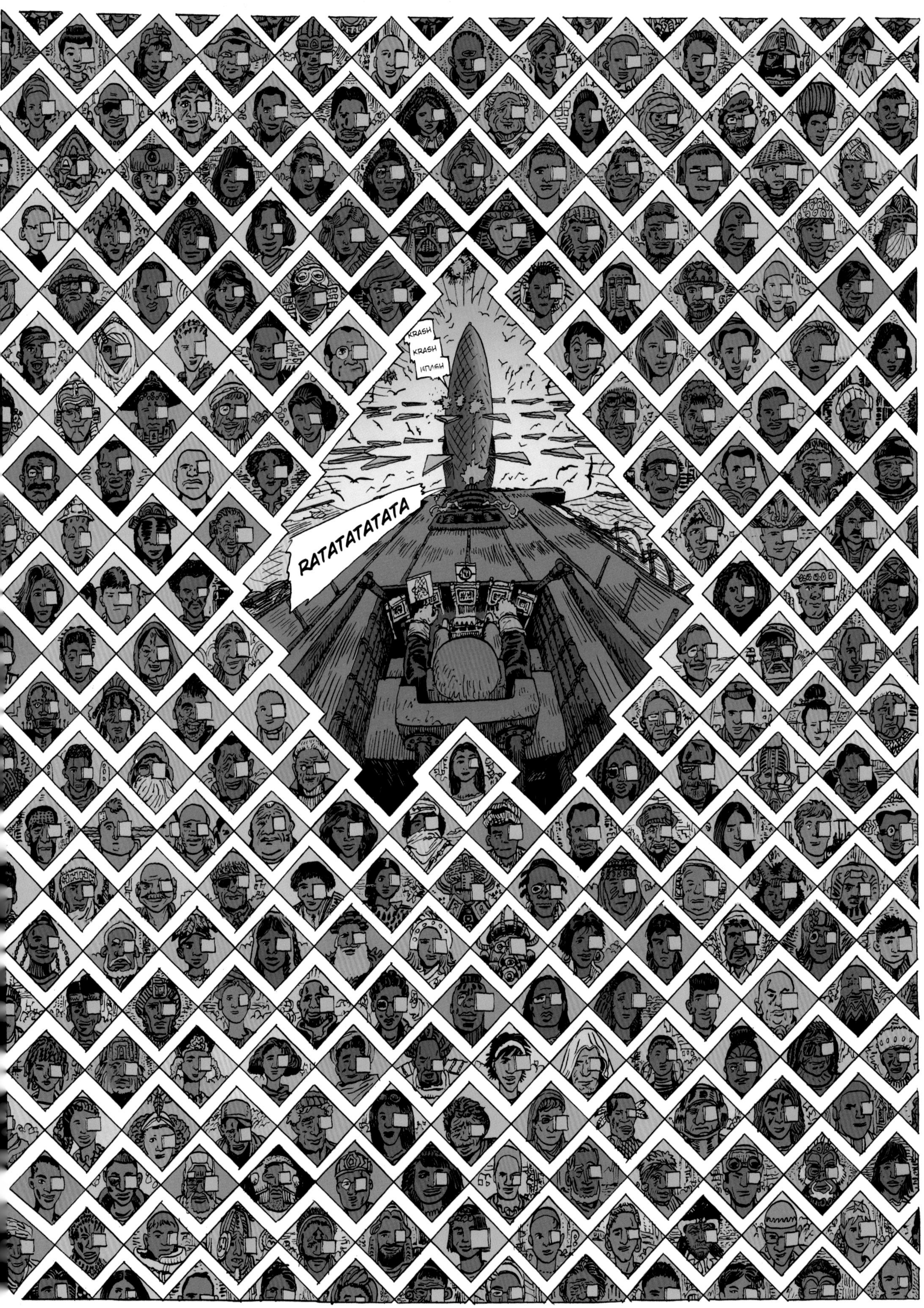
KRASH
KRASH
RATATATATA

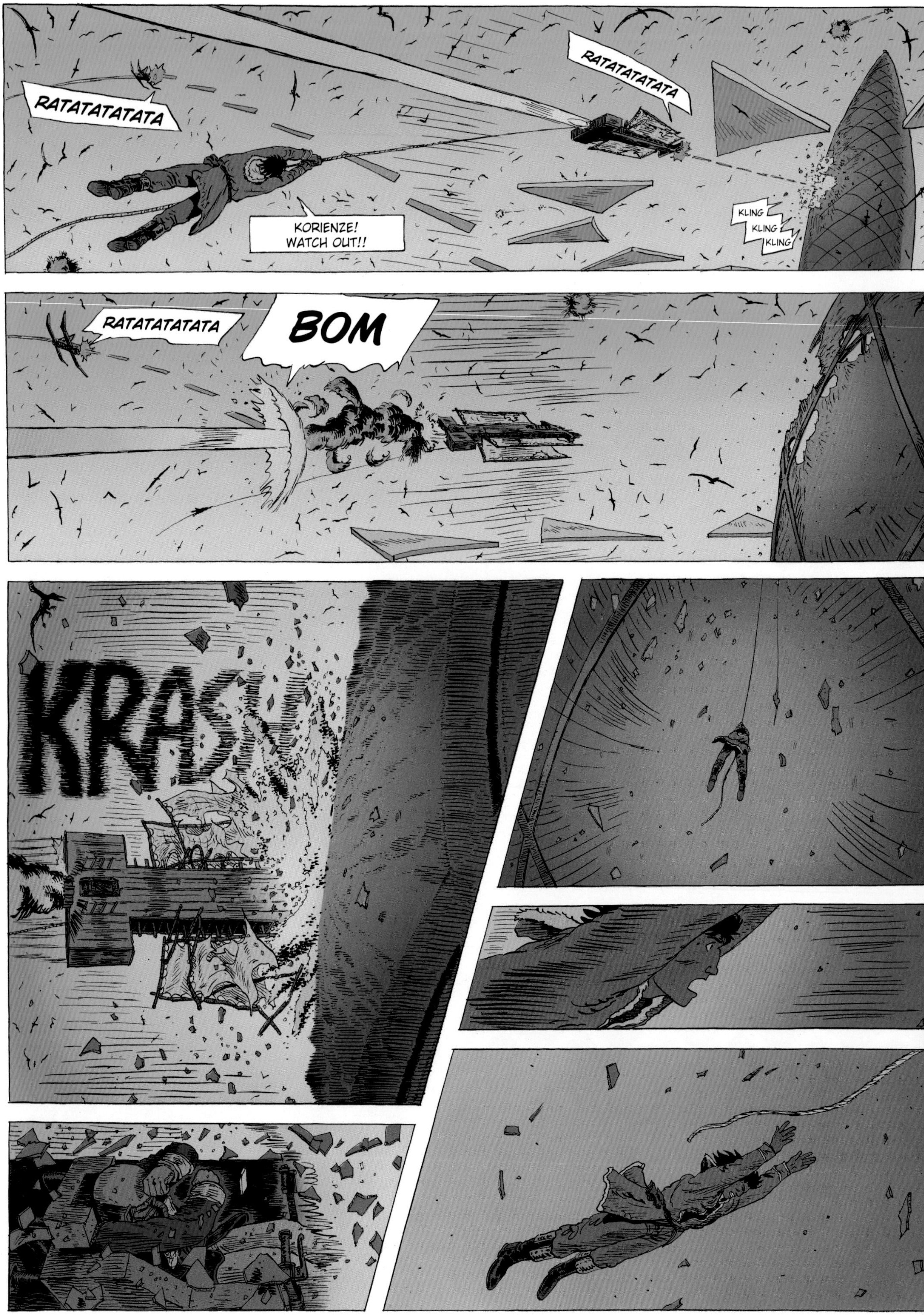
RATATATATATA
RATATATATATA
KORIENZE! WATCH OUT!!
KLING
KLING
KLING
RATATATATATA
BOM
KRASH

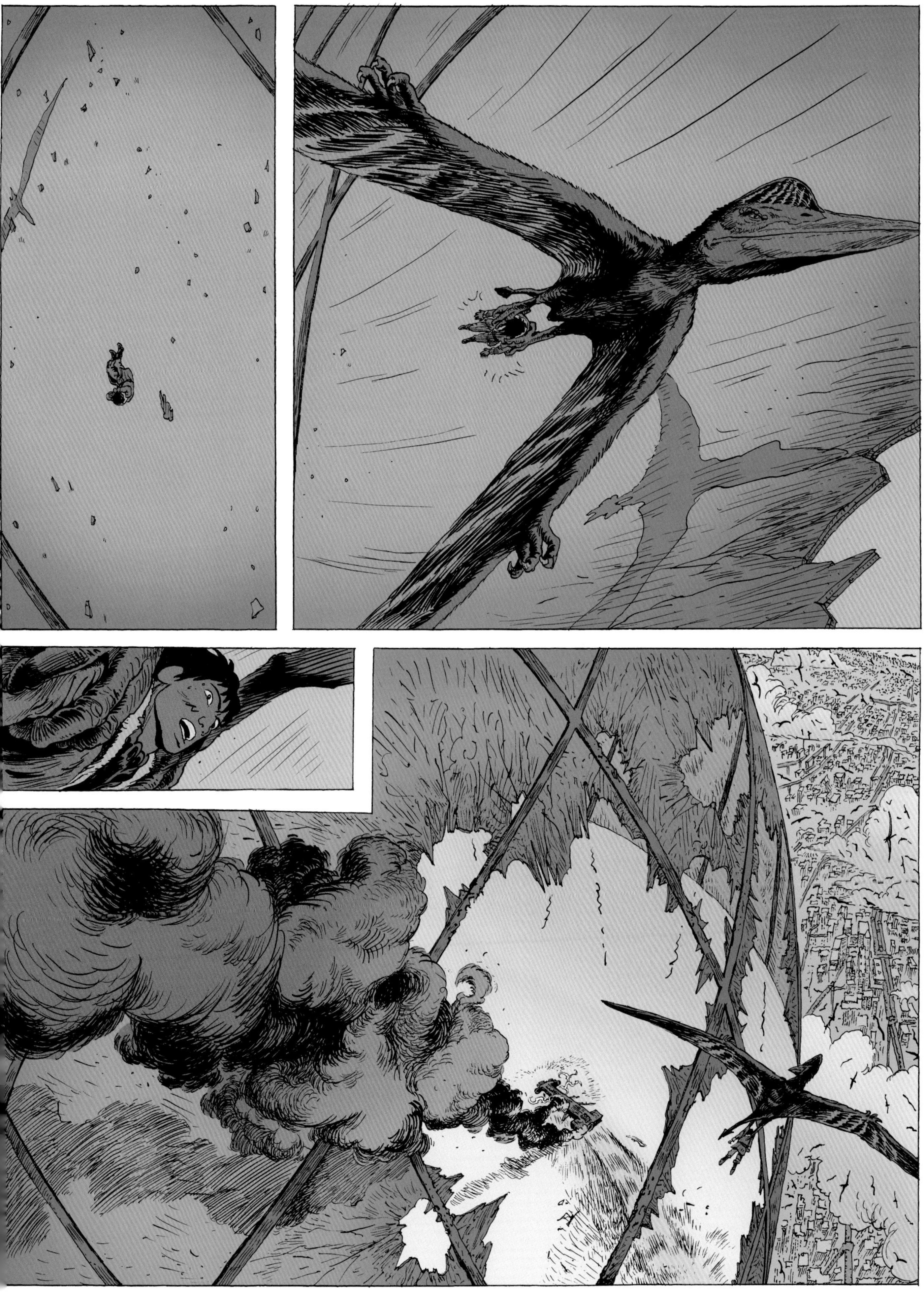

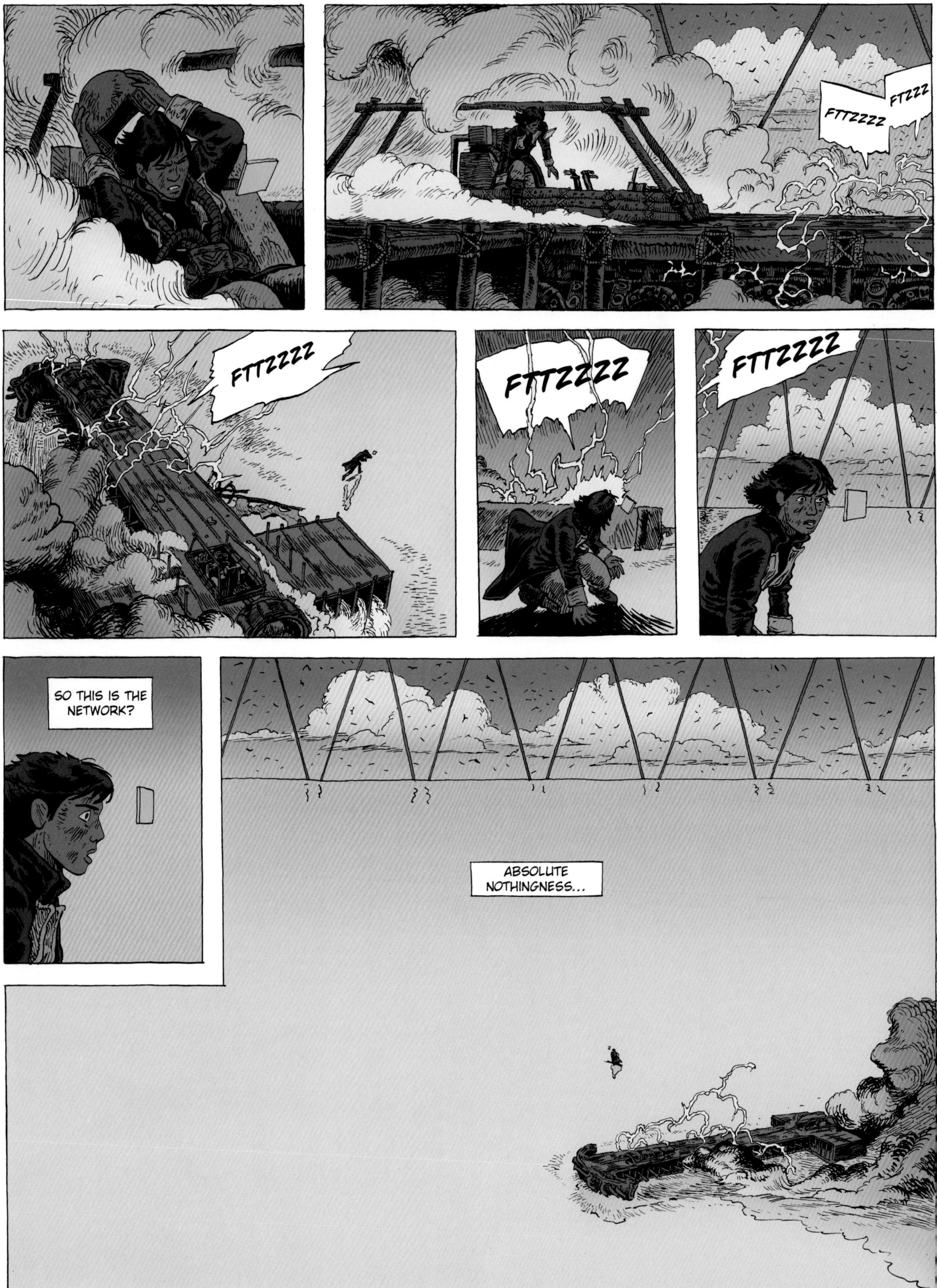
FTTZZZZ
FTZZZ
FTTZZZZ
FTTZZZZ
FTTZZZZ
SO THIS IS THE NETWORK?
ABSOLUTE NOTHINGNESS...

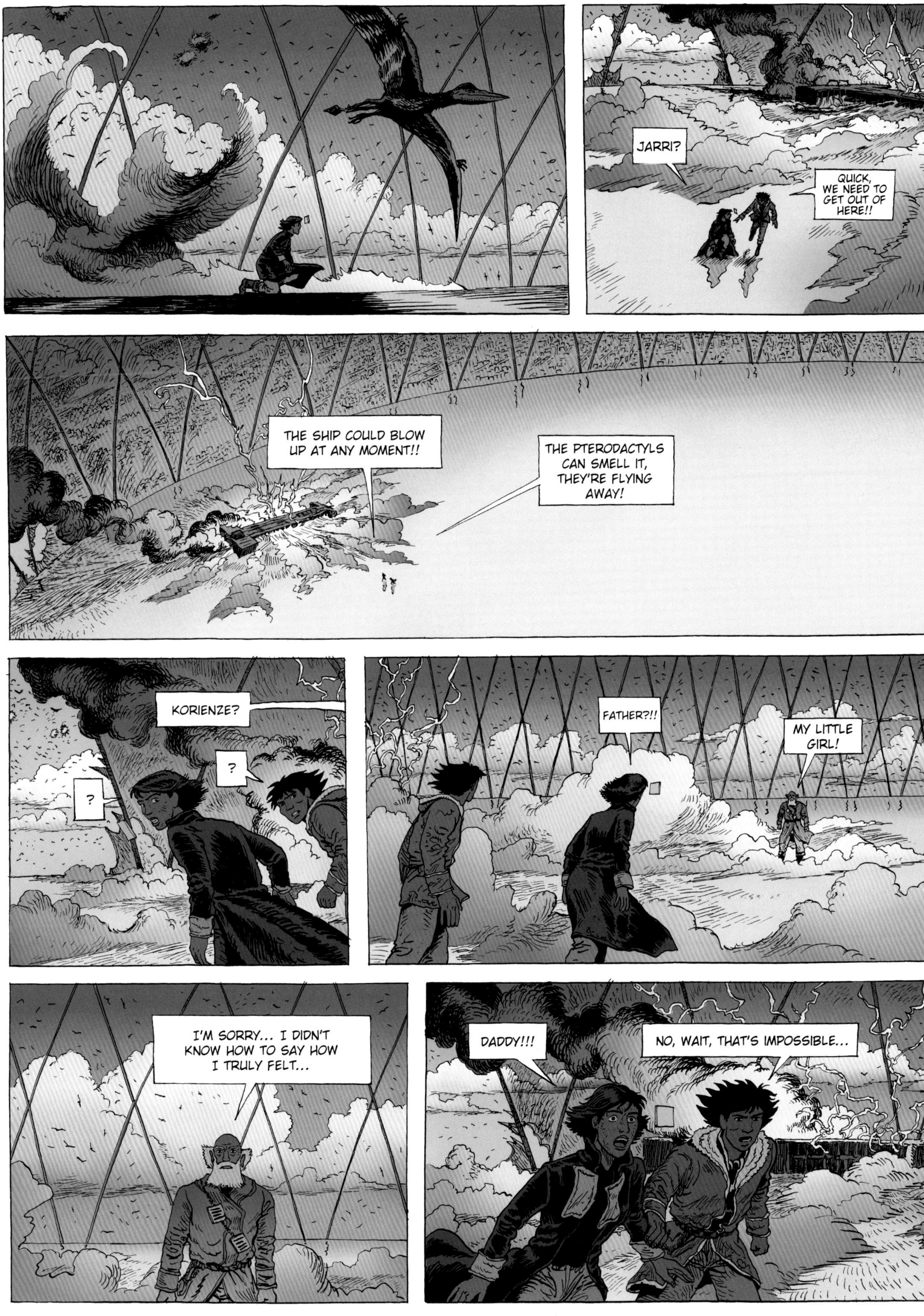
JARRI?
QUICK, WE NEED TO GET OUT OF HERE!!
THE SHIP COULD BLOW UP AT ANY MOMENT!!
THE PTERODACTYLS CAN SMELL IT, THEY'RE FLYING AWAY!
KORIENZE?
?
?
FATHER?!!
MY LITTLE GIRL!
I'M SORRY... I DIDN'T KNOW HOW TO SAY HOW I TRULY FELT...
DADDY!!!
NO, WAIT, THAT'S IMPOSSIBLE...

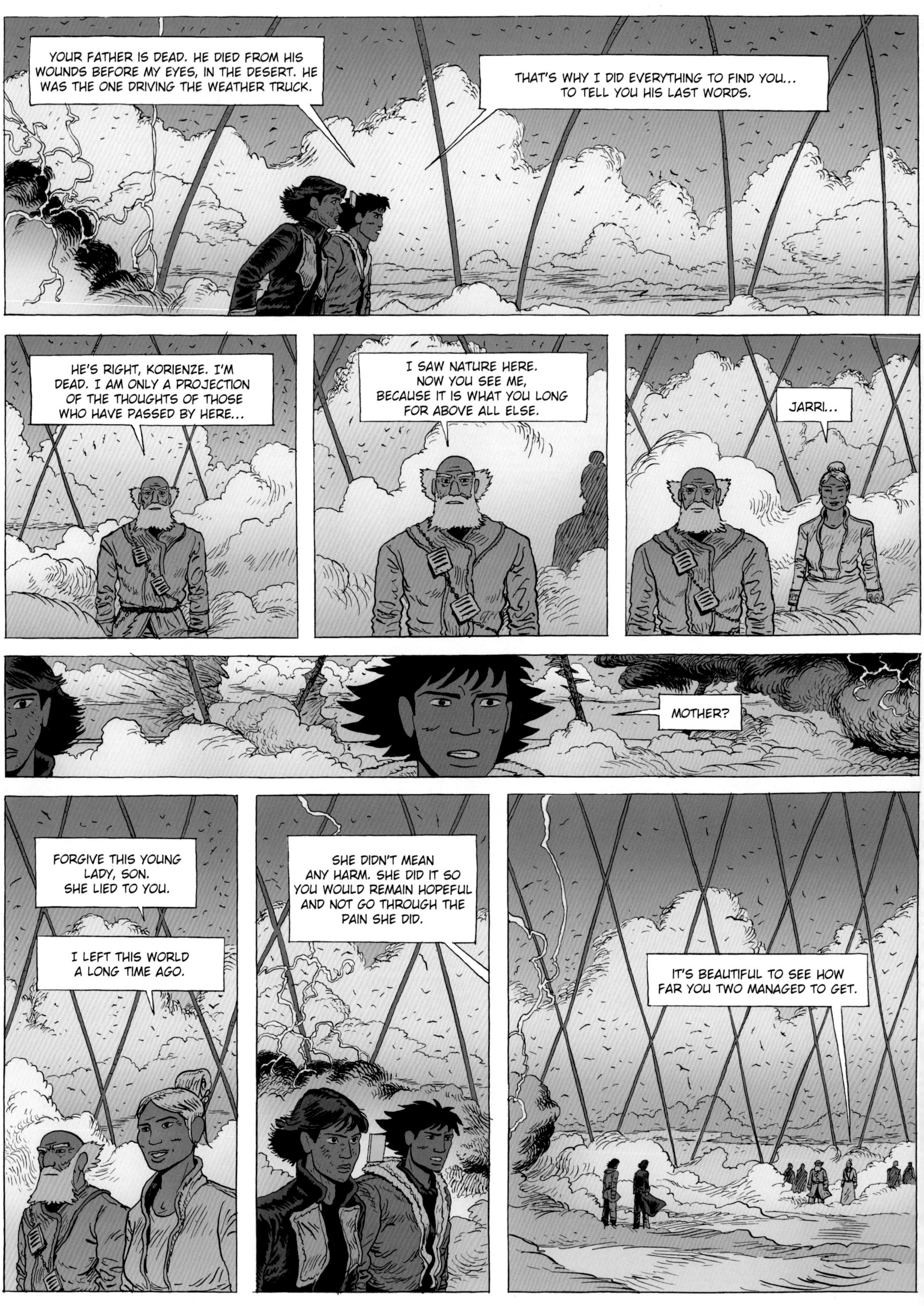
YOUR FATHER IS DEAD. HE DIED FROM HIS WOUNDS BEFORE MY EYES, IN THE DESERT. HE WAS THE ONE DRIVING THE WEATHER TRUCK.
THAT'S WHY I DID EVERYTHING TO FIND YOU... TO TELL YOU HIS LAST WORDS.
HE'S RIGHT, KORIENZE. I'M DEAD. I AM ONLY A PROJECTION OF THE THOUGHTS OF THOSE WHO HAVE PASSED BY HERE...
I SAW NATURE HERE. NOW YOU SEE ME, BECAUSE IT IS WHAT YOU LONG FOR ABOVE ALL ELSE.
JARRI...
MOTHER?
FORGIVE THIS YOUNG LADY, SON. SHE LIED TO YOU.
I LEFT THIS WORLD A LONG TIME AGO.
SHE DIDN'T MEAN ANY HARM. SHE DID IT SO YOU WOULD REMAIN HOPEFUL AND NOT GO THROUGH THE PAIN SHE DID.
IT'S BEAUTIFUL TO SEE HOW FAR YOU TWO MANAGED TO GET.

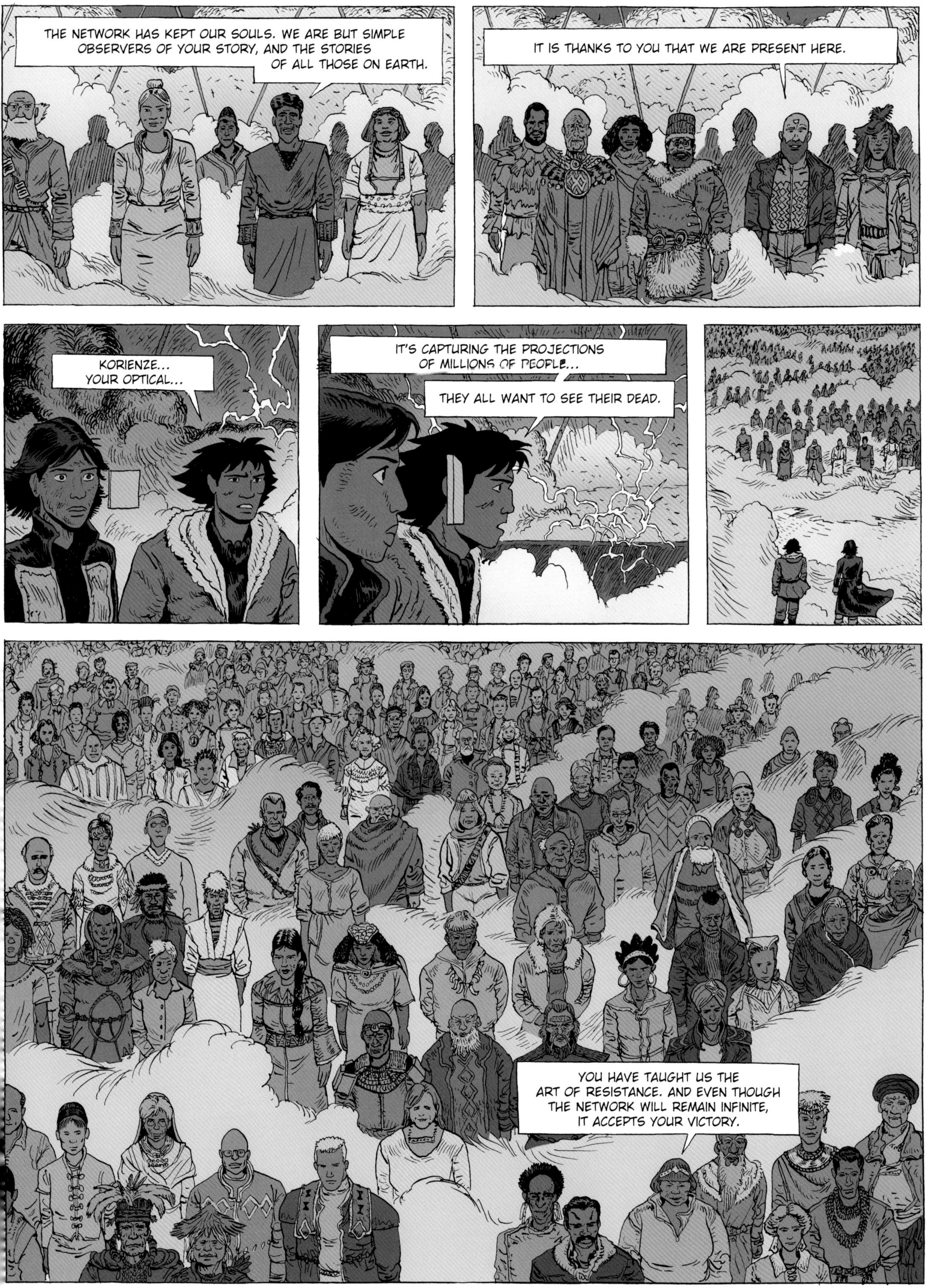
THE NETWORK HAS KEPT OUR SOULS. WE ARE BUT SIMPLE OBSERVERS OF YOUR STORY, AND THE STORIES OF ALL THOSE ON EARTH.
IT IS THANKS TO YOU THAT WE ARE PRESENT HERE.
KORIENZE... YOUR OPTICAL...
IT'S CAPTURING THE PROJECTIONS OF MILLIONS OF PEOPLE...
THEY ALL WANT TO SEE THEIR DEAD.
YOU HAVE TAUGHT US THE ART OF RESISTANCE. AND EVEN THOUGH THE NETWORK WILL REMAIN INFINITE, IT ACCEPTS YOUR VICTORY.

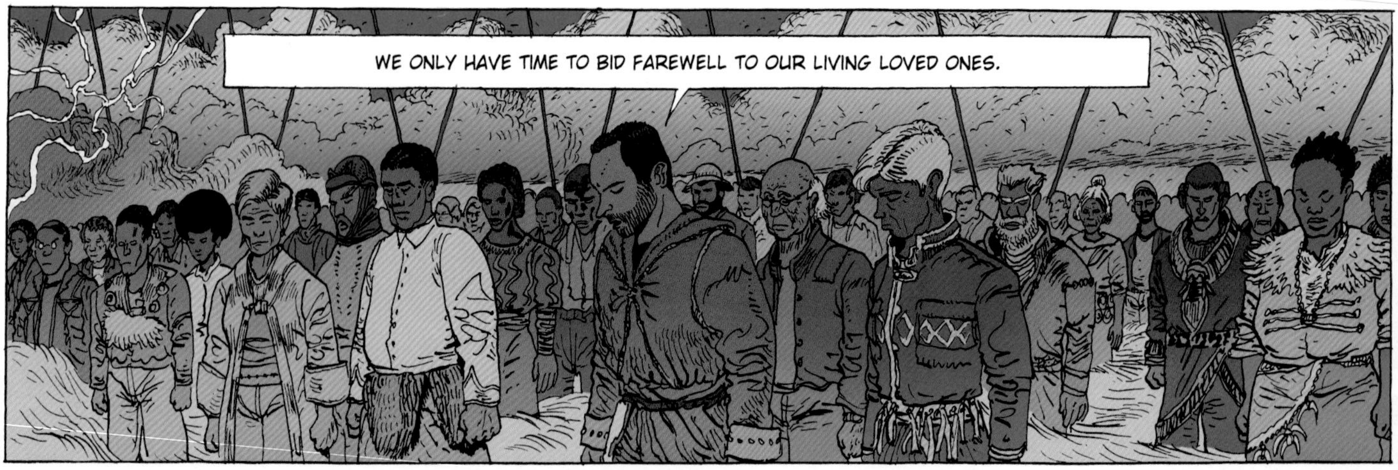
WE ONLY HAVE TIME TO BID FAREWELL TO OUR LIVING LOVED ONES.

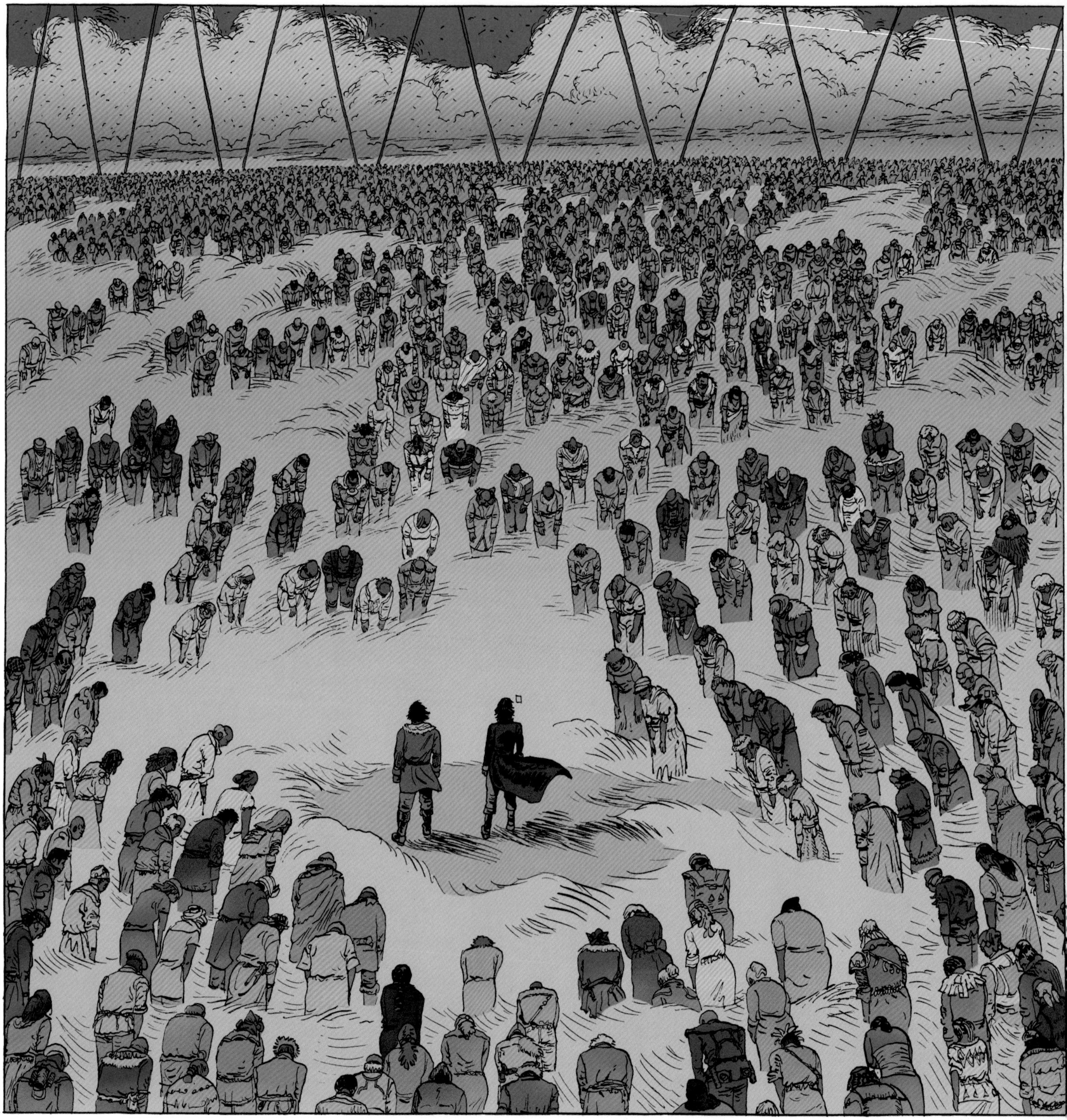

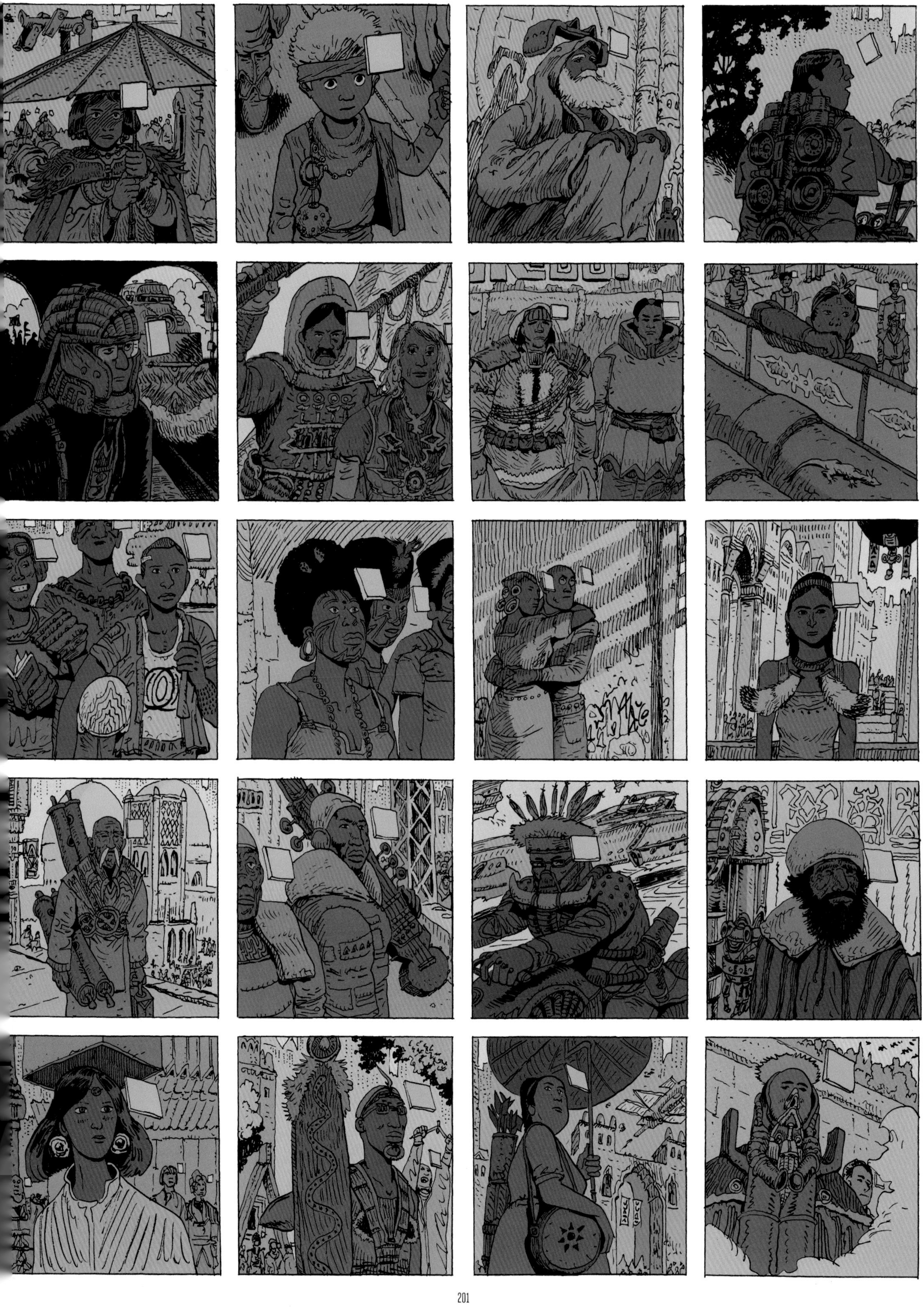

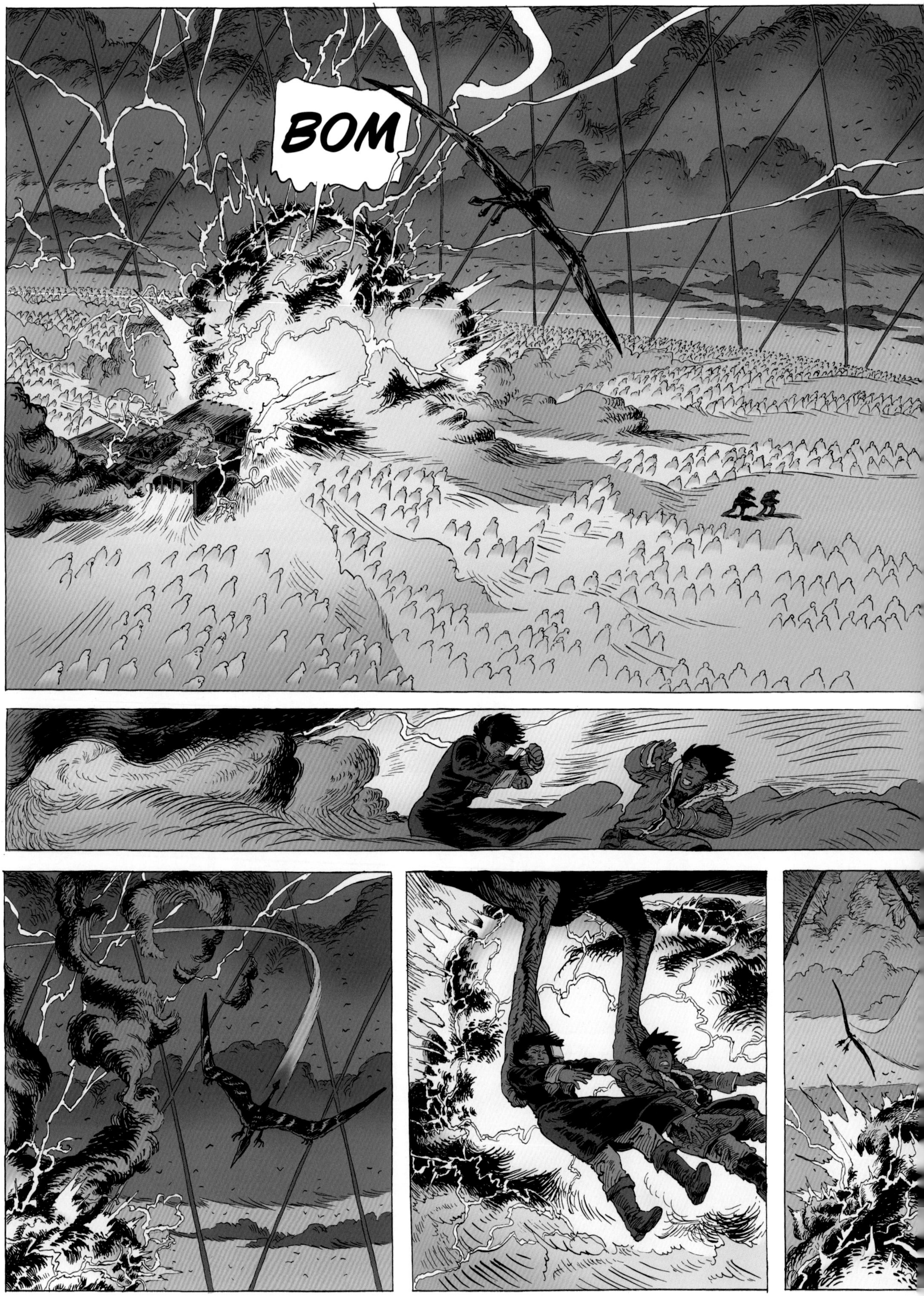
BOM

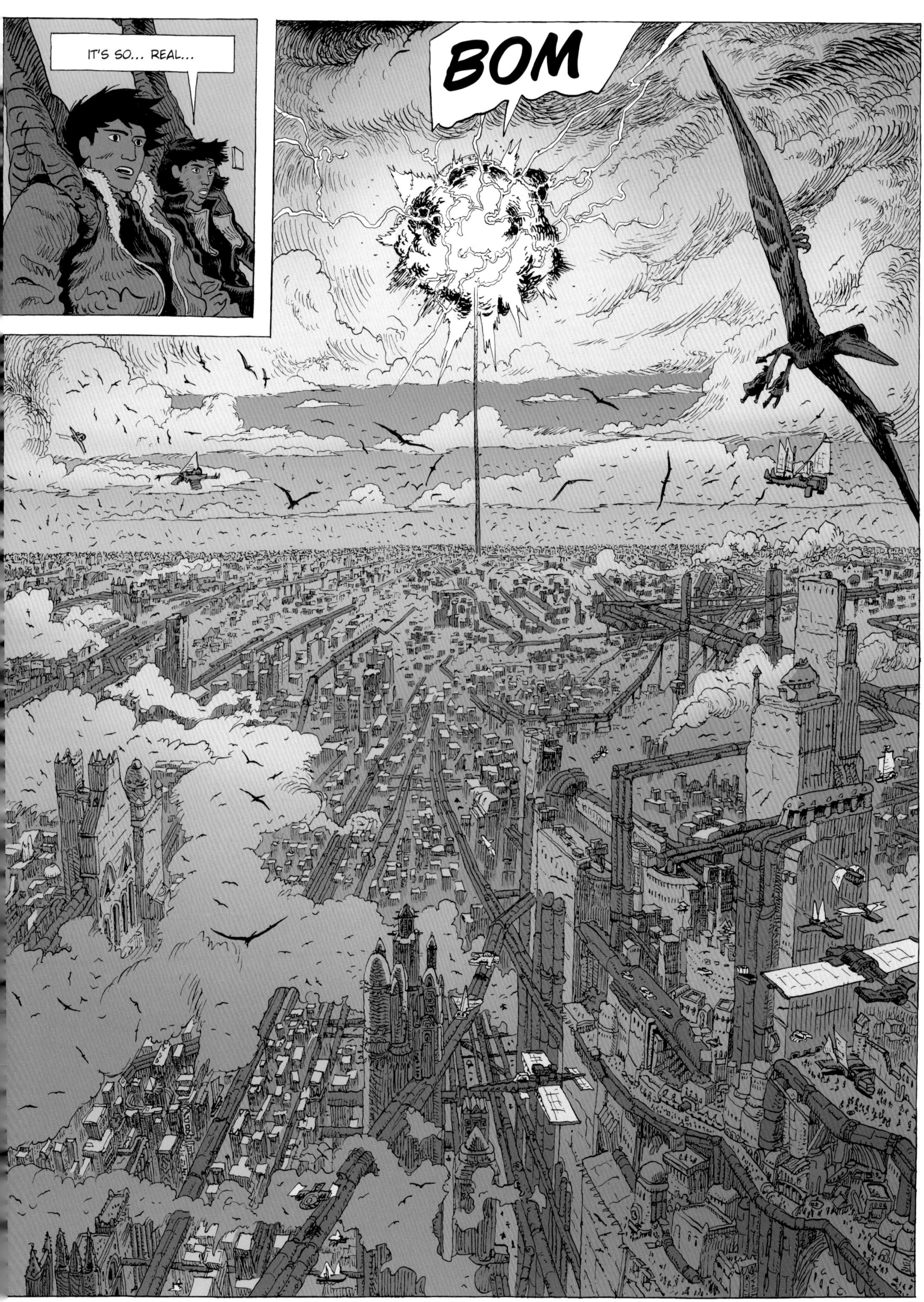
IT'S SO... REAL...
BOM

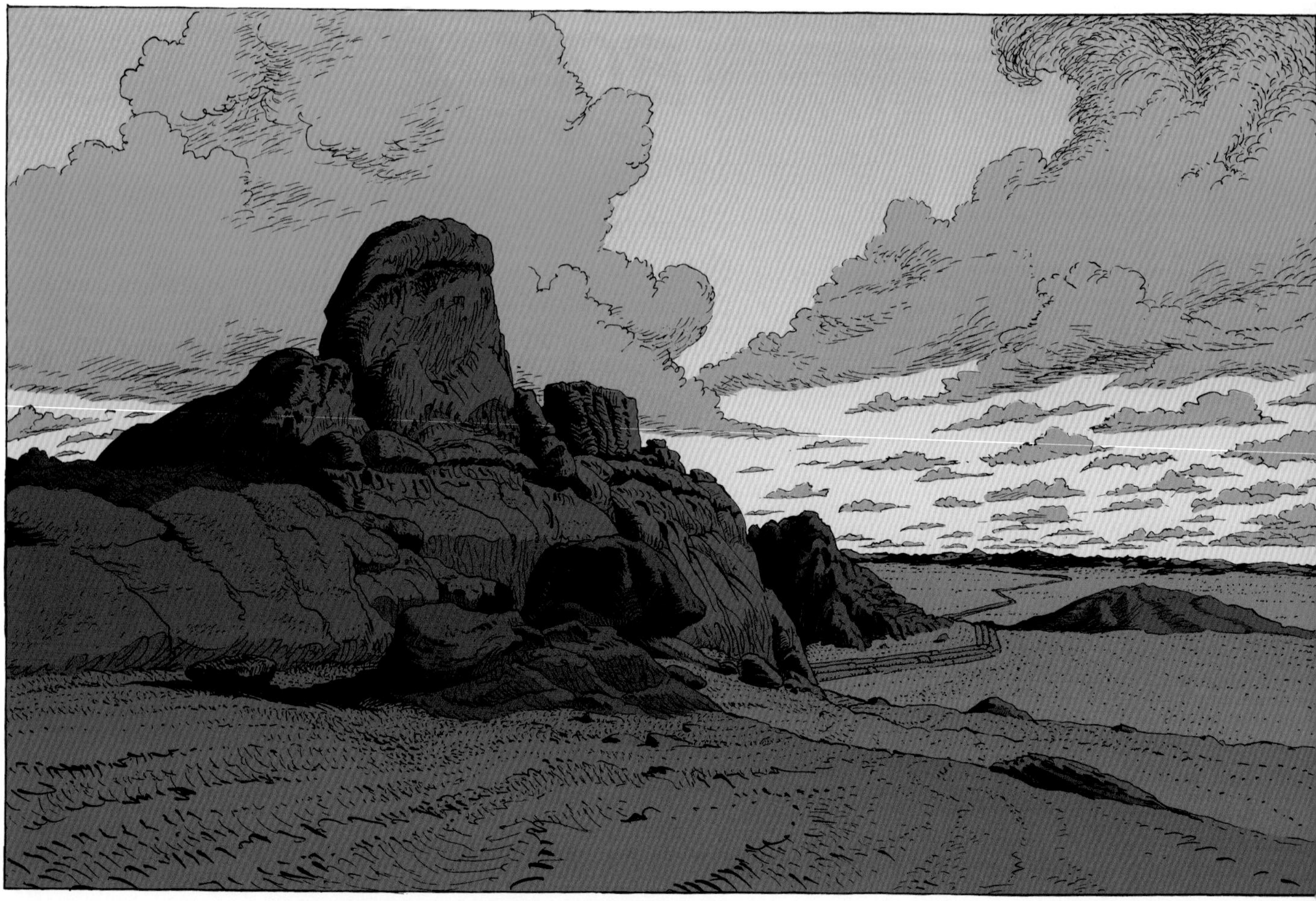

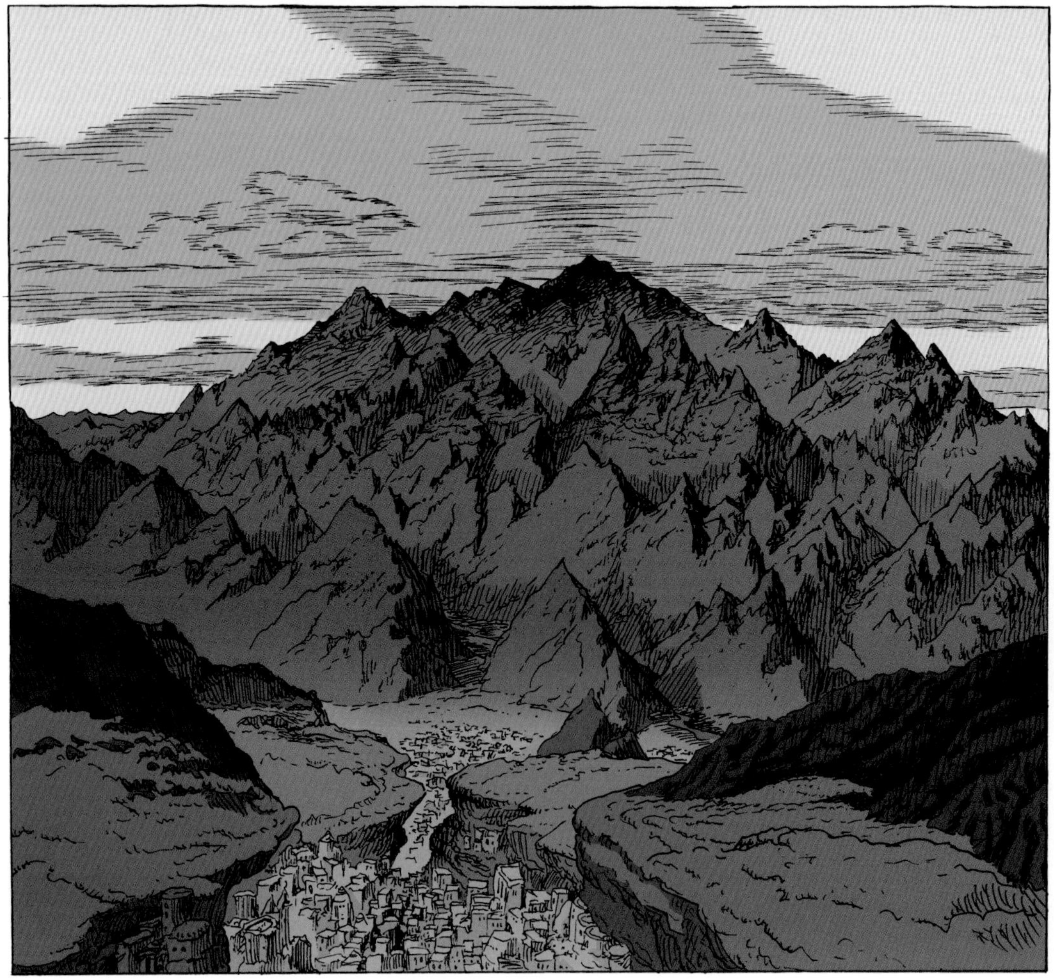

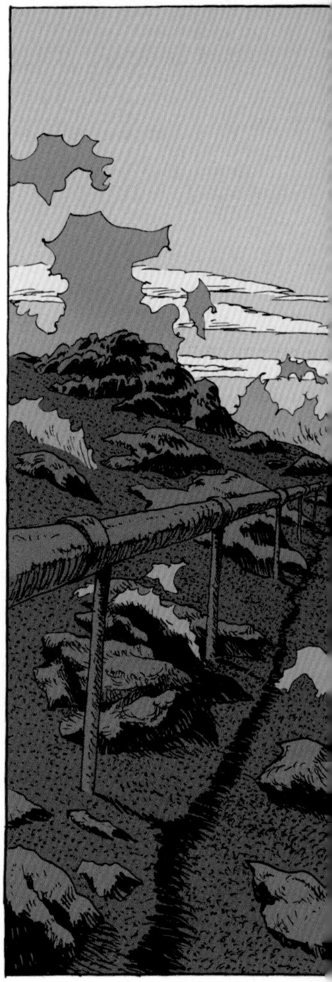

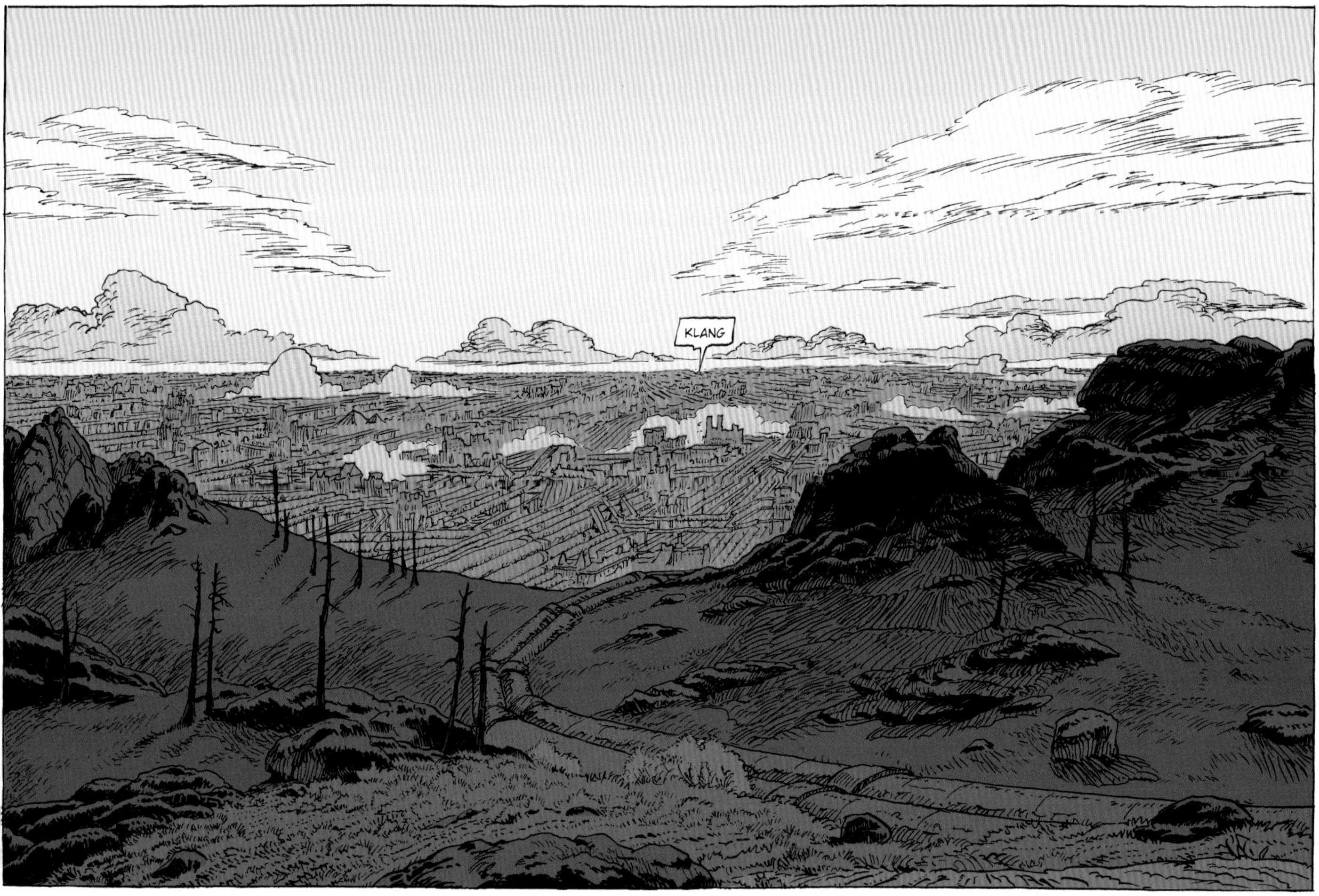
KLANG

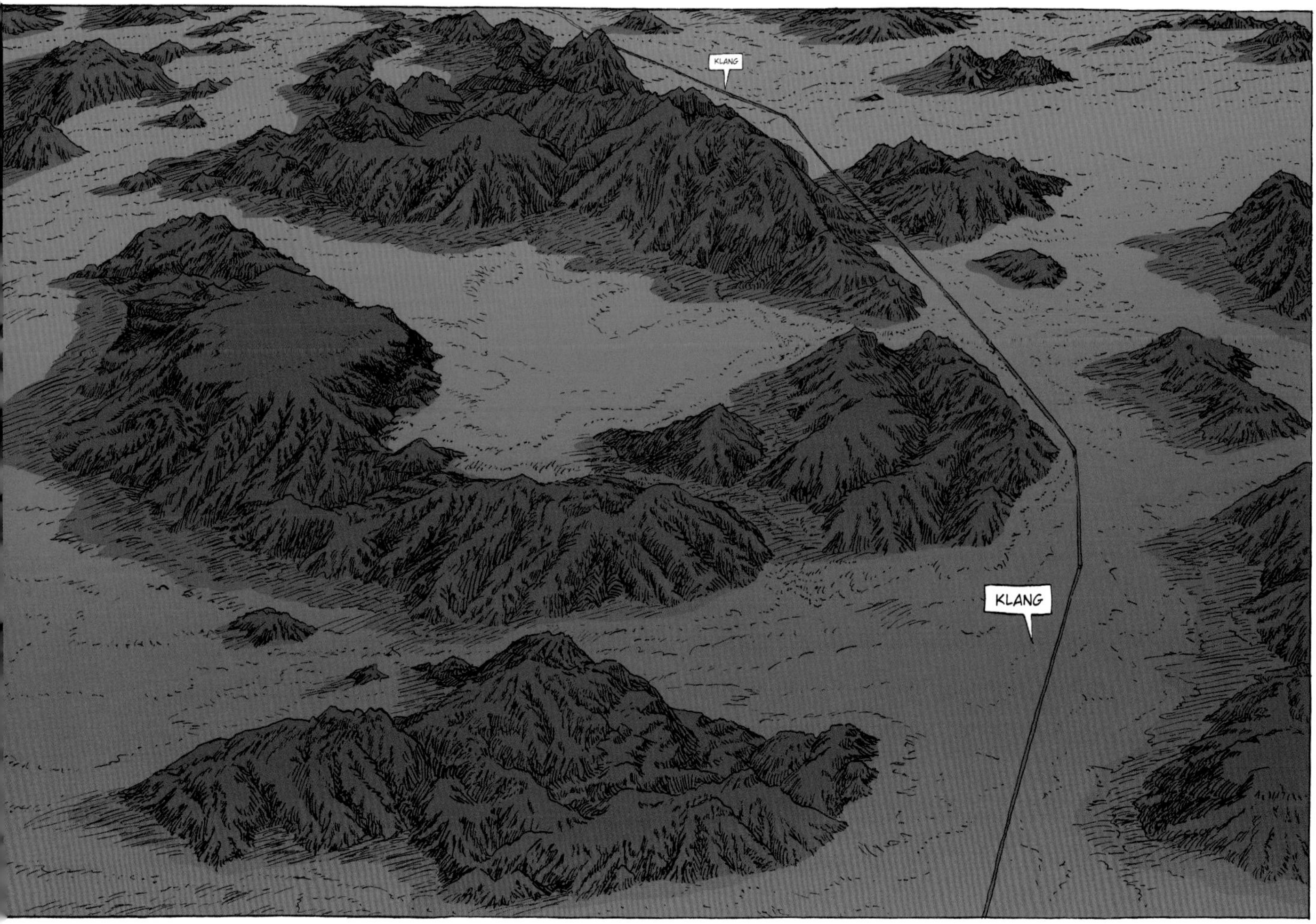
KLANG
KLANG

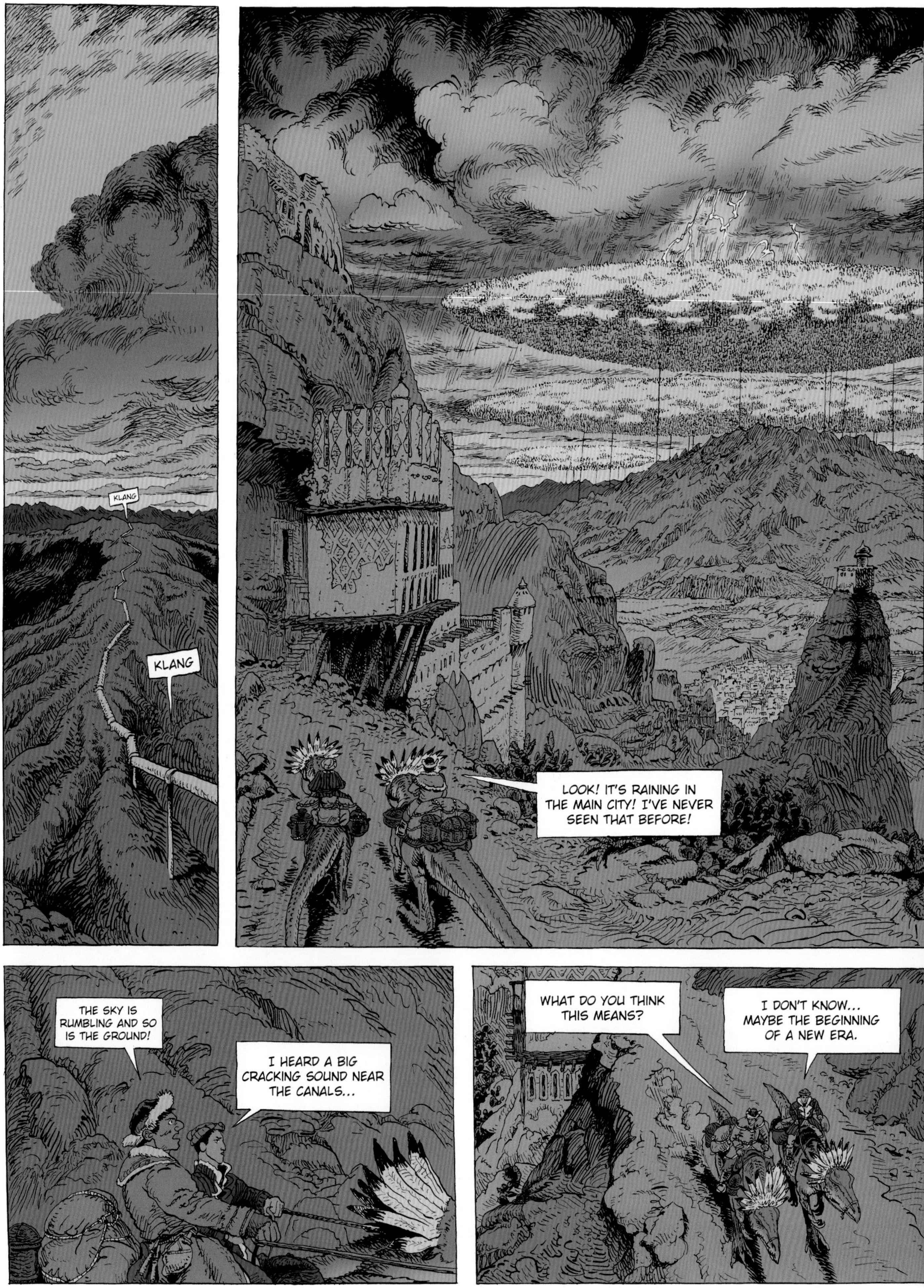
KLANG
KLANG
LOOK! IT'S RAINING IN THE MAIN CITY! I'VE NEVER SEEN THAT BEFORE!
THE SKY IS RUMBLING AND SO IS THE GROUND!
I HEARD A BIG CRACKING SOUND NEAR THE CANALS...
WHAT DO YOU THINK THIS MEANS?
I DON'T KNOW... MAYBE THE BEGINNING OF A NEW ERA.

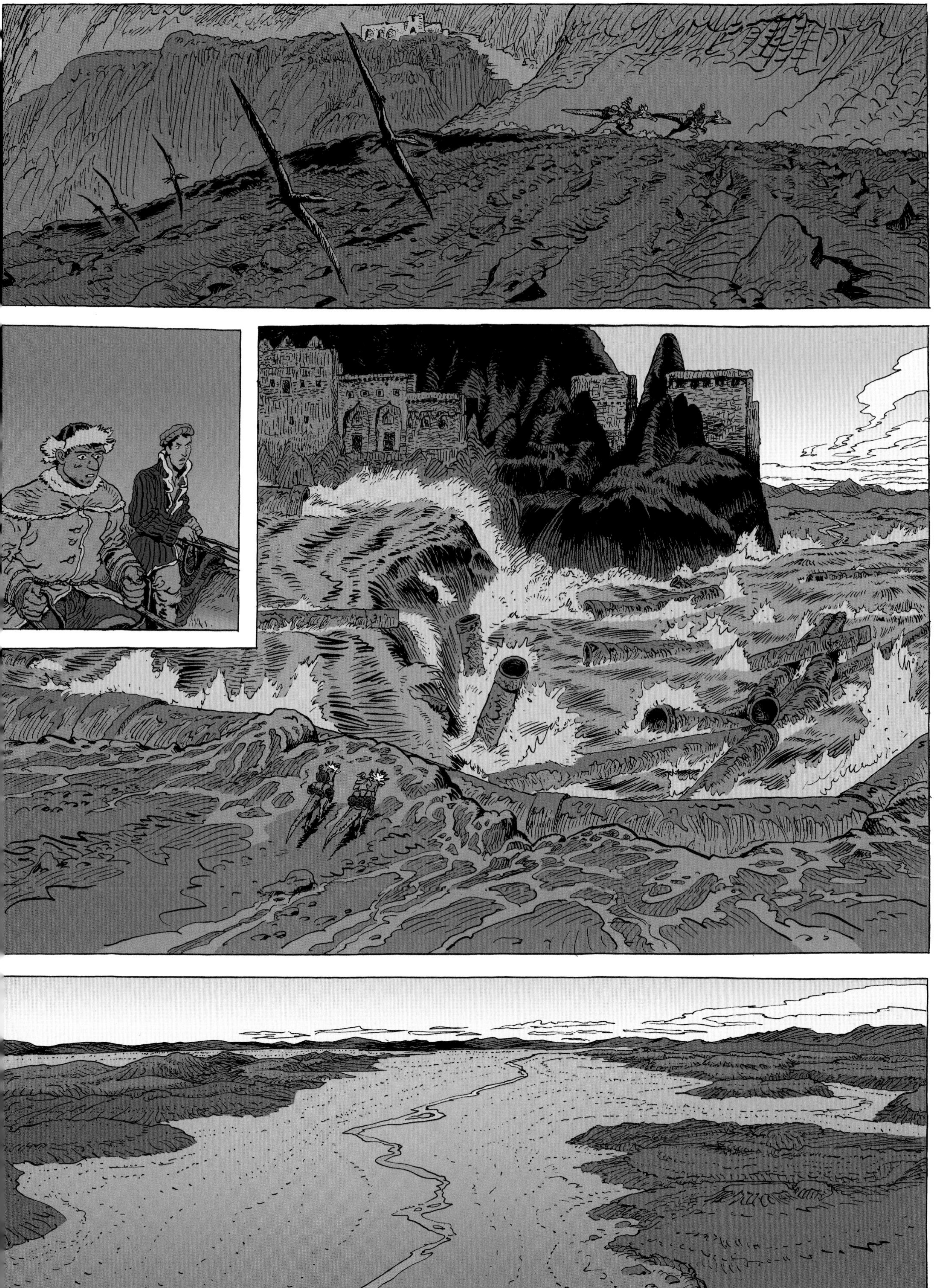

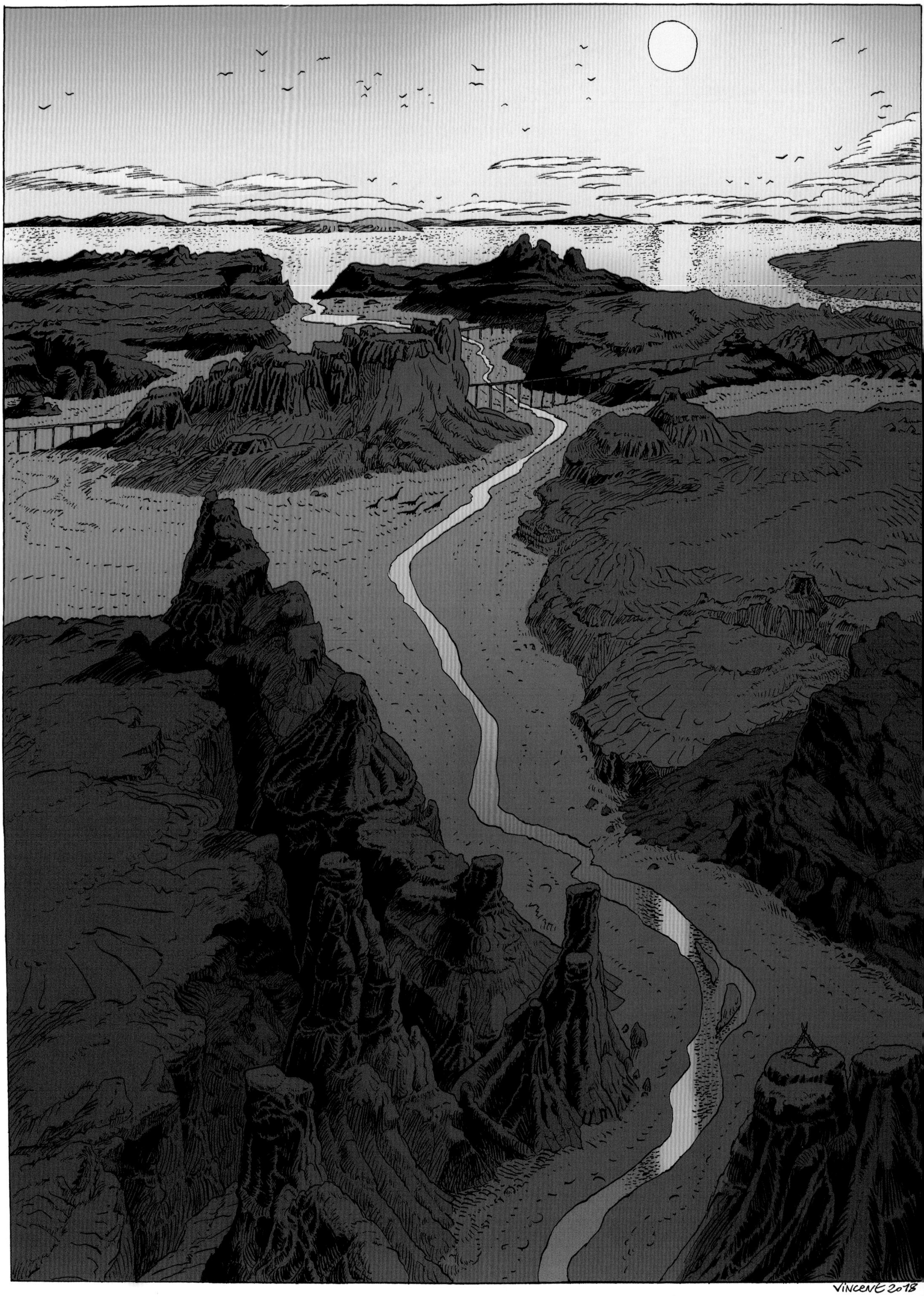
VINCENT 2018

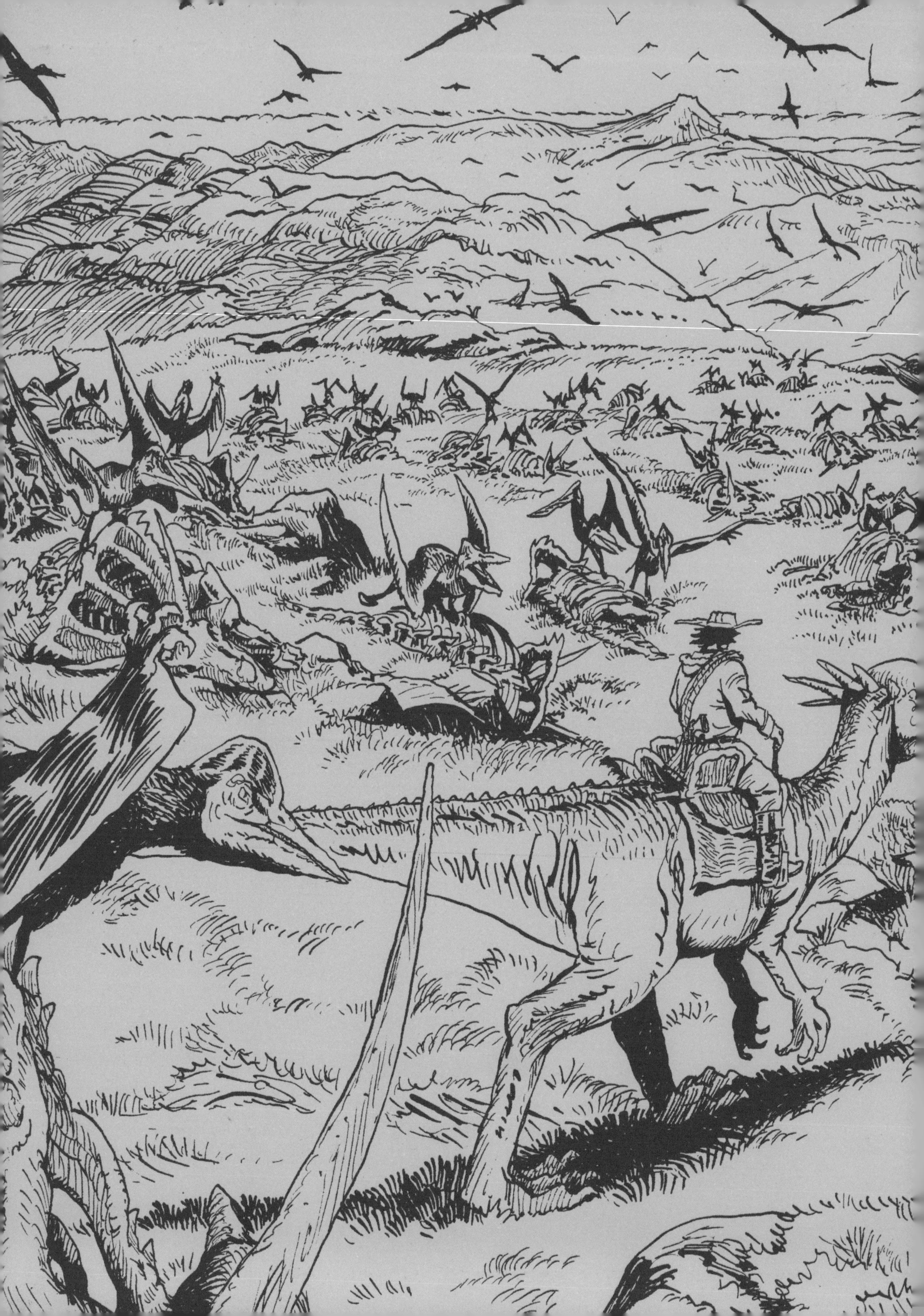